MW00811020

THE HISTORY OF THE
GERMAN

IN TEXAS 1831-1861

BY

RUDLOPH LEOPOLD
BIESELE

EAKIN PRESS * Austin, TX

CONTENTS

THIS BOOK
IS DEDICATED TO THE
GERMAN PIONEERS OF TEXAS—
TO THE MEN AND WOMEN WHO HELPED
TO MAKE TEXAS A CIVILIZED COUNTRY.
MAY IT SERVE TO INSTILL IN THEIR
DESCENDANTS A HIGH RESPECT
FOR THEIR EFFORTS AND A
PROPER APPRECIATION OF
THEIR ACHIEVEMENTS.

PREFACE

This study was accepted by the Graduate Faculty of the University of Texas for the Doctor of Philosophy degree in the spring of 1928. A few changes have been made in the arrangement of the work, and three maps and several plates of persons and places have been added. The subject is one that has interested me for a number of years. The study should, perhaps, have been made at an earlier time, while many of the old German settlers were still living, because more of the human interest could have been woven into the story. In its scope this account is confined to the history of the German settlements in Texas in the period from 1831 to 1861.

In presenting this study I have attempted to show how the dissatisfaction with the prevailing social, economic, and political conditions in Germany during the first half of the nineteenth century caused German emigrants to direct their footsteps toward Texas after that distant, promising land became known to them. Various plans were submitted to the Spanish and Mexican governments in the interest of German colonization in Texas, but these, as well as the proposals made later to the republic of Texas, proved unproductive.

The actual founding of German settlements in Texas began in 1831, when Friedrich Ernst, a former subject of the grand-duchy of Oldenburg, settled on a league of land on the west bank of Mill Creek in what is now Austin County. This first settlement received the name of Industry and became the center of a number of German settlements founded in Austin, Colorado, Fayette, Washington, De Witt, and Victoria counties in the period before 1861. With the single exception of Yorktown, no concerted effort was behind the founding of any of these settlements.

In western Texas—that is, in the counties of Comal, Guadalupe, Gillespie, Llano, Kendall, and Kerr—on the other hand, the German settlements were founded either directly or indirectly as the result of a colonization movement supported by the Society for the Protection of German Immigrants in Texas (*Verein zum Schutze deutscher Einwanderer in Texas*). Having first become interested in Texas in 1842, this society in 1844 definitely embarked on a program of directing German emigration to Texas. It acquired two colonization contracts, one from Alexander Bourgeois d'Orvanne and Armand Ducos in 1843, the other from Henry Francis Fisher and Burchard Miller in 1844. The Bourgeois-Ducos contract, however, expired before the society could make any use of its provisions, while the Fisher and Miller grant was so far in the interior of Texas that it was not very accessible. New Braunfels and Fredericksburg, the two principal settlements made by the Society, were both established on land not included in the Fisher and Miller grant. One of the greatest achievements of the early settlers in western Texas was a treaty by which the Comanche Indians allowed them to settle in the grant, a tract of over three million acres. Both before and after the society was dissolved other settlements were founded in western Texas, but it is doubtful if these would have been made had not the society carried on its pioneer work in that part of the state.

The German settlers contributed their share to the political, economic, and social life of Texas. In politics they sided with the Democratic party. Most of them engaged in agriculture, but a few among them were skilled artisans and their products had a ready market. They were interested in education, looked after their religious needs, and founded societies for promoting good fellowship, as well as for literary and political purposes. Besides the singing society, they used the newspaper as an agent of cultural development and published five of them in the German language in the period covered by this study.

In preparation for the writing of this work I used a considerable number of books and pamphlets, both contemporary with the period and of subsequent publication. I have presented material from newspapers published in Germany to show how the people there felt about emigrating to Texas and founding a new home in that distant land; and I have given numerous excerpts from newspapers published in Texas, both in the German and English languages, to show how the German settlers felt and how they were regarded by their American neighbors. Finally, I have used a considerable amount of manuscript material in the archives of the General Land Office, the office of the Secretary of State, the Texas State Library, and of the University of Texas, material hitherto unused in works on the history of the German element in Texas.

I wish to acknowledge the friendly spirit with which several newspaper editors, archivists, and librarians in Germany responded in locating and furnishing material. These men are Dr. Dertsch and Mr. Jean Kessler of the Stadtbibliothek in Mainz; Prof. Dr. Hermann Degering, the archivist of the Preussische Staatsbibliothek in Berlin; Dr. Entholt, the archivist of the Staatsarchiv in Bremen; Dr. Curt Amend, the editor of the *Karlsruher Zeitung,* and Prof. Dr. B. Mueller, the director of the Staedtisches Historisches Museum in Frankfort on the Main. Dr. Rudolf Bonnet of the University of Frankfort on the Main was especially obliging in supplying information and in locating material.

To Mr. E. W. Winkler, librarian, and Mrs. Mattie Austin Hatcher and Miss Winnie Allen, archivist and assistant archivist, respectively, of the University of Texas, to Miss Harriet Smither, archivist of the Texas State Library, and to Mrs. A. N. McCallum, Secretary of State, Austin, Texas, I desire to extend my thanks for courtesies shown me while working with material under their charge. I am greatly indebted to Mrs. Lucy Marschall, Llano, Texas; Mrs. Emmy Marschall, Cherry Springs, Texas; Mr. Alex Brinkmann, Comfort, Texas; Mr. W. A. Trenckmann, Mrs. Walter Wuppermann, and Mr. E. W. Winkler, Austin, Texas; and to Mr. C. A. Jahn, Mr. Hermann Altgelt, and Mr. Fritz Leo Hoffmann, New Braunfels, Texas, for the use of illustrative manuscripts and other material in their private possession and for valuable information furnished by them. Mr. Harry C. Seele of New Braunfels, Texas, placed the first volume of the *Neu Braunfelser Zeitung* at my disposal, and Mr. G. F. Oheim, at present editor of the same newspaper, extended me the use of later volumes. My grateful acknowledgments are due to the late Mr. S. V. Pfeuffer of New Braunfels, Texas, for letting me have access to the valuable collection of books and other material in his private library. Without this permission, so generously granted to me by Mr. Pfeuffer, I would have experienced difficulty in completing my study. I take this opportunity, also to express my thanks to the many other friends who furnished me with information.

I am especially indebted to Dr. E. C. Barker of the University of Texas for the careful reading and scholarly and constructive criticism of this study. It was a great pleasure to conduct my research under his guidance. To Dr. C. W. Ramsdell of the University of Texas I wish to extend my thanks for his friendly interest and helpful suggestions. Finally, I owe more than I can express to my wife for the hearty enouragement and active cooperation which she gave while I was engaged in this study.

R. L. BIESELE.

Austin, Texas, July, 1930.

ABOUT THE AUTHOR

Rudolph Leopold Biesele spent much of his professional life delving into the doings of the German settlers of Texas. After all, he was descended from them, and the genealogical fervor with which many of us seek our particular roots he applied broadly to all Texans of German descent. How he came to write this history is itself a story of motivation, interest, the push of circumstances, and the strong arm of events.

Rudolph Leopold Biesele was born a century ago–on January 19, 1886–in a little community once known as Bonita, on York's Creek in Guadalupe County, Texas. He was the eldest son of cotton farmer Julius Biesele and his wife, Hedwig Bading Biesele, who were Texas-born children of German immigrants from Baden and Berlin, respectively. Rudolph had two younger brothers, Hugo and Carl, and a younger sister, who died in her youth.

His grandfather, Leopold Biesele, once a lieutenant in the army of the grand-duchy of Baden, had engaged in the insurrection of 1849, had advanced through the ranks of captain and major in the rebel forces besieged in Fortress Rastatt, had been imprisioned in Bruchsal, but had escaped to come to Texas in 1851. Here he started a new life with his beloved Babette and an eventual baker's dozen children. Leopold became a teacher in rural schools of Guadalupe County, and this may have led his grandson, who suffered from maleria and became ill from working in the sun, to choose academia over agriculture. Leopold wrote a long poem about his experiences as a "Forty-Eighter," and his grandson copied it carefully in German script.

ABOUT THE AUTHOR

Rudolph attended high school in nearby Seguin and then the Southwest Texas State Normal School in San Marcos from 1903 to 1905, graduating with a teacher's certificate. He won a "Her-mannssöhne Stipendium" from the Sons of Hermann Lodge in New Braunfels for the study of German language and literature. In 1907 he entered The University of Texas, at Austin, residing for a while in old B Hall and receiving his bachelor's degree in 1909. He won his M.A. degree in German literature in 1910 with a thesis entitled "Der Einfluß Schillers 'Kabale und Liebe' auf Sudermanns 'Sodoms Ende.'" For his later doctoral work at The University of Texas from 1924 to 1928 he changed his field to history and wrote his dissertation under the supervision of Professor Eugene C. Barker on "The History of the German Settlements in Texas, 1831-1861." This dissertation became the book now before you, originally published in 1930.

The factor that led Rudolph to shift from German literature to history was World War I and the accompanying anti-German feeling in Texas. He had taught school in New Braunfels, and then before the war he taught high-school German and civics in Corsicana, Texas. On moving to Waco, Texas, he taught history in high school during and after World War I.

His college teaching began in the summer of 1925 at the East Texas Teachers College in Commerce. He also instructed history at The University of Texas, while a graduate student, from 1925 to 1928. After receiving his doctorate, he taught Latin-American history at the University of Alabama from 1928 to 1929. He returned to The University of Texas in 1929 and, in the absence of Professor C. W. Hackett, taught Latin-American history. In 1930-1931 he was chairman of the Department of History and Social Science at Louisiana Polytechnic Institute in Ruston. He returned again to Austin in 1931 to teach American history, becoming a full professor in 1941 and retiring as professor emeritus in 1957.

Besides teaching his popular sophomore course in American history and several advanced courses, Dr. Biesele found time to supervise several doctoral dissertations and more than a hundred master's theses, many of these on particular Texas subjects, such as county histories. He was a meticulous, demanding teacher but beloved by his students.

Dr. Biesele was for some years a member of the Board of Editors of the *Journal of Southern History* and of the *Southwestern Social Science Quarterly*. From 1939 to 1957 he was both Associate Editor and Book Review Editor of the *Southwestern Historical Quarterly*.

ABOUT THE AUTHOR

Dr. Biesele published six articles on Germans in Texas in the *Southwestern Historical Quarterly* between 1927 and 1946. He also gave addresses at a number of gatherings of German descendants in Texas. Notable among these was one delivered in Austin County in 1936 as part of the Texas Centennial celebration, his subject being "The Contributions of the German Settlers in the Building Up of Austin County and Texas." In New Braunfels on August 21, 1938, he presented the "Festrede" at the dedication of the memorial to the German settlers of Texas next to Comal Springs in Landa Park. He carried on his research not only with the aid of reminiscences, letters, and other documents available locally in Texas, but also on papers from the Solms-Braunfels Archiv in Germany furnished him in photostatic copies by the Library of Congress. These papers concerned activities of the "Adelsverein," the Society for the Protection of German Immigrants in Texas.

Rudolph Biesele was married in 1910 to Anna Emma Jahn, daughter of C. A. Jahn, businessman and mayor of New Braunfels. Her grandfather was Johann Michael Jahn, a cabinet maker from the Baltic coast. Like Leopold Biesele, the political refugeee, Johann Jahn did not permit himself to be photographed, for reasons not now known.

Rudolph and Anna Biesele had four children: Ferdinand Charles (1912-1975), who became Professor of Mathematics at the University of Utah; Rudolph Leopold, Jr. (1915-1984), who was Professor of Electrical Engineering at Southern Methodist University and the University of Oklahoma before entering industry; John Julius (1918-   ), who was a Member of the Sloan-Kettering Institute for Cancer Research in New York City before becoming a Professor of Zoology at The University of Texas at Austin; and Grace Annette (1920-   ), wife of Professor Robert H. Gregory of Massachusetts. There were sixteen grandchildren and a number of children in later generations. In 1964 Governor John A. Connally named Anna Jahn Biesele Texas Mother of the Year.

Rudolph and Anna were members of an Evangelical Reformed Church in Waco and later of several other churches before becoming founding members of the Westminster Presbyterian Church in Austin.

Rudolph Leopold Biesele died January 4, 1960, at the age of seventy-three in the home he and Anna had built twenty-four years before at 2308 Bridle Path, Austin. Anna put out a second edition of this book in 1964 and followed Rudolph in death in 1983.

John J. Biesele
October 24, 1986

THE HISTORY OF THE GERMAN SETTLEMENTS IN TEXAS, 1831-1861

CHAPTER I

THE GERMAN BACKGROUND

North America has been the goal of German emigration ever since the last two decades of the seventeenth century. Early in the eighteenth century, particularly after the War of the Spanish Succession, many people from the Palatinate came to America. In a few instances the love of adventure caused Germans to leave their native country; in others it was the desire for social betterment. Religious freedom served as a motive for emigration in the seventeenth and eighteenth centuries, but this motive, as far as can be ascertained, was never active in the nineteenth century and was never considered by those who came to Texas in the nineteenth century. With most of the emigrants the desire for economic betterment was the paramount consideration for seeking a new home in America. When the opportunities for making a living in Germany no longer promised a comfortable existence to the workingman, he began to migrate to those parts of North America and elsewhere that held out a prospect of a better living. During the nineteenth century, particularly in the early thirties and in the revolutionary period of 1848 to 1849, the desire for political improvement served as the outstanding motive for emigration. When the revolutionary movements of these years failed, many Germans were forced to flee from their native land in order to escape military punishment. These turned their footsteps toward the United States, where, as they thought, a man was a man and freedom was a fact.

When the Anglo-American colonization of Texas began, the eyes of the German people were directed toward this new land, which, with the North American republic, was to receive a part of the German emigration. But motives of this emigration, with the exception of the religious motive, apply to Texas quite as well as to the United States. In connection with the desire for political betterment, Texas was considered as a suitable region for establishing a German state in North America. After Texas secured her independence, her importance in this respect became all the greater. A closer examination of these motives is proper at this point.

Centuries ago, when the Germanic tribes were still living in their primitive social development in the northern part of Europe, they frequently undertook adventurous enterprises under leaders especially chosen for the purpose. These expeditions developed among the early Germans an adventurous spirit, for which, in a much later period, they used the term *Wanderlust*. This *Wanderlust* has remained with them through all the ages as one of their national characteristics. It has seized many a young German who hoped to find in a far-away land what his native country could no longer offer him. Since the earliest times these tribes have felt the impulse to leave their native country and to transplant their civilization and customs to other lands.[1] In the nineteenth century many of those who were tired of Europe *(Europamuede)* were overcome by *Wanderlust* and directed their steps toward North and South America. Among these some came to Texas. Detlef Dunt, who made a journey to Texas in 1833, mentions as characteristic of these younger Germans "the impulse to see the world."[2]

Schiller expressed in his poem, "Hope" *(Die Hoffnung)*, the thought that man is forever looking for betterment of his social condition. In the case of his own people, not only has such a need been manifest, but they have had to struggle with the various forces that have tended to retard their development. One of the principal factors which helped to keep the German people in a wretched or at least an unsatisfactory social condition was overpopulation. In

---

[1]Schuetz, Kuno Damian, Freiherr von, *Texas. Rathgeber fuer Auswanderer nach diesem Lande*, 135. At the time of writing his book, Schuetz was an official of the Society for the Protection of German Immigrants in Texas *(Verein zum Schutze deutscher Einwanderer in Texas)* and lived in New Braunfels, Texas. The Society for the Protection of German Immigrants in Texas, hereafter to be briefly referred to as the Society, was first organized in 1842 at Biebrich on the Rhine for the purpose of buying tracts of land in Texas. It sent two of its members to Texas in the same year to investigate conditions. In 1844 it decided on directing German emigration to Texas and kept up this work from the fall of 1844 until early in 1847. A full treatment of its activities will be given in later chapters of this study. (For a full treatment of this Society, see Chapters IV and V of this study.)

[2]Dunt, *Reise nach Texas nebst Nachrichten von diesem Lande; fuer Deutsche welche nach Amerika zu gehen beabsichtigen*, 1.

the preface of a book by Gottfried Duden, published in 1829, the remark appears that "most of the evils from which the inhabitants of Europe, and particularly of Germany, suffer arise from overpopulation and are of such a nature that all remedies remain without effect unless a thinning out of the population precedes them."[3] The only practicable remedy for overpopulation was emigration, to which many Germans resorted as a natural consequence, and looked upon as a necessity, even if in some quarters it was regarded as an evil. Anyway, it is certain that those who remained in Germany found it easier to make a living as a result of the emigration of their kinspeople.[4]

Some of the German states, however, opposed the reduction of their population and attempted, though not before the thirties and forties of the nineteenth century, to protect themselves against emigration. The kingdom of Bavaria was opposed to emigration but did allow it. That government, in 1835, required that those of its subjects who were anxious to emigrate should make application to the proper authorities, each application being decided upon its merits. Fairly heavy penalties were imposed upon the emigrant, such as confiscation of property or of income derived therefrom; and even persons enticing royal subjects to emigration were classed as traitors, for whom the penalty was to be a term of

[3]Duden, *Bericht ueber eine Reise nach den westlichen Staaten Nordamerika's* (second original edition), XLIII. Duden went to the United States in 1824 and spent four years in Missouri. After his return to Germany he wrote a report of his travels and experiences. Due to the rigid censorship of the press in Germany, his book was published in St. Gallen, Switzerland, in 1829. This book was widely read throughout the southwestern part of Germany and awakened in many people the desire to emigrate to America. In an article, called "America as the Political Utopia of Young Germany," T. S. Baker attributes the beginning of the emigration to America about the year 1831 to two causes, one of which was the publication of Duden's book. (See *Americana Germanica*, I (No. 2), 65.)

In Dunt, Detlef, *Reise nach Texas*, 1, appears the statement that overpopulation of the fatherland was the cause for the major portion of German emigration. Dunt probably overstated it, or else he had all of the accompanying effects of overpopulation in mind.

[4]Schultz, Joh. Heinr. Siegfried, *Die deutsche Ansiedlung in Texas*, 34. Schultz was a referendary in Bonn. He defended the colonization program of the Society for the Protection of German Immigrants in Texas by eight articles in *Der Rheinische Beobachter*, published at Bonn. These articles were subsequently published in pamphlet form under the title, *Die deutsche Ansiedlung in Texas*. Five articles by Schultz in favor of the Society and its colonization program appeared in the *Frankfurter Journal* on August 11, September 1, 4, and 28, and October 27, 1844.

imprisonment of from two to eight years.[5]   On April 23, 1847, the
grand-duchy of Baden issued a decree that no person might, without governmental permission, operate an emigration agency in
Baden. The decree sought also to protect the prospective emigrants
against unscrupulous agents by requiring that sufficient food be
taken along on the transatlantic voyage to feed the traveler
properly.[6]

But the movement was not to be stopped. Fr. W. von Wrede,
who was in Texas early in the forties, said that any action on the
part of the German state governments to prevent emigration would
be in vain.[7] Viktor Bracht, who established himself as a merchant
in New Braunfels in 1846, said that, since it was impossible to
stem the tide of emigration, it should be every German's concern
to know that his countrymen were in a land which offered the most
favorable conditions for their prosperity. It was his firm belief
that Texas was the country where every farmer with a little capital,
every skilful mechanic, and every industrious laborer could count
on a comfortable existence.[8]

The maladjustments of modern life formed a second social cause
of emigration. The industrial life of the Rhine region left many
people wretchedly poor and made a few immensely rich. There
was a very unequal distribution of wealth. The capitalist class
controlled the industrial situation; they alone reaped the profits of
industry. The worker was oppressed and was barely able to eke

[5]Treu, Georg, *Das Buch der Auswanderung*, 8-13. This law was re-
published in 1848. *(Ibid.,* 1-7.) This book is made up in part of acts,
ordinances, and decrees relating to emigration and is, for that reason, very
useful for this study. It contains also a number of announcements of
the Society.

[6]Treu, Georg, *Das Buch der Auswanderung*, 34-37. In the early forties
the liberal legislature of Baden had resolved, however, in favor of the
enforced emigration of poor communities. A similar action had been
taken in Wuertemberg. Indeed, many German communities are claimed
to have disposed of their poor by an enforced emigration in the winter
of 1847 to 1848. (Kapp, *Aus und ueber Amerika*, I, 180, 248.) Dr.
Ferdinand von Herff claims that this practice was resorted to throughout
the entire period from 1840 to 1850. (Herff, *Die geregelte Auswanderung
des deutschen Proletariats mit besonderer Beziehung auf Texas*, 9. Hereafter cited as *Die geregelte Auswanderung.)* It is readily apparent that
such a method would aid those who remained behind in their native
country, but such drastic action does not reflect credit on the communities
that resorted to it.

[7]Wrede, *Lebensbilder aus den Vereinigten Staaten von Nordamerika
und Texas*, 117.

[8]Bracht, *Texas im Jahre 1848*, 168, 301.

out an existence; his efforts were not justly rewarded.[9] It is no wonder that many of the workers looked to emigration as the only avenue of escape from these wretched conditions. It promised them freedom from external control of their actions. The uneducated and misinformed German hoped to find in America all that he had lacked in his native country—land in abundance and a table spread with all he desired, in short, a sort of Utopia.[10] A few years before the revolution of 1848 the better educated Germans felt again a growing dissatisfaction with the social status of the German people, many of whom did not seem to have enough of the necessaries of life.[11] The gradual impoverishment of the majority of

[9]Schuetz, *Texas. Rathgeber fuer Auswanderer nach diesem Lande*, 135-136. See also Steinhausen, Georg, *Geschichte der deutschen Kultur*, II, 486. Steinhausen refers to an article written by Friedrich List in 1844 for the *Allgemeine Zeitung*, published in Stuttgart. The article stated that in many regions of Germany the term, "indispensable necessaries of life," comprised potatoes without salt, soup with black bread, oatmeal gruel, and occasionally dumplings. People in better circumstances never saw meat or smoked beef oftener than once a week. Most of them knew roast meat only by hearsay. In some regions the potatoes were made palatable by rubbing them on a herring, suspended by a string from the ceiling and passed from one person to the other around the table. Steinhausen comments that the picture is somewhat overdrawn.

[10]Kapp, *Aus und ueber Amerika*, I, 280. Kapp made a journey through Texas and visited the German settlements, where he learned from the settlers what they had expected to find in Texas. Prof. J. G. Buettner, in his *Briefe aus und ueber Nordamerika*, 209, said that Texas was regarded as the land of milk and honey, where the German hoped to find all that his heart desired. Buettner thought that many would be disappointed.

Dr. Johann Gottfried Buettner, who published his *Briefe aus und ueber Nordamerika* in 1845, was born August 23, 1809, in Muenchenbernsdorf, in the district of Gera. For a time he was a professor in Hamburg, but the writer does not know at what institution nor the years of his professorship. From 1845 to 1857 he was a preacher in Volkmannsdorf and Essbach, Thuringia. In 1848 he served as substitute for the deputy in the Diet of the German Confederation from the fourth electoral district of the grand-duchy of Weimar. After his superannuation he lived at Wuerzburg, Bavaria, and Lichtenthal, Baden.

[11](Douai, Dr. Adolf ?), "Die Deutschen in Texas," in *Neu Braunfelser Zeitung*, November 26, 1852, 2, col. 5. The article is not signed, but the subscriber of the paper, Mr. Hermann Seele, wrote the name of Dr. Douai in pencil under the article. Mr. Seele was one of the first settlers of New Braunfels and knew everybody there. It is reasonably certain that Mr. Seele knew that Dr. Douai was the author of the article. The article appeared in the first number of the *Neu Braunfelser Zeitung*, founded by Ferdinand Lindheimer, a botanist of note, who came to Texas in 1836. There is only one copy of the first volume of the *Zeitung* in existence and is the prized possession of Mr. Harry C. Seele, son of Hermann Seele, of New Braunfels, Texas. It was through the kindness of Mr. Seele that the writer had access to Dr. Douai's article.

the German people made emigration a necessity. Texas was the choice of many of the emigrants.[12]

Johann Heinrich Siegfried Schultz made a laudable suggestion for reducing overpopulation and decreasing poverty. He thought that the colony which the Society for the Protection of German Immigrants in Texas wanted to establish in Texas should be made into a colony for the poor. The Society, whose work will be discussed in later chapters of this study, consisted of some twenty German noblemen who in the years from 1842 to 1844 organized themselves to direct German emigration to Texas. Schultz urged that the German states should support the movement for the creation of a colony for the poor. In this way they could continue to serve, unite, and protect their unfortunate subjects.[13] Dr. Ferdinand von Herff published a pamphlet on the subject in 1850 with a special consideration of Texas as a suitable place for a colony for German industrial workers. Dr. Herff had been a member of the German communistic colony, Bettina, founded on the Llano River in 1847.[14] Dr. Herff advocated the systematic founding of colonies in which the colonists, through their own work and industry, could become self-supporting and respectable citizens in a very short time. He wanted all the governments, both state and local, in Germany to join in sending the proletariat to the colony, the state governments to take charge of the transportation of colonists thither, the local governments to assume charge of their transatlantic welfare. The German fleet could render the fatherland no greater service than to end the saddest of wars, the revolutionary strife in Germany, by transporting the proletariat to Texas. Dr. Herff thought that Texas was especially suitable for such a colony, since the climate was healthful, land and provisions were cheap, and little work and time were required to make a crop.[15]

[12]Mgebroff, Johannes, *Geschichte der Ersten Deutschen Evangelisch-Lutherischen Synode von Texas*, 3-4.

[13]Schultz, *Die deutsche Ansiedlung in Texas*, 45, 52. Traugott Bromme, who was well informed on conditions in North Amerika, had proposed such a colony in the Diet of Saxony in 1844. (*Ibid.*, 46.)

[14]Reinhardt, Louis, "The Communistic Colony of Bettina," Texas State Historical Association *Quarterly*, III, 33-41. See also Chapter VII, p. 154, of this study.

[15]Herff, *Die geregelte Auswanderung des deutschen Proletariats mit besonderer Beziehung auf Texas*, 5-16. It was not Dr. Herff's intention, however, to promote any system, idea, or principle of socialism, but

The economic motive always occupied an important place in emigration. It was thus the hope of improving their material welfare which induced many Germans to direct their footsteps toward North America. They desired to escape the heavy taxation in their own country and hoped to get cheap land and higher wages in America. With an improvement in their economic status, they expected to improve their social condition and, in the course of time, their political condition as well. The German merchants saw in the emigration of their countrymen an expansion of trade and an opening up of new markets. The new markets would be found particularly in Texas, which would become the avenue of trade between Europe and China, as well as between Europe and Australia. These various aspects of the economic motive will be considered next.

Following the Napoleonic wars, the people of the various German states suffered considerably from the burdens of taxation. Not only were their governments forced to collect higher taxes in order to meet the heavy war debts; they must also keep up expensive military establishments. Worst of all, however, was the extravagance at the courts of many of the German rulers, which increased the already unbearable burden. The rebirth of Germany meant much to the German people, of course, but some were not willing to bear their share of the very heavy cost.[16] The reading of Gottfried Duden's book fired many with the desire to settle in North America. In the preface of his book, Duden reminded his readers of the wretched conditions then prevailing in Germany by saying: "The poverty, the administrative coercion, the oppressive financial system, the tolls and excises, form with us invisibly, and therefore the more injuriously, a kind of serfdom for the common people, which, in some instances, is worse than legally recognized slavery."[17]

In America land was still cheap and wages were relatively higher than in Germany. The German peasant, therefore, longed for the

simply to make the largest number of workers self-supporting in the least possible time and with the least possible expense.

[16] (Muench ?) "Die drei Perioden der neueren deutschen Auswanderung nach Nordamerika," *Der deutsche Pionier*, I, 244.

[17] The translation is taken from Tiling, *History of the German Element in Texas*, 14. In his bibliography Tiling lists an edition of Duden's book, published at St. Gallen, Switzerland, in 1832. The writer used the second edition of Duden's book, published at Bonn, Germany, in 1834, but did not find the passage translated by Tiling.

day when he might get away from the difficulties which he encountered at home and become the owner of land in the new world. It became known to him that in Texas land was being given away to settlers in large tracts, larger than those possessed by some of the German nobility. The German artisan looked forward to the time when he might get a living wage for his work. This information, therefore, served its purpose by directing a good number to Texas.[18]

It has been pointed out already that the emigration of the poor increased the opportunities of making a living for those who remained in Germany. Some German communities, at their own expense, are said to have transported their poor to America in the hope of alleviating the conditions of those who were allowed to remain.[19]

Some Germans were also prompted to leave their native country by the desire to provide for the future welfare of their children. German parents had apprehensions about the future economic welfare of their sons and daughters. Frederick Law Olmsted tells of a Bavarian artisan who had emigrated to Texas because he was solicitous of the future prosperity of his children. Olmsted found this man happy in his new home, although emigration had brought him many hardships and privations.[20] Viktor Bracht points out that nobody in America ever had cause to despair, because any man with the will and the ability to work could provide for himself and his family a carefree present and a happy future.[21]

But emigration for the purpose of increasing trade by opening up new markets and stimulating the demand for German manufactures was especially welcomed by the German merchants and manufacturers. These two groups could look at emigration in a

---

[18]Schuetz, *Texas. Rathgeber fuer Auswanderer nach diesem Lande*, 83-90; Bromme, *Hand- und Reisebuch fuer Auswanderer nach den Vereinigten Staaten von Nord-Amerika*, 301, 435-445; Behr, Ottomar von, *Guter Rath fuer Auswanderer*, 1 ff. Behr advises day laborers, unskilled manual workers, tavernkeepers, students, teachers, writers, and jurists to stay in Germany. Bromme's book will be referred to henceforth briefly as *Hand- und Reisebuch fuer Auswanderer*.

[19]Above, p. 4, foot-note 6.

[20]Olmsted, *Wanderungen durch Texas und im mexikanischen Grenzlande*, 135. Olmsted, who made a journey through Texas in 1853 and 1854, was very much impressed with the evidences of a high civilization in the German settlements of West Texas.

[21]Bracht, *Texas im Jahre 1848*, 169.

broader way than the individual emigrant. They could see the possibility of a colonial establishment and the advantages to be derived therefrom. This subject interested the thinkers of the time and to them we are indebted for the comments which are to follow. Traugott Bromme, who was well informed on conditions in North America through his many travels, said that trade was the great pivot about which everything turned in America; that everybody was interested and nearly everybody was engaged in it.[22] When Texas came to be considered for colonization, the trade possibilities of this new country were always emphasized.[23]

[22]Bromme, *Hand- und Reisebuch fuer Auswanderer*, 452.

[23]The earliest mention of Texas in connection with the development of German trade is found in a book which appeared in Germany in 1821. It was written by J. Val. Hecke, a retired Prussian army officer, who had made a journey through the United States in 1818 and 1819. Hecke presented an elaborate colonization scheme for Texas, which stressed also the mercantile possibilities of that country. He felt that Prussian merchants could get control of all the trade with the Indians down to the South Sea. Galveston he pictured as becoming a depot from which goods could be shipped to Mexico by the Rio del Norte and to the United States by way of the Sabine, the Red, the Mississippi, the Missouri, and the Ohio rivers. The Prussian merchants were to organize a trading company on the order of the British East India Company, bear all the expenses, and reap all the profits. Prussia could get sugar, indigo, and cotton from Texas. The trade would react favorably on Prussia's manufactures, Hecke thought. (Hecke, *Reise durch die Vereinigten Staaten von Nord-Amerika in den Jahren 1818 und 1819*, 200. For an account of Hecke's colonization plan, see below Ch. II, 41-43. F. E. Walther, *Texas in sein wahres Licht gestellt*, 5, said in 1848 that Texas would become the main avenue of trade for Europe and North America to China and Australia.)

Shortly after the Society for the Protection of German Immigrants in Texas began its colonization work in Texas, eight articles were contributed by Johann Heinrich Siegfried Schultz to *The Rhenish Observer* (*Der Rheinische Beobachter*. See above, p. 3, footnote 4). In his third article Schultz discussed the economic advantages which would accrue to Germany from the Texas colony. Schultz pointed to the imports of Texas in 1841 amounting to $1,320,000. He estimated that in 1845 Texas would import that much from Germany alone. The Texan exports of cotton, tobacco, rice, and hides could be exchanged for German manufactures. Thus Germany and Texas would become closely connected. In addition, the Society, as will be seen later, was obliged by its contracts with the emigrants to keep its magazines and storehouses filled with necessary supplies. Since every immigrant was allowed to import, duty free, goods in the amount of five hundred dollars, and since ordinarily the immigrant would not bring in over two hundred dollars' worth of goods, the Society would be allowed to bring in, duty free, $900,000 of goods for every 3000 immigrants, the number which the Society was contemplating sending into Texas in 1845. These goods would, of course, be manufactured in Germany. Once a market for German goods had been established, the German merchants could establish branch houses in Texas. Schultz looked beyond Texas even to the Santa Fé trade. He contended

So far only those forces which act silently and without much disturbance have been discussed. Political discontent in Germany attracted more attention and caused more discussion than the social and economic maladjustments. This discontent was felt by a class of people who stood higher in the social scale than the working classes, and for that reason more was said and more was written about it. Histories of Germany, whether written by Germans or by foreign writers, have devoted more space to the political agitations of the period from 1815 to 1849 than to the social and economic discontent.

When the Congress of Vienna had completed its work in 1815 and a thoroughgoing reaction against liberal tendencies had set in, the students in the German universities became interested in a movement to unite themselves into one large student association *(Burschenschaft)*.[24] It was hoped that the *Burschenschaft* would become the model for a united German fatherland *("ein vereinigtes deutsches Vaterland")*. The first of these societies was organized at the University of Jena in 1815 and soon comprised the entire student body. The movement spread to other universities, such as Halle, Leipzig, Giessen, Heidelberg, Tuebingen. The organizers of the *Burschenschaften* were imbued with liberal political principles and were in the main from the smaller German states. The constitution of the *Burschenschaft* demanded a striving for moral and scientific improvement and a thorough development of one's individuality in body and spirit, in order to place oneself later in the service of the fatherland. Its watchword was: "Liberty, honor, fatherland" *(Freiheit, Ehre, Vaterland)*.[25]

also that in 1844 the Germans in the Southern States carried the election for Polk, because they wanted a commercial treaty with Germany through which they could exchange their rice, cotton, and tobacco for German manufactured goods. With the emigration of Germans to Texas on the increase, German trade would increase; if Texas should join the Union, the votes in favor of a commercial treaty with Germany would be increased. In either case, German trade would be materially augmented. (Schultz, *Die deutsche Ansiedlung in Texas*, 23-41.)

[24]Up to that time the students at each university had organized themselves into as many *Landschaften* as there were German states represented among the student body. The *Burschenschaft*, on the other hand, was open to every student at a German university, regardless of the German state from which he came. The *Burschenschaft*, then, represented the federal idea, whereas the *Landschaft* stood for the state idea.

[25]Biedermann, K., *Deutsche Volks- und Kulturgeschichte*, III. Teil, 169; Meister, Aloys, *Gebhardts Handbuch der deutschen Geschichte*, III (sechste

The *Burschenschaften* movement spread until an incident occurred in 1819 which gave it a severe check. Karl Sand, a member of the Jena *Burschenschaft,* murdered the author Kotzebue at Mannheim on March 23, 1819. Sand had come under the influence of certain principles taught by a young professor at Jena, Karl Follen. One of these principles was that what a person considers to be right, is right. The Jena *Burschenschaft* was held to be implicated in Sand's deed, but the government could not prove it. As a result of Sand's rash act, several reactionary measures were instituted by the Prussian government, although it had for some years looked with favor on the great work in physical culture which the *Burschenschaften* promoted.[26] At the instance of Prussia, a provisional national press law, valid for five years, was promulgated by the Diet of the German Confederation in all of the German states for all publications under three hundred and twenty pages. The universities were to be under the surveillance of special government officials. All teachers whose opinions seemed dangerous were to be dismissed, and all secret organizations, especially the *Burschenschaften,* were prohibited. A central investigating commission with headquarters at Mainz was to investigate and prosecute all revolutionary plots. These measures were decided on at a conference in Karlsbad on August 8, 1819, under the leadership of Metternich and were promulgated on September 20, 1819, as the Carlsbad Decrees.[27]

These repressive measures did not, however, overcome the liberal movement, which gave new evidences of vigor in Germany from 1831 to 1833. As a result of the ordinances which the Diet of the German Confederation passed in 1832 after the July Revolution in France, the persecution of the academic world and

Auflage), 19; Henderson, Ernest F., *A Short History of Germany,* II, 328, 332-333. Henderson comments that the *Burchenschaften* were founded in 1815 "with the noblest purposes and in patriotic antagonism to the *Landschaften,* which represented the separation of the various states." (*Ibid.,* II, 328.)

[26]Biedermann, *Deutsche Volks- und Kulturgeschichte,* 3. Teil, 172. Ludwig Jahn started the movement for the teaching of physical training in the schools of Germany. The *Burschenschaften* had embodied Jahn's work in their program.

[27]Biedermann, *Deutsche Volks- und Kulturgeschichte,* 3, Teil, 180; Kaufmann, Georg, *Politische Geschichte Deutschlands im Neunzehnten Jahrhundert,* 113-127; Meister, *Gebhardts Handbuch der deutschen Geschichte,* III (6te Auflage), 20-21.

of politicians suspected of liberalism was intensified.[28]   Discontent in Germany reached a high point.   Under the leadership of Dr. John G. A. Wirth, publisher of the *German Tribune*,[29] patriotic unions, known as "press unions", were formed for the support of the liberal papers.   At Zweibruecken in the Bavarian Palatinate a central committee directed the work of sub-committees in Wuertemberg, Baden, Hesse-Cassel, Hesse-Darmstadt, Nassau, Saxony, Coburg, Altenburg, Weimar, Westphalia, Hanover, the Hansa towns, and Holstein.[30]   Wirth announced in his paper that the object of his "Press-Union" was the organization of a German empire on democratic principles.[31]

On May 27, 1832, on the occasion of the "Hambacher Fest," a great festival held at Hambach Castle in Rhenish Bavaria on Pentecost, the hope of a united German fatherland was revived. The British *Annual Register* for 1832 gives the following account of the festival:

The Bavarian government forbade the meeting. Then it changed its mind, and revoked its prohibitory rescript. The convocation was accordingly held on the 27th and 28th of May. The persons present amounted to about 20,000. It neither was, nor had ever been intended to be, a Bavarian meeting. Multitudes flocked to it from Electoral Hesse, from Nassau, Rhenish Prussia, Baden, and Wurtemberg; and its character was still better marked by the presence of Polish refugees, and French national guards. Patriotic songs were sung; patriotic speeches were delivered; and it was resolved to hold other meetings of the same kind; and the solemnity concluded with a repast laid out on the open plain. The speeches which attracted most notice, and were most loudly applauded, were of a nature to excite the fears of all regular governments. Amid their smoke and heat, nothing could be distinctly traced except democracy and revolution. Insurrection and civil war were treated as very easy and very desirable things, which would not fail to place the orators, and enlightened lovers of justice and liberty, like the orators, in their natural place at the head of the society. One of the speakers denounced all the German princes as traitors. He brand-

[28]Hazen, C. D., *Europe Since 1815*, I, 35.

[29]Wirth published this newspaper in Munich in 1831 and in Homburg in 1832.

[30]Koerner, Gustave, *The Memoirs of Gustave Koerner*, 187. These *Memoirs* were published in 1909.

[31]Treitschke, Heinrich von, *Deutsche Geschichte im Neunzehnten Jahrhundert*, IV, 261.

ished the sabre, presented to him by his admirers, when he had been compelled to give up the publication of a seditious periodical journal, crying out 'Liberty and Equality.' Songs and toasts were given in the same spirit; and the more moderate politicians, who had expected good from the meeting, now repented that it had ever taken place. The Bavarian government, which had placed itself in an unpleasant relation to its confederates by sanctioning the solemnity, now issued a rescript strongly condemning it and all assemblies of the same kind.   .   .   .[32]

Treitschke says that Siebenpfeiffer, one of the speakers, predicted that the day would come when the princes would exchange the gay ermine robes of feudalistic rulers for the manly toga of German national dignity; and he says that Wirth, the principal speaker, offered a toast to the united free states of Germany and to a confederated republican Europe and demanded that a few determined men should assume the leadership of the German opposition. Biedermann says it was not only a national German festival, but a festival of the fraternization of free people. Gustav Koerner, who participated in the political uprising at Frankfort the following year, says that an immense flag bearing the inscription, "Resurrection of Germany," was seen in the parade. He says that the speeches all expressed the prevailing opinion that "reform in the different constitutions and in the constitution of the Bund should be brought about by force of public opinion and the support of a free press enlightening and informing the masses about their rights and duties."[33]

New restrictive measures followed this outburst of democratic aspiration. On June 28 and July 5 the Diet of the German Confederation issued a number of ordinances, directed mainly against the right of legislatures to refuse appropriations and against freedom of debate and the press. Associations and meetings of a political nature were not to be tolerated. The provisions of the Carlsbad Decrees respecting the universities and teachers were re-

[32]*The Annual Register for 1832*, 372-373. See also Meister, *Gebhardts Handbuch der deutschen Geschichte*, III (6te Auflage), 183; Henderson, *A Short History of Germany*, II, 338; Ziegler, Theobald, *Die geistigen und sozialen Stroemungen des XIX Jahrhunderts*, 162.

[33]Koerner, *Memoirs of Gustave Koerner*, 193; Treitschke, *Deutsche Geschichte im Neunzehnten Jahrhundert*, IV, 263-264; Biedermann, *Deutsche Volks- und Kulturgeschichte*, 3. Teil, 183.

enacted by the Diet, which also forced Leopold, grand-duke of Baden, to revoke a liberal press law on July 28, 1832.[34]

But the restrictions brought on renewed political agitation, for "among the educated classes not a few were filled with hot indignation, and some were ready to stake their lives in an effort for the liberation and unification of Germany." Many students at German universities supported the cause of a united Germany. Among these Wislizenus took a decided stand, repeatedly representing his university at secret general councils.[35] On April 3, 1833, the so-called "Frankfort Riot" *(Frankfurter Putsch* or *Frankfurter Attentat)* occurred. In the sketch of Dr. Wislizenus's life we read the following:

The plan was conceived of seizing Frankfort, chasing off the representatives of royalty, and thus, as was hoped, striking a spark that would kindle fires of revolt throughout Germany. On the evening of April 3, 1833, a body of students assembled from various universities—Wislizenus among them—less than a hundred all told, surprised the Constables Watch and the Main Watch, two massive military buildings at either end of Frankfort's main street, *die Zeile;* disarmed the guards, seized the arms and munitions; rung (rang) the alarm bells, and summoned the citizens to rise. Only a handful joined them. Soldiers were rushed up, and in a few hours all was over.

The scheme seems fantastic, but it must be remembered that older heads had given it sanction; that the organization had ramifications throughout Germany; that the plan involved action at other places of which no account can here be given. But granting the plan of these young men to have been chimerical, it still is true that they risked not only their future career but life itself under no other inspiration than love of liberty and of Fatherland. Such motives dignify failure. The student attack at Frankfort in 1833 was a logical forerunner of the popular uprising of 1848.[36]

Dr. Gustav Koerner, who was among those wounded, says in his *Memoirs* that the plan was "to call all the Liberal members of the different legislatures of Germany together as a preliminary

---

[34]*Annual Register* (1832), 376; Koerner, *Memoirs*, 193.

[35]Wislizenus, Dr. F. A., *A Journey to the Rocky Mountains in the Year 1839*, 6. Preceding the account of the journey is a sketch of the author's life by his son, F. A. Wislizenus, Esq., of St. Louis. Dr. Wislizenus came to the United States after the uprising of 1833 had failed.

[36]Wislizenus, Dr. F. A., *A Journey to the Rocky Mountains in the Year 1839*, 7.

Parliament." This body was to "order elections for a constitu-ent assembly, which should establish either a republic of the whole nation, or a confederate one, or, if the sense of the people demanded it, a constitutional monarchy."[37]

The German state governments proceeded to mete out punishment to the Liberals. Thousands, says Kapp, left Germany. Rhenish-Prussia, Rhenish-Bavaria, Nassau, Hessen, and many of the smaller states lost a good number of their better educated citizens, who sought refuge in America and established settlements in the Mississippi and Missouri valleys. One writer comments as follows on the emigration of this period:

When the storm had subsided and quiet again restored by the liberal use of bayonets and gendarmes, a detestable system of espionage became rampant in many of the German states and principalities. Hundreds of men in all walks of life were put under rigid police surveillance, while many were even imprisoned for expressing or merely holding different political views from those of their governments. The reactionary element was triumphant, while the progressive, liberal minded men were harassed everywhere. Men of education, science, university professors and teachers, jurists and physicians, suffered most from this political persecution. The press was gagged and literary productions subjected to merciless censure.

This deplorable state of affairs naturally created in the hearts of many men of intellect and energy the desire to free themselves in some way from these intolerable political fetters. The revolution, or rather insurrection, having failed, these men were anxious to emigrate to some country with free institutions and a liberal government, and to found and establish there new homes for themselves and their families under more favorable conditions. Naturally their eyes and thoughts turned westward, where the rising young republic of the United States guaranteed to everybody that freedom of thought and action that had been banished from Europe and especially so from the German states.[38]

[37]Koerner, *Memoirs*, 217. Koerner, although wounded, made his escape into France, whence he went to the United States. He played a prominent part in the political history of the state of his adoption, Illinois. For further accounts see Biedermann, *Deutsche Volks- und Kulturgeschichte*, 3. Teil, 183-184; Meister, *Gebhardts Handbuch der deutschen Geschichte*, III, 32-33; Henderson, *A Short History of Germany*, II, 338-339; Treitschke, *Deutsche Geschichte im Neunzehnten Jahrhundert*, 4. Teil, 299-303; Ziegler, *Die geistigen und sozialen Stroemungen des XIX. Jahrhunderts*, 163; *Annual Register* (1833), 280-281.

[38]Tiling, *History of the German Element in Texas from 1820-1850*, 12-13.

Some of the emigrants of this period went to Texas, but their number was small. In 1869 the editor of the *Wochenblatt der Union,* in giving a brief résumé of a manuscript on *Die Deutschen in Texas,* wrote: "The effects of the Frankfurter Putsch or the Hambacher Fest sent only a few to Texas. . . . Most of them remained near the coast, but some of these emigrants founded the colonies on the Mill and Cummings Creek, with Industry and Frelsburg as their center.[39]

It was in the early thirties that the first German emigration societies were formed in response to the prevalent desire for emigration. Among these societies the Giessen Emigration Society *(Giessener Auswanderungsgesellschaft)* was the most important In the *Frankfurter Journal* and in the *Augsburger Allgemeine Zeitung,* in which the call for organizing an emigration society was issued, the political conditions in Germany were pictured as so hopeless that even the most persevering patriot *("ausdauerndste Patriot")* could emigrate with an easy conscience. The call was signed by Paul Follen, a superior court attorney and jurist of Giessen. Associated with Follen were Friedrich Muench, a Protestant minister, known later in America as "Far West," George Bunsen, brother of Dr. Gustav Bunsen, who was one of the leaders of the *Frankfurter Putsch,* Professor Goebel of Coburg, and Joseph Kircher of Munich, a university friend of Gustav Koerner.[40] Many other emigration societies were organized in different parts of Germany and directed emigration to the United States during the next decade and longer. Of these, only the Society for the Protection of German Immigrants in Texas was interested in German colonization in Texas.

[39]"Die Deutschen in Texas," in *Wochenblatt der Union,* XI, No. 47, September 12, 1869, 4, col. 2. The manuscript, entitled *Die Deutschen in Texas,* was written probably by Dr. A. Siemering of San Antonio, Texas, who interested himself in the subject of German colonization in Texas. Whoever the author was turned the manuscript over to Flake, the editor of the *Wochenblatt der Union,* for review before publication. Such a work never appeared in print, however, a fact which is to be seriously regretted. *The Wochenblatt der Union* was published at Galveston.

[40]Rattermann, H. A., "Sagen-Geschichte einer deutschen Auswanderungs-Gesellschaft," *Der deutsche Pionier,* I, 20-21; Koerner, *Memoirs,* 307-308. In the twelfth volume of *Der deutsche Pionier,* Rattermann, its editor, has a long article on the German element in the United States before 1848, in which he refers again to the large German emigration immediately after the Hambacher Fest and the Frankfurter Putsch. The subject seems to have interested him.

After the revolutionary period of 1830 to 1833, which had
culminated in the *Frankfurter Putsch,* the dissatisfied elements
in Germany continued their work in behalf of a united Germany.
Finally the great revolutionary movement of 1848 broke out. Its
failure sent many Germans to the United States. These "Forty-
eighters" Ernest Bruncken describes as follows:

By the year 1848, a large portion of these classes which took
an interest in public matters at all had become imbued with ultra-
democratic notions. They believed in the republican form of
government as the only one fit for civilized society. All mon-
archies, no matter how strictly limited, were merely forms of op-
pression. All kings and princes were enemies of mankind. An
enthusiastic belief in 'Liberty' was, with most of them, coupled
with fanatical intolerance of all who disagreed with them. The
strength of their convictions was usually proportionate to their
inexperience of the actual business of government. Of this inexperience there was a remarkable amount in the ranks of these
reformers. Naturally the men who were practically acquainted
with such matters were not to be found among them, for radical
or even pronounced liberal opinions were not favorable to a
man's rising very high in an official career under the Metternich
system. The great majority of the radical leaders were literary
men, journalists, advocates, physicians. Their following came
almost exclusively from the small tradesmen and workingmen of
the cities. The wealthier commercial classes, as well as large
numbers of the professional and official class, were mostly ad-
herents of a moderate Liberalism and believed in a constitutional
monarchy. Instead of a German republic, the aim of the Radicals,
the Liberals desired a Germany united under the sway of an
emperor, with an imperial parliament to represent the people.
The country population, both squire and peasant, were as a class
the staunchest of conservatives.
Such being the ranks of society from which the Radicals mostly
came, it must be mentioned in addition that they were mostly
young men; and a third circumstance important to remember is
that Radicalism had its chief strength in the Southern portions
of Germany, and along the Rhine. Elsewhere, it was on the
whole confined to the large cities, such as Berlin, Dresden, and
Breslau. In the Parliament, which met at Frankfurt early in
the summer of 1848, to deliberate on a constitution for a united
Germany, these Radicals formed the 'Democratic Left.' . . .
Even before the Parliament, the Democrats of the Palatinate
and Baden, under the leadership of Friedrich Hecker, had attempted the Republic by force of arms. . . . In addition
to the Baden insurrections, which assumed the dimensions of

warfare, there had been numerous riots and barricade fights in almost every city of any importance, and everybody who had been in any way concerned in these felt his liberty and life in danger.[41]

In connection with the German emigration the idea arose of building up a German state in North America. It was after the failure of the Hambacher Fest that a movement was started in southwestern Germany to send over to America a large number of emigrants and to establish a German state. *Niles' Weekly Register* took notice of this with the following account:

WHOLESALE EMIGRATION. The *Stuttgard Universal Gazette* of September 2d, announces that a plan is in progress in the southwest of Germany, to make up a state and ship it over to the United States, to become a twenty-fifth member of the confederacy. The following notice of the project appears in that publication: 'According to accounts from the southwest of Germany, a society of liberal men are organizing a grand plan for emigrating to North America. The emigration has hitherto been precarious, because it did not rest on any solid foundation, and because the means were not concentrated. But now it is different, as the object is to form a *New Germany* beyond the ocean, which is to receive all those whose hopes and claims to liberty and right are disappointed in old Germany . . . Many of the Germans established in North America will join their countrymen, and the plan is so popular in Germany, that scarcely any doubts are entertained of its being successful.'

The editor's comment on the plan was that the idea of forming a state was chimerical and would be injurious on many accounts.[42]

The Giessen Emigration Society *(Giessener Auswanderungsgesellschaft),* in connection with its plan of directing German emigration to the United States, was interested also in the project of founding a new Germany. According to the prospectus which it issued in 1833 its objects were stated to be: "The founding of a German state, which would, of course, have to be a member of the United States, but with maintenance of a form of government which will assure the continuance of German custom, German language, and create a genuine, free, and popular

---

[41]Bruncken, *German Political Refugees in the United States during the Period from 1815-1860,* 27-28.

[42]*Niles' Weekly Register,* XLIII (Whole Series), 148, or VII (Fourth Series), 148. The date of issue is November 3, 1832.

(*volksthuemliches*) life." Bruncken says that the intention was "to occupy an unsettled and unorganized territory, 'in order that a German republic, a rejuvenated Germany, may arise in North America.' "[43] Koerner says that the Giessen Emigration Society failed principally because it had adopted this impracticable idea of founding a new Germany. The promoters thought in the beginning of sending the first colonies to a territory not yet organized as a state, but they finally selected Missouri.[44]

Interest in this movement gained a new momentum when the announcement of the plan of the Society for the Protection of German Immigrants in Texas to make settlements in Texas appeared in 1844. Great hopes arose for the success of the plan. The Society, it was thought, would not be hampered by a lack of funds, since it was organized by some of the richer princes. The time seemed to have come when at last the idea of a German state would bear fruit. Conditions were certainly favorable. Texas was independent and its population was still small enough so that a heavy German emigration to Texas might in a short time make that element predominant.[45] To some, indeed, the plan of the Society held out the prospect of establishing a large German colony dependent upon the German Confederation. But against this proposal Johann Heinrich Siegfried Schultz raised his voice in protest. He wanted to know if its advocates realized what such a colonial establishment would cost and if Germany's navy were large enough to protect it. He pointed out also the possibility of a colonial declaration of independence from Germany, similar to the pronouncement which had freed America, as well as the possibility of seizure of the colony by its mighty neighbor, the United States. Schultz maintained that the colony must not be independent of the state in which it might be located. The colony of the Society would never exist under

---

[43]Bruncken, *German Political Refugees in the United States during the Period from 1815-1860*, 17. Bruncken cites *Aufforderung und Erklaerung in Betreff einer Auswanderung im Grossen aus Deutschland, in die nordamerikanischen Freistaaten* (Giessen, 1833), and Koerner, *Das deutsche Element in den Vereinigten Staaten von Nord-Amerika, 1818-1848*, 300; also Loeher, *Geschichte und Zustaende der Deutschen in Amerika, passim.* See also Davis, Philip, *Immigration and Americanization*, 126-127.

[44]Koerner, *Das deutsche Element*, 300. See also Benjamin, G. G., *The Germans in Texas*, 6.

[45]Koerner, *Das deutsche Element*, 360.

the black, red, and gold flag of Germany but would revere the lone star flag of the Texas republic. Some day the Germans might deem it advisable to separate from Texas, but Schultz doubted it. If they did, however, the state would be an independent state made up of German emigrants, a new Germany, in which German nationality and German life would be preserved.[46]

The German state plan was never seriously considered by the large mass of these emigrants, who thought first and foremost of the pressing problem of making a living. They went to America to escape the prevailing oppressive conditions in the social, economic, and political life and wanted to enjoy the blessings of liberty. Only a small educated minority was interested in the state plan, which was, as Bruncken says, "essentially a greenhorn's scheme." As far as Texas was concerned, too, the advocates of the plan left out of consideration the likelihood that this region would some day abandon its independence and join the American union.

In various ways, then, the German people learned about Texas and began to consider that vast country as a suitable place for establishing a new home. Texas interested both those who were no longer satisfied to endure the social conditions in Germany and those who saw in emigration a means of improving these conditions at home. Those who could no longer make a satisfactory living at home felt that in Texas they could acquire economic independence, while merchants and manufacturers saw the opportunity of opening up new markets for the expansion of German business. In Texas the immigrant hoped to enjoy the blessings of liberty and the full rights of citizenship, free from the ever-present police supervision with which he was so familiar at home. By a small minority, too, Texas was considered favorably for establishing a German state, in which German ways and customs would be observed, the German national characteristics preserved, and the desire for liberty and self-government realized.

[46]Schultz, *Die deutsche Ansiedlung in Texas*, 7-15.

CHAPTER II

INTEREST IN THE GERMAN COLONIZATION OF TEXAS

While Texas was still a part of the Spanish possessions in North America various persons developed an interest in bringing German colonists into Texas. This interest was carried over into the period when Texas was a Mexican possession. Some sponsored the proposal as a means of helping Spain to defend her Texas frontier against the foreign aggressor; some were empresarios who wanted to carry out their contracts with Mexico by settling their colonies either in whole or in part with German settlers; one wanted to settle Germans in Texas to produce raw materials for a projected industrial development in Spain; one wanted his country, Prussia, to buy Texas and reap the rich profits of her trade and agriculture; while still another desired to encourage Swiss and German immigrants to come to Texas because these, as he said, did not have the mania for speculation and would oppose slavery. When Texas became an independent republic there was a renewed interest in the proposal. In this later period the interest was predicated on the general desire to aid in the development of Texas. It is the object of this chapter to give an account of the various plans that were suggested.

The earliest proposal for settling Germans in Texas was made by Morphi, the Spanish consul at New Orleans. In 1812 he proposed to the Spanish government that German and Polish soldiers be sent to Texas to serve as a buffer against Napoleonic aggressions in Texas. Morphi wanted to detach German and Polish soldiers in Napoleon's army from their allegiance to the great general and induce them to settle in Texas, "where they could devote themselves to agriculture and the useful arts, thus securing their own happiness and the welfare of the province. He wished to grant them *seven square leagues* of land upon the Gulf of Mexico near the Louisiana frontier, to exempt them from taxation, to allow them free trade with all nations, and to invest them with local authority. Only artisans and mechanics of good character were to be introduced." The plan was not approved either by the local authorities or by the Cadiz Regency. The Regency saw danger in placing foreign soldiers in a region that was in ferment and unrest and feared that the crafty Napoleon, once he learned of the plan, would induce a great number of German and Polish soldiers to desert from the French legions, who, at the word of their master, would revolt against the Spanish authorities and deliver Texas into the hands of France, thus defeating the very purpose for which they were to be settled in Texas. One member of the Regency offered as a substitute that German Catholics should be persuaded to desert, that they be sent over in small detachments in loyal Spanish regiments, and that they be settled on lands given them in regions where defense against the Indians was needed. But the Regency rejected all proposals and insisted "upon the enforcement of the law forbidding all intercourse with foreigners."[1]

Don Ricardo Reynal Keene addressed a memorial to the king of Spain in 1814 on the subject of placing foreign settlers in Texas. He proposed that both Irish and Germans be brought to Texas because they could aid in building up the agriculture and commerce of Texas and in protecting the frontier of New Spain. He pictured the sufferings and poverty of the Irish people, but thought that the Germans, especially in the Rhine region, because of Napoleon's despotic rule, were even worse off. Hence he thought they would gladly emigrate to Texas and place themselves under Spanish rule.[2] A grant for making a settlement in Texas, which Keene had received in 1813, required that two-thirds of his settlers should be Spaniards, while the others might come from any foreign country except France.[3]

On May 3, 1819, Charles Henry Du Pasquier, P. H. Leuba, and William Wohlleben, citizens of Switzerland, but then in Philadelphia, proposed to Don Luis de Onis, Spanish minister to the United States, the establishment of a colony of Swiss and Germans on the Trinity River in Texas. Five days later they asked

---

[1]Hatcher, M. A., *The Opening of Texas to Foreign Settlement, 1801-1821*, 219-221. Mrs. Hatcher refers to various documents in the *Archivo General de las Indias*.

[2]Keene, *Memoria presentada a S. M. C. El Señor Don Fernando VII*, 19-21. This memorial, in printed form, is to be found in the University of Texas Library.

[3]Hatcher, *The Opening of Texas to Foreign Settlement*, 241.

for permission to substitute either the Sabine, the San Antonio, or the Guadalupe River for the Trinity. The colonists were to engage in agriculture, sheep raising, and silkworm culture, in order to furnish Spain with the raw materials for the manufacture of cotton, woolen, silk, and linen goods.[4] Du Pasquier pointed out that these colonists could be used to protect the frontier of Texas against the enemies of Spain. Action on the plan was delayed, however, while the king of Spain was making up his mind on the Florida treaty which Onis had negotiated with the United States.[5] The delay was fatal to the plan, for by the time final action was taken on the treaty Mexico had struck for independence.

The most ambitious plan proposed for German colonization in Texas came from a retired Prussian army officer, J. Val. Hecke, who published a book in 1821 about his travels in North America made in the years 1818 and 1819. He expressed his opinion of the value of Texas as a Prussian colony in the following words: "If there is a tract of land on the trans-Atlantic continent that is suited as a colonial possession for Prussia, it is the province of Texas, the acquisition of which by purchase from Spain, to which. country it is neither useful nor of political worth, should be very easily accomplished." If Prussia were unable to buy Texas, then, Hecke suggested, the merchants should advance the money for its purchase. A trading company on the order of the British East India Company should be organized and should bear all expenses and reap all profits, but the Prussian government should furnish the troops for protection of the province. Ten thousand soldiers, recruited from the veterans of the Napoleonic wars, would be sufficient to hold the colony against all attacks. Each of these men should receive one hundred acres of land. Hecke thought highly of the agricultural, political, and commercial possibilities of Texas. He advocated that Prussia

---

[4]Du Pasquier to Onis, May 3 and 8, 1819. Archivo General de Indias, Sevilla; Audiencia de Guadalajara; Dunn Transcripts, 1821, pp. 3-10, 15-19. These transcripts are in the University of Texas. The paging used is that found in the French section of the transcript.

It was a part of the plan, also, to send skilled factory workers to Spain from Switzerland and Germany to aid in setting up the machinery and to teach Spanish youths the operation of the machines.

[5]Du Pasquier to Onis, May 3 and 8, 1819. Dunn Transcripts, 1821, pp. 2 and 27.

should take advantage of the prevailing emigration, give the unhappy emigrants free transportation on Prussian ships, and give them land or some other assistance, even if only in the form of a loan. In five or ten years, he estimated, each settler would have fifty acres in cultivation, would earn over fourteen hundred dollars from part of his land sown in wheat, and would produce enough feedstuffs for his stock and food for himself on the remainder of his land to sustain himself and his family. In ten years, Hecke thought, the population might reach one million persons, when a constitution should be granted to satisfy the political needs of the colony. Since the mountains of Texas are in the same range with those of San Luis Potosi, Mexico, he predicted the discovery of gold and other precious metals in Texas. He would send incorrigibles and minor criminals to Texas to engage in agriculture and would deport all thieves and swindlers to Texas. Prussian merchants would get control of all the trade with the Indians down to the South Sea. Galveston would become a depot from which goods could be shipped to Mexico by the Rio del Norte and to the United States by the Mississippi, Missouri, Ohio, Sabine, and Red rivers. Prussia could get sugar, cotton, and indigo from Texas, either through actual production or through purchase from nearby states. This trade would react favorably on Prussian manufactures. Texas could furnish the Antilles and all the northern and eastern shores of South America, including Brazil, with grain, butter, salt meat, and other products.[6]

[6]Hecke, *Reise durch die Vereinigten Staaten von Nord-Amerika in den Jahren 1818 und 1819*, I, 199-203.

The Baron de Bastrop, after whom the town of Bastrop, Texas, was named, is said to have planned an extensive German colonization in Texas when the first American settlements were made in that Mexican province. Bastrop's death, so the story goes, prevented the execution of his plans. Where Dr. Ferdinand Roemer, the author of the statement, got his authority for making it is not ascertainable. It is certain that nowhere in the histories of Texas is the statement made that Bastrop was interested in bringing German settlers into Texas, and no documentary authority for the statement has been discovered.

(For the statement see Roemer, *Texas*, 208; Koerner, *Das deutsche Element*, 359; Eickhoff, *In der neuen Heimath*, 321; Tiling, *History of the German Element in Texas*, 9-10; Weber, *Deutsche Pioniere in Texas*, 12.)

In his *Texas*, 56, Prince Charles of Solms-Braunfels, the first commissioner-general of the Society for the Protection of German Immigrants in Texas, errs in saying that Bastrop founded the town of Bastrop. According to the records, Bastrop was founded on June 8, 1832, by Miguel

On October 5, 1826, Joseph Vehlein granted power of attorney to Dr. John Lucius Woodbury, who was to secure for Joseph Vehlein and Company a contract for establishing a colony in the province of Coahuila-Texas. Doctor Woodbury's application for the contract contains the following words: "Desirous to undertake the project of Colonizing the vacant lands in the Department of Texas, appertaing *(sic)* to this State, the aforesaid Mr. Jose Vehlein, has authorized me to solicit Your Excellency, for permission to effect this object, offering to execute it with Three hundred industrious families, professants of the Catholic religion, and of good moral habits, part of them to be Germans and Swiss, and part of them from the States of North America." The colonization contract was issued at Saltillo on December 21, 1826, but does not state from where the colonists were to come. Article 8 of the contract reads: "The families of which this Colony has to be composed, besides being Catholics, must be of good moral habits, accrediting these qualifications by certificates from the authorities of the place of their emigration."[7] In his petition for a second grant, Dr. Woodbury stated that Joseph Vehlein and Company wanted to settle one hundred families of Germans, Swiss, and English, "all natives of Europe."[8] Vehlein, then, was interested in settling Germans in Texas, but he did not carry his plans into execution, although in 1830, he, David G. Burnet, and Lorenzo de Zavala organized the Galveston Bay and Texas Land Company with certain New York and Boston capitalists and "prepared to promote colonization on a great scale from the United States and Europe."[9]

In 1830 Stephen F. Austin was considering the project of inducing Swiss and German immigrants to come to Texas. He valued the character and industry of the Swiss and Germans and

Arciniega, who had been appointed in 1827 by the Mexican government to lay out new towns for Austin's Colony. (See Translations of Empresario Contracts, 133-134. General Land Office, Austin, Texas. See also Barker, E. C., *The Life of Stephen F. Austin*, 143.)

[7]Translations of Empresario Contracts, 116-119. The land granted by this contract was situated between the Sabine and the San Jacinto, north of the ten league coast reserve and south of the old San Antonio and Nacogdoches road.

[8]*Ibid.*, 172-177. The land contained in this grant was located on the coast reserve, below Vehlein's first grant, east of the San Jacinto to a line parallel with the Sabine, twenty leagues west thereof.

[9]Barker, *Life of Stephen F. Austin*, 144.

said that "they have not in general that horrible *mania* for speculation which is so prominent a trait in the English and North
American character, and above all they will oppose slavery."[10]
Archibald Austin, who was acting for Stephen F. Austin, wrote
on May 31, 1830, that he had had conversations with several
Swiss gentlemen and that one of them, a Mr. Richard, "approved
very much of the project." Archibald Austin called also on
Theodore Meyer, consul for Hanover, from whom he secured the
information that "it would be difficult to prevail on his countrymen to go there," but that, if three or four respectable families
could be induced to go to Texas and should be pleased with the
country, then Stephen F. Austin "would have no difficulty in
prevailing on as many to follow" as he could wish. An extract
from Stephen F. Austin's letter, inserted in the *Journal of Commerce,* had a good effect on Meyer, for "it paid his Countrymen
a compliment."[11]

On July 14 Archibald Austin wrote that since his previous letter
of May 31 he had spoken with various Swiss and Germans in
New York, but that it would be difficult to induce them to go to
Texas, since they had either made up their minds to go to Ohio,
where some of their friends were living, or else they feared the
Texas climate. He intended to communicate on the subject with
Mr. Gildermeister of Havana, but then in Germany.[12] In his
letter to Gildermeister, Archibald Austin "stated the low price
of the land, the inducements held out by the Mexican Government to Swiss & German Emigrants, & urged him, to endeavor
to prevail on some of the most capable, & inteligent to visit it,
and judge for themselves of the qualities, & advantages of the
Country."[13]

In 1830, also, while Austin was considering the advisability
of inducing German and Swiss immigrants to settle in Texas,

[10]Quoted in Barker, *The Life of Stephen F. Austin*, 254, from a letter
by Austin to Thomas F. Leaming of Philadelphia. The explanation for the
remark on slavery is that Austin favored the perpetual exclusion of
slavery from Texas. On this point see *Ibid.*, 254.

[11]Archibald Austin to Stephen F. Austin, New York, May 31, 1830.
Austin Papers, University of Texas.

[12]Archibald Austin to Stephen F. Austin, New York, July 14, 1830. MS.
Austin Papers, University of Texas.

[13]Same to same, New York, September 5, 1830. MS. Austin Papers,
University of Texas.

'Tadeo Ortiz[14] proposed to Lucas Alamán, Mexican Secretary of State for Interior and Exterior Relations, that settlements be established at Sabine Bay, Galveston, and at the mouth of the San Bernard River and that the settlers should be obtained either in Germany or in Switzerland.[15] The proposal was looked on with favor by Manuel de Mier y Terán, Commissioner of Colonization, who wrote to Alamán that "it would be very advantageous to locate about a hundred Swiss or German families in Galveston without an empresario and under the immediate supervision of the government."[16]

In 1832 Dr. J. C. Beales of New York secured two contracts for settling foreign families in Texas.[17] Dr. Beales left New York on the *Amas Wright* in the fall of 1833 with his first contingent of colonists. An interesting account of the journey was written by Eduard Ludecus, a German, who accompanied Dr. Beales. Ludecus had intended to go to St. Louis but gave up that trip when Dr. Beales approached him about going to Texas. At that time, Ludecus wrote, "people in Germany were beginning to talk of Texas and the condition of Austin's colony was pictured as flourishing."[18] There were some fifty persons on the *Amas Wright,* including besides Beales, the leader, Power, Little, Plunkuet (Plunkett), Paulsen, Addicks, Ludecus, Talloer, three English families, three German families, and twenty-seven men of diverse handicrafts. The German families were those of Dippelhofer, Wetter, and Schwarz. These German families went along on the condition of getting their transportation and

[14]Tadeo Ortiz de Ayala was a Creole of Guadalajara who was dominated by two great purposes, the establishment of the independence of Mexico and the protection of the integrity of the national domain by the formation of colonies to develop the unsettled regions and to serve as a barrier against foreign aggressions.

[15]Ortiz to Alamán, June 26, 1830. Department of *Fomento* on Colonization, *Legajo* 7, *Expediente* 57, 33; West Transcripts, 1833-1834, University of Texas.

[16]Terán to Alamán, October 14, 1830. *Ibid.*, 36.

[17]Translations of Empresario Contracts, 194 ff. The first of the contracts, dated March 14, 1832, specified two hundred foreign families; the second, dated June 30, allowed Dr. Beales to bring four hundred and fifty families into Texas.

[18]Ludecus, *Reise durch die Mexikanischen Provinzen Tumalipas, Cohahuila und Texas im Jahre 1834*, 56-67. Ludecus kept his account in letter form. The date of the letter in which the passage quoted occurs is November 4, 1833.

one hundred acres of land free in return for six months of free labor for Dr. Beales. Ludecus gives two indications that Dr. Beales was considering Germans for a part of his colonists. The first of these is that Paulsen, a German, would probably go to Germany after the expedition had arrived in Texas for the purpose of securing emigrants for the colony.[19] The second is seen in the account of a dispute between Beales and Ludecus, during which Ludecus finally said that he would never make any attempt to secure Germans for Beales's colony.[20] Beales failed in his undertaking, although a settlement was made and an election held, in which Ludecus was elected syndic.

On September 17, 1832, Sebastian Mercado, minister of Mexico to Holland, wrote to his government from The Hague that Baron Johann von Racknitz Ludwigsburg of Wuertemberg was going to the Republic of Mexico with the object of proposing the founding of a German colony in Texas, to consist of from two hundred to one thousand families.[21] Baron Johann von Racknitz became interested in Texas during a brief stay in Texas in 1817 at the time of the ill-fated Mina expedition into Tamaulipas. Racknitz claimed he had written a pamphlet early in 1832 on the proposed establishment of a German colony in the province of Texas, on the banks of the Colorado or Brazos, for the purpose of giving an asylum to industrious German emigrants. Racknitz believed that many thousand German families desired to go to America; hence his proposal to establish a colony.[22] Thomas Murphy, Mexican minister in France, wrote to Don N. Gonzales Angulo on the same matter and said that Baron von Racknitz had been particularly

---

[19]Ludecus, *Reise durch die Mexikanischen Provinzen Tumalipas, Cohahuila und Texas im Jahre 1834*, 68, 73.

[20]*Ibid.*, 128. The dispute arose over a severe beating which the cook of the expedition gave to Schwarz for quarreling with one of the English women. Ludecus wanted Beales to take some action as a preventive of further altercations, but Beales refused to punish the cook. After the dispute, Beales treated the Germans with more consideration.

[21]Mercado to the Secretary of State, The Hague, November 7, 1832. Department of *Fomento* on Colonization, *Legajo* 1, *Expediente* 1, 58, West Transcripts, 1822-1835, University of Texas. The transcript of the documents bearing on the Racknitz plan comprises thirty-seven typewritten pages.

[22]Racknitz to ———— ————, Paris, October 27, 1832; West Transcripts, 1822-1835, pp. 60-62. Racknitz had conferred with Don Fernando Mangino, Minister of Foreign Relations for Mexico.

recommended to him by the minister from Wuertemberg.[23] Almost a year later Baron von Racknitz, after his arrival in Mexico, wrote to the Secretary of State for Interior and Exterior Relations and enclosed the two recommendations from Mercado and Murphy, as well as a copy in German of two plans for making German settlements in Texas and New Mexico. He claimed that he had circulated these plans in his country.[24]

Racknitz did not, however, establish a colony on the banks of either the Colorado or the Brazos River. On August 10, 1841, General Mariano Arista reported to the Mexican Minister of War that Baron von Racknitz had told him, Arista, that his first undertaking to make a settlement on the banks of the Colorado had been frustrated by the cholera.[25] One writer claims that Racknitz "had received a land grant from Mexico in 1832, along the lower Nueces River, and had induced some German families to settle on his land, who had to experience all the hardships and privations of pioneer life in a new country."[26] Writers on Texas history have recorded nothing about a German colony on the banks of the Nueces in 1832, nor do the public records of the state of Tamaulipas, Mexico, reveal anything about such a colony.

Baron von Racknitz did receive a colonization contract from

[23]Murphy to Angulo, Paris, May 7, 1833; *Ibid.*, 58-59.

[24]Racknitz to Secretary of State for Interior and Exterior Relations, Matamoras, March 13, 1834. Department of *Fomento* on Colonization, *Legajo* 1, *Expediente* 1, 65-66, West Transcripts, University of Texas. Copies of the plans mentioned by Racknitz are not included in the documents.

[25]Arista to the Minister of War (Mexico City ?), August 10, 1841. *Ibid.*, 78.

[26]Tiling, *History of the German Element in Texas*, 20. Tiling must be in error about this colony. He states that Racknitz (called Rackwitz by Tiling) returned to Germany in 1834 and in 1836 published a pamphlet at Stuttgart, entitled *Kurze und treue Belehrung fuer deutsche und schweizerische Auswanderer, die an der Colonie Johann von Rackwitz theilnehmen wollen.* (Brief and true instructions to German and Swiss emigrants who wish to participate in the founding of the Colony Johann von Rackwitz in Texas.) Since Tiling does not list this pamphlet in his bibliography, it must be assumed that he did not use it, but based his statements on some other work. It is not quite clear why Racknitz should have waited until 1836 to publish a pamphlet of instructions for a colony which he is said to have founded in 1832. However, one writer says that while he was in San Antonio in 1834 he saw an orphan boy nine years old, whose parents had been members of the expedition of Baron von Racknitz. The boy's parents had died from the cholera and only a few of the other settlers had survived the disease. (See Ludecus, *Reise durch die Mexikanischen Provinzen Tumalipas, Cohahuila und Texas im Jahre 1834,* 135.)

the state of Tamaulipas on April 10, 1835. Racknitz obligated himself to establish a colony "composed of German families or from any other nation that is not and never has been at war with the Mexican Republic." Racknitz was allowed to choose the tracts of land which best suited him, provided they were not "occupied by another colony to whom they had been granted first." The government of Tamaulipas was obligated to mark the boundaries and location of the town and adjacent tracts desig-nated by the empresario. Thirty leagues and labors were granted for the first and as many more for the second colony. Within four years and at his own expense, Racknitz had to bring into the colony a number of families sufficient to occupy the land. If less than two-thirds of the minimum number of families had been brought in within four years, the contract was to lapse, but the settlers were to retain the lands which they had cultivated by that time. No taxes, except municipal taxes, were to be collected for five years; the franchise and civic privileges were to be enjoyed from the time of entrance in the colony; and the colonists were not to be molested in their political and religious views, provided they did not disturb the public order. Racknitz was allowed to sell to the colonists the tracts which might be granted to him at the "rate of 400 pesos for each labor or place for cattle."[27]

No actual colonization followed the awarding of this contract. On April 1, 1838, Racknitz, then in Matamoras, wrote that he thought he would collect two hundred and fifty German families from Bremen and New Orleans at the latter port. For these he asked permission to settle on the Nueces and added that if the political conditions would not permit the founding of a colony there, he would be glad to have lands assigned to him on the Rio Grande or in the vicinity of Victoria, the capital of Tamaulipas, at the foot of the Sierra Madre range.[28] More than a year later Racknitz petitioned for a four-year extension of his contract of 1835, pointing out that the Texan Revolution, the French block-

[27]Department of *Fomento* on Colonization, *Legajo* 1, *Expediente* 1, 75-78, West Transcripts, University of Texas.

[28]Racknitz to the Minister of the Interior, Matamoras, April 1, 1838. Department of *Fomento* on Colonization, *Legajo* 1, *Expediente* 1, 69-70, West Transcripts, University of Texas. The Prussian Secretary of Foreign Affairs asked Cuevas, Mexican Minister of Exterior Relations, to consider the petition favorably. (Cuevas to Minister of Interior Relations, April 23, 1838. *Ibid.*, 71.)

ade of the Mexican ports in 1838, and the turbulent political situation in Mexico had prevented him from establishing his colony.[29] Racknitz was persistent, to say the least, and madé a final proposal that his colony be located on the Rio Grande for frontier protection, but the Mexican government refused any longer to consider his plan.[30]

All of the plans discussed so far for settling Germans in Texas failed to accomplish their object. The idea, however, continued to live. After Texas became an independent republic other plans for establishing German settlements in Texas were presented. The remainder of the chapter will be devoted to a discussion of these later plans.

Major A. Bullman, who served as aide-de-camp to one of Napoleon's generals and had received the cross of the Legion of Honor, wrote to President Sam Houston from New York on December 24, 1837, and presented a plan for bringing German settlers to Texas. He estimated the number of prospective settlers at three hundred but felt that the number might exceed one thousand if Texas would bear the cost of transportation. These prospective settlers were to come from Hessia, Franconia, and Thuringia, from the regions of the Rhine, the Main, and the Moselle. They were experienced farmers, horticulturists, artisans, and mechanics. All could farm, if necessary. Bullman vouched for their morals and industry and said they were "induced by their love of liberty and independence to emigrate with their families to Texas." He declared that the settlers would prove themselves valuable citizens and could be of great help in defending the Republic of Texas. Bullman asked for information about the amount of land that would be granted to settlers, the acquisition of citizenship and its privileges, the taxes on farming lands, the duties on implements and tools which the settlers might bring along, and about the prospects of a loan for the expenses of the journey to Texas. He wanted to know also about the amount of land he would get for his "trouble and ex-

---

[29]Almonte to the Minister of the Interior, Mexico City, August 10, 1841. Department of *Fomento* on Colonization, *Legajo* 1, *Expediente* 1, 72, West Transcripts, University of Texas.

[30]General Arista to the Minister of War (Mexico City ?), August 10, 1841. *Ibid.*, 78-80.

penses to organize and engage the settlers,"[31] John Birdsall,
acting Secretary of State, replied to Bullman on March 19, 1838,
that the law under which land was granted to immigrants had
expired by limitation the previous October, but that land could
be bought "at very low prices, compared with their intrinsic value," and that it was "the decided policy of the government to
encourage and invite the emigration of industri(ous) and good
citizens of all countries." Birdsall informed Bullman that a
residence of six months and the usual oath of allegiance were
required to entitle the settler to all the rights and privileges of
a citizen, that the settler was protected in his person, property,
and religion, that "all the implements and utensils of any trade
or business and all such provisions and stores" which the immigrant might bring with him for his own or his family's use were
duty free, and that the immigrant would never be discrimi-
nated against in the matter of taxation.[32]

In his second letter Major Bullman wrote:

Concerning the answer to my letter received through the kindness of your honor, for which I beg leave to tender my most
humble acknowledgments, I take the liberty to state that I consider it to convey but a part of the desired information. Therefore, to bring the matter to a speedy close I have drawn up the
enclosed articles of agreement, subject of course to such altera-
tions and amendments as may be required by your constitution
and as are compatible with common justice and equity, soliciting
a candid perusal of the same. It only remains for me to make
a few additional remarks. It has long been a favorite idea of
mine to settle in Texas, as I conceive the most glorious days of
political existence to be those of a republic in its infancy, where
all outward strife has subsided and party bias has not yet developed itself. Thus I offered my services to your Government
as I have some influence more particularly across the Atlantic
and my simple word would induce at least 50 families to come out
instanter to join the colony. I think it is needless for me to
observe that the safest guarantee for the performance of the
settlement is my personal interest. If now you should sustain
my proposition I expect an (amended) copy of the enclosed articles duly authenticated to be returned to me. I do not insist

[31]Bullman to Houston, New York, December 24, 1837. Correspondence
Secretary of State, Vol. 49 (Letter Book No. 2), 116-117, Texas State
Library.

[32]Birdsall to Bullman, March 19, 1838. Domestic Correspondence,
Texas State Library.

upon any particular remuneration but if you should hereafter deem my operations worthy of your acknowledgment it will be left to your discretion altogether.[33]

R. A. Irion, Secretary of State, acknowledged the receipt of Bullman's second letter and of the "Articles of Agreement." He replied that it was not within the province of the Department of State to make the contract desired by Major Bullman and referred him to the Congress of Texas, with the comment that "it is hardly to be presumed that in the present condition of the public domain the Government would wish to make Colonization Grants."[34] A very careful search of the "Memorials" and of the bills and resolutions of the Congress of Texas for the year 1838 reveals no further documents on Bullman's plan. This fact would indicate that Bullman let the project drop after the receipt of Irion's letter.

The second inquiry from New York about settling Germans in Texas came from Theodore Frontin, who introduced himself by letter to President Lamar as the president of a German Association of about one hundred and fifty persons. Frontin asked for a tract of land suitable for agricultural purposes. He was interested in developing manufactures and trade and for that reason asked for a location at the mouth of either the Rio Grande, the Nueces, or the Colorado. He asked for information on the amount of land to be granted to each settler and on the cost of surveying the land. He implied that relatives and friends of the settlers, both from Germany and the United States, would settle in the colony, and for that reason he asked the government to reserve, for a period of five years, a tract of land ten times as large as that required for the initial group of settlers.[35] The

[33]Bullman to Birdsall, New York, May 21, 1838. Correspondence Secretary of State, Vol. 49 (Letter Book No. 2), 157, Texas State Library.

[34]Irion to Bullman, August 24, 1838. Domestic Correspondence, Texas State Library.
The "Articles of Agreement" are not to be found among the records.

[35]Frontin to Mirabeau B. Lamar, New York, February 22, 1839. Lamar Papers, II, 460-461, No. 1082.
Besides the signature of Theodore Frontin, the names of Dr. M. Fr. Griel, secretary, F. P. Gaertner, C. Mueller, Johann Esser, Geo. Sonne, Christian Heintz, N. Rossi, and H. Hempel appear on the letter. These names are taken from the original in the Lamar Papers and differ slightly from the published list.
A letter by Charles H. Forbes, vice consul for Texas at New York, to

request of the association to have the reply addressed to the care
of Mr. Woodworth (Woodward) seems not to have been heeded
by Lamar, since no reply is to be found in the executive or consular correspondence.

While the foregoing plans were being worked out by people
in New York, interest developed also in Philadelphia. On May
17, 1839, Edward Hagedorn wrote to Lamar for an appointment
as Texan consul to the Hanseatic Cities. He was the principal
partner of the commercial firm of E. Hagedorn & Company of
Bremen. Hagedorn's main interest was the promotion of trade
with Texas, but he implied in his letter that he could direct German emigration to Texas. His memorial stated in part that the
Hanseatic Cities would form one of the principal European
markets for the tobacco, rice, cotton, sugar, and other products
of Texas and would send, "besides the manufactures of the workshops, the hardy and industrious race of emigrants to till and
defend" the soil. He did not desire the office "for its pecuniary
emolument" but for the honest pride of representing "the young
and growing Republic" in some official capacity.[36] But Hagedorn
did not get the appointment.

On June 9, 1839, Valentine Pabstmann outlined a plan to General R. G. Dunlap, then minister of the Republic of Texas at
Washington. He proposed to establish a German colony of 500
to 1000 families in Texas. He thought he could send probably
100 families from Pennsylvania that fall. His "extensive ac-
quaintances and influence in Germany," he thought, would enable
him to secure enough colonists in Germany. His brother, a merchant in Cologne, would second him in the project "with all his
ardor and influence." Pabstmann intended to go to Germany
in order to get emigrants for his colony. He asked that Dunlap
send the letter on to Texas so that President Lamar could lay

Barnard E. Bee, Secretary of State, says that nearly all of the applications
at the consulate referred to contemplated emigration and that the recent
act of the Texan Congress relative to land would cause more applications
to be made. Forbes asked that the consulate be furnished with documents
and papers that gave "information in regard to the condition of the
country." (Forbes to Bee, New York, February 13, 1839. Department
of State, Consular Letters, 1836-1840, Vol. 57, 14. Office Secretary of
State.)

[36]Hagedorn to Lamar, Philadelphia, May 17. 1839. Correspondence
Secretary of State, Vol. 49 (Letter Book No. 2), 238-239. Texas State
Library.

the plan before the special session of the Texas Congress to be held some time in the summer of 1839. Pabstmann informed Dunlap that he had been a commissioned officer in two campaigns against France, that he was then captain of a volunteer company in Philadelphia, many of whose members were ready to follow him to Texas, and that he would, in case of hostilities with either Mexico or the Indians, form a company or a battalion for the defense of the country. As a remuneration for his expenses in securing the emigrants Pabstmann desired 500 acres of land for every ten persons brought to Texas. He said, too, that he would make it his "sacred duty" to use his "influence in Germany for the welfare of the Commonwealth of Texas."[37] A few months after Pabstmann's plan was presented to him, Dunlap reported to President Lamar that he had attended a meeting of Germans in Philadelphia in September, that they wished to emigrate and settle together, that some had good business connections in Germany, and that, if the law granting donations of land to immigrants[38] were extended for one year, thousands would emigrate to the republic.[39] No action was taken by President Lamar on Pabstmann's plan and the records do not reveal that he even replied to either Dunlap's or Pabstmann's letter.

The year 1839 was not to be wholly unproductive, however, in bringing German settlers to Texas. One expedition of German settlers reached Texas from New York late in December, 1839.

[37]Pabstmann to Dunlap, Philadelphia, June 9, 1839. Lamar Papers, III, 14-16, No. 1325.

[38]The Texas land law then in force provided for giving six hundred and forty acres of land to heads of families and three hundred and twenty acres to single free white men over seventeen years of age. It required the immigrant to live on the land for three years and to pay the "fees of office and surveying," whereupon the government would grant an unconditional title to the land. (Gammel, H. P. N., The Laws of Texas, II, 35-36.)

[39]Dunlap to Lamar, Washington, October 23, 1839. Lamar Papers, III, 142, No. 1500.

Dunlap's statement on the desire of Philadelphia Germans to emigrate to Texas is borne out in a letter by Cyrus Joy, Texan consul at Philadelphia, to David G. Burnet, acting Secretary of State. Joy recommended that the President of Texas should suggest to Congress an extension of the Texas land law, because many families in and around Philadelphia desired to remove to Texas early the following spring if they could obtain lands from Texas on terms then in force. (Joy to Burnet, Philadelphia, November 28, 1839. Department of State, Consular Letters, 1836-1840, Vol. 57, 20-21. Office Secretary of State.)

The expedition was sent out by the "Germania Society," which was organized on January 24, 1835, in the City of New York. The printed constitution recites the following objects of the society:

To unite more closely the Germans living in the United States, in order to maintain and promote a vigorous German character, good German customs, and German culture; to support the principles of a pure Democracy in the new home; nourish love and attachment for the old country; and to work towards the end that as soon as possible better conditions may be brought about in Germany, similar to those enjoyed in the United States; and to support, with counsel and deed, German political refugees.[40]

Prof. J. G. Buettner gives some additional information about the Society and its plan. The members of the first expedition agreed to till the soil in common for three years, after which the land was to be divided among the members by lot. Provisions for from six to eight months, all kinds of tools and materials for building houses, and skilled workmen, such as carpenters, joiners, and locksmiths, were to be furnished by the Society. A town was to be built at some suitable place and each member was to get a house and a lot. The payment of fifty dollars, the enrollment fee for first class members, entitled each single man and head of a family to the use of the Society's provisions, tools, and munitions. Some of the wealthier members paid in from one hundred to eight hundred dollars. These larger deposits were to bear interest and form the funds for a proposed bank. Less fortunate persons were to be enrolled in the second and third class on the payment of thirty and twenty dollars, respectively, but were to receive correspondingly less land in the final division. As a reward for their usefulness, activity, and special talent the members of the second and third class were to be allowed admission to the first class. The society was to be governed by a mayor or president, elected for a six months' term, and by six senators, who were to be approved monthly by the society. The more educated members were to be senators in turn, in order that each might appreciate the importance and responsibility of that

[40]Bruncken, E., *German Political Refugees in the United States during the Period from 1815-1860*, 23. The German version of the constitution is found in Koerner, G., *Das deutsche Element in den Vereinigten Staaten von Nordamerika, 1818-1848*, 108, and in *Der deutsche Pionier*, IV, 83.

position. When new rules were to be made, at least seven-eighths of the members had to attend the meeting and majority rule was to prevail. In Galveston a station was to be erected in which the members of a second immigration could remain until leaving for the rendezvous of the colony. Special care was to be taken of the families of those members who might die during the three-year period of communal work. No discrimination was to be made against the later immigration and all were to find a real home in the new republic of Texas.[41]

The Germania Society found some difficulty in deciding on the location for its colony. Some members favored Wisconsin, others declared in favor of Oregon, while still others favored Texas. Since the founding of a German state was another object of this society, some of the members declared that such a state should be a member of the American Union, while others wished to be assured that the state would be an independent one. Most of the members felt that the plan of founding a pure German state in the midst of the American Union would arouse the opposition of the American people; hence it was decided that Texas should be the field for the experiment.

The Society bought a brig, the *North,* and sent out its first expedition from New York on November 2, 1839. This group of colonists numbered 130 persons and comprised men of all trades. Mr. Woodward, the Texan consul general at New York, sent recommendations along to the President and the Congress of Texas. After landing in Galveston the colonists went to Houston, where they separated. The leader and those members of the expedition who still had money returned to New York.[42]

[41]Buettner, *Briefe aus und ueber Amerika,* II, 209-211.

[42]Loeher, F., *Geschichte und Zustaende der Deutschen in Amerika,* 281. Loeher was a contemporary of the period. His book appeared in Leipzig in 1847.

Tiling's account of the expedition and its disbanding reads, in part, as follows: "The vessel arrived at Galveston on Christmas Day, 1839. There they heard the unwelcome news that a few days previous the last victim of a yellow fever epidemic, a German, had been buried at Houston, which was almost depopulated. This deterred most of the colonists from disembarking and many returned with their ship and their leader, Dr. Schuessler, to New York. The more courageous remained and went to Houston." (Tiling, *History of the German Element in Texas,* 45.)

Those who remained suffered want and were forced to seek employment. Thus ended the Germania Society's project.[43]

The Germania Society's colonization plan attracted attention in France. L. Harper, a doctor of philosophy, wrote to President Lamar for a tract of land and requested a location which would enable his colony to engage in commercial enterprises. He asked also that the tract of land be as close as possible to the German colony, *Teutonia,* in order that his own colony might be able to establish trade relations with it.[44] Harper, however, did not get a grant of land for a colony.

On December 30, 1839, H. Rutter wrote a letter of introduction to President Lamar for Mr. De Witt, a native of Germany, who had brought a number of German families to Texas a few weeks previous. These German families, under the care of Mr. De Witt, wished to have a settlement of their own. Mr. Rutter besought Lamar's consideration for these new settlers both for a suitable place on which to settle and for information and advice to the settlers.[45] The records do not indicate that Lamar did anything for this group of settlers.

[43]Cronau, Rudolf, *Drei Jahrhunderte deutschen Lebens in Amerika,* 298-299; Buettner, *Briefe aus und ueber Amerika,* II, 211; Eickhoff, *In der neuen Heimath,* 322-323; Benjamin, G. G., *The Germans in Texas,* 7; Loeher, *Geschichte und Zustaende der Deutschen in Amerika,* 291; Tiling, *German Element in Texas,* 45.

Tiling says that the families Usener, Schweikart, Habermehl, Bottler, and Karcher, and a single man by the name of Schnell, were among those who settled in Houston, and that most of the single men of the expedition went to Cat Spring in Austin County, where they bought land from the Klebergs.

Dr. Buettner comments on the failure of the undertaking and asserts that many members of the expedition were forced to work by the side of slaves ("an der Seite schwarzer Sclaven zu arbeiten"). He claims also that the editor of the *New Yorker Staats-Zeitung* ended a report of the unhappy expedition with the question: "How long will our countrymen allow themselves to be ruined by such schemes?" (Buettner, *Briefe,* II, -211.) The writer of this study cannot vouch for Buettner's statement, since he was unable to find the files of the *New Yorker Staats-Zeitung* for 1839. The New York Public Library does not have a file, and the *Check-List of Newspapers in the Library of Congress* does not list the *Neu Yorker Staats-Zeitung.*

[44]Harper to Lamar, Poissy, France, September 17, 1839. Lamar Papers, III, 111, No. 1452. Harper stated in his letter that the German colony, *Teutonia,* had arrived in Texas in May, 1839. He must have had reference to the Germania Society's colony, but he was misinformed about the date.

[45]Rutter to Lamar, Houston, December 30, 1839. Lamar Papers, III, 218, No. 1599.

A former artillery officer in the Prussian army, H. Moellhausen, who lived in Austin, Texas, in 1840, tried to secure a contract from the Republic of Texas for making three large maps of Texas. It was his intention, had he secured the contract, as he says in a "Sketch," to go to the courts of Prussia, Russia, Austria, and other powers "in order to give accounts of the many advantages which would result from an intercourse with Texas." Moellhausen was interested both in the recognition of Texas by Prussia and Russia and in the emigration of Europeans to Texas. Moellhausen was confident that his accounts of Texas would be well received and that he would one day return to Texas as the diplomatic representative of some European court. His desire to help Texas is very evident in his "Sketch."[46] He did not want to establish a colony in Texas but was confident that he could induce German emigrants to go to Texas.

It is well at this point to state that none of the various plans discussed in this chapter resulted in the establishment of a single German settlement in Texas. The only movement which carried an organized group of German settlers to Texas was that of the

[46]Moellhausen's "Sketch," which is undated, is found in the Lamar Papers, III, 346-348, No. 1738.

The following extract from his "Sketch" is reproduced here to show what Moellhausen had in mind. The extract reads: "The King of Prussia, for whom I fought during three great campaigns and for whom I shed my blood, and who decorated me with his badge of honor, would listen to me, his former subject, with a certain degree of confidence and satisfaction. I say it with pleasure (that) I could relate to him very favorable things about Texas and might greatly influence him to promote an agreeable intercourse.

The mercantile interest of Prussia wants connections with South America, and the acknowledgement of Texas by Prussia would have in its consequence that of Russia whose ambitious politic (sic) only can wish a friendly intercourse and point of alliance in this part of the world, particularly in regard of her ever increasing rivalry with England. The Emperor of Russia is in such matters greatly guided by the King of Prussia, his father-in-law.

There are many inducements which would make it very desirable for Texas to be more known to the mighty Nations and Governments of Europe. Many products of her soil, now scarcely noted as useful, would find a ready and favorable market in Europe; her rich lands would be more valuable; but particularly her mineral riches, now slumbering in the earth, might be brought to light by German industry and capital. . . . But looking more to the future, the Emigration from Europe might greatly be turned to Texas instead of the United States, if some attention were paid to this so very important object, particularly when Europe, teeming with revolutions, sooner or later will experience horrible wars and persecutions of the subdued political party."

Germania Society of 1839, but no settlement resulted from it. The group which Dr. De Witt brought to Texas from Germany in 1839 does not even seem to have been organized. In spite of the failure of the various plans, however, some Germans came to Texas during the thirties. Some of them came from the German centers in the United States and others came from Germany. Most of them remained in or near Houston. Henry Thompson estimated their political strength in and around Houston at 400 in 1840.[47] The following extract from the *Morning Star,* published in Houston, indicates something of the number of German immigrants and of the esteem in which they were held. It read:

Amongst the newcomers we are delighted to see the florid-complexioned and blue-eyed sons and daughters of Germany. To those people we extend the hand of welcome. A large number of these hardy and industrious persons are now in our place, seeking for employment and an honest livelihood. Amongst them are farmers, mechanics, and persons of almost every trade and vocation. They are ready and anxious for work. Whoever wants assistance to cultivate his soil, servants for his house, artisans to work in the shop, day-laborers, shoemakers, and so forth, can find in the honest Germans, who now have possession of the Capitol (capital city?), the very persons who will suit him. They will add to the wealth, the physical power, and numerical force of our infant nation; they will be good citizens in times of peace and invaluable soldiers in the hour of war.[48]

The question of German immigration became so important in

---

[47]Thompson to Lamar, January 10, 1840. Lamar Papers, III, 304-305, No. 1682. Thompson estimated there would be 2000 German voters in 1842.

[48]*Morning Star,* December 17, 1839, 2, col. 1.
In its next issue the *Morning Star* printed an editorial, "The Germans in Texas," which made mention of the German immigrants in Houston. The editor wrote: "In the afternoon, a discourse was pronounced to a congregation of German adventurers, by a minister of their own nation. As we looked upon the earnest and honest faces of these deserving people and observed the ardor with which they engaged in the services of the day, we could not but feel proud that we were the citizens of a government whose laws tolerated all doctrines, all sects, all religions, a government which enabled us, undisturbed, to honor the great Jehovah in our own way, and threw the aegis of its protection over the children of a foreign clime, whilst worshipping the God of their faith, in the loved language of 'Fadderland'." *(Ibid.,* December 24, 1839, 2, col. 1.)
The same paper carried an announcement on January 11, 1840, of German services of the German Protestant congregation regularly every Sunday morning at eleven o'clock at the home of Mr. Thiel.

1840 and the number of immigrants who needed aid so great that the Germans of Houston sent a memorial to the Congress of Texas on December 8 of that year. They had formed an association for philanthropical purposes and submitted *By-Laws* with their petition for a charter of incorporation. Article II of the *By-Laws* stated the objects of the association to be: I. "To promote the prosperity of our German fellow-citizens to the best of our means; 2. to assist the stranger with counsel and action; 3. to minister the necessaries to the sick and needy; and 4. to inspire confidence to the immigrants and to encourage them through the agency of the association with counsel, in cases when by application to individuals their exertions might prove abortive.[49] On January 21, 1841, the Texan Congress granted a charter to this association under the name of "The German Union for Texas" and authorized it to make such by-laws, rules, and regulations for its own government as were not contrary to the laws and the constitution of the Republic of Texas.[50] The opportunities to do philanthropic work were numerous and the German Union did not fail to aid German immigrants in their hour of need.

Not all of the German immigrants who came to Texas during the thirties, however, remained in Houston and Galveston. Some went into the interior and, either singly or in very small groups, laid the basis for a number of German settlements in Austin, Fayette, and Colorado counties. From these settlements in turn other settlements were founded in the forties and fifties in the counties just named as well as in Victoria, De Witt, and Washington counties.

[49]MS. Records Office Secretary of State, Memorial No. 12, File Box No. 32, Letter No. G. The memorial bore the signatures of Frederick Lemky, J. Hermann, Henry Levenhagen, Theodore Miller, Wm. Dankwerth, Karl Fischer, Ulrich Fischer, Henry F. Fisher, Heinrich A. Kuckenthal, George Fisher, Robert Levenhagen, Charles F. Gerlach, Charles Kesler, Dr. De Witt, Charles Bowman, Gustav Erichson, John Koop, Dr. C. Herman Jaeger, and C. Franke.

[50]Gammel, *Laws of Texas*, II, 553-554. With the exception of Wm. Dankwerth and Dr. De Witt, all of the memorialists were named as incorporators.

CHAPTER III

THE GERMAN SETTLEMENTS ON THE LOWER BRAZOS, COLORADO, AND GUADALUPE RIVERS

Some Germans went into the state at various times before any German settlements were founded in Texas. A few German adventurers came into Texas in 1821 with Dr. James Long, whose expedition of fifty-three men was overpowered and captured by Mexican forces at Goliad on October 9, 1821. Among these were Eduard Hanstein, Joseph Dirksen, Ernst von Rosenberg, Wilhelm Miller, Carl Cuans, Gaspar Porton, and August Blaccher.[1] Five Germans secured grants of land in Stephen F. Austin's Colony. These men were Gabriel Strawsnider (very probably Americanized from Strohschneider), John Keller, Peter Conrad, Francis Keller, and F. W. Grassmeyer.[2] J. Becker, of Bevil Settlement, and F. Swetenburg, of San Augustine, had settled in

[1]Nacogdoches Archives for 1821, Texas State Library. In several books on the Germans in Texas, only the first six of these men are listed. (See Tiling, *History of the German Element in Texas*, 9; Penniger, *Fest-Ausgabe*, 18; Rosenberg, *Kritik. Geschichte des Vereins zum Schutze deutscher Auswanderer in Texas*, 6; Benjamin, G. G., *The Germans in Texas*, 13.) Ernst von Rosenberg, who had been an officer in Germany during the Napoleonic wars, went to Mexico, where he was promoted to the rank of colonel. When Iturbide was overthrown, however, von Rosenberg was shot to death. (See Brown, John Henry, *Indian Wars and Pioneers of Texas*, 283.) The records in the General Land Office, Austin, Texas, do not show that these men ever got any grant of land from the Mexican government.

[2]Austin, Stephen F., *List of Titles*, 8, 15, 19, 23, 40; University of Texas. The dates and the locations of the grants of land made to these men are given on the pages listed. Other Germans received grants of land in Austin's Colony, but that was after the founding of the first German settlement at Industry, which is now in Austin County, Texas. These were John Dokanski (Dombrinski?), Abraham Darst, Francis G. Keller, Charles Fordtran, Henry Thierwester (Thuerwaechter), Charles A. Bettner, Joseph Biegel, John Peske, Peter H. Fullenwider, Jno. D. H. Varrelmann, Peter Pieper, Samuel Wolfenbarger, and Solomon Rumpfeldt. These names are listed at different places from page 27 to page 63 in Austin, *List of Titles*. The name of Jacob Lentz is entered on page 32, but no grant is recorded. According to a petition for a pension filed by Henry Thuerwaechter in 1851, Thuerwaechter came to Texas in 1827 and lived at Harrisburg until 1836. (MS. Records Office Secretary of State, Memorial No. 127, File Box No. 40, Letter No. H.)

'Texas before 1831.[3] These two Germans, as well as those who
settled in Austin's Colony, were attracted by the liberal grants
which the government of Mexico made to actual settlers.

The cradle of the German settlements in Texas is the little
town of Industry in Austin County. It was founded by Friedrich
Ernst on a league of land granted to him in Austin's Colony.
Friedrich Ernst came to the United States in 1829 and intended
to settle in New York. Like so many others, however, he read
Duden's book and decided to go to Missouri. He interested Charles
Fordtran in making the journey with him. When they arrived at
New Orleans, a fellow-passenger gave Ernst a pamphlet containing
a description of Texas, probably a prospectus of Austin's Colony.
Ernst changed his plans again and went to Texas.[4] They landed
at Harrisburg on April 1, 1831, and went from there by ox cart
to San Felipe de Austin, fifty miles inland. On April 16, 1831,
Ernst received a league of land on the west side of the west fork
of Mill Creek, a region then still inhabited by Indians. These
Indians, however, were quiet and friendly and did not molest
the new settlers. Ernst gave Fordtran one-fourth of his league
for surveying it for him.[5]

It was a matter of great significance for the history of the
German settlements in Texas that Friedrich Ernst changed his
plans about going to Missouri. One of the immediate effects of
Ernst's going to Texas was that other German families followed
him. Ernst wrote a long letter from Texas to a friend by the
name of Schwarz in Oldenburg. The letter was published in an

[3]Census Records for 1828-1836 in Nacogdoches Archives, Texas State
Library. In a lengthy article on the Germans in Texas before the heavy
immigration of the forties, L. F. Lafrentz states that Henry Rueg, a
German Swiss, was *jefe politico* in Nacogdoches in 1821. (Lafrentz, "Die
Deutschen in Texas vor der Masseneinwanderung im Jahre 1844," *Deutsch-
Texanische Monatshefte*, XI, 49.) Lafrentz is mistaken about the date,
since Rueg was *jefe politico* in 1835. (See Nacogdoches Archives, Texas
State Library.)

[4]Dunt, *Reise nach Texas*, 52. Friedrich Ernst was born at Varel, in the
duchy of Oldenburg. In his young manhood he was a bookkeeper. In
1829, becoming dissatisfied with conditions in Germany, he emigrated to
America with his family. For about a year he kept a boarding house in
New York. John Jacob Astor tried to interest him in buying a dairy farm
on the East River, but Ernst rejected the offer. In New York he met
Charles Fordtran, a tanner by trade, who was born in Minden, Westphalia, on May 7, 1801. (Tiling, *German Element in Texas*, 17-18.)

[5]Austin, *List of Titles*, 25; Tiling, *German Element in Texas*, 17-19;
'Trenckmann, W. A., *Austin County*, 22.

Oldenburg newspaper and was widely read. It was reprinted
also in Detlef Dunt's *Reise nach Texas,* a book which was published
in 1834 and was among the earliest to appear in Germany about
Texas.[6] In his letter Ernst pictured Texas in very glowing
terms. He wrote that every married settler got a league of land,
the only expense being one hundred and sixty dollars for surveying and recording. He described the land as slightly rolling and
the climate similar to that of southern Italy. Plots of wooded
land alternated with large grassy prairies. From his own land
Ernst said he could have gathered several thousand cart-loads of
hay. He pictured the prairies in their festive beauty of wild
flowers. Up to the time of writing there had been ice only twice
that winter. Ernst wrote that it was very easy to raise all the
live stock necessary, and that a cow and calf could be sold for
ten dollars. Some planters, he said, had seven hundred head of
cattle. Pork cost four cents a pound, corn seventy-five cents a
bushel. The land produced from thirty to forty bushels of corn
per acre. Ernst wrote that every farmer could become well-to-do
in a very few years. Dunt comments on Ernst's letter as follows:
"In Oldenburg, a country in which the people were generally
poor, this letter could not fail to create a big sensation, especially
since the emigration fever had recently seized hold of the people.
The letter was copied many times."[7]

It is difficult to say how many Germans were induced to emi-

---

[6]Dunt, *Reise nach Texas,* 4-16; Tiling; *German Element in Texas,* 197-
200. See also Benjamin, G. G., *The Germans in Texas,* 17-19, where a
translation of a letter signed by Fritz Dirks is found. About the "Fritz
Dirks" letter, Benjamin comments as follows: "When the above was
written I had not seen an article by Mr. L. F. La Frentz, of San Antonio,
Texas, in *Deutsch-Texanische Monatshefte,* vol. 11, no. 4. This article
contains a résumé of the letter which Fritz Ernst sent to his compatriots
in Germany and which was published in a newspaper in the Duchy of
Oldenburg. The similarity of the Ernst letter to that quoted above leads
me to believe that either the author of the work in which the letter signed
Fritz Dirks is quoted . . . misunderstood the name or that the name
Dirks is a misprint and should read Ernst. In many paragraphs the
words of the two letters are identical. The letter of Ernst as stated
above had a great influence on German immigration." Benjamin, *The
Germans in Texas,* 20. In a footnote for the Dirks letter, p. 19, Benjamin
cites Achenbach, Hermann, *Tagebuch meiner Reise in den Nordamerikanischen Freistaaten oder das neue Kanaan,* 132-135. The writer
of the present study is convinced that there must have been a mistake
about the name Dirks, especially after reading the Ernst letter in Dunt,
Reise nach Texas, 4-16.

[7]Dunt, *Reise nach Texas,* 16.

grate by reading the Ernst letter. Mrs. Ernst, who after her husband's death in 1858 married a Mr. Stoehr, said that in 1833 the families of Wm. Bartels, Zimmerschreib (Zimmerscheidt,) and J. Juergens and in 1834 the families of Marcus Amsler, Karl Amsler, Jacob Wolters, Robert Kleberg, Louis von Roeder, Wm. Frels, Siebel, F. W. Grassmeyer, Joseph Biegel, and some others came to live near the Ernst farm.[8] Some of these, as the families of Karl and Marcus Amsler, Ludwig Anton Siegmund von Roeder, and Robert and Louis Kleberg, settled as far away as Cat Spring. All of them, however, came to Texas as a result of reading the enticing descriptions of Texas by Friedrich Ernst.[9] Robert Kleberg, Sr., who kept a memorandum of his experiences, records also the families of Wm. Bartels, Damke (Geo. Dannker), John Heinike, George Herder, John Reinermann, and R. D. Stoelje. These families were in the main from the duchies of Oldenburg and Westphalia.[10] Another writer lists, in addition, the families of Pettus, Benninghof, Kleekaemper, Wm. Schneider, and Peter Pieper.[11] To this list must be added the name of Dr. John D. G. Varrelmann, the first man who went to Texas from Oldenburg after reading the Ernst letter.[12]

Friedrich Ernst, who had been chief gardener for the grand-duke of Oldenburg, chose an ideal location for a settlement. He built his house in the friendly little valley of Mill Creek. The house was six-cornered, in the style of his summer-house in Oldenburg, and hence was quite a departure from the conventional pioneer log hut. A small wood formed a pleasing background for his cornfield. But the family suffered often from the lack of corn meal and flour. Since San Felipe de Austin was some distance away and at times could not be reached on account of the bad roads, the family improvised its own grist mill in the form

[8]Tiling, *German Element in Texas*, 19.
Tiling did not list the given names of the settlers in this group. The writer of the present study, in order to make his own narrative as complete as possible, has tried to supply the given names of the persons. He has followed the same practice in regard to other lists of German settlers. In a few instances, however, he has been unable to get the information.

[9]Trenckmann, *Austin County*, 16.

[10]Benjamin, *The Germans in Texas*, 15-16.

[11]Lafrentz, "Die Deutschen in Texas vor der Masseneinwanderung im Jahre 1844," in *Deutsch-Texanische Monatshefte*, XI, 53.

[12]Dunt, *Reise nach Texas*, 95.

of a mortar shaped out of a stump. Softened corn was placed in this mortar and ground into meal, from which small cakes were baked and served for bread. Coffee and sugar were luxuries seldom served. Dried or smoked meat was at times the only article of food in the house. The prices of the plainest kinds of cloth were almost prohibitive. A yard of domestic cost fifty cents, a yard of calico even seventy-five cents.[13]

By 1838 Ernst had a large orchard planted with peach trees, and a vegetable garden with all kinds of vegetables. His former employment under the duke of Oldenburg was serving him in good stead. He had become interested in the cultivation of tobacco and had been fairly successful in his first trial with the Havana variety.[14]

The town of Industry was not laid out until 1838. On November 28, 1838, Friedrich Ernst announced that he had laid out a town for German immigrants on his plantation. He offered building lots, 50 feet front by 150 feet deep, at the low price of twenty dollars, saying that he was not a speculator who desired to turn German immigration to his advantage, but that he wanted to attract educated fellow-countrymen to his town. He pointed out that a good number of Germans were then living in the neighborhood of Industry.[15]

Industry grew very slowly, a characteristic of all of the German settlements in that part of the state. Its name was chosen by the American settlers in recognition of the enterprising and industrious spirit of Friedrich Ernst. In 1838, J. G. Sieper became the first postmaster of Industry. About this time, too, the first drug store was opened.[16] About the year 1840 Mrs.

---

[13]Dunt, *Reise nach Texas*, 93-95; Trenckmann, *Austin County*, 16, 22-23.

[14]Wrede, *Lebensbilder aus den Vereinigten Staaten von Nordamerika und Texas*, 132. According to Lafrentz, "Die Deutschen in Texas vor der Masseneinwanderung im Jahre 1844," in *Deutsch-Texanische Monatshefte*, XI, 52, B. Scherer taught Ernst how to make cigars. Scherer accompanied Dunt on his trip to Texas. (See Dunt, *Reise nach Texas*, 93.)

[15]Ernst to N. A. Bonzano, November 28, 1838. Henry Francis Fisher Papers, University of Texas. Bonzano, to whom Ernst sent the announcement of the laying out of the new town, was then living in Houston and was in touch with the Germans at that place. Ernst's announcement said that Bonzano would be glad to give additional information about the new town.

[16]Lafrentz, "Die Deutschen in Texas vor der Masseneinwanderung im Jahre 1844," in *Deutsch-Texanische Monatshefte*, XI, 52. Alwin Soergel,

Ernst opened a hotel, "an oasis in the desert," which became a gathering place for Germans who were going from Galveston and Houston into the interior of Texas. Count Boos-Waldeck and Prince Victor Leiningen lodged at this hotel in 1843 while they were in Texas studying conditions for the Society for the Protection of German Immigrants in Texas. When Prince Solms, first commissioner-general of this Society, was a guest at the hotel in 1844, the Germans in the vicinity of Industry came there to meet him.[17] Other guests of the hotel were the countess of Stolberg, Fr. W. v. Wrede, von Specht, two brothers von Wedel, von Blank, and various other members and emigrants of the Society just mentioned.[18] The family of Adolphus Fuchs, who came to Texas as immigrants of the Society, wanted to go to Industry, where they hoped to find Ernst, known to all as the "father of the immigrants," because he assisted everyone in a most unselfish manner.[19]

The population of Industry remained predominantly German. In 1860, when the eighth census was taken, the list of farm owners for the beat comprising Industry, Cat Spring, and New Ulm contained three hundred and fifty German names in a total of four hundred and eight.[20]

The second German settlement that developed in Texas was

who went through Industry in 1846, said that there were only three houses, but he had reference only to the central part of the settlement. (See, Soergel, *Fuer Auswanderungslustige*, 37.)

[17]*Texas. Ein Handbuch fuer deutsche Auswanderer*, 78. This book was prepared by the Society for the Protection of German Immigrants in Texas for emigrants desiring to go to Texas.

[18]Lafrentz, "Die Deutschen in Texas vor der Masseneinwanderung im Jahre 1844," in *Deutsch-Texanische Monatshefte*, XI, 52.

[19]Goeth, Mrs. Ottilie, *Was Grossmutter erzaehlt*, 31. Mrs. Goeth was the daughter of Adolphus Fuchs. This family did not go to the Fisher and Miller grant, which the Society mentioned above undertook to colonize, but remained for some years in the neighborhood of Cat Spring, where Fuchs taught school. Later the family moved to Cypress Mill in Blanco County. Mrs. Goeth tells of the experiences of this pioneer family in a very interesting manner.

[20]Eighth United States Census, Schedule 4: Productions of Agriculture, I. Texas State Library. This census, as well as the ones for 1850, 1870, and 1880, is a compilation of the original census sheets used by the census takers in those years. Schedules 1 and 2 for the white and slave population of the years 1850 and 1860 and for the white and negro population of the years 1870 and 1880 are not included in the collection. The remaining schedules, 3 to 6, especially 4 and 5, on the productions of agriculture and industry, are invaluable for this study. The population schedules are still in Washington, D. C.

Biegel's Settlement, later known as Biegel Post Office. It was founded in 1832 by Joseph Biegel when he laid out his farm on the waters of Cummins Creek. Like Industry, it did not assume the proportions of a settlement until a few years later. Biegel is in Fayette County about eight miles east of LaGrange on the road to Fayetteville. Little is known of the early settlers of Biegel, but besides its founder there were B. Scherer, who came to Biegel in 1834 from Switzerland, J. O. Tschiedel, Andre, J. D. Meyer, and John C. Helble, who settled there in 1844. Helble went to California in 1849 and returned in 1851. The eighth census does not list Biegel separately, but the settlers Beagle (Biegel) and Schirrer (Scherer) are listed for LaGrange and Meyer for Fayetteville.[21]

Cat Spring in Austin County was founded in 1834 as a direct result of reading the Ernst letter and the desire to "live under a republican form of government, with unbounded personal, religious and political liberty, free from the petty tyrannies and the many disadvantages and evils of the old countries."[22] Cat Spring lies southwest of Bellville on the edge of the Post Oak Woods and about ten miles west of Sealy on the Missouri, Kansas and Texas Railway. The place was named Cat Spring, because one of the young von Roeders killed a wild cat at one of the springs on the San Bernardo. The first persons to locate there were: Marcus Amsler, Karl Amsler, Louis von Roeder, Albrecht von Roeder, Joachim von Roeder, and Valeska von Roeder. The Amslers did not have the means to have their land surveyed, an act which Louis von Roeder performed for them for one-third of a league. The von Roeders came to Texas in 1834 as the advance party of a group of emigrants consisting of Lieutenant Ludwig Anton Siegmund von Roeder and wife, his daughters Louise and Caroline, his sons Rudolph, Otto, and Wilhelm, Robert Kleberg and his wife, née Rosalie von Roeder, Louis Kleberg, Mrs. Otto von Roe-

---

[21]Eighth United States Census, Schedule 4: Productions of Agriculture, I. Texas State Library. See also Lotto, F., *Fayette County, Her History and Her People*, 350, 376. F. Lotto secured the information for his book while he was traveling agent of the *LaGrange Deutsche Zeitung* in 1901 and 1902. For other information about this book and the men to whôm Lotto was under obligations, the preface should be read. Later references to the book will be made under the title, *Fayette County*.

[22]Tiling, *German Element in Texas*, 24. Tiling quotes here from notes by Robert Kleberg, Sr., the founder of Cat Spring.

ROBERT JUSTUS KLEBERG
Founder of Cat Spring
From a photograph in the possession of Mrs. Rudolph Kleberg,
Austin, Texas

der, *née* Pauline von Donop, Miss Antoinette von Donop, who later became Mrs. Rudolph von Roeder, John Reinermann and family, William Frels, and others. They sailed from (Bremen?) on the last day of September, 1834, in the ship *Congress,* Captain J. Adams, and landed at New Orleans after a voyage of sixty days. They heard discouraging news about Texas in New Orleans, but they decided to go on, since they did not want to disappoint the others who had preceded them. From New Orleans they sailed for Brazoria, but were wrecked off Galveston Island on December 22, 1834. All of the passengers were brought safely on shore with enough provisions. Robert Kleberg and Rudolph von Roeder went to Brazoria to charter a boat, but found none there. At San Felipe de Austin Captain W. Harris wanted one thousand dollars to charter them the steamer *Cuyuga,* but they considered that too high. Finally they chartered a small steamer from Mr. Scott, father-in-law of S. M. Williams, for one hundred dollars. On this steamer and a sloop, hired from Captain Smith in Velasco, the stranded immigrants were moved to Harrisburg in three trips, the last reaching Harrisburg in the fall of 1835. From Harrisburg they travelled in ox-carts to their destination in Austin County, a distance of more than fifty miles. The roads were almost impassable.[23]

These early settlers of Cat Spring suffered all of the hardships and privations of pioneer life. After their arrival at Cat Spring it was necessary to build log houses. Mr. M. Hartmann, who came to Cat Spring in 1847, says that the sons of von Roeder cut down trees about four inches thick, set them in the ground at intervals of two feet, nailed shingles on the outside, made the roof, doors, and windows likewise of shingles, and filled out the spaces between the upright posts with clay and wood. One of the two houses had a floor and ceiling made from planks sawed by hand from post oak trees. Over the interior wall von Roeder pasted pictures from illustrated magazines. When Mrs. von Ploeger, his sister, arrived from Germany and entered this pioneer palace, she is said to have swooned. Robert Kleberg says in his memorandum that in the summer of 1835 they enclosed a field of ten acres and planted it in corn and cotton. After that they moved as much of their furniture as they had use and room

[23]Tiling, *German Element in Texas,* 25-28.

for from Harrisburg to Cat Spring. They left a fine piano, belonging to Mrs. Kleberg, many valuable oil paintings, music, books, and other articles in Harrisburg, where they were destroyed by the fire in the following spring during the Texas Revolution.[24]

Cat Spring continued to attract Germans. When Hartmann arrived there in 1847 he found his boyhood friend, John Baptiste Dros, Wm. Flato, Albert Hagemann, Hermann Bolten, Wm. Mersmann, Fritz Sens, W. Kinkler, John Glaum, C. Dittert, Charles Wellhausen, Levermann and J. Hollien. The family of Adolphus Fuchs settled in Cat Spring in 1846, although they had intended to go to Industry. Besides the original settlers mentioned above, the Engelking family had come there in the early days. Other settlers who lived in Cat Spring before 1850 were Kaspar Stuessel, Joachim Kaeding, Jacob Kaeding, Heinrich Siewert and wife, Heinrich Dethloff, Heinrich Wack, and Fritz Eckelberg.[25]

[24]Trenckmann, *Austin County*, 29-30; Tiling, *German Element in Texas*, 28. M. Hartmann, from whom Trenckmann got his information about Cat Spring, was born in 1817 in Berg-Rheinfeld, Unterfranken. He studied to be a merchant. In 1847 he came to Texas with the intention of going to Castro's Colony on the Medina River, but he went instead to Cat Spring. In 1856 he became alternate for the first secretary of the Agricultural Society of Austin County *(Landwirthschaftlicher Verein fuer Austin County)*. He served as a trustee of the Cat Spring school for fifteen years and also as justice of the peace for nearly as long.

[25]Trenckmann, *Austin County*, 30; Goeth, *Was Grossmutter erzaehlt*, 32. The minutes of the Agricultural Society of Austin County *(Landwirthschaftlicher Verein fuer Austin County)*, organized June 7, 1856, give some additional, though not very definite, information about the population of Cat Spring, but only the names of the officers, of committee members, and of persons who took an active part in the discussions are given. The roster of the members is not given in the minutes for the first five years. The society was organized originally for Cat Spring and vicinity, but at the meeting in October, 1856, it was decided to have the society take in all of Austin County. Since the minutes are silent about the residence of the members, except in rare instances, it is not possible to say which members were from Cat Spring. The initials of persons are also generally omitted in the minutes. The list up to March, 1861, ending the period covered by this study, follows. Rev. Ernst Bergmann (Cat Spring), E. Kloss (Millheim), Andreas Friedrich Trenckmann (San Bernard), M. Hartmann, Louis Kleberg, J. Soder, John Schluenz, Andreas Schulze, Alex Himly, Charles Reibenstein, F. Engelking, A. Hagemann, Subrar, Ch. Wellhausen, Reymershofer, Plenow, H. Siewert, C. Reinecke, H. Amthor, W. Schneider, Wm. Gaedecke, W. Kretschmar, F. Eckelberg, Sr., Franz Meyer, Reichard, Robert Kloss, L. Constant (Bellville), H. Umland, E. G. Maetze, R. Berner, H. Glaum, K. Amsler, Gottlieb Hibbold, Sam Swearingen, H. John, J. H. Kraucher, Frank Dros, John Laas, Kay, J. Hollien, Max Meisner, Adolf Schulz, F. Fissler, Robert Wagner and Richard Poth (New Ulm), Robert Dehnisch (San Bernard), Johann Kohlhof, W. Mersemann, H. Nagel, W. Kaeuffel, Arthur Kopisch, Friedrich

The first German settlement to be established in Colorado County was Frelsburg. It is located a few miles east of the main branch of Cummins Creek in the extreme northern corner of the county. The place was named after William Frels, the first German settler of that region. This man was on the ship *Congress* with Lieutenant von Roeder, Robert Kleberg, and others who settled at Cat Spring in 1835. Just when Frels, former subject of Oldenburg, moved to Frelsburg is not definitely known; it could hardly have been before 1837, because Frels participated in the storming of San Antonio in the fall of 1835 and saw service at the battle of San Jacinto.[26]

Frelsburg did not develop rapidly. One description of the place in 1846 says that the settlement was rather extended with great distances between the different houses. Most of the settlers were from Oldenburg and Holstein.[27] The other description of it, written in 1852, says that there was a store, a post-office, a blacksmith shop, a few houses, and a Catholic church located near by. In 1856 the congregation at Frelsburg was admitted into the synod of the Evangelical-Lutheran Church in Texas, and in 1857 the annual meeting of the synod was held at Frelsburg. Two years later the Evangelical-Lutheran congregation under Rev. J. C. Roehm built a church at Frelsburg.[28] The census for 1860 lists one hundred and three landholders with German names for Frelsburg.[29]

Eckelberg, Heinicke, Heinrich Wellhausen, Charles Amsler, C. Wellhausen, C. Sturm, Koppisch, C. H. Stuessel, J. Hintze (Millheim), C. Luetcke, Bubach, C. Severin, Howe, and H. Bruno. (See Photostat Copy, Minutes of the Agricultural Society of Austin County, University of Texas.)

[26]Wiggin, Edith E., *Anstandslehre fuer Schule und Haus*, 77, where reference is made to Kleberg, Rosa, "Early Experiences in Texas," Texas State Historical Association *Quarterly*, II, 172. A footnote, p. 172, says that the information came from Robert Kleberg's memorandum. Wiggin's *Anstandslehre* contains an appendix, in which Wm. Eilers, who lived in Fayette County for over forty years, gives a history of a number of Germans in that part of the state. Tiling, *German Element in Texas*, 34-35, gives a list of one hundred and two names of Germans who fought in the Texas Revolution.

[27]Solms-Braunfels, *Texas*, 56.

[28]Mgebroff, Johannes, *Geschichte der ersten deutschen Evangelisch-Lutherischen Synode in Texas*, 50, 100, 107, 115. Cited subsequently as *Evangelisch-Lutherische Synode in Texas*.

[29]Eighth Census (1860), Schedule 4: Productions of Agriculture, I; Texas State Library.

Blumenthal had become a settlement of considerable importance by 1840, for in that year L. C. Ervendberg went there from
Houston and organized a congregation which was composed of
seventy-two men, women, and children.[30] It was located in Colorado County, probably on Cummins Creek in the neighborhood
of Frelsburg and not far from the other German settlements at
Cat Spring, Bernardo, and New Ulm. The name *Blumenthal*
means "valley of flowers." The place is not listed on any of the
maps of the period. Blumenthal was described in 1846 as having
many farms owned by Germans.[31]

In its issue for April 30, 1840, *The Morning Star* contained
the following news about German immigrants and settlements:
"It is a fact, that notwithstanding the troubled state of the country
about La Baca Bay, large numbers of English and German emigrants have come, during the spring and are still coming into that
part of the country, and forming settlements. Protection and
quiet are the only things needful for the west."[32] No record exists,
however, of any such German settlements. It is probable that the
immigrants all went into the interior to Cat Spring, Industry,
and Frelsburg.

Shelby, sometimes called *Roedersmuehle,* owes its name to the
first American settler of that region, David Shelby. It lies in
the northwestern corner of Austin County. The real beginning
of Shelby dates from the early forties, when Otto von Roeder
built a mill there on the upper stretches of Mill Creek. For that
reason it was called Roedersmuehle by the Germans. In 1845
August Vogelsang bought the mill. The families of John Vanderwerth, Andrew Rothermel, Charles Ohlendorf, and others settled
there in 1845, and in 1846 the families Witte, John Bern(s)hausen,
Henry Wagner, Harry Marburger, and others arrived. In the
next few years H. Schmidt, known as cigar-maker and surveyor

---

[30]Mgebroff, *Evangelisch-Lutherische Synode in Texas*, 8. Mgebroff says
that Ervendberg came from Illinois to Houston, Texas, in 1839 and
organized a German congregation of fifty-eight men, women, and children.
Between 1840 and 1844, when Ervendberg became the Protestant minister
for the Society for the Protection of German Immigrants in Texas, he
organized congregations at Industry, Cat Spring, Biegel, LaGrange, and
Columbus. Dr. Joseph Anton Fischer was associated with him in teaching school at these places. *(Ibid.,* 8.)

[31]*Texas. Ein Handbuch fuer deutsche Auswanderer*, 45.

[32]*The Morning Star*, April 30, 1840, 2, col. 1. This paper was published at Houston, Texas.

Schmidt, C. Henniger, F. Hetzel, P. Albrecht, Dr. Reisig, Christian Rudloff, Fentrop, Jacob Schneider, Sassenberg, Rosky, Walther, Freibig, Eisenberg, Krebs, H. Voelkel, C. Doss, H. Wunderlich, Henry Brandt, Rudolph Goebel, Suerth, H. Otto, and others settled there. Most of the early settlers of Shelby came to Texas with the Society for the Protection of German Immigrants in Texas, but decided to remain in the eastern portion of Texas when they heard of conditions prevailing in New Braunfels in the spring and summer of 1846. These people were interested in the promotion of the arts and sciences. The first school was organized by Suerth and the first school house was built in 1854. F. Fisseler, who did much to promote the settlement of the region and was especially interested in the school, started the movement to organize an agricultural society (*Landwirthschaftlicher Verein*).[33] A singing society, another evidence of culture among these people, existed in Shelby as early as 1852.[34]

In 1843 Count Boos-Waldeck, representing the Society for the Protection of German Immigrants in Texas, bought the W. H. Jack league in Fayette County and named the plantation Nassau, in honor of Adolf, the duke of Nassau and Protector of the Society for the Protection of German Immigrants in Texas. Charles Fordtran, who was appointed overseer by Prince Leiningen, in turn placed William Etzel in charge of Nassau.[35] The Society for the Protection of German Immigrants in Texas did not promote a settlement at Nassau. Some of the Society's immigrants, however, acquired land around Nassau Farm, so that a settlement developed there.

In the eastern part of Fayette County, between Fayette and Ellinger, a German settlement was started at Ross Prairie about the year 1845. The first settlers, John H. Meyer, from Hanover, and Joseph F. M. Sarrazin, from Westphalia, moved there in 1842 and 1843, respectively; Dietrich Hattermann from Oldenburg and Henry William Luecke from Westfeld, Hanover, estab-

---

[33]Fisseler was one of the members of the Agricultural Society of Austin County. See above, footnote 25.

[34]Trenckmann, *Austin County*, 24-25. This author says that Doss was instrumental in the organization of a singing society in 1858.

[35]Count Boos-Waldeck and Prince Leiningen were sent to Texas in 1843 to make an inspection for the Society just mentioned and, on the basis of conditions in Texas, to suggest a plan of procedure in establishing a colony.

lished themselves there in 1845; Hinrich Eilers, an Oldenburger,
Jacob Laferre and Henry Kurtz moved to Ross Prairie in 1847.
Other old settlers were John F. Meyer, H. G. Cook (an Olden-
burger who Americanized his name), John Neimann, Friedrich
Neumann, Dietrich Wacker, Baumbach, Sommer, Anton Sommer,
G. Mueller, F. T. Doni, August Beyer, Girndt, Richard Zedlitz,
and Jacob F. Dirr.[36] Ross Prairie was described in 1851 as a
very large German settlement by Rev. P. F. Zizelmann, a minister
of the Evangelical-Lutheran Synod of Texas. He believed that
the Germans living there were devout Christians. In 1859 the
St. John's Evangelical-Lutheran congregation built a church at
Ross Prairie, but it was not until 1861 that the congregation got
its own pastor, the Rev. R. Jaeggli.[37]

Millheim, lying in the fertile valley of the Mill Creek northeast of Cat Spring in Austin County, was founded about the year
1845, but the date is not certain. Millheim was an offshoot of
Cat Spring. It did not get its name until some time in the fifties,
when a meeting was held in the community at the store of
Engelking and Nolte. Wilhelm Schneider, an immigrant from
the Palatinate, suggested the name *Muehlheim,* which the American settlers pronounced Millheim, the name which clung to the
place. The German settlers of the community were Louis Kleberg, Hugo Zapp, F. Engelking, Carl Wenmohs, Marcus and
Fritz Amsler, H. Vornkahl, H. Bolton, Ernst Kleberg, Louis
Constant, W. Mersmann, A. Hagemann, F. Langhammer, E. Kloss,
Alex. Kloss, J. R. Wilm, Robert Kloss, J. H. Krancher, Rudolph
Goebel, Wilhelm Schneider, Carl Schneider, August and Otto Goebel, F. Buntzel, Theodor Brosig, B. Siegert, E. G. Maetze, Andreas
Friedrich Trenckmann, F. Heinecke, Dr. H. Nagel, A. Regen-
brecht, and A. Kluewer.[38] Most of these settlers became farmers,

---

[36]Lotto, *Fayette County,* 350.

[37]Mgebroff, *Evangelisch-Lutherische Synode in Texas,* 40, 113-116.

[38]Trenckmann, *Austin County,* 34-35. Trenckmann secured the information from S. Engelking, the son of the storekeeper, F. Engelking, and a
nephew of Louis Kleberg. The names of some of these men appear in the
minutes of the Agricultural Society of Austin County. See above, 50,
footnote 25.

Louis Constant wanted to make Mill Creek navigable; A. Hagemann
made tomato cider; E. Kloss was a lawyer and the first secretary of the
Agricultural Society of Austin County; J. R. Wilm built the first cotton
gin in Millheim; J. H. Krancher was the first constable of Millheim; E.

but there were also "blacksmiths, wheelwrights, carpenters, shoemakers, tailors, brickmasons, a cabinetmaker, a saddler, a tanner, and a tinner. The ordinary farm-laborer received free board and fifty cents per day. . . . The farmers of Millheim lived in frame dwelling houses, but some of the pioneer settlers still lived in block houses. . . . The Bernard Prairie extending from the Brazos to the Colorado and from Catspring to Brazoria County was a ranch free for cattle and horses. Therefore, many settlers were cattle and horse raisers. Some raised sheep, but with no success on account of depredations by wolves. Corn bread, bacon, molasses, and coffee, occasionally fish and venison, were the principal food of the pioneers. In 1856 the settlers had better vegetable gardens and orchards and more milk, butter and cheese. There were more stores. . . . There was a singing society in Millheim."[39]

About ten miles west of Cat Spring a German settlement was made at San Bernard on the south bank of the San Bernardo in Colorado County. A few of the early settlers came to Texas as colonists of the Society for the Protection of German Immigrants in Texas, but they preferred to remain in this section of the state where a good number of Germans had established themselves and where the frontier conditions were not as exacting as in the Fisher and Miller grant. The Society just mentioned, however, had nothing to do with the founding of this settlement. The census for 1860 lists twenty farmers with German names in San Bernard. These were: Jacob Marz (Merz), F. Kornsteiner, J. Wilburg, Anth. Geistmann, John Weigel, Charles Benzung, F. Pesserchek, J. B. Neihus (Neihaus), Wm. Goedke (Gaedeke), F. W. Hengst, Ludwig Litzmar, John Schaberda, Robert Denisch (Dehnisch), Stephen Schimera, Alex Himly, Franz Kortzbue (Kotzebue), Franz Ordner, H. E. Jordt, F. Schiller, B. Schiller, Charles Reichard (Reichart), and A. Braden.[40]

The fertile lands in the western part of Austin County proved very attractive to those German immigrants who came to Texas

G. Maetze founded the old Millheim school; and Andreas Friedrich Trenckmann was the founder of the Agricultural Society of Austin County.

[39]Regenbrecht, Adalbert, "The German Settlers of Millheim before the Civil War," in *Southwestern Historical Quarterly*, XX, 29-30.

[40]Trenckmann, *Austin County*, 18; Eighth Census (1860), Schedule 4: Productions of Agriculture, I.

after 1845 to engage in agriculture. The first settlers of New Ulm came from Nassau, Industry, and Shelby. The settlement grew rapidly and a Mr. Ebeling (?) was made post-master. In 1850 Franz Pille, F. Lingnau, J. Schuette, M. Hartmann, John and F. Luedecke, Eduard Brune, F. Dorbritz, Seiller, F. Mueller (cabinet-maker), "Post Oak Point" Mueller, Joseph Mueller, Adam and Ernst Wangemann, the post-master Ebeling, and Lorenz Mueller lived there.[41]   At Christmas time in the year 1858 the Rev. Adolphus Fuchs, then a resident of Cypress Mill, Blanco County, visited New Ulm with his daughter Ottilie in the home of Ferdinand Wolters.[42]   For Ottilie Fuchs this visit was very important, since she met Carl Goeth, her future husband. Goeth was in the saddlery business at New Ulm with his brother-in-law, Ferdinand Wolters.

Washington County received a good number of German settlers, especially during the great immigration after 1848. Just east of the line between Fayette and Washington counties, in the La Bahia prairie, the settlement of *Latium* was established in the late forties. Its name indicates that some of its settlers were so-called "Latin Farmers" and that it was a "Latin Settlement." Viktor Witte, who had been a large landowner in Hanover and who, rather than allow a railroad to be built across his land, had sold his possessions and come to Texas, was one of the first settlers. His immediate neighborhood was called the Rock House community because of the large rock house which he built. Bernhard Witte had studied medicine in Germany but did not actually practice in Texas, although the early settlers frequently consulted him for medical advice. Two of his sons in turn became physicians. Dr. Henry (?) Brandt interested himself in the production of commercial fertilizer. Carl F. Giesecke of Clausthal, Germany, an immigrant of the Society for the Protection of German Immigrants in Texas, who left Germany late in 1845, was another settler, as was also George Christian Friedrich Giesecke, his brother. Hermann R. von Bieberstein was a civil

---

[41]Trenckmann, *Austin County*, 26, 63. The place was called Duff's Settlement before the arrival of the Germans. It is said that Lorenz Mueller suggested the name New Ulm and carried his point when the change of name was discussed by treating those present to a case of Rhenish wine *(Rheinwein)*.

[42]Goeth, *Was Grossmutter erzaehlt*, 46.

engineer by profession and did much work as a surveyor in Texas. He married Miss Adele Hagedorn, a daughter of Carl Dietrich Hagedorn, another of the settlers of this community. Carl Wilhelm Apollo Groos, three of whose sons established the Groos Bank in San Antonio, lived in Latium until his removal to New Braunfels. Hermann Otto Cornitius was another of the "Latin Farmers," while Professor Krug, whose descendants are to be found in Brenham to-day, was the school teacher of this settlement. Mr. Albert Eversberg lived in Latium from the early days and married Miss Anna Schmidt of Austin County.[43]

The second German settlement founded in Washington County was Berlin, which was begun about 1849. It received a good number of the immigrants who came to Texas after 1848. Valentin Hoffmann and his family were the first settlers. By 1861 the community had grown large enough to engage the services of Rev. Jacob Graul, an Evangelical-Lutheran minister.[44]

Among the German settlements in the lower Brazos-Colorado-Guadalupe region, Yorktown enjoys the distinction of having become the largest and of having come into existence as the result of a definite plan to establish a town. Yorktown lies in De Witt County and was originally laid out in 1848. The place was named after John York, owner of the Alexander Pendaris headright in De Witt County. On April 1, 1848, York entered into certain "Articles of Agreement" with Charles Eckhardt, Theodore Miller, C. DeSchutz, and John L. Mueller.[45] Under the agreement York conveyed a half interest in his league of land for one dollar in cash, while Eckhardt and his associates agreed to lay out the league into town or building lots, blocks and acre lots, and were to bear the expenses of surveying, mapping, recording, and advertising. York was to keep each alternate lot, block, and acre lot. The agreement stipulated that the town was to "be known and named 'Yorktown' in honor of the former proprietor."

[43] I am indebted to Mr. W. A. Trenckmann, Mr. C. R. von Bieberstein, and Mr. Ernst H. Eversberg, all of Austin, Texas, to Dr. F. E. Giesecke of College Station, Texas, and to Mrs. E. P. Stein of New Braunfels, Texas, for the information about the early settlers of Latium.

[44] Pennington, R. E., *The History of Brenham and Washington County*, 111; Mgebroff, *Evangelisch-Lutherische Synode in Texas*, 116. According to Mrs. Pennington, Valentin Hoffmann came to Galveston on October 6, 1846, and his wife lived to be 102 years old.

[45] Charles Eckhardt and Theodore Miller lived in Indian Point, Calhoun County; C. DeSchutz and John L. Mueller were from New Braunfels.

On July 24, 1848, Eckhardt and his associates wrote to York from New Braunfels that they were sending him a copy of the town plat and that Eckhardt had full power of attorney to bring the transaction to a close.[46]

Yorktown became at once a German settlement. Charles Eckhardt's sterling qualities had much to do with attracting settlers to the community. Of the one hundred and twenty persons whose names appear on the census rolls for 1860, ninety-seven have German names.[47] Wm. T. Eichholz says that the first settlers were Andreas Strieber, Peter Metz, C. G. Hartmann, and Mrs. Hoppe.[48]

About nine miles west of Victoria the settlement of Coletoville was founded in 1849 by Carl Steiner, for which reason it is sometimes called Steiner's Settlement. It was located right on the western edge of Victoria County. When the post office was established the place was named Coletoville. It is one of the few German settlements that did not survive, for in 1884 both the post office and store no longer existed.[49] In one of a series of articles, entitled "Meine Erlebnisse in Texas," Julius Schuetze, editor of the *Texas Vorwaerts,* gave some information of a few of the early settlers of the Coletoville neighborhood. He moved there with his mother and sister in the fall of 1853 and rented a small farm from Jacob Schiewitz. The year before he had rented on the farm of Gustav von Frauenstein, three miles from Yorktown. He added to his income by hauling freight from

[46]MS. Records, Office Secretary of State, Memorial No. 5, File Box No. 99, Letter No. Y. The memorial includes one document duly executed and acknowledged by C. DeSchutz and J. L. Mueller, granting the power of attorney to Charles Eckhardt, and a second, duly executed and acknowledged by Theodore Miller, selling to Charles Eckhardt all of his rights, title, and interest in the league for twenty-nine dollars and thirty cents. These highly important documents were probably filed in the Secretary of State's office in connection with the case of *Riedel vs. York & Eckhardt.* One of the documents is endorsed: "Reidel vs. York & Eckhart (A) Filed May 16th A. D. 1855 W. A. Blair Clk."

[47]Eighth Census (1860), Schedule 4: Productions of Agriculture, I; Texas State Library.

[48]Eichholz, "Die deutschen Ansiedlungen am Colletto," in Schuetze, *Jahrbuch fuer Texas* (1884), 85. Eichholz was for a number of years editor of the *Cuero Deutsche Rundschau* and well-informed on the early history of the German settlements of DeWitt County.

[49]Eichholz, "Die deutschen Ansiedlungen am Colletto," in Schuetze, *Jahrbuch fuer Texas* (1884), 86.

Indianola to Victoria, Goliad, New Braunfels, and San Antonio. Louis Schuetze, his brother, moved to the region from Indianola early in 1854. Other settlers were George and Fritz Witting, Baron von Lochhausen, Dr. Wolff, E. Froboese, and A. Wundt. Two former German officers, von Hoyer and von Zobel, kept a country store where the road from Victoria to Yorktown crossed the 12-mile Coleto. William Westhoff, a young man, was in their employ. Among the agricultural products of the Coletoville neighborhood was the Irish potato, which the German settlers had found to grow well in the light soil of the region. On April 7, 1854, the Coleto *Gesangverein* was organized with ten active members, and Julius Schuetze, then hardly nineteen years old, was made director.[50]

Another German settlement in the Coleto neighborhood is Meyersville. It was named after Adolph Meyer, who founded the place about 1849. Meyer had made a contract with the Society for the Protection of German Immigrants in Texas to go to the lands of the Fisher and Miller grant, but he, as so many others, preferred to remain in the lower part of the state. Meyersville really grew up in two sections about two miles apart, on both banks of the 12-mile Coleto, in De Witt County, south of Cuero. Lower Meyersville became the real business center of the community. As early as 1852 there was an Evangelical-Lutheran church in Meyersville with Rev. Christoph Adam Sager in charge. In 1859 the Evangelical-Lutheran Synod of Texas held its annual meeting there. Out of eighty landowners listed for Meyersville in the eighth census, seventy-two were of German extraction. The settlement had a fairly rapid growth.[51]

Seven miles southwest of La Grange, on O'Quinn's Creek, is situated the O'Quinn settlement. Lotto says that it was named after an Indian chief by that name, but that another version claims that it was named after an Irishman by that name. The

---

[50]Schuetze, Julius, "Meine Erlebnisse in Texas," *Texas Vorwaerts*, February 1, 1884, p. 2, cols. 2-4. *Texas Vorwaerts*, a newspaper published in the German language at Austin, Texas, made its initial appearance on October 26, 1883, under the very able editorship of Julius Schuetze. This paper remained in continuous publication until September 4, 1914.

[51]Eichholz, "Die deutschen Ansiedlungen am Colletto," in Schuetze, *Jahrbuch fuer Texas* (1884), 83; Mgebroff, *Evangelisch-Lutherische Synode in Texas*, 63, 110; Eighth Census (1860), Schedule 4: Productions of Agriculture, I, Texas State Library.

majority of its first settlers in 1850 were Germans, among them the families of A. Duellberg, Fred. Melcher, Charles Luck, H. Bruns, and John Voigt. Together with the Germans of the Black Jack community, a few miles farther south, there were thirty German landowners in 1860. One of the Germans on Black Jack Creek was J. C. N. Romberg, a man of considerable poetic ability and by whose pen a whole volume of verse was produced.[52]

In the northern part of Austin County lies another German settlement, Welcome. The earliest American settlers of the community were Carothers, S. A. Shelburne, N. Davis, and others, but they did not give a name to the place. It was not until the early fifties, about 1852, that German settlers moved into the region. Four Oldenburger schoolmasters, A. Vogelsang, J. F. Schmidt, D. H. Schelling, and Carl Kruse, were the chief persons interested in establishing this German settlement. One of these, J. F. Schmidt, selected the name "Welcome," because "everything—forest, field, meadows, and flowers—seemed to give them a friendly welcome."[53] Schmidt also organized a singing society. A school was built on the right bank of Pecan Creek near the center of the community. The early German settlers were A. Wangemann, Harde, H. Peters, K. Stoelje, Barings, Wittner, H. Huebner, Lange, Otto Boeker, H. Meier, Eben, Albert Spreen, Mahlmann, Bockelmann, F. Hachfeld, Haverlah, Giesel, and others.[54]

Near the southern boundary of Fayette County, north of Schulenburg, the settlement of High Hill is located. It was originally in two parts, the upper being called Oldenburg, the lower Blum Hill. In the year 1855 the settlers named the place Blum Hill, in honor of Robert Blum,[55] who was murdered in

---

[52]Lotto, *Fayette County*, 401-402; Eighth Census, Schedule 4: Productions of Agriculture, 1, Texas State Library. Two daughters of Johannes Romberg, Luise and Lina, married William and Hermann Fuchs, respectively, brothers of Ottilie Goeth. (See Goeth, *Was Grossmutter erzaehlt*, 46-47.)

[53]Trenckmann, *Austin County*, 28-29. The article on this settlement was written for Mr. Trenckmann by Theodore Buehrer.

[54]Trenckmann, *Austin County*, 28-29.

[55]Robert B. Blum was born in Cologne on November 10, 1804, of poor parents. He was ten years old before he went to school. As an author he contributed poems and articles to the Berlin *Schnellpost*. The revolutionary period of the thirties influenced him greatly. On August 13, 1845, in the absence of Prince Johann of Saxony, Blum quieted a disturbance

MAP 1

COUNTIES IN THE LOWER BRAZOS, COLORADO, AND GUADALUPE RIVER
REGION WITH GERMAN SETTLEMENTS AND A GERMAN
ELEMENT IN 1860

The counties which are shaded are those which had definite German
settlements by 1860; the others which are named had only a German
element. The figure with each county indicates the approximate percentage ratio of the German population to the total white population in
1860. See also Table I on next page.

Table I.—Showing Percentage Ratio of Foreign (German) Population to Total White Population in Counties with German Settlements and a German Element.

Counties	Native	Foreign	*Total	†German	Percentage	‡Probable Percent- age
Austin	5020	1205	6225	840	13	20
Colorado	3160	1166	4326	696	16	24
De Witt	2587	788	3475	750	21	32
Fayette	5781	2027	7808	1350	17	25
Victoria	1863	894	2757	510	18	27
Washington	6020	1251	7271	1000	14	21
Bastrop	3715	700	4415	525	12	18
Calhoun	1490	738	2228	402	18	27
Galveston	3982	2725	6707	1360	20	30
Harris	4787	2221	7008	1480	21	31
Lavaca	3987	251	4238	162	04	06
Matagorda	1116	231	1347	77	06	09

*Figures secured from Kennedy, Joseph C. G., *Population of the United States in 1860,* pp. 487-489. The figures for the foreign population represent more than only persons of German nativity.

†In Walker, Francis A., *The Statistics of the Population of the United States* (Volume I of the Ninth Census, 1870), pp. 372 and 373, is found a table on Selected Nativities by Counties. On the basis of figures given in that table the writer estimated the number of Germans in the above Texas counties in 1860.

‡Among the records in the archives of the University of Texas is to be found a photostat copy of the original census sheets of the Seventh as well as of the Eighth Census (1850 and 1860) for Gillespie County. From a very careful check of the original census sheets for 1860 it was found that the children of German extraction, who were listed as native-born, amounted to about one-half of the number of persons classed as foreign-dorn Germans. It may be concluded fairly accurately, it seems, that the same conbition held true for the counties in the table above. Hence the percentages should be increased about one-half, thus giving the figures listed in the last column.

Vienna on November 9, 1848. When the post-office was established there in 1858, the place was named High Hill. The pioneer German settlers were L. Zahrenthold, L. Eschenburg, E. H. Bauch, F. G. Seydler, H. Ebeling, and J. H. Hillje. Ebeling built the first general merchandise store in 1858, and Seydler and Hillje each built a steam grist mill. Other old settlers of High Hill are Joseph Heinrich, Sr., F. Kleinemann, George Herder, Gerhard Siems, P. Stuelke, Gerhard Nordhausen, Charles Hinkel, Edward Schubert, Captain Charles Wellhausen, August Kuechler, and Ernst Goeth.[56]

The last German settlement that needs to be mentioned in this chapter is Round Top in the eastern part of Fayette County on the banks of Cummins Creek. It is located two miles above the old Nassau Plantation of the Society for the Protection of German Immigrants ·in Texas. In its early days there were only American settlers in this region, but in the middle fifties it developed into a German community. Among its early German settlers we find: George Fricke, a veteran of the Mexican War, C. E. Bauer, Weyand, William von Rosenberg, Ferdinand Kneip, Henry Kneip, Adolph Kneip, C. W. Rummel, Charles Schiege, Robert Zapp, C. Henkel, Weikel, and Rev. John G. Lieb. In the year 1860 the synodal meeting of the Evangelical-Lutheran Church in Texas was held at Round Top, where the St. John's congregation had been organized in 1858. According to the census of 1860 one hundred and twenty-nine farms were owned in Round Top by German settlers.[57]

in Cologne after the military had fired on the mob. In 1848 he organized the *Vaterlandsverein*, to which 40,000 members belonged at one time. As a member of the Diet of the German Confederation he tried to keep the Radical Left in control. In 1848 he and Froebel, another member of the Diet, were chosen by the Left and Extreme Left to present an address to the people of Vienna. For his participation in the uprising in Vienna he was tried by a military court and sentenced to be hanged, but the sentence was reduced. On November 9, 1848, he was assassinated in Vienna while out walking. (*Allgemeine Deutsche Biographie*, II, 739-741.)

56Lotto, *Fayette County*, 393-395; "Kurzer Umriss der Geschichte von High Hill, Fayette County, Texas," reprinted in *Der Deutsche Pionier*, I, 349-351, from the *San Antonio Freie Presse*. Presumably Siemering, editor of the *Freie Presse*, wrote the article, since the history of the Germans in Texas interested him.

57Lotto, *Fayette County*, 355; Mgebroff, *Evangelisch-Lutherische Synode in Texas*, 110, 113; Eighth Census, Schedule 4: Productions of Agriculture, I, Texas State Library.

A total of twenty German settlements is listed in this chapter. A few definite conclusions may be drawn from the account. With the exception of Yorktown, none of the settlements came into being as the result of any concerted plan. They grew up, for the most part, around the farm of some individual settler, as for instance, Industry, Biegel, Frelsburg, Shelby (Roedersmuehle), Ross Prairie, Coletoville, and Meyersville. Some were named after the first settler, either American or German, in the neighborhood, as Biegel, Frelsburg, Shelby, Yorktown, and Meyersville. Some grew up in localities after the original American settlers were out-numbered. Shelby, Welcome, and Round Top are examples of this type. Some have English names, for which an explanation was given in nearly every instance. These are Industry, Cat Spring, Shelby, Yorktown, Welcome, High Hill, and Round Top. This use of English names indicates an Americanizing influence as well as a feeling on the part of the settlers that German names would not be appropriate for settlements in Texas. One of the settlements, *Latium,* in Washington County, had a considerable number of highly educated men, so that it was called the Latin Settlement *(Lateiner Settlement).* But in the other settlements there were educated men also, notably in Shelby *(Roedersmuehle),* Millheim and Cat Spring. The settlers, as a rule, believed in schools and tried to provide the elements of an education for their children. They did not neglect their religion either. Rev. L. C. Ervendberg founded German Protestant churches at Industry, Cat Spring, and Biegel between 1840 and 1844. After the Evangelical-Lutheran Synod was organized in Texas in 1851, congregations of this denomination were started and churches were built in Meyersville (1852), Frelsburg (1857), Round Top (1858), Ross Prairie (1859), and Berlin (1861). Most of the Germans in these settlements were from Oldenburg, Holstein, and Westphalia, in the northwestern part of Germany. Friedrich Ernst's letter brought a number of Oldenburgers to Texas. When these wrote back to their former homes, relatives and friends were induced to settle in Texas, where it seemed easier to make a living. The failure of the revolutionary movement from 1830 to 1833 proved to be an additional incentive for emigration, especially in the case of the early settlers of Cat Spring. After 1845 a number of the colonists of the Society for the Protection of German Immigrants in Texas preferred to remain in the previously established settlements and in some instances helped in the founding of other settlements, as New Ulm, Yorktown, and Meyersville. The Society itself, however, was not interested in the founding of any of these settlements. After 1848 the exodus of revolutionists from Germany added to the population in these settlements, but no settlements are traceable to these newcomers. The settlements discussed in this chapter were confined to six counties. Victoria County had one German settlement, Washington and De Witt had two each, Colorado had three, and Austin and Fayette each had six. A slow but steady growth was characteristic of all of them, and only one, Coletoville, did not survive.

CHAPTER IV

THE SOCIETY FOR THE PROTECTION OF GERMAN IMMIGRANTS IN TEXAS: ITS ORGANIZATION AND ITS ACQUISITION OF TWO COLONIZATION CONTRACTS

The second significant event in the history of German settlements in Texas was the organization of the "Society for the Protection of German Immigrants in Texas" *(Verein zum Schutze deutscher Einwanderer in Texas)*. This society was known also in Germany and by the German settlers in Texas as the *Mainzer Adelsverein,* or just briefly the *Adelsverein.* German emigration to Texas was well under way by the forties and would have continued, but the organization of the Society for the Protection of German Immigrants in Texas gave a new impetus to the movement and furnished the German settlements in the lower Brazos, Colorado, and Guadalupe region with settlers who, as was pointed out in the preceding chapter, preferred to remain in the settled portions of Texas rather than to go to the uninhabited frontier. Up to the time of the founding of the Society for the Protection of German Immigrants in Texas, no concerted effort had been made to induce German emigrants to go to Texas; the Society, however, undertook, as one of several objects, to direct emigration there.

It is the object of the writer to show in this chapter how a few German noblemen organized themselves in 1842 for the purpose of purchasing lands in Texas, how they determined the following year on a colonization scheme, how they reorganized themselves in 1844 into the "Society for the Protection of German Immigrants in Texas," and how they acquired two colonization contracts in order to carry out the work which they had planned.

On April 20, 1842, a small number of German counts and princes met at Biebrich on the Rhine, near the old city of Mayence, and organized themselves into a society. The moving spirit of this society was Carl, the Count of Castell, an officer of the Austrian garrison in the fortress of Mayence. He and other members of the nobility had read the widely disseminated accounts of Texas and of her struggle for independence[1] and conceived the idea of doing something for Texas by assisting German emigrants who were going there. At the meeting in Biebrich they signed, the following document:

"We, the undersigned, hereby make known that we have to-day constituted ourselves as a society for the purpose of purchasing lands in the Republic of Texas."[2]

The original purpose of the society was simply the purchase of land on which they were planning to settle German emigrants. The society decided on the day of the meeting in Biebrich to send Prince Victor of Leiningen and Count Joseph of Boos-Waldeck to Texas. In May, 1842, these two noblemen left for Texas with ample funds and full power to buy land for the society. From Galveston, where they arrived early in September, they went to Houston, arriving there on September 13. Then they went to San Felipe and Industry. After a brief stay, Prince Leiningen went to Austin to confer with President Houston about a land grant and concessions for the society. Leiningen asked that the society's colonists be exempted from taxation for a number of years, but President Houston could not grant the exemption, nor would the Congress of Texas make any change in the colonization law to that effect.[3] Leiningen did not accomplish anything, but after his return to Germany in 1843 he reported in favor of coloniza-

[1]Some of these accounts were: Scherpf, G. A., *Entstehungsgeschichte und gegenwaertiger Zustand des neuen, unabhaengigen, amerikanischen Staates Texas;* Dunt, *Reise nach Texas;* Hecke, *Reise durch die Vereinigten Staaten von Nord-Amerika in den Jahren 1818 und 1819;* Kennedy, Wm., *Texas: the Rise, Progress, and Prospects of the Republic of Texas;* and Sealsfield, Charles, *Das Kajuetenbuch oder Nationale Charakteristiken.*

[2]Penniger, *Fest-Ausgabe*, 23; Tiling, *German Element in Texas*, 59-60. The following noblemen belonged to the society: Duke Adolf of Nassau, Prince Victor of Leiningen, Prince Maurice of Nassau, Prince Guenther of Schwarzburg-Rudolstadt, Prince Ferdinand of Solms-Braunfels, Prince Hermann of Wied, Count of Colloredo, Prince Alexander of Solms-Braunfels, Prince Carl of Solms-Braunfels, Count Carl of Castell, Count of Colloredo, Count August of Neu-Leiningen-Westerburg, Count Christian of Neu-Leiningen-Westerburg, Count Frederick of Alt-Leiningen, Count Victor of Alt-Leiningen, the Countess of Ysenburg-Meerholz, Count Edmund of Hatzfeld, Count Clemens of Boos-Waldeck, Count Joseph of Boos-Waldeck, Count Anton of Boos-Waldeck, and Count Renesse.

[3]For a discussion of the colonization laws of Texas, see below, pp. 69-70.

tion in Texas on a large scale.[4] Count Joseph of Boos-Waldeck,
in the meantime, busied himself with the task of purchasing a
tract of land. Not far from Industry, the home of Friedrich
Ernst, he found a league of land that appealed to him. This was
the W. H. Jack League in the eastern part of Fayette County on
Cummins Creek. When Count Boos-Waldeck bought the league,
January 9, 1843, it was the property of Robert Mills of Brazoria
County. The purchase price was three thousand three hundred
and twenty-one dollars, or seventy-five cents an acre.[5] Count
Boos-Waldeck named the league Nassau Farm, in honor of Duke
Adolf of Nassau, who was the Protector of the society. In January, 1844, Count Boos-Waldeck returned to Germany and reported to the society against colonization on a large scale, since
it would require too large a financial outlay. He advised also

[4] Tiling, *German Element in Texas*, 60-61; Penniger, *Fest-Ausgabe*, 23-24.
The writer did not find any documentary evidence on Leiningen's proposal.

[5] Fayette County Transcribed Deed Record Book C, 205-206. W. H. Jack
had received this league of land from the Mexican government as a colonist
by a deed dated March 19, 1831, and conveyed it to Robert Mills on
January 20, 1840.

Nassau Farm, as this league came to be called, remained in the possession of the Society for the Protection of German Immigrants in Texas
for only a few years. In the meanwhile the Society came to be called the
German Emigration Company. Gustavus Dresel, lawfully constituted
attorney of the Lavaca, Guadeloupe, and San Saba Railroad, *alias* the
German Emigration Company, on July 28, 1848, conveyed Nassau Farm
with all of its farming utensils, plantation tools, horses, mules, swine,
sheep, household and kitchen furniture, carpenters' and blacksmiths' tools,
all other personal property whatsoever, and twenty-five slaves to Otto von
Roeder for the sum of fourteen thousand dollars. (Fayette County Deed
Record Book E, 113-114.) Otto von Roeder agreed, however, that, if the
German Emigration Company repaid him the sum of six thousand dollars
by July 28, 1849, he would reconvey the league to the company. (Fayette
County Deed Record Book G, 130-131.) On February 22, 1850, L. Bene,
Trustee of the German Emigration Company, surrendered the deed of
reversion (reversion— in Scots Law the right of redemption of an estate
that is security for a debt or judgment) granted by Otto von Roeder, who
paid an additional eight thousand four hundred and seventy-five dollars
and seventy-six cents. Otto von Roeder thus became the owner of Nassau
Farm. (Fayette County Deed Record Book G, 132-133.) But on May 3,
1853, Otto von Roeder lost Nassau Farm by a sheriff's sale of the property
to satisfy a judgment secured in the Bexar County District Court on
November 24, 1852, by P. Bremond and W. A. Van Alstyne against the
German Emigration Company for two thousand four hundred and forty-
four dollars and sixteen cents. Sheriff J. Moore of Fayette County levied
upon Nassau Farm and sold it to James A. Chandler of Bristol County,
Massachusetts, as the highest bidder for one hundred and seventy-seven
dollars and seventy-six cents, or about four cents an acre. (Fayette
County Deed Record Book I, 426.) Chandler and McFarland were attor-
neys for the plaintiffs, Bremond and Van Alstyne.

·against accepting a proposition by Alexander Bourgeois (d'-Orvanne) for acquiring a colonization contract.[6] Count Boos-Waldeck severed his connection with the society when it did not follow his advice but accepted instead the suggestion of Prince Leiningen to embark on a large-scale colonization.[7]

While Count Boos-Waldeck was still in Texas, some changes took place in the society. Some of its members dropped out and new ones were added. The society was reorganized into a stock company with a capital stock of eighty thousand dollars (two hundred thousand florins), divided into forty shares of two thousand dollars each. On March 25, 1844, at a general meeting of the stockholders a new society was formed. This society was called the "Society for the Protection of German Immigrants in Texas." A resolution was adopted that speculation and political projects were not contemplated and that the society, out of purely philanthropical reasons, would devote itself to the support and direction of German emigration to Texas. On May 3, 1844, the government of ·the duchy of Nassau issued a charter to the society.[8]

It is desirable at this point to give a brief statement of the

[6]For a discussion of the Bourgeois contract and proposition, see below, pp. 71-74.

[7]Penniger, *Fest-Ausgabe*, 24-25; Tiling, *German Element in Texas*, 61-62.

[8]Penniger, *Fest-Ausgabe*, 25. The members of the Society for the Protection of German Immigrants in Texas in 1844 were: Duke Adolf of Nassau, Protector of the Society, Prince Victor of Leiningen, President, the duke of Meiningen, the duke of Coburg-Gotha, Prince Frederick of Prussia, the landgrave of Hessen-Homburg, the duke of Schwarzburg-Rudolstadt, Prince Maurice of Nassau, the duke of Neuwied, the duke of Solms-Braunfels, the duke of Colloredo-Mansfeld, the duke of Schoenburg-Waldenburg, Prince Alexander of Solms-Braunfels, Prince Carl of Solms-Braunfels, the count of Neu-Leiningen-Westerburg, Count Victor of Alt-Leiningen-Westerburg, Count Friedrich of Alt-Leiningen-Westerburg, the count of Ysenburg-Meerholz, Count Hatzfeld, Count Knyphausen, Count Renesse, Count Lilienburg, the count of Colloredo-Mansfeld, Count Carl of Castell, business director, and Alexander Bourgeois d'Orvanne, colonial director. (Schuetz, Freiherr Kuno Damian, *Texas. Rathgeber fuer Auswanderer nach diesem Lande*, 137-138; Roemer, Dr. Ferdinand, "Geschichte der deutschen Ansiedlungen in Texas und im Besonderen der durch den Mainzer Verein veranlassten," in *Der deutsche Pionier*, VII, 95, footnote. Neither of these references gives Alexander Bourgeois d'Orvanne as a member, probably because the society dismissed him as colonial director during the summer of 1844. D'Orvanne's name is correctly included in the list of members accompanying the announcement of the Society for the Protection of German Immigrants in Texas. (See Republic of Texas, Colonization Papers, 1843-1845, Texas State Library.)

land and colonization laws of the Republic of Texas, because it was through an amended colonization law that the Society for the Protection of German Immigrants acquired two colonization contracts. On October 1, 1837, the Congress of Texas passed a law to discontinue the practice of giving land to immigrants.[9] On January 4, 1839, however, a law was enacted that all free white persons who had emigrated to Texas since October 1, 1837, and who might emigrate to Texas before January 1, 1840, would be entitled to a conditional grant of land. The head of a family was to receive six hundred and forty acres and a single free white male over seventeen years three hundred and twenty acres. Such grantees, however, had to pay the fees of office and surveying and were required to reside and remain within the Republic of Texas for three years.[10] On January 4, 1841, Congress passed an act which authorized the President to "make a contract with W. S. Peters (and others named in the act) to introduce colonists . . . for the purpose of colonizing and settling a portion of the vacant and unappropriated lands of the Republic."[11] This act was amended on February 5, 1842, so that its provisions were extended to any "other company or companies, which may be organized for like purposes, as the President may, in his judgment, approve."[12] Dissatisfaction arose in Texas over the colonization law during 1843 and Congress passed a bill for the repeal of all laws then in force which authorized the President to grant colonization contracts. The repeal provided also for forfeiting all colonization contracts the terms of which had not been strictly complied with. Houston vetoed the repeal bill on January 10, 1844.[13] Congress exercised its constitutional privilege on January 30 by passing the bill over the President's veto.[14]

[9]Gammel, H. P. N., The Laws of Texas, 1822-1897, I, 264. Cited hereafter as Gammel, Laws of Texas.

[10]Gammel, Laws of Texas, II, 35-36.

[11]Gammel, Laws of Texas, II, 555.

[12]Ibid., II, 786.

[13]Republic of Texas, Records Department of State, Vol. 40, 299, Texas State Library. Houston gave as a reason for the veto that the bill would "directly impair the obligation of existing contracts." The veto message praises the society of German noblemen at Mayence, as the following passage shows: "The Executive is assured from many sources, both in Europe and America, that many emigrants are already on their way to the colonies to be settled under existing contracts—many have already arrived, and many more will (unless all faith in the government is destroyed)

As far as this study is concerned, only two colonization contracts made under the amended act have any bearing on German colonization in Texas. The first is that made by President Houston with Alexander Bourgeois and Armand Ducos on June 3, 1842, the second was made with Henry Francis Fisher and Burchard Miller on June 7, 1842, and renewed on September 1, 1843.[15] The Bourgeois grant will be considered first.

The Bourgeois-Ducos colonization contract called for the settlement of twelve hundred families or single men, with the privilege of increasing the number to sixteen hundred. One third of the colonists had to be settled on the grant within eighteen months, that is, by December 3, 1843, or else the contract would expire and Bourgeois and Ducos would lose all of their rights under it. Each family was to receive a section of land and each single man over seventeen years was to receive half a section. Each alternate section and half-section was reserved for the Republic of Texas. The contractors had to pay all the expenses of surveying their own lands and the government reserve. The lands designated in the contract were situated as follows: "Commencing at the junction of the Rio Potranca with the Rio Medina, thence extending up the Potranca to its source, thence due North to the Sabinas, thence extending along the Sabinas to the source of that Stream, thence in a direct line to the source of the Arroyo de Ubalde, thence in a direct line to the source of the southern branch of the

make our vacant territory their future home. A very powerful and wealthy association at Mayence in Germany is on the eve of commencing the introduction of a large number of German families into western Texas. By affording a few facilities and observing a strict regard for the laws, much may be done towards the settlement and protection of that portion of our vacant territory by a population distinguished for its industry and thrift."

[14]Gammel, *Laws of Texas*, II, 958-959.

[15]Binkley, W. C., *The Expansionist Movement in Texas, 1836-1850*, 100.
Alexander Bourgeois was a Frenchman who added "d'Orvanne" to his name in order to be considered of noble birth. He felt that this was necessary to approach the Society for the Protection of German Immigrants in Texas, whose members belonged to the German nobility. At any rate, he succeeded in interesting the Society in his grant as early as September 19, 1843. Eickhoff calls him an adventurer and Tiling calls him and Henry Francis Fisher the "evil spirits" of the society. (Eickhoff, *In der neuen Heimath*, 324; Tiling, *German Element in Texas*, 73.) On June 14, 1842, d'Orvanne made an agreement with the government of Texas to negotiate a loan of a million dollars in Europe, but the loan fell through ultimately. (Rives, G. L., *The United States and Mexico*, I, 474.)

MAP 2
BOURGEOIS-DUCOS AND FISHER AND MILLER GRANTS
From a map in Solms, *Texas*.

Rio Frio, thence extending down the said stream to the junction of the Rio Frio with the Arroyo de Ubalde, thence extending along the line of the grant made to Henri Castro & John Jaussand to the northeastern Corner of said grant, thence in a direct line to the place of beginning."[16] According to their colonization contract, Bourgeois and Ducos were to receive ten sections of land for every hundred families and ten half-sections for every hundred single men introduced. The Republic of Texas was pledged also to give them title for any land that the colonists agreed to give Bourgeois and Ducos for the privilege of settling on their grant.[17]

When Bourgeois d'Orvanne learned about the plan of the German noblemen he hurried to Germany to see them. He gained their confidence and on September 19, 1843, he induced them to take the first steps to acquire the colonization rights of the Bourgeois-Ducos grant. As yet Bourgeois and Ducos had not placed any colonists on their land. Furthermore, if they should not settle at least four hundred colonists on the land by December 3, 1843, they would suffer forfeiture of their contract and all rights under it. Bourgeois realized that the grant might be forfeited but tried to secure a renewal. On October 1, 1843, he wrote Anson Jones that he had associated himself with a large society in Mayence which planned to send 10,000 families to Texas. On October 14 he wrote again, called attention to the forfeiture clause, expressed the hope that he might get a renewal, and said that forfeiture would deprive Texas of a large number of settlers ready to depart from Europe at that very time.[18] It is not conceivable that Bourgeois kept the German noblemen in the

16Waples, Acting Secretary of State, to President Houston, July 6, 1842. Colonization Papers, 1829-1842, Texas State Library. On June 18, 1842, Anson Jones, Secretary of State, replied to a petition from Bourgeois and Ducos for a grant of the lands between the Frio and the Rio Grande that President Houston would not make a contract for colonizing these lands before November of that year, in order to let Bourgeois and Ducos present proposals for colonizing the region. (See Jones to Bourgeois and Ducos, June 18, 1842. Colonization Papers, 1829-1842.) The Waples letter indicates that by July 6, 1842, a second grant had been made to Bourgeois and Ducos for five hundred families. This grant was located along the Rio Grande from its mouth up to the town of Reynosa. (See also, Jones to Ashbel Smith, June 7, 1842. Foreign Letters Book, Vol. 44, 60-61, Texas State Library.)

17Republic of Texas, Colonization Papers, 1829-1842, Texas State Library.

18Bourgeois to Jones, Paris, October 1 and 14, 1843. Colonization Papers, 1843-1845, Texas State Library.

dark about the forfeiture clause. They must have believed, as he
did, that the contract would be renewed. They secured from him
a three months' period of grace in which to approve or reject his
proposition. In fact, it was not until April 7, 1844, after another
extension of time, that they closed the deal with him.[19] In the
meantime, however, the Bourgeois-Ducos contract had been forfeited by the Congress of Texas.[20]

At the general meeting on March 25, 1844, when the Society
for the Protection of German Immigrants in Texas was formed,
Bourgeois was elected to membership and was placed with Prince
Carl of Solms-Braunfels on the Society's Commissariat for
Colonization. Almost a month later, April 20, 1844, the Committee of Directors resolved to appoint Prince Carl of Solms-
Braunfels Commissioner General for the colonial establishment
in Texas and Bourgeois Colonial Director.[21] These two men were
dispatched to Texas to get everything in readiness for the colonists.
On July 1, 1844, they landed at Galveston, from where they went
to Houston and then to Nassau Farm.[22] Bourgeois was still hopeful about the renewal of his grant. On July 10 he wrote to
Jones to the effect that he might get his grant confirmed during
the approaching session of Congress. He stated frankly that his
services to Texas, the esteem of Jones and the consideration of
the President for him, the "high respectability" of the Society
for the Protection of German Immigrants in Texas, and the interest he had shown in Texas were the reasons for his hopefulness.
He pointed out, too, that the concessions of Peters and of Fisher

[19]Penniger, *Fest-Ausgabe*, 24-25. Bourgeois, after the Society for the
Protection of German Immigrants in Texas had dismissed him from office,
said that they had asked for the three months of grace in order to get as
much information as possible from him about colonization and then to
write to Count Boos-Waldeck, who was still in Texas, to get a tract of
land for them. (Bourgeois to Jones, San Antonio, Texas, August 28,
1844. Colonization Papers, 1843-1845, Texas State Library.

[20]See above, p. 73.

[21]Colonization Papers, 1843-1845, Texas State Library. This document
is in the form of a communication from Prince Leiningen, President, to
Prince Carl of Solms-Braunfels and was to serve as a credential for the
commissioner general and the colonial director. It was presented to
Ashbel Smith, *chargé d'affaires* of Texas in France, on May 13, 1844, and
was stamped at his office on that day.

[22]Solms-Braunfels, Carl, Prinz von, *Texas*, 20.

DUKE ADOLF OF NASSAU
Protector of the Society
From a portrait in the office of the city secretary,
New Braunfels, Texas

PRINCE CARL OF SOLMS-BRAUNFELS
First Commissioner-General of the Society in Texas
and Founder of New Braunfels

From a portrait in the possession of Mr. H. V. Dittlinger,
New Braunfels, Texas

and Miller had been renewed.[23] To this letter Jones replied on July 13 and Bourgeois expressed his thanks for Jones's "new manifestation of friendship and good will."[24] On August 28, however, Bourgeois announced that he had been dismissed as colonial director.[25]

Prince Solms, too, seemed to be hopeful about the prospects of getting either a renewal of the Bourgeois-Ducos grant or else new concessions. In his first report from Texas, dated Nassau, July 15, 1844, and addressed to the Society for the Protection of German Immigrants in Texas, he said: "The colonial director has reported about our conferences and our correspondence with the Secretary of State, Dr. Anson Jones, and I can confirm that he (Jones) expressed the opinion that our presence during a part of the coming session of Congress in Washington, Texas, would secure everything for us that we might desire."[26] In his second

[23]Bourgeois to Jones, Nassau Place, July 10, 1844. Colonization Papers, 1843-1845, Texas State Library.

[24]Bourgeois to Jones, San Antonio de Bexar, August 11, 1844. Colonization Papers, 1843-1845, Texas State Library.

[25]Same to Same, San Antonio de Bexar, August 28, 1844. Colonization Papers, 1843-1845, Texas State Library.

In this letter Bourgeois continued to plead for the renewal of his contract, but only for himself and Ducos, not for the Society. He said: "My labors, and my large expenses, to do a good office for the Texian Republic in Europe, and to elevate her futur (sic) prospects will, I hope, not be overlooked by the Congress and the administration."

On September 24, 1844, William Kennedy, British consul to Texas at Galveston, wrote to his government and enclosed the following letter from Bourgeois, explanatory of his dismissal by the Society. The Bourgeois letter is dated San Antonio, August 30, 1844, and reads as follows:

Dear Sir:

It is painful to inform you of a fact as unexpected as extraordinary. The German Association forgetting the Conditions of the Contract entered into between themselves and me, which bound us together, has violated the Condition of our joint obligation.

I would not give you this notice, if, in soliciting the favour of the English Government, I had not taken on myself the responsibility of all the acts of the Association. Now, I am compelled to decline this same responsibility.

"Signed"   A. S. Borgeau d'Orvanne.

In a postscript to this letter, Bourgeois requested Kennedy to forward an enclosed letter to His Royal Highness, Prince Albert, but this letter could not be found by Mr. E. D. Adams, who edited the British diplomatic correspondence concerning Texas.

For the above correspondence see Adams, E. D., *British Diplomatic Correspondence Concerning the Republic of Texas, 1838-1846*, 367-369.

[26]Solms-Braunfels, Carl, Prince of, "Berichte des Prinzen Karl zu Solms-Braunfels an den Mainzer Adelsverein," *Kalender der Neu Braunfelser*

report, dated San Antonio de Bexar, August 20, 1844, Solms stated that he had made an inspection of the Bourgeois grant, but that he "considered it good fortune that the contract had been annulled." The good lands on the grant had all been located, a fact which would have forced the Society to place the colonists on the remaining bad land or else on the hilly country of the grant.[27]

The result of the deal with Bourgeois, then, was that the Society for the Protection of German Immigrants in Texas had acquired neither land nor a renewal of the Bourgeois-Ducos colonization grant. On December 14, 1844, the Society announced, rather tardily, that it had nothing else to do with Bourgeois and that his land grant had been forfeited.[28]

On February 8, 1842, Henry Francis Fisher,[29] Burchard Miller, and Joseph Baker applied to President Houston for a grant of land under the amended act of February 5, 1842, and proposed to introduce one thousand families of German, Dutch, Swiss, Norwegian, Swedish, and Danish emigrants. They asked for a tract of land lying between the Llano and Colorado Rivers and reaching far into the western portion of Texas.[30] President Houston endorsed the application with the following notation: "Let the contract be made." On June 7, 1842, Fisher and Miller re-

Zeitung fuer 1916, 17-18. Hereafter the reference will be "Berichte an den Adelsverein," in *Kalender*.

[27]Solms-Braunfels, "Berichte an den Adelsverein," in *Kalender*, 20-21.

[28]Tiling, *German Element in Texas*, 71.

[29]In the Archives of the University of Texas there is a collection of papers called the Henry Francis Fisher Papers. This collection contains, among other things, numerous letters written to Fisher which throw much light upon his work in Texas. Many of these letters are from his relatives in Germany, who wrote their name *Fischer*. Others are from persons in Texas who besought Fisher's aid in all sorts of matters, chiefly financial. This collection should be edited some day.

The Henry Francis Fisher Papers show that Fisher left Germany late in 1833. On January 13, 1834, he was in London. On September 14, 1834, Otto Graeve of London gave him a letter of introduction to Ernst Fiedler of New York; on June 1, 1835, Fisher was in the employ of H. Riedel of New York. A tavern bill for $11.51 included in the collection shows Fisher to have had a fondness for cigars and light wines. In March, 1836, Mr. Matthieu of Stuttgart, Germany, wrote to Fisher in New Orleans. On January 22 and February 5, 1837, Fisher bought a bill of goods from Valentin & Buddecke of New Orleans for $197.25. By April, 1838, Fisher was in Harrisburg, Texas, as a letter from B. Oelreich of New Orleans indicates.

[30]Fisher, Miller, and Baker to Houston, Austin, Texas, February 8, 1842. Colonization Papers, 1829-1842, Texas State Library.

ceived their first colonization contract, which in its main points is similar to the renewal contract of September 1, 1843.[31]

Fisher must have become interested in colonization in Texas as early as 1839, for in that year he served as acting treasurer for an exploration company called the San Saba Company. A number of business accounts in the Henry Francis Fisher Papers indicate that as early as 1839 the San Saba Company was making purchases of supplies preparatory to an exploration of the San Saba country.[32] President Lamar seems to have thought well of the company, for on May 4, 1839, it adopted a resolution to thank President Lamar for his approval of its object and for extending the facilities of the Texas armory to it. The San Saba Company was convinced of the "feasibility of the plan contemplated" and "was buoyed up by the bright anticipation of success."[33]

Up to 1843 the San Saba Company does not seem to have been very active, at least the writer did not find any mention of it either in the newspapers or in the manuscript material of the period from 1839 to 1843. But in May, 1843, two Houston newspapers reported about the company as follows:

The party of gentlemen who left this city a few weeks since, to survey the tract of country on the head waters of the San Saba, are returning without effecting the object of the visit. On arriving at Washington they were informed by the President that he had recently sent Commissioners to treat with the Indians in that section, and he feared the presence of an armed party of whites in that region at this juncture would induce the Indians to fear that they intended to resume hostilities, and thus the treaty would be prevented. Satisfied that these objections were reasonable and just, they, with a commendable forbearance, concluded to relinquish their expedition, although they had expended a very large sum in preparing for it. They intend, however, to

[31]For a summary of the terms of the renewal or second contract, see below, pp. 80-81.

[32]The company was organized on a military basis with J. L. Davis as captain and A. H. Moore as first lieutenant, as the records in the H. F. Fisher Papers indicate. The company was not, however, a part of the Texas military organization, at least the writer has not been able to find anything in the military records of the War Department of the Republic of Texas about the company.

[33]Winn, W. H. G., Secretary of the San Saba Company, to Lamar, Houston, Texas, May 4, 1839. Lamar Papers, II, 559, No. 1246. The name is W. H. Grimes instead of W. H. G. Winn, which can be verified from the original.

make another attempt to visit that beautiful section in autumn, as they are desirous to examine minutely every portion of the country designated in the Colonization grant of the German Association, in order that they may furnish information respecting it to the emigrants who may be desirous to settle upon it.[34]

Henry Francis Fisher was still interested in the company, being its agent at that time, as the following advertisement indicates:

SAN SABA COLONIZATION COMPANY

Having given notice some time since that a Company was about to start for the San Saba for the purpose of exploring that region, I deem it my duty as the Agent of the San Saba Colonization Company, to state that circumstances have rendered a temporary delay in the execution of the object unavoidable. Measures for entering into negotiations of amity with the Indians who visit that portion of the country being in progress, it has been thought that such a step might frustrate the object of the government, and perhaps endanger the lives of the Commissioners. To those who have made preparations to accompany us, I return, in the name of the company, my sincere thanks, with the assurance that due notice will be given when the party will again set out.

Industry, Austin County, May 13th, 1843.

Henry F. Fisher, Agent, &c.[35]

It is the writer's opinion that Fisher and Miller revived the former San Saba Company, or else, if the San Saba Company had a continuous existence from 1839 to 1843, reorganized it into a colonization company after they had secured their first colonization contract. The equipment purchased by the company in 1839 was such that it could be used to advantage by Fisher and Miller in making the necessary preparations for placing settlers on their grant. Certainly it was highly desirable for the grantees to find out everything possible about their land grant, such as the fertility of the soil, the nature of the country, the supply of water and wood, and the number of Indians, as well as their feeling toward the whites. It is possible that Fisher interested Prince Leiningen in the Fisher and Miller grant, for, as was pointed out above, Leiningen reported in favor of colonization on a large scale. But the newspaper account of the San Saba Company simply assumed

---

[34]*Morning Star*, May 23, 1843, 2, col. 1; *Telegraph and Texas Register*, May 24, 1843, 2, col. 5.

[35]*Telegraph and Texas Register*, May 24, 1843, 3, col. 2.

a "colonization grant of the German Association" out of two facts, namely, that Fisher and Miller had a colonization contract and that the German Association had two representatives, Prince Leiningen and Count Boos-Waldeck, in Texas at that time.

It was nearly a year later before Fisher arrived in Germany to secure colonists for the San Saba Colonization Company. Among the records in the General Land Office of Texas dealing with German colonization the writer found eight manuscript certificates for land issued by Henry Francis Fisher at Bremen in May, 1844, to prospective colonists of the San Saba Colony. A copy of one of the certificates follows:

This is to certify that Thomas Schwab, a native of Rumbach, Cr. Hessen (Kurhessen ?— Electorate of Hesse) in Germany, by occupation a Mason, and being a single man over the age of 17 years is entitled to One hundred and Sixty acres of Land in the San Saba Colony by virtue of authority granted to Fisher, Miller & Co., and in accordance with the stipulations of a certain Colonization Contract entered into between the President of the Republic of Texas and the said Fisher, Miller & Co. at Washington, September 1, 1843.

Bremen, May 10, 1844.   Henry F. Fisher
                                   Agent of the S. Saba Col. Comp-[36]

Fisher did not, however, go to Germany for the sole purpose of securing colonists. He managed to get an appointment as Texan consul for Bremen,[37] a position, it is true, that he could and did

[36]These records are found in the General Land Office, Austin, Texas, in one of six large bundles marked "Records of the German Emigration Company." Besides the certificate issued to Thomas Schwab there are certificates for Valentin Vey (Fey), Peter Reis, Johannes Schneider, and Johannes Arnholt (Arnold) all of Rumbach, for one hundred and sixty acres each, for J. A. Koch of Eisleben for one hundred and sixty acres, and for Sebastian Heinrich Christof Moeschen and Johann Valentin Schulmeyer of Manterota, Saxe-Gotha, for three hundred and twenty acres each. The last two listed were married men and received, therefore, twice as much land as the others.

These eight men, together with the wives and children of the last two, twenty-seven single men, and nine other families, reached Galveston on the brig *Weser* on July 8, 1844, as the first colonists for the Fisher and Miller Colony. (Colonization Papers, 1843-1845, Texas State Library.)

For an extended treatment of the San Saba Colonization Company, see my article on the subject in *The Southwestern Historical Quarterly* in its issue of January, 1930.

[37]On May 8, 1843, Fisher wrote to John Hall, acting Secretary of State, that he was preparing to leave for Germany in a short while. Since he would reside in Bremen, he requested Hall to inform President Houston that he would be glad to serve Texas in the capacity of consul

use to advantage in enlisting colonists, but which enabled him also to interest the German noblemen in the Fisher and Miller colonization contract and, as we shall see, to dispose of it to them.

Before Fisher was appointed consul for Bremen and subsequently sailed for that port, he received for himself and Miller a renewal of their contract. The Fisher and Miller second or renewal contract is very significant in this study. Its salient points are the following: *first,* that Fisher and Miller were allowed to introduce six hundred families and single men; *second,* that the grant included a vast expanse of land (over three million acres); *third,* that each family was to get six hundred and forty acres and each single man over seventeen years was to get three hundred and twenty acres, for which each would get a full and absolute title after having built a comfortable cabin and having kept fifteen acres in cultivation and under a good fence; *fourth,* that Fisher and Miller, upon request, could get title from the Republic of Texas for one-half of the amounts of land for families and single men, respectively, provided Fisher and Miller had made such an agreement with the immigrants; *fifth,* that premium lands of ten sections for every hundred families and of ten half-sections for every hundred single men introduced be given to Fisher and Miller as a compensation for their expense; *sixth,* that one section of land was to be set aside near the center of every settlement of one hundred families, for aiding and assisting them "in the erection of buildings for religious public worship and for schools"; *seventh,* that the contract would be forfeited if less than two hundred families or single men had been introduced within a year, but such forfeiture was not to prejudice the rights of the settlers in any manner; *eighth,* that only persons of good moral character were to be introduced; *ninth,* that the settlers would not be permitted to sell intoxicating liquors, powder, lead, firearms, or other weapons to the Indians; *tenth,* that Fisher and Miller were to designate and survey within three years all the lands required for settlement as well as the premium and church lands; *eleventh,* that Fisher and Miller were to be permitted, upon giving written notice to certain officials named in the contract, to increase the

at that port. (Fisher to Hall, Washington, May 8, 1843. Letters to Department of State, No. 42, 338, Texas State Library.) Houston nominated Fisher as Texan consul for the port of Bremen on December 20, 1843. (Records Executive Department, Vol. 40, 287, Texas State Library.)

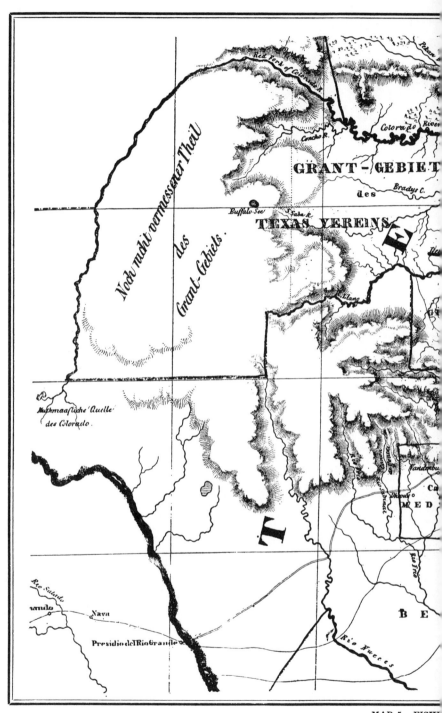

MAP 5. FISHE
From a map in a folder of i

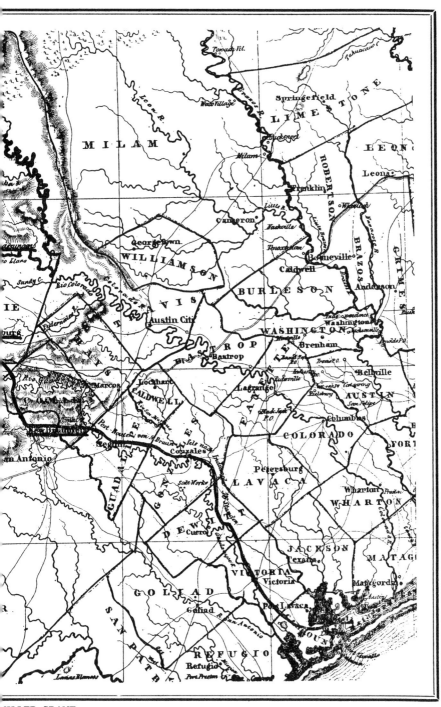

MILLER GRANT
issued by the Society in 1851

number of settlers up to six thousand families and single men; and *twelfth,* that the time for introducing the first third of the whole number of settlers be extended for six months over the one year stipulated in the contract.[38]

Fisher and Miller gave due notice to Anson Jones on January 6, 1844, of their intention to increase the number of families and single men to six thousand.[39]   Considering the resources of Fisher and Miller, one must feel that this number was too ambitious, but Fisher and Miller may have believed that they could dispose more easily of a contract calling for a large number of settlers.

On March 12, 1844, Fisher wrote to Jones that he was on that day going on board the brig *Weser,* bound for Bremen. He expressed some anxiety about securing a sufficient number of ships on which to send emigrants from Germany, since no commercial treaty had yet been made between Texas and Bremen. Ships were being taxed a five per cent additional duty and a twenty per cent tonnage duty, a fact which would tend to keep them away from Texas ports.[40]

On June 27, 1844, Fisher wrote to Jones from Mayence that he was in Bremen on May 20. He informed Jones that on June 26 he had associated himself with the Society for the Protection of German Emigrants to Texas (Immigrants in Texas). To Count Castell, Prince Leiningen, and other members of the Society he pointed out the impracticability of obtaining a new grant for Bourgeois. They decided, therefore, to get rid of Bourgeois, "in order to be able to concentrate all their means for the colonization and improvement" of the Fisher and Miller grant.[41]   On June 26,

---

[38]For the full text of the second Fisher and Miller contract, see MS. Colonization Papers, 1843-1845, Texas State Library.

For a brief discussion of several maps made in the period from 1845 to 1851 and showing the location and extent of the Fisher and Miller grant, as well as of the Bourgeois-Ducos grant, based on what was then known of the topography of western Texas, see Appendix A.

[39]Fisher and Miller to Jones, Washington, January 6, 1844. MS. Colonization Papers, 1843-1845, Texas State Library.

[40]Jones, A., *Memoranda and Official Correspondence Relating to the Republic of Texas, Its History and Annexation,* 326-327. Cited hereafter as Jones, *Memoranda and Official Correspondence.* Fisher believed that the prospect of the annexation of Texas to the United States had caused the delay in the ratification of a commercial treaty with Bremen.

[41]Jones, *Memoranda and Official Correspondence,* 367-368. Fisher told Jones that he was entrusted with the management of affairs in Texas. He must have written this for the effect it might have on Jones. Prince

1844, they bought an interest in the Fisher and Miller colonization contract for 100 Friedrichsd'or cash, 14000 florins payable at Frankfort on the Main on July 5, 1844, and $2000 payable at New Orleans on September 1, 1845.[42] In addition the agreement provided: 1. the Society was to take the place of Fisher and Miller, their associates, heirs, and assigns in the colonization contract; 2. after reimbursing itself for all expenses incurred, including the money consideration, the Society, on a capitalization of $80,000 (200,000 florins), was to pay Fisher and Miller one-third of the profits derived annually from the sale of land and from industrial establishments; 3. there was to be a colonial committee of six members, five from the Society with one vote each and Henry Francis Fisher with three votes, to protect the interests of both contracting parties; 4. Fisher and Miller were not to transfer their rights under the agreement before September 1, 1848, without the consent of the Society; and 5. the heirs of Fisher and Miller were not to be entitled to membership or vote on the committee without the consent of the Society.[43]

On August 1 Fisher left Mayence and arrived in Texas on September 15, 1844. In the meanwhile the Society was busy making preparations to meet its obligations under the Fisher and Miller colonization contract. The two succeeding chapters will discuss, first, the work carried on by the Society in Germany in preparation for its colonization work, and second, the actual settlements made by the Society in Texas at New Braunfels, Fredericksburg, and on the tract of land known as the Fisher and Miller grant.

Solms was the Society's first commissioner general in Texas and in that capacity had the management of affairs in his hands.

[42]Since the Friedrichsd'or was worth $4.00 and a florin 40 cents, the total money consideration involved was $8000.

Penniger, *Fest-Ausgabe*, 27, says that the Society paid $9000 and asserts that the Society could have bought over 100,000 acres of land for that sum. Tiling, *German Element in Texas*, 69, says also that the Society paid "$9000 in three deferred payments." Eickhoff, *In der neuen Heimath*, 324, says that Fisher got $16,000 and a part of the profits. Kapp, *Aus und ueber Amerika*, 257-258, says Fisher got one-third of the profits and a doomage (penalty for retarded delivery) of $14,000.

[43]*Gesammelte Aktenstuecke des Vereins zum Schutze deutscher Einwanderer in Texas*, 20-23. Future references to this pamphlet will be made briefly as *Gesammelte Aktenstuecke*.

CHAPTER V

COLONIZATION PREPARATIONS MADE BY THE SOCIETY FOR THE
PROTECTION OF GERMAN IMMIGRANTS IN TEXAS

In the preceding chapter the founding of the Society for the
Protection of German Immigrants in Texas was discussed. It
was pointed out that this Society had its origin in April, 1842,
at a meeting of German noblemen at Biebrich on the Rhine and
that after a period of almost two years it was reorganized at
Mayence in March, 1844. At the meeting in Mayence the Society
adopted its name and broadened the scope of its work. It is the
object of this chapter to give an account of the preparations made
by the Society both in Germany and in Texas for carrying on its
colonization work. The actual founding of settlements will be
discussed in later chapters.

In the spring and summer of 1844 the Society announced its
organization, its objects, and its readiness to aid those desiring to
emigrate. The newspapers of Germany, especially in the region
around Frankfort on the Main, gave their space to the announcement. One of these papers was the *Mainzer Zeitung,* which, in
its issue of Sunday, June 16, 1844, contained the following announcement:

SOCIETY FOR THE PROTECTION OF GERMAN IMMIGRANTS IN TEXAS

A Society has been organized whose purpose is to direct German
emigration, as far as possible, to one single, favorably located
point, to protect the emigrants on their long journey and in their
new home, and to employ every means to secure for them their
new home across the seas.

The Society does not make this announcement with the intention of interesting capitalists in its undertaking, since the necessary funds have been secured already. But conscious of the good
purpose, the Society owes it to itself and to the public to state
the reasons for its founding, the manner in which it hopes to solve
its problem, and the principles which guide it in this work.

The Society wishes neither to encourage nor to excuse emigration. The desire exists, a fact which can not be denied any more
than it is possible to arrest the progress of emigration. Many
causes are working together to increase emigration: the displace-

ment of manual labor by machinery, the great periodic depressions which affect commerce, the increasing poverty, caused by over-population and the lack of employment, the reported productivity of the land in the new country, and the hope of improving one's condition across the seas.

The emigrants would, indeed, improve their condition if they were kept together and found the right guidance and a real pro-tection in foreign lands. Hence the Society will try to regulate and direct emigration, so that it may be possible for the Germans in America to find again a German home and to build up an industrial and commercial intercourse with the Fatherland for the material and spiritual benefit of both. In this manner the Society wants to do its part to add to Germany's honor and wel-fare, to find a remunerative occupation for Germany's poor, to open new markets for German industry, and to expand the Ger-man overseas trade.

After a long and careful examination the Society has decided that Texas is the land which will best suit the emigrant. The healthy climate, the fertility of the soil, the abundance of its products, and the ease of communication with Europe have drawn many German emigrants to Texas. But without aid and assistance these have become separated and have frequently failed. The Society has sent capable men to Texas to get first-hand informa-tion and, on the basis of their reports, has selected Texas as the field of its operations.

In the western part of Texas, in its most healthy region, the Society has acquired a large unsettled tract of land on which it will promote the settlement of those Germans who want to leave their Fatherland.

Before his departure each emigrant gets a written assurance from the Society that he will get a piece of good land upon his arrival in Texas. The number of acres in the donation will depend upon the size of the family. In order to get a clear title to the land, the emigrant must live upon it for three years, but the products of the land during the three-year period belong to him.

The Society will provide large and commodious ships as well as enough wholesome and cheap food for the trip across the ocean. It will have agents in Texas to assist the emigrants when they land and it will furnish enough wagons to transport them and their belongings to the place of settlement. Care will be taken of their needs on the way. As soon as they arrive at the place of settle-ment, each family will get its own house built after the fashion of the country of logs laid and fitted upon one another. Ware-houses filled with provisions, gardening and farming implements, and seeds and plants of all sorts, will provide the emigrants with all they need for working and living. They will find also all the necessary oxen, horses, cows, hogs, and sheep. All of these will be sold cheaper at the warehouses of the Society than they can be bought at the nearest market. Such emigrants whose conduct and work are especially commendable will receive advances from the Society and may pay them back from the first crop. The emigrants may dispose of their products of agriculture and industry to the storehouses of the Society.

The Society regards it a sacred duty to provide for the moral and religious education of the emigrant children and will cause schools and churches to be erected in the colony according to the needs of the settlers. The Society will care for the employment of doctors and druggists and will look after the erection of a hospital.

As soon as advisable the colonial directorate will create a municipality and tribunals of justice after the model of those recognized in Texas.

If any of the emigrants should desire to return to Europe, they will receive transportation on the Society's ships at the same rates as for the journey to Texas.

The first group of emigrants will leave for Texas this coming September. In May two members of the Society will journey to Texas in order to make preparations for the reception of the emigrants and to arrange temporarily for the administration of the settlements.

The Society will devote three per cent of its income to pay the costs of transportation and settlement of needy emigrants. For the present, however, and until the Society can carry out this purpose, only those will be allowed to settle in the colony who possess the necessary means. The unmarried emigrant needs a capital of at least three hundred florins ($120.00); the head of a small family needs six hundred florins ($240.00).

For the purpose of facilitating the settlement of a small number of poor families, the Society, in order to respond to the noble intentions with which it has been credited, will open a list of voluntary subscriptions. The sums subscribed and their disposal, together with the names of the benefactors, will be published annually in the most widely read journals of Germany.

Although the Society uses all the means in its power to assure the success of its undertaking, nevertheless, success will depend in the main upon the earnest and indefatigable activity of the emigrants themselves. The new Fatherland beyond the ocean will flourish only if the Germans will be industrious, persevering, faithful to good morals, and obedient to the laws, as in their former home.

Although the Society is certain that such will be the case, it will accept only one hundred and fifty families for emigration this year (1844) and will not aid any further emigration until the first settlement has been firmly established.

Further information may be secured, upon postpaid written request, from the directorate of the Society in Mayence and from L. H. Flersheim, banker for the Society in Frankfort on the Main. Done by the Executive Committee of the Society.

(Signed)   Prince of Leiningen.

Count of Ysenburg-Meerholz.

(In the absence of Count Carl of Castell.)[1]

In its general meeting at Mayence on March 25, 1844, the Society transacted a considerable amount of business. It elected Prince Victor of Leiningen president, Count Carl of Castell vice-president, and placed on its executive committee of three members the two officers just mentioned and Count Christian of Leiningen. Counts Victor and Friedrich Leiningen were chosen as alternate members of the committee and Count Castell was made business director. This meeting drew up a constitution which announced the following threefold purpose of the Society: (1) improvement of the conditions of the working classes and a decrease of pauperism; (2) opening of new markets for the products of German industries; and (3) the development of maritime commerce.[2]

The elective executive committee of three members and the elective business director mentioned in the preceding paragraph were to have charge of the administration of the affairs of the Society. The annual general business meeting of the stockholders, according to the constitution, was also entitled to deal with matters of a general interest affecting the Society. One share of stock had one vote, two or three shares two votes, and four or more

---

[1]Translation made by the writer from a transcript of the *Mainzer Zeitung*, June 16, 1844, furnished and attested by Dr. Dertsch, director of the City Archives of Mayence (Stadt-Archiv Mainz).

For the German original, see Appendix B.

See also an English translation from a French original manuscript in Colonization Papers, 1843-1845, Texas State Library. This document names Prince Carl of Solms-Braunfels and Mr. Bourgeois d'Orvanne as the members whom the Society would send to Texas.

Another copy of the announcement is found in *Gesammelte Aktenstuecke des Vereins zum Schutze deutscher Einwanderer in Texas.*

Other copies are found in Treu, Georg, *Das Buch der Auswanderung*, 140-145; Tiling, *German Element in Texas*, 221-225; and *Ein Handbuch fuer deutsche Auswanderer*, 63-68.

From Prof. B. Mueller, director of the City Historical Museum of Frankfort on the Main (Staedtisches Historisches Museum, Frankfurt a/M.) the writer has the information that the announcement appeared in the *Frankfurter Journal* on June 1, 1844, and again on June 7.

[2]See Constitution of the Society, Art. I, par. 3, in *Gesammelte Aktenstuecke*, 3.

shares three votes. Owners of land or of land concessions could be admitted to membership, were entitled to participate in the discussion of all matters affecting the colonial establishments made on the land, but in no case were to have more than three votes. The executive committee had the power to appoint and remove all employees and agents, as well as to fix the duties and salaries of such persons. The committee, however, could neither appoint nor recall the colonial director; only the general meeting of the Society possessed these powers. The executive committee prepared the budget of the expenditures and income of the Society for the general meeting of the stockholders. The business director was to be chosen from the members of the executive committee and was its chairman. He had the power to sign all documents in the name of the Society, to make all agreements with governments, to draw up all contracts, and to oversee the employees and to dismiss them. It was his duty to plan the work of the Society, to prepare a digest of the reports from the settlements and from the Society's agents in European ports, to carry on all of the correspondence, and to keep all of the documents. A general agent assisted the business director in accepting and making arrangements for transporting the colonists.[3]

It is interesting to observe that the Society expected to reap profits from its colonial establishment, for its constitution provided for the distribution of profits in the following manner: 80 per cent among the stockholders, 10 per cent to the reserve fund, 5 per cent among the employees, 3 per cent among charitable institutions, and 2 per cent for exploration, promotion of the sciences, the founding of institutions, and similar objects.[4]

For its colonial establishments the Society worked out very elaborate regulations. Each settlement was to be under a director and council of five appointed by the executive committee. The colonial council (Colonial-Rath) was composed of a minister of the gospel, a physician, a civil engineer, a bookkeeper, and the commercial agent of the Society. The bookkeeper was ex-officio secretary. This council was required to reside in the colony. The colonial director was to select the sites for town and village settle-

---

[3]See Constitution of the Society, Chapter VI, par. 26-43, in *Gesammelte Aktenstuecke*, 7-11.

[4]Constitution of the Society, Chapter VII, in *Gesammelte Aktenstuecke*, 11-12.

ments and to conduct the drawing for building lots in each of them. The Society guaranteed the transportation of the settlers from the coast to the colony lands by furnishing wagons for the women, children, and personal chattels of the immigrants. The Society promised to build houses for each settler in the value of twenty-four dollars (sixty florins), if time and circumstances allowed. The day laborers employed by the Society were to receive the wages determined by the còlonial council either in goods or in drafts on the Society. The Society was to advance each settler the material for fencing and cultivating fifteen acres, as well as the necessary oxen, cows, and horses, but no interest was to be charged for the first year. Separate accounts were to be kept for each settler. After the crop was made the settlers were allowed to pay their accounts with farm products on the basis of current prices. For the protection of life and property it was required that all male settlers between the ages of seventeen and fifty were to be formed into a militia company. The Society was to erect a church building in which both Protestant and Catholic services were to be held. One or more free schools were to be built in which instruction was to be given in morals, religion, reading, writing, arithmetic, and the German and English languages. In connection with a well-stocked apothecary, the Society was to maintain a hospital for the free care of the sick. There was to be a public building for holding the meetings of the colonial council, for depositing the archives, and for the use of the provisional civil officials. A large storehouse in each settlement was to be well supplied with articles of general use and with agricultural implements. Each settlement was to have a grist-mill, a sawmill, and a cotton gin, and, as the settlement grew, such other industrial establishments as were needed. Provision was made for the building of streets, canals, bridges, and other public works. When the population justified it, a newspaper was to be published in each settlement to discuss topics of general and special interest and to inform the settlers about their duties as citizens and about trade and agriculture.[5]

Besides the general regulations *(General Statut)* for the colonial establishments the Society adopted an organic statute of coloniza-

---

[5]General Statut fuer die Colonial-Niederlassungen des Vereins, *passim*, in *Gesammelte Aktenstuecke*, 29-37. The General Statut is also given in Tiling, *German Element in Texas*, 211-220.

tion *(Organisches Statut der Colonisation)*. In the organic statute many of the provisions of the general regulations given in the
preceding paragraph are duplicated. In addition, however, the
following provisions occur. As a prerequisite for acceptance as a
colonist, each emigrant had to present a birth certificate, a marriage certificate, a character certificate, and a certified copy of the
emigration permit.[6] Each emigrant was to present evidence that
he had sufficient means to pay the costs of the ocean voyage and
for his support in the colony for six months. The emigrants had
the option of letting the Society furnish their meals or to provide
them themselves. Before sailing, each emigrant was to receive a
provisional title for his land, three hundred and twenty acres if
married, one hundred and sixty acres if single. The Society was
to organize a savings bank and pay five per cent on deposits. A
widows' and orphans' home was to be built as soon as the population of all of the settlements warranted the expense. The settlers
were to have a share in the management of the home.[7]

For accepting an emigrant and entering into an agreement with
him, the Society made use of printed forms. For 1844 and 1845
these forms were alike, except that on the form for 1845 the seal of
the Society, reproduced herewith, was printed instead of being
stamped on sealing wax. The lone star on the seal was symbolic
of the Republic of Texas, while the bundle of arrows symbolized

[6]In my research work I found copies of a birth certificate, of an emigration permit, and of a character certificate, but not of a marriage certificate. The birth certificate of Anna Maria Klein on the next page
was furnished me by her son, Mr. C. A. Jahn, of New Braunfels, Texas.
The emigration permit of Johann Heinrich Petri, reproduced on page 91, was
secured from valuable papers in the possession of Mr. Fritz Leo Hoffmann
of New Braunfels, a relative of Mr. Petri. The original of the following
translated character certificate was furnished me by the late Mr. S. V.
Pfeuffer of New Braunfels.

"This is to certify that Mr. Edward Quirin Kriegner, a merchant of
this place, who intends to emigrate to Texas and settle there, has been
irreproachable in his moral behavior and that nothing disparaging has ever
happened to injure his reputation. He must be felicitated upon his
intention.

Merseburg, August 31, 1846.
                                The Municipal Council
                                  by (. . . . . ?)"

[7]Organisches Statut der Colonisation, *passim*, in *Gesammelte Akten-
stuecke*, 38-43. This Organisches Statut is given also in Tiling, *German
Element in Texas*, 204-210, and in Benjamin, G. G., *The Germans in
Texas*, 144-148.

ZWANZIG KREUZER 4

Anzeige Wattenheim Amts Zelle

aus dem Verzeichnisse der Gebornen in dem Kirchspiele.

Nummer.	Zeit der Geburt im Jahr 1818			Des Kindes				Des Vaters Familien- und Tauf-Name, Stand, Gewerbe, Confession, Wohn- und Geburtsort.	Der Mutter Tauf- und Geburts-Name, Stand, Confession, Wohn- und Geburtsort.	Bemerkungen.
	Monat.	Tag.	Stunde.	Familien-Name.	Tauf-Name.	Geburts-Ort.	Geschlecht.			
				Klein	Anna Maria	Wattenheim				

Wattenheim, 18ten April 1818.

(90)

Decret

Dem Gesuch des Johann Heinrich Petri von
Dornscheid hiesigen Amts

um Entlassung aus dem Herzogl. Nassauischen
Unterthanenverbande, behufs der Aus=
wanderung nach Texas

wird hiermit willfahrt und demzufolge
1. das Supplicant
2. dessen Ehefrau Anna Elisabetha geboren Kgl.
3. seine Kinder, namentlich

    a. Johannes, geboren am 16 Mai 1830
    b. Jacob Heinrich „ „ 8t November 1832
    c. Catharina Louise „ „ 7 November 1836
    d. Johannes Heinrich „ „ 24 August 1839
    e. Margaretha Henriette „ „ 7 Januar 1845

aus hiesigem Unterthanenverband entlassen und
diese Decret zufolge Genehmigung Herz: Landes=
Regierung vom 5t Juni c. J. ad Num: 25987
nach Freigrzen ertheilt.

Herborn, d. 11 Juni 1845.
Herzoglich Nassauisches Amt

Leidscheid

Dem p. Schultheiß zur
Nachricht d. Obigen.

Chef
geschrieben Chn des Sypph. d. pnar
Chfmn d. Unterschreiben.

Vann Nassau Wilhelm 1848.
Dem 28 Juli zur Ausgabevers
Meine Nassau Augusta Maline
Dem 26 Februar 1851

the presence of Indians on the Fisher and Miller grant.   In 1846 neither form of the seal was used.

Seal of the Society

In order to show the essential points of the agreement made between the Society and the settlers, the form used in 1844 and 1845 is reproduced herewith.   It read as follows:

Immigration Agreement.

Between the Society for the Protection of German Immigrants in Texas, represented by Count Carl of Castell, the director especially authorized to make contracts, and in his absence by his fully authorized substitute, Dr. jur. B. Hill, secretary of the Society, party of the first part, and ...., party of the second part, the following agreement has been made.

Paragraph 1.

The Society for the Protection of German Immigrants in Texas grants to ...., who accepts the same for himself, his family, his heirs, and assigns, ... acres of land, to be taken from the Society's lands, located in the present county of San Antonio, Republic of Texas, in the present condition of the grant, and to be designated to the immigrant by an agent of the Society.

Paragraph 2.

The immigrant will use the tract assigned to him as owner, fully protected in all of the rights of property, from the day of taking possession, without, however, being allowed to alienate the tract in whole or in part, during the next three years following.

Paragraph 3.

This transfer of land is made under the following conditions. The immigrant must

(1) live on the land granted to him for three consecutive years, counted from the day he takes possession;

(2) fence and keep in cultivation fifteen acres of land during the three years;

(3) build a dwelling on his land;

(4) submit to the colonization plan of the Society and to the laws of the land.

Paragraph 4.

The respective costs of surveying are to be borne by the immigrant, but the Society will advance the money to him for this purpose. The land given to the immigrant, and the buildings and improvements made thereon, are to be security for this advance, as well as for all others made by the Society, until the debt is entirely paid.

Paragraph 5.

The present provisional deed will be exchanged in Texas with a final deed drawn in favor of the immigrant by the government of Texas, three years after taking possession, provided all of the above conditions shall have been met by the immigrant.

Paragraph 6.

The tardy fulfillment of the above conditions by the immigrant will cause the loss of his rights to the present donation, and the land, as well as all buildings erected on it, will revert to the Society by way of compensation.

The present agreement is to be dutifully and faithfully observed in all respects by the contracting parties, as their own signature witnesseth.

Done at Bremen, the........day of................., 1844.

Signed   In the name and under the
   The Immigrant   authority of the Society,
                          the Secretary,
                                    Dr. B. Hill.[8]

[8]For a copy of the form used in 1844 and 1845, see the accompanying illustration. Johann Michael Jahn, whose name appears on the agreement, was the grandfather of the writer's wife on her father's side. Jahn was one of the first settlers introduced into Texas by the Society. It will be seen from the agreement that Jahn was a single man when he emigrated, since he was to get only one hundred and sixty acres of land. The agreement was signed by Johann Michael Jahn and by Dr. B. Hill, secretary of the Society. The certificate of the Texan Consulate at Bremen, the port of embarkation, was attached to the agreement, a requirement made by the government of the Republic of Texas.

Einwanderungs-Vertrag.

Zwischen dem Vereine zum Schutze deutscher Einwanderer in Texas, repräsentirt durch den zur Abschließung der Contrakte speciell beauftragten Direktor, Herrn Grafen Carl zu Castell, und in dessen Abwesenheit durch seinen mit Specialvollmacht versehenen Stellvertreter, Herrn Dr. jur. B. Hill, Sekretär des Vereins

Eines Theils

und dem *Herrn Johann Michael Jahn und Bath Altzünsbach*

Andern Theils

ist nachfolgender Vertrag verabredet und abgeschlossen worden.

§. 1.

Es verleiht der Verein zum Schutze deutscher Einwanderer in Texas dem Herrn *Johann Michael Jahn, und Bath, Altzüns. Bezirk besser Naudort*

welcher dies für sich, seine Familie, seine Erben und Rechtsinhaber in bester Form Rechtens annimmt *160. sage hundert und sechzig* acres Landes, zu entnehmen von seinen Ländereien, gelegen in der jetzigen county San Antonio, Republik Texas, sowie jener Landstrich gegenwärtig daliegt, in dem Zustande, in welchem er sich derzeit befindet, und wie solche dem Einwanderer durch einen Agenten des Vereines an Ort und Stelle werden bezeichnet werden.

§. 2.

Es benutzt der Einwanderer den ihm überwiesenen Landstrich als Eigenthümer, ungefährdet in allen im Eigenthume liegenden Rechten, vom Tage der Besitz-Einweisung an gerechnet, ohne jedoch während einem Zeitraume von drei Jahren, von bezeichneter Epoche an gerechnet, diesen Landstrich ganz oder theilweise veräußern zu können.

§. 3.

Es findet dieser Uebertrag des Landes unter folgenden weiteren Bedingungen Statt. Es hat der Einwanderer

(94)

1) drei nacheinanderfolgende Jahre, vom Tage der Besitz-Einweisung an gerechnet, auf den bewilligten Ländereien zu verweilen;

2) in demselben Zeitabschnitt fünfzehn acres Land zu umzäunen und in Cultur zu erhalten;

3) ein Wohnhaus auf seinem Grund und Boden zu errichten;

4) sich dem vom Vereine entworfenen Colonisations-Plane und den gesetzlichen Bestimmungen des Landes im Allgemeinen zu unterwerfen.

§. 4.

Die betreffenden Landes-Vermessungskosten fallen dem Einwanderer zur Last, der Verein aber legt dieselben vor: es haften für diesen Vorschuß sowohl, als alle andern dem Einwanderer durch den Verein etwa gemachten Vorschüsse, die umsonst bewilligten Ländereien und die darauf aufgeführten Gebäude und Vorrichtungen als Pfand, bis zur gänzlichen Abtragung der Schuld.

§. 5.

Gegenwärtiger provisorischer Erwerbstitel wird in Texas selbst durch eine von der texanischen Regierung ausgestellte, auf den Namen des Einwanderers lautende, definitive Eigenthums-Urkunde, umgetauscht, und zwar drei Jahre nach der Besitz-Einweisung, und wenn die oben festgesetzten Bedingungen von Seiten des Einwanderers erfüllt worden sind.

§. 6.

Bei nicht pünktlicher Erfüllung obiger Bedingungen durch den Einwanderer, verliert derselbe seine Rechte auf gegenwärtige Verleihung, und es fallen die auf den vom Vereine ihm verliehenen Ländereien aufgeführten Gebäulichkeiten, so wie die Ländereien selbst dem Vereine als Entschädigung anheim.

Gegenwärtiger Vertrag soll pflichtgemäß und treu von den Contrahenten in allen Punkten gehandhabt und beobachtet werden, was dieselben anmit durch eigenhändige Namensunterschrift geloben.

So geschehen Bremen, den 23 September 1844

F. Fahn.

Consulate of the Republic of Texas for the port of Bremen.

These are to certify, that appeared before me Mr. I. Fahn and made oath, that the whole content of the above going Agreement, was well comprehended and consented by him and both parties signed the same in my presence.

Done in Bremen the 23 April 1844.

Wm. Fehrmann

Vice-Consul.

(95)

The form of the immigration agreements for 1846 differed somewhat from the earlier form. The agreement for 1846 contains ten paragraphs. The immigrant was to receive an unconditional grant of ten acres for the purpose of making a crop the first year, provided the land promised him could not be assigned to him immediately upon his arrival in the grant. In case of forfeiture of the land, it was provided that the immigrant was not to have any claims for damages whatsoever. If the immigrant should die before the expiration of the three years, his rights and obligations were to fall on the rest of his family or nearest heirs in Texas; if he died after the three years and after fulfilling his obligations, his heirs in Europe were to inherit the land, provided he had no heirs in Texas. From the day of embarkation the Society undertook to provide the emigrant with food, shelter, and transportation to New Braunfels, Texas, for ninety-eight florins ($39.20) and a hospital fee of one dollar.[9] The hospital fee was to be returned to the settler, however, if the immigrants of the Society were to be relieved from its payment by the municipal council of Galveston. After his arrival on the lands of the Society (evidently New Braunfels is meant), the immigrant was to make no further claims for support upon the Society, but was to pay for all provisions and other articles bought from its storehouse. In case he could not pay for his supplies, however, the Society was to give him employment to earn enough to pay for his purchases. The Society was not to be held responsible for any injury to the immigrant or damage to his property sustained on the voyage from Europe.[10]

The writer did not find a copy of an immigration agreement for either 1847 or 1848, although he had available for inspection in the General Land Office, Austin, Texas, a list of over two thousand agreements made between the Society and individual German emigrants.[11] In fact, the only document dated 1847 which was found

[9]The hospital fee of one dollar was charged by Galveston against every immigrant to Texas arriving at that port.

[10]For a copy of an immigration agreement made in 1846, see Appendix C.

[11]This large number of agreements is contained in six fairly large packages among the records of the General Land Office at Austin, Texas. The packages are marked "Records of the German Emigration Company," the name under which the Society for the Protection of German Immigrants in Texas was known in this state. The writer secured quite a bit of information from these agreements. Their greatest value lies in the fact that from them a fairly complete list of German immigrants can be

HEINEMANN REDEMPTION CONTRACT

From an immigration agreement in the General Land Office, Austin, Texas among the agreements was a certificate of admission issued to one of the Society's colonists. Because the certificate contains some of the essentials of the customary agreement, a translation follows:

Certificate of Admission

Of the Society for the Protection of German Immigrants in Texas for the Year 1847.

The Society for the Protection of German Immigrants in Texas grants to .... 100 acres of its lands situated in Travis County, Texas, in absolute possession for himself and his heirs, as soon as he reports on the grant to the colonial directorate. But the condition is attached hereto that in three years 15 acres must be cultivated and properly fenced.

The costs of surveying are to be borne by.................. ....

On his arrival in Galveston the bearer of this certificate must report to Mr. G. Dresel, the agent of the Society, who will give him additional necessary information.

Bieberich, September 30, 1847.

The General Agency of the Society,
By M. W. Settegast.

An examination of the immigration agreements in the General Land Office revealed the fact that twenty of the two thousand immigrants were unable to sign their own names. The sign used in place of the signatures consisted of three cross marks. Generally two witnesses signed the agreement.[12]

The most novel fact, however, which the writer discovered in his research work was that some of the Society's settlers came to Texas under a modified form of the redemptioner system. The practice was not widespread, however, since there were only fifteen agreements in which redemptory clauses were inserted. The clauses were added in writing to the printed form of the immigration agreements. In seven cases the Society furnished the emigrant with money for transportation and provisions on the voyage; in the remaining eight cases some individual furnished the money. The Society agreed to let the redemptioner pay back the amount either in cash or in services within three years with interest at 5 per cent annually. Caspar Herber, for instance, was allowed to

made for the years 1844 to 1846. Future references to these agreements will be listed as "Records of the German Emigration Company."

12For a copy of an agreement signed by three cross marks, see the illustration facing this page.

pay back the sum of 320 florins ($128.00) either in cash or in
services as a civil engineer. The conditions imposed by an individual on a redemptioner were threefold: first, the transfer to the
benefactor of a certain part of the land, generally 110 acres;
second, the cultivation of not more than 12 acres of the benefactor's land for a period of six years; and third, the payment to
the benefactor of one-third of the produce of the land so cultivated.[13]

The preparatory work of the Society in Germany created an
interest among those also who were not planning to emigrate to
Texas. These persons wanted to know more about the colonization
program of the Society. Some of them doubted the wisdom and
practicability of the plan to direct emigration, others believed in
the plan and supported it. Newspaper articles and pamphlets
appeared on both sides of the question. The German press, in the
main, seemed to support the project.

Some opposition to German emigration was expressed by cor-
respondents in the *Frankfurter Journal* in 1844. On January 18
a correspondent from the Taunus region spoke of the Society and
its project of taking 10,000 families to Texas and expressed the
opinion that neither speculation nor any other unworthy motive
prompted the Society, but he urged it to beware of any phantastic
dreams and not to bring ruin on the German emigrants, as
Las Casas had brought untold suffering on the negroes of Africa
through his appeal for the protection of the natives of the Caribbean
islands. The Taunus correspondent considered it every patriot's
duty not to further the work of the Society until it had announced
its program.[14] On February 23 a correspondent from the Main
indulged in a discussion of the slavery question in its relation to
the annexation of Texas. He considered Texas unsafe for German
emigrants because of its unsettled political condition.[15]

Georg Franz attacked the Society in a pamphlet which he published at Munich in 1844. He called it a warning to the nation.

[13]For a copy of a redemptory agreement with the Society, see the preceding illustration, and for a copy of a redemptory agreement with a private
individual, see the next illustration.

[14]*Frankfurter Journal*, January 21, 1844. Prof. B. Mueller, who is now
director of the City Historical Museum (Staedtisches Historisches Museum)
of Frankfort on the Main, sent the writer transcripts of a number of
articles and editorials which appeared in the *Frankfurter Journal* during
1844 on the subject of German emigration to Texas.

[15]*Ibid.*, February 26, 1844.

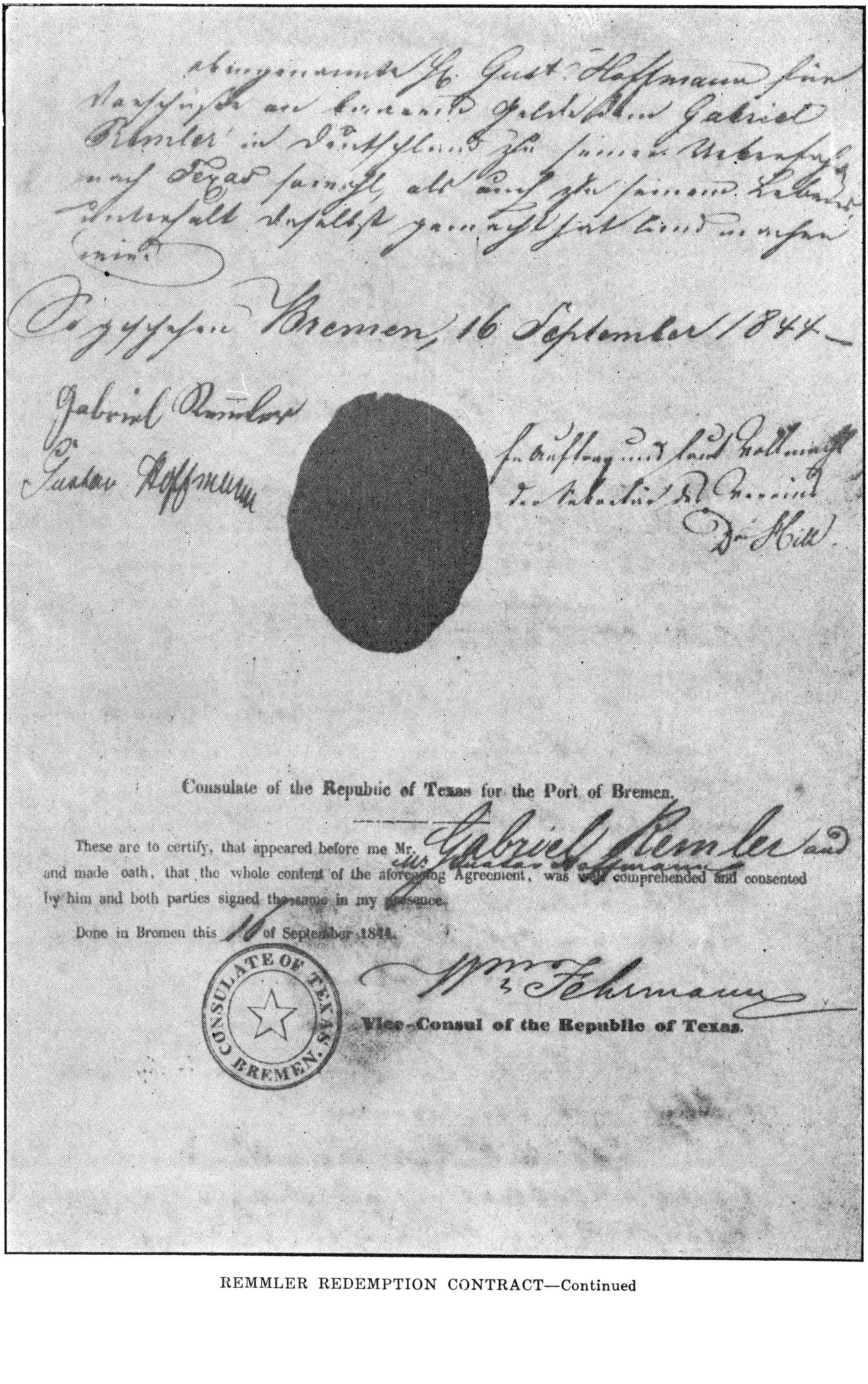

obengenannte H. Gust. Hoffmann für das[...] an benannten [...] Gabriel Remmler in Deutschland zu seiner Ueberfahrt nach Texas sowohl, als auch zu seinem Lebens Unterhalt daselbst gemacht hat und machen wird.

Geschehen Bremen, 16 September 1844 —

Gabriel Remmler

Gustav Hoffmann

Im Auftrag und laut Vollmacht des [...]

Dr. Hill

Consulate of the Republic of Texas for the Port of Bremen.

These are to certify, that appeared before me Mr. Gabriel Remmler and Mr. Gustav Hoffmann and made oath, that the whole content of the aforegoing Agreement, was well comprehended and consented by him and both parties signed the same in my presence.

Done in Bremen this 16 of September 1844.

Wm. Fehrmann

Vice-Consul of the Republic of Texas.

REMMLER REDEMPTION CONTRACT—Continued

REMMLER REDEMPTION CONTRACT
From an immigration agreement in the General Land Office, Austin, Texas

He felt that the German press had ignored the important subject
of German emigration to Texas. His attack was directed especially against the German princes and noblemen and charged that
the German press did not dare to question their motives. The
German press had praised the undertaking as one of national importance, since it would aid in freeing Germany of over-population. The press, he said, had not made a close examination of the
Society's plans, had not called for a full explanation of its project,
and had not raised the voice of doubt, but had expected the nation
to give its approval. If, on the other hand, Franz said, the plan
had been formed by a group of lowly German subjects, there would
have been no end to the attacks by the press against the absurdity
and the speculative nature of such an undertaking. In brief, the
German press would then have discussed the issue in an impartial
manner. Only two German newspapers, the *Deutsche Allgemeine
Zeitung* and the *Karlsruher Zeitung,* met with Franz's approval
for picturing the dangers of emigration to Texas and for demanding a full explanation of the Society's plans. Franz wanted the
German people to ponder upon the Society's project. He believed
that there was much trouble ahead for Texas, since Mexico had
not given up her claim to Texas, and that, if war should break out
between Texas and Mexico, the German settler could not remain
a disinterested bystander but would have to take up arms. The
institution of slavery in Texas was objectionable to Franz, who
thought that contact with it would demoralize the German settlers.[16]

In the *Karlsruher Zeitung,* which was praised by Franz for its
stand on German emigration and the project of the Society, an
editorial described the population of Texas as consisting of the
refuse of the United States, of fugitives from justice, and of bank-
rupts. Other objections to Texas were raised by the editorial, as
the subordination of law to the will of the desperado, the enslaving
of poor immigrants by the rich planters, the unhealthy climate,
and the depredations of the Indians. The editorial finally quoted
at length from the pamphlet by Franz, mentioned in the preceding
paragraph.[17]

[16]Franz, *Die Auswanderung der Deutschen nach Texas, Nordamerika,
und Ungarn,* 3-16.

[17]*Karlsruher Zeitung*, July 23, 1844. The writer secured a copy of the
editorial from the present editor of the *Karlsruher Zeitung.* The editorial

But the Society had its friends as well as its enemies. On January 28 a correspondent from the Main spoke of the return of Count Boos-Waldeck, adjutant of the duke of Nassau, from Texas, and said that not only people from the lower classes but even Count Castell would move to Texas with his family in the fall.[18] On May 13 a correspondent from Hamburg reported the renewed efforts of Hamburg and Bremen to enter into a commercial treaty with Texas which would facilitate emigration as well as promote trade. The Texan *chargé d'affaires* at the Hague, Col. William Henry Daingerfield, had instructions to conclude such a treaty.[19] Friedrich von Wrede, a citizen of Texas since 1836, entered the lists for his adopted fatherland and answered two scathing articles which had appeared in the *Frankfurter Journal* on March 25 and 27. Wrede contended that Texas still had available land, that it could protect its citizens, that the climate was good, and that the Texans were not all disreputable characters.[20] Probably the strongest supporter of the Society and its colonization work was Siegfried Schultz. In an article on the Society and its relation to the slavery question, he said, in conclusion: "Let us rejoice that the regulation of German emigration and the founding of German colonies has at last found consideration at the hands of those circles of society which are capable of directing this work to the advantage of Germany, and let us hope that their undertaking, supported by the united Fatherland, may soon become a national interest. Above all, however, let us hope that the attacks of a part of the German press on the founders of the Society may not make them waver in their noble, humane work."[21]

also calls attention to the sufferings of the colonists sent to Texas by Henry Castro, which probably explains the caustic remarks in the editorial. On April 27, 1844, there appeared an article in the *Frankfurter Journal* which spoke in derogatory terms of Castro's colonization work.

[18]*Frankfurter Journal*, February 5, 1844.

[19]*Ibid.*, May 24, 1844.

[20]*Ibid.*, July 6, 1844.

[21]*Frankfurter Journal*, July 17, 1844. The article just quoted was contributed by a correspondent "from the Rhine" (Vom Rhein) and signed S. S. Prof. B. Mueller, director of the City Historical Museum of Frankfort on the Main, in a letter to the writer expressed the opinion that Siegfried Schultz was probably the correspondent "from the Rhine," since one correspondence, dated October 21, 1844, is signed Siegfried Schultz. The writer, too, is convinced that Schultz contributed the articles, because they contain, in the main, the arguments and the line of thought found in Schultz, Joh. Heinr. Siegfried, *Die deutsche Ansiedlung in Texas*, a

MAP 4

THE GERMAN CONFEDERATION (WESTERN PART) ABOUT 1845

Most of the emigrants of the Society for the Protection of German Immigrants in Texas came from the states which are shaded. Smaller numbers of emigrants left the other states of western and southwestern Germany.

It is not easily determined how many Germans emigrated to Texas as a result of the opportunity of securing a new home offered by the work of the Society for the Protection of German Immigrants in Texas. The population of Comal and Gillespie Counties, and of the region which was organized into Kendall County in 1862, was almost exclusively German in 1850 and still in 1860. A considerable number of the emigrants did not go to these counties of western Texas but remained in the counties on the lower Brazos, Colorado, and Guadalupe rivers, as was pointed out in the third chapter of this study. The Records of the German Emigration Company in the Office of the Commissioner of the General Land Office in Austin, Texas, indicate that most of the settlers of that company in the years from 1844 to 1846 came from the states of western and northwestern Germany, especially from Nassau, Hesse, the Electorate of Hesse, and Hanover. With its seat at Mayence and Frankfort the influence of the Society for the Protection of German Immigrants in Texas was especially strong in Nassau, Hesse, and the Electorate of Hesse. The availability of Bremen as a port of embarkation caused many subjects of Hanover to emigrate to Texas under the auspices of the Society.

While the Society was making its preparations in Germany for carrying on its colonization work, and while it was receiving both favorable and unfavorable criticism, it was making preparations in Texas as well. It was quite as important for the Society to be able to take care of the colonists which it would send to Texas as it was to draw up the regulations for its colonial establishment and to enter into agreements with those Germans who were willing to settle in Texas. The most reliable source from which to draw information on this phase of the Society's work is the series of reports made to it by Prince Carl of Solms-Braunfels, its first commissioner-general in Texas.

It will be recalled that in the previous chapter mention was made of the fact that Prince Carl of Solms-Braunfels and Alexander Bourgeois were sent to Texas in the spring of 1844 to get every-

pamphlet published at Bonn in 1845 and containing eight articles contributed to the *Rhenish Observer (Rheinischer Beobachter)* by Schultz. Bonn is on the Rhine. Schultz, the writer thinks, signed himself briefly "Siegfried Schultz" because he was proud of the fact that he was named after the great hero of German mythology, Siegfried. Schultz was a referendary, according to information received by the writer from Dr. R. Bonnet, who holds a lectorship at the University of Frankfort.

thing in readiness for the colonists to be sent over by the Society, and that on August 28 Bourgeois announced that he had been dismissed by the Society.[22] With the dismissal of Bourgeois as colonial director, Prince Solms was left to carry on the preparatory work alone, until Henry Francis Fisher arrived in Texas as colonial director.

In his first report from Texas, dated Nassau, July 15, 1844, Prince Solms stated that he agreed with the suggestion of the colonial director, Alexander Bourgeois, to parcel out and sell Nassau Farm,[23] since it was about one hundred and forty miles from the Bourgeois-Ducos grant and too difficult to reach from there. He reported that he had met many prominent men who had all expressed their happiness over the colonization work to be carried on by the Society. Many of the Germans then living in Texas visited him and asked to be accepted as settlers. Prince Solms told them that he was not authorized to give them land but that they might buy land very cheaply and have an equal share with immigrants in the churches, schools, and charitable institutions. During Prince Solms's visit in Industry Friedrich Ernst offered the toast: "To the health of the noble and generous German princes who think of the welfare of their subjects even on this side of the ocean!" Prince Solms stated that he had secured the services of Dr. Emil Meyer, who would help him in making the preparations for the first settlement and who, because he had lived in warm climates and knew the methods of treating the diseases of those regions, would be especially valuable to the settlers and to the physician whom the Society would send to the colony.[24]

[22]See above, Chapter IV, p. 75.

[23]Nassau Farm was the name given to the plantation on the W. H. Jack league which Count Boos-Waldeck bought from Robert Mills of Brazoria County on January 9, 1843.

Prince Solms reported about Nassau Farm that Bryan, the overseer, had so mistreated the negro slaves that three had run away. Two of them were shot on a plantation near San Antonio during a robbery; the other was recaptured and brought back. He became a model worker, almost overworking himself for the new overseer, Denman. Charles Fordtran, appointed as inspector by Count Boos-Waldeck, had taken care of the plantation for two hundred and fifty dollars and was left in charge by Prince Solms until the arrival of a physician whom the Society was to send to Nassau Farm. William Etzel was left as general manager of Nassau Farm until the arrival of the physician. Prince Solms promised to give him one hundred acres of land if he would come to San Antonio, but Etzel insisted on getting fifty acres on Nassau Farm according to the promise made him by Count Boos-Waldeck.

[24]"Berichte an den Adelsverein," in *Kalender*, 15-19.

In his second report, dated at San Antonio de Bexar on August 20, 1844, Prince Solms stated that he had made an inspection of the Bourgeois-Ducos grant, had found land suitable for agriculture along the rivers and creeks and in the Uvalde and Sabinal canyons, but that all of this good land had been previously located. Consequently the Society had no land on which to start its colony. He considered it fortunate that the grant had been annulled.

It thus became necessary for the Society to secure land in some other way. Acquisition by purchase was not deemed advisable by Prince Solms, since it would not be possible to buy a compact tract that would be large enough for the needs of the Society. Prince Solms considered it equally inadvisable to make agreements with owners of leagues to settle half of the leagues, for the Society's lands would thus always be split up and the colonization work would enhance the value of the remaining half leagues at the expense of the Society. He argued, in addition, that a compact tract could never be secured, since some owners would not be willing to make agreements with the Society. Temporarily, however, he and Bourgeois had begun negotiations with a Mr. Cassiano and others under the half-league settlement plan just stated. The land was situated at the confluence of the Cibolo with the San Antonio River not quite half way to the coast.[25] A settlement at that place would serve as a station for those settlers who would desire to go farther up into the republic. Since the San Antonio River, which was four feet and deeper up to this point, could be made navigable, the settlement would become a trading center in the course of time. The place was on the way from the coast to the Medina and from Victoria to Laredo. Merchants from Mexico, because of the shorter distance, would go there to trade instead of going to San Antonio.[26] But Prince Solms did not push the San Antonio-Cibolo proposal. Only two

[25]Prince Solms estimated the distance at fifty-five miles from San Antonio and fifty miles from Aransas Bay. Why he wrote Aransas Bay is not clear, because the San Antonio River does not flow into Aransas Bay but flows into the Guadalupe River about ten miles above San Antonio Bay.

[26]Prince Solms was probably too enthusiastic, since the road from Laredo to San Antonio was an old established one, well known, and only a few miles longer than the other. Then, too, the trade connections between Laredo and San Antonio were well established and would not be given up readily.

leagues were offered him on the partial settlement plan, making the equivalent of only one league available for settlement. There would not have been enough land for fifty families allowing only one hundred acres per family. Besides, the Society intended to place at least one hundred families on each settlement. The proposal had one other disadvantage, namely, it did not leave any lands for the Society to sell profitably at a later time when they had enhanced in value.[27]

Prince Solms tried also to make an agreement with McMullen to settle half of his tract of sixteen leagues on the Medina. Although McMullen was favorable at first to the proposition, he decided finally that he would dispose of his land by sale alone. Prince Solms liked the land, since it was very fertile and had numerous springs.

After presenting these propositions to the Society, he advised as follows: *first,* secure enough land at the confluence of the Cibolo with the San Antonio in any manner possible in order that all of the settlers coming the first year might be settled there; *second,* acquire the McMullen tract on the Medina in whole or in part so that it could be used for another settlement and another station on the way to the interior; *third,* purchase the land in the Uvalde canyon, which, if bought soon enough, might be bought at five cents an acre.

[27]On October 30, 1844, the *Telegraph and Texas Register* contained an article about the proposed San Antonio-Cibolo settlement, which read as follows: "M. Bourgeois d'Orvanne has treated for a large tract of land in the forks of the Cibolo and San Antonio rivers. These lands are considered as the best in this part of the Republic, very fertile and perfectly suited to cultivation of any kind of production. The waters are pure and healthy, the timber is abundant and good for every purpose.

M. Bourgeois d'Orvanne has already made some preparations to receive the emigration on this tract. Some settlements are established on it, and a new town, called "San Bartolo," is to be erected in a beautiful situation. This city, situated midway from the sea to San Antonio, by the road of La Bahia, is about 48 miles from Copano. It is destined to become an excellent stopping place for travelers and emigrants and to give great security to this part of the country—distant from Laredo, on the Rio Grande, about 140 miles, its commercial prospects have a large chance of success.

It is believed that the Rio San Antonio, from its mouth to the junction of the Cibolo, may be navigable. M. Bourgeois d'Orvanne, therefore, has the intention to execute this important work, the expense of which will be almost without importance to him. In this case, San Bartolo will gain a large consideration and become the principal market in the West. The rich lands in this part of the Republic will then soon acquire a great value." (See *Telegraph and Texas Register*, October 30, 1844, 2, col. 4.)

Prince Solms planned to ask the Texas Congress for a grant of land which would include the fertile unlocated lands on the Medina and extend out toward the southwest. Such a grant would lie nearer the Rio Grande and might secure some of the overland trade with Chihuahua, which he estimated lay four hundred and fifty miles west of San Antonio. He said that he would try to get a reduction in the duties on all goods brought into Texas by the ships of the Society. If he should succeed in all of this program, Prince Solms said that the Society would find its whole position changed and, if the Bourgeois-Ducos grant were not renewed, Bourgeois's membership in the Society would cease.[28]

To assist him, Prince Solms asked for several capable older men, preferably officers, to be sent to Texas to serve as commandants in the different settlements and for several young men to act as messengers. He recommended also the organization of a mounted company of twenty to fifty men for outpost and patrol duty. He requested that he be allowed to return to Germany the following spring, since he could explain better verbally than in writing the changed position of the Society, the prospects of the colony and of German trade, as well as the advantages which Germany in general and the Society in particular would derive from trade with Mexico. He felt, too, that his personal presence in Germany would enable the Society to induce the various governments in Germany to join the Society, thus assuring the colonization work of becoming a national movement.[29]

On August 26, 1844, Prince Solms made his third report. Bourgeois, he said, was so disgruntled over his dismissal as colonial director that he would not consider accepting employment by the Society at a salary of five per cent of its net proceeds, nor would he accept a position for five per cent of the net proceeds derived from land sales in the Fisher and Miller grant. About the Fisher and Miller grant Prince Solms wrote that the land along the Colorado was all located but that there was still a large

---

[28]Prince Solms wanted the Society to send him appropriate instructions for dealing with Bourgeois, whom he considered self-seeking, indifferent to the interests of the colonists and of the Society, and incapable of directing, as well as of securing obedience. He believed Bourgeois to be arrogant, as was also the case with Ducos, whom Solms had taken along to Texas on the recommendation of Bourgeois.

[29]"Berichte an den Adelsverein," in *Kalender*, 19-27.

.amount of desirable unlocated land in the grant. He regretted, however, that the grant was not in the direct line of trade from San Antonio to Mexico, a fact which might prevent the accomplishment of one of the three objects of the Society—the enlarging of German trade. From Col. Jack Hays he heard that Henry Francis Fisher believed that it was impossible to make the first settlement on the grant itself, since it was too far from the coast, .an opinion for which Solms gave Fisher great credit. For the first settlement Fisher had acquired, as Hays reported, eleven leagues of land on the Guadalupe beginning twenty miles above Seguin and running thirty-three miles to the source of the Guadalupe,[30] from where it was only fifteen miles to the Llano, the beginning of the grant. Prince Solms pointed out that the northwestern part of the grant consisted of the hunting grounds of the Comanche Indians, whom he proposed to force into a treaty ·or else administer such a crushing defeat to them that they would not molest him for a long time. Twenty or more of Castro's colonists, who had been in San Antonio since May, offered to serve under Prince Solms against the Indians. Solms would not, however, estrange them from Castro, not wishing to give Castro .a pretext for complaint against the Society.[31] Prince Solms re-

[30]Either Prince Solms misundertood Col. Hays about the distance, or else that doughty Indian fighter and scout certainly made a mistake. Taking all of the turns of the Guadalupe into consideration, it must be .at least one hundred miles from Seguin to its source.

[31]In his second report Prince Solms called attention to the fact that Henry Castro had enlisted colonists in France, Switzerland, and Germany. After they arrived in Galveston, these colonists were sent on to Port Lavaca at their expense and arrived there just before Easter, 1844, .practically penniless. On the way to Castro's grant, which lay west of San Antonio on the Medina, all of them took sick and twenty-eight died in San Antonio. Castro would not do anything for them, not even sending them a physician. Prince Solms, therefore, asked that the different German governments be requested to restrain Castro's emigration agents. Among Castro's unfortunate immigrants were Germans from the Rhenish and Bavarian Palatinate, from Baden, and from Wuertemberg. For services rendered these unfortunate people by Col. Hays and one of his soldiers, Joseph Rahm, from the Swiss canton of Schaffhausen, Prince Solms suggested that the Society make Hays a present of a rifle and Rahm a musket.

William Kennedy, British consul in Texas, reported to his government about the sufferings to which emigrants from Continental Europe had been needlessly subjected and observed that "it would be a worthy and becoming service if the respective governments would supply their emigrating people with means of precise and accurate information, protect them from fraudulent speculators, and keep them paternally in view until they had made a lodgment on their adopted soil." (See Kennedy

quested that the Society send over as many emigrants as possible
by the end of March, 1845, since the probability of success would
be greater with a larger number of settlers.[32]

On September 1, 1844, Prince Solms, on the order of the executive committee, arrived at Nassau Farm, from where he made
his fourth report on the twentieth of that month. He included
in this report a statement about the arrival of the brig *Weser* at
Galveston in July with the immigrants enlisted by Henry Francis
Fisher.[33] These immigrants were assured by Prince Solms that
the land promised them by Fisher had not been forfeited. Prince
Solms wanted to know if these immigrants were entitled to the
same rights as those to be sent by the Society.[34]

In his fifth report, dated Galveston, October 25, 1844, Prince
Solms announced his selection of D. H. Klaener of Galveston as
agent of the Society. Klaener was to have charge of transporting
the settlers from Galveston to Matagorda Bay, where Prince Solms
and Fisher were to purchase sufficient land for a landing place
and leave a manager in charge to receive the settlers. From Indianola, or Carlshafen, as this place came to be known, Solms
and Fisher were to go to the Guadalupe along the route to be
taken by the colonists, and then to the Fisher and Miller grant in
company with Major Hays and a detachment of his rangers.
After returning from the grant, Prince Solms wanted to go to
Washington in order to be present at the meeting of the Texan
Congress in December, whereupon he was going to Indianola to
make his headquarters there.[35] Prince Solms advised the Society

to Aberdeen, Galveston, September 9, 1844, in Adams, E. D., *British Diplomatic Correspondence Concerning the Republic of Texas, 1838-1846*,
361.)

On February 26, 1845, the *Telegraph and Texas Register* printed an
extract from an article on Texas which appeared in a newspaper in
Basel, Switzerland, on October 26, 1844. The article, on the whole, was
unfriendly to Texas. Quoting the *Cologne Gazette* about Castro's colonists, it said: "Texas is fallen with us into great discredit, because
the immigrants from Alsace, Switzerland, and Germany, according to
the official reports of all the French consuls, have become the victims of
innumerable miseries." (See *Telegraph and Texas Register*, February
26, 1845, 2, col. 5.)

[32]"Berichte an den Adelsverein," in *Kalender*, 29-34.

[33]Mention was made of the arrival of the Fisher colonists in Chapter
IV, p. 79, footnote 36.

[34]"Rerichte an den Adelsverein," in *Kalender*, 34-36.

[35]Prince Solms, however, did not go to Washington. Instead, Henry
Francis Fisher went there to request the aid of the Texan Congress for

to acquire lands to the south of the Fisher and Miller grant and to get a foothold on Corpus Christi Bay by the purchase of land belonging to McGloin. Prince Solms had in mind a tract of land reaching from the Colorado along the Llano and San Saba westward to the Rio Grande and southward through the Uvalde canyon to the mouth of the Nueces River—verily, a kingdom! On the subject of the annexation of Texas to the United States he essayed the role of prophet and predicted that very few voices would be raised in Texas in behalf of annexation, unless the land-grabbing policy *(raubgierige Politik)* of the United States should force Texas into approving annexation. A treaty of peace between Texas and Mexico, recognizing the independence of Texas, would be of especial interest and benefit to the Society, Prince Solms wrote.[36]

On November 22, 1844, Prince Solms arrived at Fort Lavaca

the Society's enterprise. (See Solms to Jones, Houston, November 2, 1844, in Jones, *Memoranda and Official Correspondence*, 391.) A month later Prince Solms wrote again and "recommended Mr. Fisher and his bill" to Jones's "kind consideration." (See Same to Same, in *Ibid.*, 408.) The "bill" referred to was passed in the form of a resolution on January 29, 1845. The second and principal section of it allowed Fisher and Miller until March 1, 1846, to introduce the first third of the six thousand families and entitled them to compensation, pro rata, for the number of families actually introduced, even if they failed to introduce the required number by that time. The third section repealed the requirement that each settler should cultivate fifteen acres for three years and build a cabin on his land. (See Gammel, *Laws of Texas*, II, 1091-1092.)

[36]"Berichte an den Adelsverein," in *Kalender*, 36-40.
The annexation of Texas to the United States interested Prince Solms and the Society very much. On November 2, 1844, he wrote to Anson Jones as follows: "By the last steamer from Galveston I got dispatches from home, by which I see that the Association is very anxious about the annexation question, stating, by good sources, that it would be a case of war between the European powers and the United States—as I am sure you, my dear and honored sir, are best aware of. The Association requested me to write to the government, and especially to you, dear sir, whose favorable disposition and feelings toward the Association I duly reported, to get, as far as it is possible for you to give, a slight notice whether the probability is for the independence of our beautiful Texas; whether we may flatter ourselves with the hope of a man with enlightened views, like you, dear Dr. Jones, at the head of the government, or whether Texas should fall into the condition of a territory of the United States." (See Jones, *Memoranda and Official Correspondence*, 391-392.)
A month later Prince Solms wrote again on the same subject and offered to go to Mexico to see Santa Anna, stating that he could not prove his feelings for Texas and his interest in its welfare in any more suitable manner. (See *Ibid.*, 408.)

with a party of men who had engaged themselves to work for the Society. During the next four days he cruised on Lavaca and Matagorda Bay to find a suitable harbor and fresh water. He decided on Indian Point because it had fresh water, some wood, a healthy location, a good harbor for all ships that could cross the bar at Paso Cavallo, and provided the shortest possible road through the low country. On November 28 Prince Solms sailed for Galveston to meet the first ships bringing immigrants to Texas for the Society. A storm delayed his arrival there until the morning of December 2. During the previous night, however, the immigrant ships sailed for Port Lavaca and reached there probably before the next stormy period on December 4 which forced Prince Solms, on board the Texas revenue cutter *Alert,* Captain Simpton, back into Galveston harbor. On December 9 the weather allowed Prince Solms to sail for Port Lavaca, where he arrived on the 11th and found the immigrants already ashore. On December 17 Prince Solms arranged with a Mr. White for the purchase of a tract of land in Indian Point for the use of the Society. This location was named Carlshafen, since Prince Leiningen, Count Castell, and Prince Solms all had the given name of Carl.[37]

The writer feels it advisable to drop Prince Solms's preparations at this point, since the first immigrants had arrived and new problems confronted the commissioner-general. The following chapter will take up the narrative again at this point and will follow Prince Solms and the immigrants to the first German settlement made in the interior of Texas by the Society for the Protection of German Immigrants in Texas.

---

[37]"Berichte an den Adelsverein," in *Kalender,* 40-44.

The *Texas National Register,* published at Washington, Texas, by W. D. Miller, contained the following news about Prince Solms: We learn from Capt. Simpton that the Prince of Solms is at Lavaca, fully furnished with wagons, provisions, etc., to remove the immigrants for his colony from the coast to the settlement, as fast as they arrive. (See *Texas National Register,* December 7, 1844, 2, col. 3.)

NEW BRAUNFELS

From a print in the possession of Mr. Walter Heidemeye:, New Braunfels, Texas. The original was made by Carl G. Iwonski

CHAPTER VI

NEW BRAUNFELS: ITS FOUNDING AND ITS EARLY HISTORY

The arrival of the immigrants at Indianola (Carlshafen) in December of 1844 increased the work of Prince Solms to a considerable degree and brought him face to face with the necessity of securing a tract of land on which to make the first settlement. The time had passed for making suggestions to the Society about different suitable places for a settlement on the way to the Fisher and Miller grant; the time for action was at hand. Prince Solms proved himself equal to the occasion. It is the object of this chapter to give an account of what Prince Solms did after the arrival of the immigrants to get them into the interior of Texas and to establish the first settlement for the Society for the Protection of German Immigrants in Texas. Following an account of the founding of New Braunfels, its history will be told briefly up to the time when Texas declared for secession from the Union.

Prince Solms pointed out again the impossibility and impracticability of founding the first settlement on the Llano and praised the region between the Guadalupe and San Antonio rivers as especially suitable. He considered the so-called "fountains"[1] thirty miles from San Antonio on the way to Austin, as an ideal location for the first settlement, because of the fertile soil, the beautiful region, the excellent cedar and oak woods, the good water, and the abundant water power. The proximity to San Antonio and Seguin would enable the settlers to get aid and protection readily. Lying at the foot of the hill country, this settlement was to become the center of the colonization work, since it was equidistant from the coast and the colony lands.[2]

Having made up his mind on the location of the first settlement,

---

[1]The "fountains" are the Comal springs, called "las fontanas" by the Mexicans.

[2]How correct this prediction would be, Prince Solms could not know, of course, when he made it. After his return to Germany in 1845, Prince Solms must have secured quite a bit of satisfaction from observing that the Society was using this settlement as the base of operations for founding other settlements.

Prince Solms turned next to the problem of reaching the settlement. He proposed to establish several stations on the way from Carlshafen to the point where the Guadalupe was to be crossed, about twelve miles below Victoria. The first station out of Carlshafen was to be located on Chocolate Creek, also called the Agua Dulce, about twelve miles distant.[3] In honor of the several members of the Leiningen family who belonged to the Society, the station on Chocolate Creek was to be called *Leiningen.* The second station, called *Castell,* in honor of the Count of Castell, the Society's business director, was twelve miles farther up the low country, at a place where the Guadalupe could be crossed easily.[4] How many other stations would have to be made on the way to the first settlement and from there to the grant, as well as for the protection of the principal settlement and the mines on the grant, Prince Solms said he could determine only after a personal inspection. Below Victoria, at the proposed station of Castell, the road was to cross the Guadalupe and run in as direct a line as possible to the settlement along the watershed between the Guadalupe and the San Antonio, with its tributary, the Cibolo. Wherever necessary, bridges were to be built. In fact, Prince Solms planned to lay out the road from Carlshafen to the settlement in such a way that in the summer of 1845 a railroad could be built on it, similar to one then used near the Ruhr in Westphalia. The railroad was to use live-oak rails and, until locomotives could be brought over, horses were to draw the cars. The railroad would mean a considerable saving of time and expense, Prince Solms estimated.[5]

---

[3]Prince Solms bought 1100 acres of land on Chocolate Creek from Captain Sylvanus Hatch. The tract contained a good amount of timber, which Prince Solms planned to use for building the Society's warehouses both at Carlshafen and on the tract itself. This station was to be used as headquarters by Prince Solms. At Carlshafen the Society was to have a wharf and a large storehouse. Several of the immigrant families agreed to remain at Carlshafen. For protection against attack, a large trench with breastworks was to be dug around the storehouse. Ludwig Willke, formerly lieutenant in the 30th Prussian Infantry, was made commandant and placed in charge of Carlshafen.

[4]Prince Solms does not state in his report that he purchased any land for this station, but says at one point that the place should be made safe from attack. He mentions a Mr. Trailor in connection with this station.

[5]This railroad was never built, but the idea was kept alive for several years. In a previous chapter, in discussing Nassau Farm, mention was made of the Lavaca, Guadalupe, and San Saba Railroad Company, an

Mindful of the personal welfare of the settlers, as well as of the interests of the Society, Prince Solms saw fit to call the attention of the Society to the apparent negligence of two persons connected with it. He believed that Dr. B. Hill, the agent of the Society at Bremen, had not been careful enough about the food supplies used on board ship and those bought for the Society. The salt pork was hardly usable, the peas would not turn soft from boiling, the barrel of brandy was not good, and the claret was of an inferior quality. Several of the immigrants had inquired about flour and other articles of food for infants and offered to purchase these before leaving Bremen. Dr. Hill had assured them that these articles were included in the ship's food supplies and the Society's stores, but such was not the case. As a result, many complaints were made to Prince Solms. Dr. Theodor Koester, the physician for the first settlement, complained that there were not enough medicines aboard the several immigrant ships. If the Society intended to keep Dr. Hill in the service of forwarding ships from Bremen, Prince Solms advised that Dr. Hill be cautioned to be more careful.

Henry Francis Fisher came in for much more criticism at the hands of Prince Solms. Fisher had lost too much time protecting his own interests before the Texan Congress at Washington. He had collected only fifteen of the fifty wagons specified for transporting the settlers, had not bought any of the draft oxen and cattle for the first settlement, nor had he provided any beef cattle and corn meal. Until the last of January Prince Solms was willing for Fisher to use the Society's funds for purchasing everything that was still lacking, but after that date Fisher was to pay for the needed articles out of his own pocket, since Prince Solms was determined not to let either the Society's or the settlers' interests suffer through Fisher's negligence. Apparently, however, Fisher did not purchase all that was still lacking, for on February 8, 1845, Prince Solms reported that the colonial council had decided to send Captain F. W. von Wrede to New Orleans to procure those articles which were still needed.[6] There

alias under which the Society was sometimes known. (See Chapter IV, 68, footnote 5.)

[6] In his eighth report Prince Solms mentions the minutes of meetings held by the colonial council. The writer has been unable to get any in-

was some friction between Prince Solms and Fisher over the Society's agent in Galveston. Solms had appointed D. H. Klaener in September, 1844, but Fisher, claiming he had been empowered by the Society's executive committee to appoint agents, wanted to have the firm of E. Kauffman & Co. act as agent in Galveston. Prince Solms refused to dismiss D. H. Klaener as agent, but did consent to have the firm of E. Kauffman & Co. appointed as agent at Carlshafen. He asked the Society for directions for dealing with Fisher.[7] He advised the Society never to give Fisher the actual management of its affairs in Texas, saying that its interests would not be promoted by Fisher's appointment.[8]

Having followed this far the continued preparations of Prince Solms for getting the immigrants to the first settlement, as well as given an account of the reports made by him in the interests of the Society on Dr. B. Hill and Henry Francis Fisher, we are now ready to go back to the immigrants at Carlshafen and follow them to the first settlement.

formation concerning the whereabouts of the minutes of the Society's colonial council. Judging from Prince Solms's reference to the minutes, the writer believes that they contain some very useful information.

[7]The friction between Solms and Fisher continued and Prince Solms notified the Society that he would hold Fisher responsible to the colonial council on five matters: *first*, for the sum of $13,360, of which $11,000 had been given to Fisher by the Society before he left Germany and $2360 given by Prince Solms for buying draft oxen, but for which Fisher had not bought enough and had not made an accounting; *second*, for his neglect in getting the necessary number of wagons, causing thereby a prolonged stay on the coast and an increase in the expenditures; *third*, for rendering the making of a crop almost impossible because of the delay occasioned by his neglect; *fourth*, for employing various persons and thus adding to the Society's expenses; and *fifth*, for the costs of transporting emigrants from Galveston to Carlshafen under Burchard Miller.

The persons mentioned in the fourth count were Burchard Miller, in charge of the transport of immigrants from Carlshafen, Theodore Miller and Eggers as agents of Kauffmann & Co. to receive the Society's goods at Carlshafen and at Port Lavaca, respectively, Moser and Schwarz for carpenter work, and Bollinger, Morewood, and Wirths for work not specified. (See "Berichte an den Adelsverein," in *Kalender*, 55-56; Photostat *Original Berichte*, 83-84.) Prince Solms does not mention either the initials or given names of the last six men in the list.

[8]"Berichte an den Adelsverein," in *Kalender*, 43-58, Photostat *Original Berichte*, 65-87. Three of Prince Solms's reports, the sixth to the eighth, are included in this reference. The sixth was made from Carlshafen on December 23, 1844; the seventh from the camp on the Agua Dulce (Chocolate Creek) on January 5, 1845; and the eighth from Galveston on February 12, 1845.

On December 23, 1844, Rev. L. C. Ervendberg[9] conducted Protestant services in camp at Carlshafen and touched the hearts of his hearers. For the Christmas Eve services a large oak tree was provided by Prince Solms, decorated with many lights and hung with many presents for the children, a fact which endeared him to the children and to their parents.[10] In connection with the Christmas Day services the sacrament of the Lord's Supper was celebrated. Thus even on the soil of Texas the German immigrants did not forget the sacred precepts of their religious training. The last of the immigrants, under the leadership of Jean J. von Coll,[11] bookkeeper for the first settlement, arrived in Carlshafen from Galveston on December 29, 1844. By January 5, 1845, Prince Solms had established his headquarters at Agua Dulce (Chocolate Creek), twelve miles from Carlshafen. The last of the immigrants were expected to arrive from Carlshafen on the afternoon of that day. In the morning Rev. Ervendberg conducted the first services at that camp. For the protection of his settlers Prince Solms organized a company of twenty men. Out of the remaining one hundred and eight men the able-bodied ones were formed into a reserve corps, to be used for assisting the regular company and for service outside of the settlement, while the others were to be organized into a second reserve *(Landwehr)*.[12] One writer described these soldiers of the Society as follows: "The neat young fellows in their high riding boots, their gray woolen blouses with black velvet collars and brass buttons, their cocked-hats with the long black feather, with their swords

[9]Rev. L. C. Ervendberg was secured by Prince Solms to serve the settlers as Protestant minister. The Rev. Father Alexander of Baltimore had not as yet sent a Catholic priest to Texas for the Society, as Prince Solms had requested.

[10]*Neu Braunfelser Zeitung*, July 22, 1926, 9, col. 3.

[11]Jean J. von Coll, before going to Texas, was a lieutenant in the service of the duke of Nassau. He made the Society a capable official. Once he foiled a plan of changing the name of New Braunfels to Comal by calling a mass meeting and announcing that those who would vote for Comal would get no more advances from the Society. In 1847 he was appointed as director or manager of the settlement of Fredericksburg in place of Dr. Schubert and brought order back into the management of that settlement. He was the father of Mrs. Katinka Clemens, widow of State Senator William Clemens of New Braunfels, Texas. Coll Street in New Braunfels was named after von Coll.

[12]"Berichte an den Adelsverein," in *Kalender*, 45-50; Photostat *Original Berichte*, 68-76.

strapped on and armed with a good rifle, made a good impression."[13]

During the two months from January 5 to March 5 the immigrants were moved farther up into the interior, some to Victoria and others to McCoy's Creek, forty-two miles up the left bank of the Guadalupe River from Victoria. Nicolaus Zink[14] was in charge of this work. He accomplished it by using the fifteen wagons which Henry Francis Fisher had bought for the Society, by renting others from the settlers of the vicinity, and by using fourteen two-wheeled carts, which the blacksmiths among the immigrants made in three camp forges. Jean J. von Coll rendered the Society a valuable service during this period, beause he kept up the spirits of the immigrants and preserved obedience in the military company through his correct and tactful conduct.[15]

[13]Seele, Hermann, "Meine Ankunft in Neu Braunfels," in *Kalender der Neu Braunfelser Zeitung fuer 1914*, 38.

In M. Maris's *Souvenirs d'Amerique. Relations d'un Voyage au Texas et en Haiti*, 90, the soldiers are described as follows: "Les attelages sont toujours conveyés par des soldats à la solde de la Société, faisant partie de la compagnie de cavalerie légère formée par le prince de Salms; ils ont une espece d'uniforme qui consiste en longues bottes, pantalon gris, blouse gris et chapeau de feutre blanc à larges bords surmonté par quelques plumes de dinde sauvage. Leurs armes sont un long sabre de cavaleris, une paire de pistolets d'arçon et une carabine de fabrique allemande portant l'inscription suivante: Fuer die Auswander(er) in Texas."

[14]Nicolaus Zink was the Society's civil engineer for the first settlement. The stockade, built in 1845 on the east bank of Comal Creek in New Braunfels for protection against the Indians, was named *Zinkenburg* (after him). In 1847 he built a cabin on Sister Creek, about forty miles above New Braunfels on the Guadalupe River. Later he sold his two farms to Ottomar von Behr and Edward Degener. For a while he owned a grist mill on Baron Creek, south of Fredericksburg. Finally he settled at Spanish Pass between Boerne and Comfort, on which farm he died in 1890. (Tiling, *German Element in Texas*, 123; Kapp, *Aus und ueber Amerika*, I, 292; Penniger, *Fest-Ausgabe*, 78; Weber, *Deutsche Pioniere*, part II, 9.) Zink Street in New Braunfels was named after him.

[15]Henry Francis Fisher, according to Prince Solms, had been active both at Victoria and at McCoy's Creek, in speaking unfavorably of the Society and of its representatives. Fisher aroused a spirit of opposition to the Society and to its officials among the immigrants. He put ideas of freedom and equality in the minds of the immigrants, and tried to win over some of the officials by promising them an increase in salary.

Before the settlers were moved again from the camp on McCoy's Creek, the colonial council had a meeting, with Henry Francis Fisher present. One complaint after the other was made against him and finally it was resolved to ask the Society to place Fisher under bond or else to buy out Fisher's right to one-third of the net proceeds derived from the colonial establishment. In this meeting Fisher offended Prince Solms

The Society's physician, however, seems to have made himself unpopular with the immigrants. At any rate, Prince Solms wrote that he had found it necessary to suspend him until he could get a reply from the Society, and announced that he had appointed Dr. Emil Meyer to serve as the Society's physician.[16]

On Monday, March 10, everything was in readiness to leave the camp on McCoy's Creek. Prince Solms left a few days ahead of the immigrants, after having inspected the mounted company

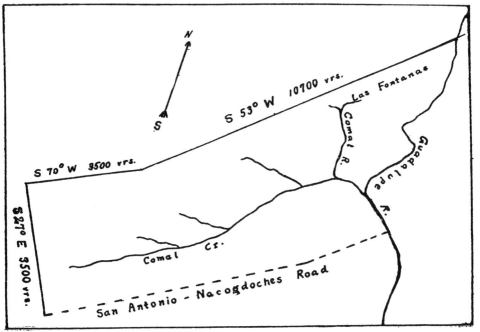

MAP 6—COMAL TRACT
Bought for the Society by Prince Solms on March 14, 1845.

of twenty men. His destination was San Antonio. From the eleventh to the fourteenth of March he carried on negotiations with Juan A. Veramendi and Rafael C. Garza for a tract of land containing two leagues, a plat of which is submitted herewith.

by refusing to recognize the powers of the commissioner-general and by saying that the commissioner-general occupied a position subordinate to the colonial council. ("Berichte an den Adelsverein," in *Kalender*, 59-60; Photostat *Original Berichte*, 88-90.)

16"Berichte an den Adelsverein," in *Kalender*, 59-60; Photostat *Original Berichte*, 88-90.

On the next day, March 15, Prince Solms, Rafael C. Garza, and his wife, Maria Antonio Veramendi Garza, signed the deed. The consideration was one thousand one hundred and eleven dollars. The sum of five hundred dollars was paid for one equal undivided fourth part of the tract, and the sum of six hundred and eleven dollars was to be paid upon the successful termination of a suit in favor of Garza and his wife, said suit to be instituted by them to clear their title to the land. Then a proper conveyance for the land was to be executed by Garza and his wife.[17]

What Prince Solms thought of the tract of land which he had purchased is best seen in his own description of it, in which he said: "Here (at the Guadalupe) the land which I purchased for the Society begins. On the right bank of the Comal Creek, which flows through it, lies a fertile prairie which reaches south to a ridge of hills. On its left bank there is richly-wooded bottom land stretching to the cliffs, which are covered with cedar, oak, and elm. These cliffs, with the hills rising gradually back of them toward the north resemble the Black Forest. Through the bottom land flows the Comal River, which, gushing out of the rock in seven large springs, shortly reaches a width of twenty paces and, becoming larger and larger, rushes along like a swift mountain stream. Its water is very deep and clear as crystal."[18]

---

[17]For the Articles of Agreement by which Prince Solms acquired this tract of land, see Comal County Deed Records, Vol. E, 58. The Articles of Agreement are dated March 14, 1845.

In 1854, in its spring term, the Supreme Court of Texas decided a suit instituted to clear the title to the Veramendi tract in favor of the Veramendi heirs. Thus the sum of six hundred and eleven dollars became due, but when the citizens of New Braunfels offered to pay the principal, together with the accrued interest, the Veramendi heirs refused to accept the money and filed suit for damages against the several owners as trespassers. A committee consisting of Dr. Theodor Koester, Franz Moureau, G. H. Judson, James Ferguson, and H. Seele represented the citizens in this case, which was finally won by the New Braunfels citizens. (See Comal County Deed Records, Book L, 478, for a certified copy of the judgment of the District Court of Guadalupe County in this case. The judgment is dated November 18, 1869.) Some years later another suit was filed against Maria Albrecht, the City of New Braunfels, et al. by various claimants under the old Veramendi title, but the New Braunfels citizens were again given the judgment. (See Comal County District Court Minutes, Book E, 344-352, and Comal County Deed Records, Book N, 556-565.)

On August 4, 1845, another tract of land was purchased, lying to the northwest of the original tract. It consisted mainly of cedar brakes, but also of some farming land along Comal Creek.

[18]"Berichte an den Adelsverein," in *Kalender*, 61; Photostat *Original Berichte*, 91-92.

On March 16 Prince Solms rode from San Antonio to Seguin, where Zink and von Coll arrived on the 17th with thirteen men of the mounted company. That night Prince Solms camped on the Guadalupe River about six miles above Seguin and on the following day he forded the Guadalupe at the place where the San Antonio-Nacogdoches road crosses it.[19] Three days later the immigrant wagons forded the river at the same place and halted on the east bank of Comal Creek.[20] The date, March 21, 1845, thus marks the beginning of the settlement of New Braunfels, named in honor of Prince Solms's estate, Braunfels, on the Lahn River, a tributary of the Rhine and noted for the many castles and ruins along its course.

It is not possible to state with any certainty or correctness the names of those who were present at the founding of New Braunfels. Some of the immigrants remained at Carlshafen to live, according to the sixth report made by Prince Solms, but their names are not given.[21] Some others remained at Carlshafen until the beginning of April, 1845, when the Society's teamsters took them up to New Braunfels. After an overland journey lasting a month, this second group reached the Guadalupe opposite New Braunfels, where high water delayed them for a few days.[22] It can not be ascertained how many of the Fisher and Miller immigrants who arrived in Galveston on July 8, 1844, decided finally to leave Galveston and join the Society's immigrants at Carls-

[19]In his tenth report, dated Camp on Comal Creek, March 27, 1845, Prince Solms reported that he and his small company of men saw a sight on the morning of the 19th that made them think of home, for the ground was covered with snow. On the 20th he rode to the top of the hill northwest of the tract of land which he had purchased and described the view from there as "enchanting." ("Berichte an den Adelsverein," in *Kalender*, 62; Photostat, *Original Berichte*, 92.)

[20]*Neu Braunfelser Zeitung*, May 27, 1870, 4, col. 1. March 21, 1845, was Good Friday. (For the route taken by the immigrants, see map, Chapter VII, 152.)

[21]See above, 112, footnote 3. There is extant a map of Indianola (Carlshafen) which shows the farms of George Thielepape and Theodore Mueller, both of whom were among the first immigrants. The map shows also numerous town lots, but it does not give the names of the owners. From Mr. E. W. Winkler, Librarian of the University of Texas, who owns a copy of this map, the writer was able to get a copy, which is given in Appendix D.

[22]Seele, H., "Meine Ankunft in Neu Braunfels," in *Kalender der Neu Braunfelser Zeitung fuer 1914*, 36-43.

hafen.[23]   Then, too, there were some Germans in Galveston and
on Cummins Creek east of La Grange in Fayette County who
expressed a desire to Prince Solms to become colonists of the
Society.[24]   Prince Solms, in his tenth report, made in camp on
Comal Creek on March 27, 1845, wrote that thirty-one wagons
had arrived and that he expected the remaining half of the settlers
to arrive in a few days.[25]   The five Bremen brigs, *Weser, John
Dethard, Ferdinand, Herrschel,* and *Apollo* brought only four hundred and thirty-nine men, women, and children to Galveston and
Carlshafen in July, November, and December, 1844.   With these
facts taken into consideration, the conclusion is that only about
two hundred persons were present at the founding of New Braunfels on Good Friday, March 21, 1845.[26]

Very little time was lost in giving the immigrants some land.
Each head of a family and single man over the age of seventeen
got a half-acre town lot and a ten-acre farm lot, which, however,

[23]"Berichte an den Adelsverein," in *Kalender,* 37; Photostat *Original Berichte,* 57.   Prince Solms said that only a few families of this
group survived the summer of 1844.

[24]"Berichte an den Adelsverein," in *Kalender,* 37; Photostat *Original
Berichte,* 57.

[25]"Berichte an den Adelsverein," in *Kalender,* 62; Photostat *Original
Berichte,* 93.

[26]The five immigrant ships arrived at Galveston on the following
dates: The *Weser,* July 8, the *John Dethard,* November 29, the *Ferdinand,* December 14, the *Herrschel,* December 18, and the *Apollo,* December 20, 1844.   There were one hundred and three families listed on these
five ships, but in three instances the immigrant's wife and children
were to come later, and one man came over as a widower with four children.   There were one hundred and thirty-four children, while the number of single men over the age of seventeen was one hundred and three.
Thus the five ships brought over a total of four hundred and thirty-nine
men, women, and children.   The immigrant lists from which these figures are taken are found in Colonization Papers, 1843-1845, Texas State
Library.   It should be stated that there is another immigrant list in
the Colonization Papers, 1846-1873, which gives a total of 318 men,
women, and children, instead of 299, the number given in Colonization
Papers, 1843-1845, for the immigrants brought over by the *John Dethard,*
the *Ferdinand,* and the *Herrschel.*
The *Neu Braunfelser Zeitung,* in its issue of May 27, 1870, gave a
list of 167 names with the comment that the list was as complete as it
could be made.   It is claimed for this list that it contains the names of
immigrants who were present at the founding of New Braunfels.   On
May 8, 1895, the *Neu Braunfelser Zeitung* published another list in
which 207 immigrant names appeared, but it is not claimed that these
persons were all present at the founding of New Braunfels.   A third
list, containing 220 names of pioneer settlers of New Braunfels and
vicinity, appeared in the *Neu Braunfelser Zeitung,* July 22, 1926, 6,
cols. 2 and 3, and 7, col. 1.   (See Appendix E for lists.)

THE SOPHIENBURG

From a print in the *Alamo Magazine* of April, 1914

were not to take the place of the 160- and 320-acre tracts specified in the immigration agreements. Some of the immigrants set to work at once to get their farm lots into condition for planting, but others, feeling that the Society was obligated to support them, planted neither corn nor potatoes, although it was not too late in the season for either.[27] After the farm lots were planted, as well as during spare moments before that time, the settlers began to build their cabins to replace the tents which the Society had furnished them upon their arrival at the settlement. For the protection of the settlers a stockade was built on the east bank of Comal Creek and named the *Zinkenburg,* in honor of Nicolaus Zink, the surveyor, who platted the settlement into town and farm lots. Work was started, too, on the Society's buildings on the *Vereinsberg.*[28] In his last report, dated April 30, 1845, Prince Solms said that the cabins of the settlers were gradually beginning to go up. He regretted, however, that the Society's buildings were not making much headway and that very little had as yet been done on the Society's large storehouse. A shed, built for taking care of some of the Society's goods, was so leaky that many of the food supplies spoiled, especially four wagonloads of corn. Zink, in charge of construction work for the Society, offered as an excuse that there was a scarcity of workers, since each man was looking after his own interests first. On April 28 Prince Solms laid the cornerstone of the fort which was erected on the *Vereinsberg* for the protection of the settlers. The fort was named the *Sophienburg,* in honor of Sophia, princess of Salm-Salm, Prince Solms's lady love. For the cornerstone laying the Prince gave the officials

[27]Photostat *Original Berichte,* 95. No reference is given here to the "Berichte an den Adelsverein," in *Kalender,* because in this, as in a few other instances, the *Kalender* omitted a part of the original.

Hermann Seele, who arrived in New Braunfels on May 6, said that his friend, Eduard von Hartz, one of the first settlers, told him that there was dissatisfaction among the settlers and that only a few understood that Prince Solms had done the best under the circumstances. Some accepted their town and farm lots with great reluctance and demanded to be taken to the grant; others sold their lots for a song, abused the Society for not keeping its promise, and demanded to be supported by the Society. (See Seele, H., "Meine Ankunft in Neu Braunfels," *Kalender der Neu Braunfelser Zeitung fuer 1914,* 41.)

[28]The *Vereinsberg* is a hill just west of the present freight depot of the Missouri Pacific Railroad and rises about thirty feet above the flat on which the principal business and the old residence section of New Braunfels lies.

See also Appendix D, *Karte der Stadt Neu Braunfels.*

and employees a holiday. In the absence of a German flag the black and yellow flag of Austria was raised on the site of the fort and salvos of cannon were fired to add to the effect. At the same time the settlers assembled on the market place, raised the flag of the Republic of Texas on an improvised flagstaff, elected Lt. Oscar von Claren commandant, and organized a company for the protection of the settlement against the Indians.[29]

Prince Solms remained in New Braunfels for only a short while after the settlement was founded. The Society had acceded to his request to send some capable person in his stead, in order that he might return home. In his last report, the eleventh, dated April 30, he said that Baron von Meusebach, whom the Society sent to Texas as its second commissioner-general, had written from New Orleans on April 6 that he was on his way to New Braunfels. Prince Solms set Thursday, May 15, for the date of his departure from New Braunfels. He wanted to reach Boston by the middle of June, in order that he might get a boat bound for Europe at that time. He was anxious to give the Society some first-hand information about a few necessary changes in the Society's colonization program.[30] The changes that Prince Solms had in mind were, in brief, as follows: *first,* to select the emigrants with great care, for only efficient and worthy persons could make the colony prosper; *second,* to charge the settlers five times as much as formerly for the trip from Galveston to the colony lands and to require them to pay cash for all goods bought by them from the Society after their deposit with the Society had been used up; *third,* to require that those settlers sent over by the Society at its own expense should bind themselves to work for the Society for one year, during which time the Society was to furnish them with the necessary supplies; and *fourth,* to establish from four to six settlements between New Braunfels and the Fisher and Miller grant, promising the emigrants land in the grant as before, but

---

[29]"Berichte an den Adelsverein," in *Kalender,* 63; Photostat *Original Berichte,* 94; Seele, H., "Meine Ankunft in Neu Braunfels," in *Kalender der Neu Braunfelser Zeitung fuer 1914,* 40-41.

Seele says that when he and other immigrants arrived in New Braunfels in May the view that presented itself to them was a large grass-grown flat on which a few trees, tents, fences, and huts stood scattered about, with here and there a cabin, and the *Vereinsberg* with the huts, sheds, and tents of the colonial officials.

[30]"Berichte an den Adelsverein," in *Kalender,* 63-64; Photostat *Original Berichte,* 95-96.

JOHN O. MEUSEBACH
Second Commissioner-General of the Society and
Founder of Fredericksburg
From a photograph in the possession of Mrs. Ernst Marschall,
Llano, Texas

requiring them to accept temporarily ten acres in one of these settlements. Prince Solms also wanted to have the Society establish settlements between Carlshafen and New Braunfels.

Late in May Baron von Meusebach[31] arrived in New Braunfels. He found the finances of the colonial establishment in a very unsatisfactory condition, but his university training in political economy and finance enabled him to bring order into the financial affairs. The financial muddle existing at the time of Meusebach's arrival in New Braunfels had come about because the commissioner-general, the treasurer, the doctor, and the engineer all had contracted debts in the name of the Society without making any record of them. They had signed promissory notes and had issued certificates of credit. Meusebach could not determine immediately the amount of the debts incurred and, although he had a letter of credit from the Society for $10,000, decided to set out for Galveston to confer with Prince Solms. He found Prince Solms still there, but he got no definite information from him.

[31]Baron Ottfried Hans von Meusebach, known in Texas by the name of John O. Meusebach, under which he was naturalized as a citizen of Texas and of the United States, was born in Dillenburg, Nassau, on May 26, 1812, where his father held the position of solicitor. Meusebach studied mining and natural science at the academy of mining and forestry in Clausthal in the Harz Mountains. At the universities of Bonn and Halle he studied law, political economy, and finance. For a while he served the Prussian government as an official connected with the Supreme Court of Justice at Naumburg and Stettin, after which he held an administrative position at Stettin. The royal government at Stettin sent him as a commissioner to Anclam to bring order into the communal affairs of that place. On February 24, 1845, he was appointed to succeed Prince Solms as commissioner-general of the Society for the Protection of German Immigrants in Texas. During his tenure of this position he founded Fredericksburg, Castell, and Leiningen, and made a treaty with the Comanche Indians. On July 20, 1847, he was succeeded by Hermann Spiess. In 1851 he was elected State Senator for the district comprising the counties of Bexar, Medina, and Comal. On September 28, 1852, he married Agnes, the countess of Coreth. In February, 1854, Governor E. M. Pease appointed him commissioner for the "Colony of the German Emigration Company," in which capacity he issued land certificates to the immigrants brought to Texas by the Society for the Protection of German Immigrants in Texas. For a while he farmed at Comanche Springs in Bexar County, where he was also justice of the peace. Then he moved to Waco Springs on the Guadalupe, a few miles above New Braunfels. After living in Fredericksburg for a few years, he moved to his farm half way between Fredericksburg and Mason and laid out the town of Loyal Valley, where he was justice of the peace, notary public, and postmaster. On May 27, 1897, he died at Loyal Valley, one of the noted pioneers of the Republic of Texas. (Penniger, *Fest-Ausgabe*, 56-58; *San Antonio Express*, January 10, 1926, 17, cols. 1-8.)

In fact, he had to use a part of the ten thousand dollars to rescue Prince Solms from the clutches of creditors by paying the bills which they presented. Meusebach got the promise from Prince Solms that he would prevail upon Count Castell to send Meusebach another letter of credit for $20,000, an amount which Meusebach estimated was necessary to meet the demands of those creditors who had presented bills to him on his first trip from Carlshafen to New Braunfels, as well as in New Braunfels. Upon his return to the settlement Meusebach set to work to draw up a statement of the Society's financial affairs and found that a debt of at least $19,460.02 had been contracted by his predecessor for transportation and provisions. He sent this statement to the Society, but no new credit was sent him.[32] Through strict economy and sound business methods he succeeded in quieting the creditors of the Society and in winning the confidence of the settlers. The dissatisfaction among the settlers disappeared and they set themselves to the tasks before them.

The settlement at New Braunfels attracted attention immediately among the Anglo-American population. Almost three years had passed before they had heard that a German colony of 10,000 settlers was to be founded in Texas. Now that the first settlement had been made, the *Telegraph and Texas Register* printed the following news:

We have learned with pleasure that the Colony of Germans near Seguin is in a remarkably flourishing condition. The Colonists are located on the tract of land about six miles above Seguin. They have erected many comfortable houses, have enclosed many acres of excellent arable land, and have planted it with corn and garden vegetables. They are also collecting a large stock of sheep and cattle. They appear to be remarkably contented with their

---

[32]Penniger, *Fest-Ausgabe*, 46-47.

When Prince Solms got to New Orleans, other creditors molested him and subjected him to a number of indignities. Fortunately Meusebach had given Prince Solms $6000 to settle accounts in New Orleans. Prince Solms wrote from New Orleans on June 11 that a balance of $2626.40 remained, which sum he had turned over to F. W. von Wrede, Jr. Prince Solms blamed Henry Francis Fisher for the insults offered him by the New Orleans creditors. (See Prince Solms to (Meusebach?), New Orleans, June 11, 1845; Henry Francis Fisher Papers, 1840-1849, University of Texas.

In his *Reminiscences*, Sam Maverick mentions that Prince Solms stopped over night with him at Deckrow's Point on his way to Galveston. (Maverick, Sam, *Reminiscences*, p. 20 of typewritten copy in University of Texas Library.)

new homes, and are confident of success. The Prince de Solms
has left the Colony and intends to return to Europe. His place
has already been supplied by a new agent from Germany, who is a
gentleman of great intelligence, and is much respected by the
Colonists.[33]

Early the following year the *La Grange Intelligencer* published
the following correspondence from New Braunfels, dated December
17, 1845. It read:

There are already about 300 frame buildings, and the people
appear to be busily employed in constructing more. The present
population is estimated at 1500. . . . There is now in New
Braunfels one good variety store, (owned) by Messrs. Ferguson
and Hesler, six groceries, one silver smith shop, one copper smith,
one saddler, six shoemaker shops, one painter, three tailor shops,
three blacksmith shops, two gunsmith shops, four cabinetmaker
shops, one wagon maker shop, one lock maker, two tanyards, three
cigar manufacturers, and one baker. Besides these, there are
other mechanics who are intended for the upper settlements. The
company have two engineers, one of whom will proceed with the
expedition soon to set out for the upper part of the grant. The
present prosperity and rapid growth of this colony must equally
delight and surprise every person who visits it. The director,
Baron Menseback (*sic*), offers encouragement to all people, especially Americans, to settle in the colony, and enter into unrestricted
intercourse, with the colonists. The enlightened and republican
liberality is in remarkable contrast with the policy of his predecessor, and deservedly recommends the colony to the favorable consideration of their future government. It is proper here to remark that Baron Menseback has the reputation of being an accomplished scholar of superior scientific attainments. He has
turned his attention to the geological characters of the country,
and has already discovered some valuable minerals. I understand
he has found coal of a good quality on the Guadalupe, and iron ore
on the Pirdenales. . . . The soil in this place is of the best
quality; it is of a light mulatto color, and of a waxy texture, and
is apparently easy cultivated. Yet I do not see much attention
bestowed on agriculture. This is a point of great importance in
the present stage of the colony. A little neglect in planting at
the proper time must be the occasion of inconvenience, if not
suffering another year.[34]

[33]*Telegraph and Texas Register*, May 28, 1845, 2, col. 4.
[34]*La Grange Intelligencer*, January 24, 1846, 1, col. 4 to 2, col. 1.
This same description of New Braunfels is found in *Democratic Telegraph and Texas Register*, March 4, 1846, 2, col. 4, although differently
arranged.

The first summer in Texas was, indeed, a trying one for the immigrants, but there was much work to do for those who were in earnest about making a success. Those who had come early enough to get a plot of ground into cultivation were kept busy for a few months with their crops. With the exception of the single men, the others were all interested in getting their cabins built. Some, of course, were so well supplied financially that they did not have to work and could spend their time as their desires dictated. Others found employment with the Society. When the weather permitted, Rev. L. C. Ervendberg conducted services regularly every Sunday under a beautiful group of oak trees at the foot of the *Vereinsberg*. A rustic table covered with a white cloth, on which was embroidered a black cross, served the combined purposes of an altar and a pulpit. The Society's officials sat on a long bench made of a thick board, the rest of the people stood. On October the fifth the German Protestant congregation was organized by the election of presbyters and became thus the oldest corporation in Comal County. The Society helped the congregation to build its first church, a frame structure of medium size. The dedication services were held on March 22, 1846. At the same place where Rev. Ervendberg conducted the first services, Hermann Seele opened the first German-English school in West Texas on August 11, 1845.[35] By the end of the summer the settlement had become definitely established. What might have become of it without the steadying influence of Meusebach's presence is a matter of speculation.

The arrival of new immigrants in the winter of 1845-1846 increased not only the financial and managerial burdens of Meusebach but added also considerably to the population of New Braunfels. About the first of November, 1845, Meusebach received word from the Society that it was sending 4304 emigrants to Texas and that it had established a credit for $24,000 with a New Orleans firm. By this time, however, the Society's debts in Texas had reached almost this sum, so that in reality there was not a dollar in the treasury when the new immigrants landed at Carlshafen. The situation was distressing. Meusebach decided not to let the immigrants know that the Society was practically bankrupt, since

---

[35]Seele, H., "Ein Beitrag zur Geschichte von Neu Braunfels," in Schuetze, *Jahrbuch fuer Texas* (*1882*), 39-40.

L. C. ERVENDBERG
First Minister of the Society
From a photograph in the possession of Mr. Carl Roeper,
New Braunfels, Texas

HERMANN F. SEELE
First Teacher of the Society
From a photograph in the possession of Mrs. George Eiband,
New Braunfels, Texas

they had trusted the promises of the Society. He did not even let the Society's officials know. He hoped that new credits might arrive from Europe. Meusebach spent much thought on the problem of the Society's finances in Texas. He was absent from New Braunfels at various times for the purpose of establishing a credit for the Society with some of the large plantation owners and merchants in the lower part of the State. Meusebach bought large quantities of food supplies, mainly corn, in order to be able to properly care for the immigrants. Some of the settlers mistook his trips as efforts to dodge them and to avoid paying them the deposits which they had made with the Society before leaving Germany. Meusebach's patience with the Society gave out finally in the spring of 1846 after he had made a trip to New Orleans and had been unable to get the correspondent of the Society's banker to accept Nassau Farm as security for a loan. On his return trip, Meusebach conferred with D. H. Klaener, the Society's agent, who had mortgaged his business and everything he had in the interests of the Society. About this conference and its results, Meusebach says in his *Answer to Interrogatories:* "I told him that our last remedy would be the public press in Germany, that I could not do it in my capacity as trustee of the Company, but that he might make a correct statement of the sufferings of the emigrants on account of the failure of the Company to come up to their promises. He did so, and that action had the desired effect. Then, and not until then, *extraordinary efforts were made to raise money on a larger scale.* A credit of $60,000 was opened at once, and the notice was brought over to me by an extraordinary messenger, Mr. Cappes."[36]

---

[36]Penniger, *Fest-Ausgabe*, 48-49; Meusebach, *Answer to Interrogatories*, 16-21.

Meusebach, in his invaluable pamphlet, *Answer to Interrogatories*, estimated that he needed about $140,000 to take care of the Society's financial needs. His figures follow:

1. For paying off the floating debt........................$ 24,000.00
2. For goods and provisions to take care of 5000 persons or less, for three months................................ 45,000.00
3. For land transportation of 4304 immigrants............ 33,161.60
4. For houses to be built in the colony.................. 12,000.00
5. For paying drafts or orders for deposits made by immigrants 26,067.00

Total $140,228.60

(See Meusebach, *Answer to Interrogatories*, 16-18. These figures are

It is impossible, of course, to say how many of the immigrants actually went to New Braunfels. Some, it should be pointed out, went on to the next settlement at Fredericksburg; others remained in Galveston, Houston, Carlshafen, and in some of the German settlements in the lower Brazos, Colorado, and Guadalupe region; while still others, as will be shown, died either at Carlshafen or after leaving there in the spring and summer of 1846.[37]

given also in Penniger, *Fest-Ausgabe*, 49; Tiling, *German Element in Texas*, 82; Benjamin, *Germans in Texas*, 48, footnote 100.)

The Klaener letter was addressed to Mr. Schmidt, mayor of Bremen, and was given to the press. Although the letter of credit for $60,000 was dated in Germany on July 14, 1846, it was not until September, 1846, that word was received in New Braunfels. Count Castell, in writing to Meusebach on June 10, said that the Klaener letter had "made the worst impression" and that various German governments were calling for an explanation.

In a correspondence from Wiesbaden, dated July 10, 1846, entitled "Die Deutschen in Texas," which appeared in a prominent newspaper in Bremen, the assertion is made that at a general meeting of the stockholders of the Society a total credit of $120,000 (300,000 florins) was voted in two sums of 50,000 and 250,000 florins on July 10 and 14, respectively. It seems, however, that $60,000 was the actual amount that was sent; at least that is what Meusebach received. Since the Society did not have the money on hand, it was necessary for Count Castell to go to Frankfort to secure a loan from the banking firm of the Rothschilds. Duke Adolf of Nassau furnished the security for the loan. (*Weser-Zeitung*, July 15, 1846.)

The new credit, large as it was, did not suffice to meet the Society's obligations, which had reached the total of almost $100,000. The creditors of the Society in New Braunfels, especially the settlers who had deposited money with the Society, now demanded that they be paid. Cappes, the messenger, it seems, intrigued with Henry Francis Fisher and incited the dissatisfied element against Meusebach. On December 31, 1846, a group of persons appeared at the *Sophienburg* and wanted to hang Meusebach, but they did not molest him, for he faced his opponents in his courageous and fearless manner. He declared that he had already sent in his resignation to the Society and offered to turn over the affairs between the Society and the immigrants to Cappes. But Cappes declined to assume the responsibility. (See Meusebach, *Answer to Interrogatories*, 20-21; Kapp, *Aus und ueber Amerika*, I, 264; Loeher, *Geschichte und Zustaende der Deutschen in Amerika*, 332; Tiling, *German Element in Texas*, 88-90; Roemer, *Texas*, 219; Hermes, Wm., Sr., "Erlebnisse eines deutschen Pioniers in Texas," *La Grange Deutsche Zeitung*, August 19, 1915, 11, col. 1.)

[37]The records in Colonization Papers, 1843-1845, Texas State Library, indicate that between October 22, 1845, and February 15, 1846, including the "*John Dethard*" and "*Ferdinand*," which arrived in Galveston on June 24, 1845, a total of 27 ships brought 3236 immigrants to Galveston for the Society. Of this number four ships came from Antwerp, eighteen from Bremen, and the others from New York and New Orleans. In Adams, *British Correspondence Concerning Texas*, 574, a list of twenty-one ships is given in a report by Consul Kennedy. These ships had on board 3084 immigrants. The list omits some of the ships given in the records of the Colonization Papers, but includes three ships not

The increase in the population of New Braunfels had some direct results for the settlement. Early in the year 1846 New Braunfels was organized as a precinct of Bexar County. G. F. Kirchner was elected county commissioner and Arnold Henkel von Donnersmark justice of the peace.[38] This arrangement did not last long, however, for on March 24, 1846, the first legislature of the State of Texas passed an act creating Comal County.[39] On July 13, 1846, the first election for county officers was held. The following officers were elected: M. A. Dooley, chief justice; L. C. Ervendberg, probate judge; Henry Bevenroth, Stephan Klein, John W. Kreitz, and Gabriel Sacherer, county commissioners; Conrad Seabaugh, county clerk; Hermann Seele, district clerk; Henry Gervin, sheriff; Carl Wiedenfeld, county treasurer; Julius Rennert, justice of the peace; and Carl Bellmer, constable.[40] Dr. Ferdinand Roemer, who was in New Braunfels at the time, says that the people were greatly excited over the election.[41]

The spring and summer of 1846 proved very trying on the inhabitants of New Braunfels. The winter of 1845-1846 had brought with it a considerable amount of rain, so that very few of the immigrants could be moved from Carlshafen to New Braunfels.[42]

---

[38]Seele, H., "Ein Beitrag zur Geschichte von Neu Braunfels," in Schuetze, Albert, *Jahrbuch fuer Texas* (*1882*), 38.

[39]Gammel, *Laws of Texas*, II, 1319.

[40]Seele, *A Short Sketch of Comal County*, 5; Seele, "Ein Beitrag zur Geschichte von Neu Braunfels," in *Jahrbuch fuer Texas* (*1882*), 41-42. Although he was not a candidate, Viktor Bracht says that he got as many votes for the office of district clerk as Hermann Seele. (See Bracht, *Texas im Jahre 1848*, 241-242.)

[41]Roemer, *Texas*, 218.

[42]D. H. Klaener, agent of the Society at Galveston, who was under contract to transport the immigrants from Galveston to Carlshafen and to supply them with provisions, became the object of a scathing, adverse criticism. The *Weser-Zeitung*, published at Bremen, was the medium through which the criticism was brought before the people of Germany. Klaener was accused of delaying some of the immigrants at Galveston and at Carlshafen in order that he might reap a maximum profit from his contract for furnishing supplies. The delay crowded more and more people into the insufficient accommodations provided by the Society at Carlshafen, thus bringing on disease that developed into a terrible epidemic, for which Klaener was held responsible. He was also charged with refusing to pay out to the immigrants the deposits which they had made with the Society in Bremen and Antwerp. (*Weser-Zeitung*, July 15, 1846.)

In defense of Klaener two of his friends, Friedrich Leo Quentell and

Disease broke out among them and developed into an epidemic. The germs of the disease were brought to New Braunfels when the immigrants were finally moved from Carlshafen. The warmer the weather became, the more the disease spread.[43] Dr. Roemer says that two and three persons died in New Braunfels every day. Precautionary measures were taken and efforts were made to provide suitable shelter for the many sick persons who were coming up from Carlshafen. On the banks of the Comal a long shed, which

John A. Droege of Bremen, published excerpts from four letters written to them by Klaener, which, they claimed, were not written for publication. In these letters, dated New Orleans, March 19, and Galveston, April 30, and May 8 and May 15, 1846, Klaener regretted that the accommodations at Carlshafen were insufficient, stated that the unusually long rainy season was the reason why the immigrants were not being moved up to New Braunfels, said that he was negotiating with capitalists in New Orleans to operate a steamship line from Galveston to Carlshafen for transporting the immigrants, and claimed that he had advanced $20,-000 of his own means to prevent the immigrants from starving. He feared that an epidemic might break out at Carlshafen and stated that the authorities of Galveston were pressing him to remove the immigrants from the island in order to prevent the occurrence of an epidemic. Because these statements were made by Klaener before the charges, his friends thought that they were a sufficient answer to the charges. (*Weser-Zeitung*, July 17, 1846.)

Klaener wrote a reply to the charges on September 5, 1846, for publication in the *Weser-Zeitung*. His answer to the charges, which he branded as a finely-spun fabrication, is in the main a repetition of the statements made in the letters to his Bremen friends. He stated that the Society had adopted a resolution expressing confidence in him and approval of his work. (*Weser-Zeitung*, November 8, 1846.)

On the same day on which he replied to the scathing article he wrote a long letter to Smidt, the burgomaster of Bremen, in which he discussed the charges. He repeated what he had said in the letter to the *Weser-Zeitung* and in the letters to his friends. He pointed out that Cappes, whom the Society had sent to Texas as a special commissioner in the summer of 1846, had approved his policy of detaining immigrants at Galveston. Meusebach, too, who had been in Galveston from December 24, 1845, until February 16, 1846, at the very time when so many immigrants were arriving, had never uttered one word in disapproval of the way in which Klaener was handling the situation. (*Ibid.*, November 8, 1846. The date of publication of this letter was not stated by the archivist of the Bremen Library when making the transcript. Since it was written on the same day with the letter addressed to the *Weser-Zeitung*, it may be presumed that it was published about the same time.)

[43]The epidemic was caused by a disease known as petechial fever (*Blutfleckenkrankheit*), as Dr. Wm. Hermes, Sr., called it. Dr. Hermes, who came to Texas late in October, 1846, and lived for a while in Fredericksburg and Castell, said that he experienced the disease himself and when he studied medicine later on he found the symptoms described in Schoenlein, *Pathology and Therapeutics*. (Hermes, Wm., Sr., "Erlebnisse eines deutschen Pioniers in Texas," *La Grange Deutsche Zeitung*, August 19, 1915, 11, col. 2.) The disease was accompanied by a very severe fever, during which small crimson spots, caused by an extravasation of

came to be called the hospital, was erected, where the sick were taken and visited daily by Dr. Theodore Koester. Dr. Wm. Remer was engaged to give medical attention to the immigrants on their way from Carlshafen to New Braunfels.[44] It became necessary, in view of the many deaths, to provide for an orphans' home. The total number of deaths is variously estimated; some say that only about 400 persons died, others place the number as high as 1200. Ervendberg, who was probate judge and later manager of the orphans' asylum in New Braunfels, estimated the number at 400, but his estimate does not take into account those who died in Fredericksburg, probably about 100. Bracht estimated the number at between 450 and 500, exclusive of the deaths at Fredericksburg; Olmsted listed 304 deaths in New Braunfels alone; and Penniger, who included the deaths for Fredericksburg, gave an estimate of 850.[45] To a certain extent the Society must be held responsible for the many deaths that resulted, because it sent too many immigrants to Texas in the winter of 1845 to 1846. The Society did not have enough accommodations at Carlshafen to take care of the immigrants, especially when the rainy season set in. However, the Society could not foresee the rainy winter. When the war between the United States and Mexico broke out, the United States paid such high wages to private teamsters that the Society

blood into surrounding tissues after a rupture of the vessels, appeared on the body. Petechial fever is called epidemic cerebro-spinal meningitis in Webster, *New International Dictionary*. Others described the disease as scurvy accompanied with dysentery. (See Penniger, *Fest-Ausgabe*, 83.)

The epidemic gave the opponents of the Society an opportunity to indulge in a merciless criticism. Among these were Kapp, *Aus und weber Amerika*, I, 269-275; Loeher, Franz, *Geschichte und Zustaende der Deutschen in Amerika*, 352; Eickhoff, *In der neuen Heimath*, 331; Soergel, *Neueste Nachrichten aus Texas*, 23-24.

Sam Maverick makes mention of this epidemic in his *Reminiscences*, p. 21.

[44]The writer found a day book kept by Dr. F. B. Webb of Leesburg, Gonzales County, in which Dr. Webb recorded in alphabetical order the various immigrants of the Society to whom he gave medical attention in 1846. In all there were 72 patients and the amount of the charges made for consultation and medicine was $1059.92¾. Dr. Webb generally stated the formula for each medicine he prescribed, together with the cost of each ingredient. (See Republic of Texas Colonization Papers, 1846-1873, No. 2825, File Box 29, Texas State Library.)

[45]Bracht, *Texas im Jahre 1848*, 244; Olmsted, F. L., *Wanderungen durch Texas und im merikanischen Grenzlande*, 129; Penniger, *Fest-Ausgabe*, 50; Roemer, *Texas*, 218, 220; Tiling, *German Element in Texas*, 87-88; Benjamin, *Germans in Texas*, 49; Goldbeck, Fritz, *Seit fuenfzig Jahren*, 13; Mgebroff, *Evangelisch-Lutherische Synode in Texas*, 4-7.

had to rely almost wholly on its own transportation equipment to take the immigrants to New Braunfels.[46]

When Dr. Roemer, the geologist, reached New Braunfels in 1846 he recorded various observations about the place and its people. These observations are given here in condensed form:

There were about 100 houses of different sizes, in which the people lived very crowded. On the main street, called Seguin Street, I noticed a house with three signs: "Apotheke," "Dr. Koester," and "Baeckerei." The combination of a bakery *(Baeckerei)* with the practice of medicine and the business of selling drugs struck me as very unusual. On the same street stood the Evangelical Church of the settlement and beside it the small cabin of Rev. Ervendberg, who preached on Sundays, taught on week days, and in his spare time tilled his cornfield and his garden "in the sweat of his brow." On the market place stood the principal tavern, owned by von Coll and von Wedemeyer, both in the employ of the Society. Ferguson and Hessler owned a variety store on the square and enjoyed a good business. The third house on the square was the inn, whose owner, Arnold Henkel von Donnersmark, came with the first settlers. At the end of the main street stood a small blockhouse, the restaurant of the place, where daily ten or twelve young men, mostly former lieutenants, adventurers, and students, gathered for three square meals of coffee, corn bread, and meat, and sometimes wild turkey or venison.[47]

In January, 1847, Alwin Soergel visited New Braunfels and described the settlement as follows:

The old clumsy huts have disappeared and have given place to a number of neat and permanent houses, about 300 in number. The fields are no longer neglected on account of the more pressing need of providing shelter. The fields are being fenced and plowed, so that in the coming summer a good crop of corn, potatoes, and vegetables may be expected. The inhabitants have a good income from business with the new arrivals and with travelers between San Antonio and Austin. Wages fluctuate but are never lower than fifty cents per day. A town lot costs from sixty to three hundred dollars, and land is sold for from two to five dollars an acre. The number of settlers in New Braunfels and vicinity is probably between 1500 and 2000.[48]

---

[46]Penniger, *Fest-Ausgabe*, 50.

[47]Roemer, "*Texas*, 118-124. Before coming to New Braunfels, Ferguson and Hessler had been engaged in business on the island of St. Thomas in the West Indies. (Bracht, *Texas im Jahre 1848*, 233-234.)

[48]Soergel, *Neueste Nachrichten aus Texas*, 27. Soergel admits that

Although New Braunfels was incorporated by act of the legislature on May 11, 1846,[49] the election for the ratification of the charter was not held until 1847. Since the chief justice of Bexar County failed to call the election, as was his duty under the act, the chief justice of Comal County ordered an election for June 7, 1847, at which time the charter was ratified and the first officers were elected.[50] The first city officials were: Gustav Hoffmann, mayor; A. Forcke, Julius Rennert, Dr. Theodor Koester, F. W. Specht, G. Ullrich, H. Zuschlag, F. Heidemeyer, and J. Jahn, aldermen; G. Dreiss, city secretary; Carl Bellmer, city treasurer. On July 1, 1847, Gabriel Remmler was made city marshal, and on July 12, 1847, Johannes Ludewig succeeded Carl Bellmer as city treasurer.[51]

Although agriculture continued to be the occupation of most of the settlers in New Braunfels, the various crafts were always represented in the population. It was not industry on any appreciable scale that developed in any of these trades. But in the sawmill and flour mill business considerable progress was made. In 1847 Wm. H. Merriweather built the first grist and sawmill, now Landa's Mills, on a channel dug from the Comal River in 1846 and 1847. By 1850 the United States Census showed that Merriweather's mill, using water power, turned out 10,000 bushels of meal and 50,000 feet of lumber, valued at $10,000.[52]

he had changed his opinion of New Braunfels since his former visit in March of the previous year. (See Soergel, *Fuer Auswanderungslustige*, 43-46.) Alwin Soergel, a merchant of Eisleben, Germany, was one of the Society's colonists and came to Texas on the Bremen bark *Franciska*, which arrived at Galveston on February 5, 1846, with 234 immigrants on board. Not desiring to go to Carlshafen and wait there until the Society would take him to New Braunfels, he and two companions left the others at Galveston, went to Houston, and then by way of the German settlements in Colorado and Fayette County to Carlshafen and thence to New Braunfels. He was so displeased with conditions there, however, that upon his return to Fayette County he bought a hundred acres of land on Cummins Creek. His book, *Fuer Auswanderungslustige*, is unfriendly to the Society.

49Gammel, *Laws of Texas*, II, 582-585.

50Gammel, *Laws of Texas*, III, 393-394. This statute, March 16, 1848, validated the election of mayor and aldermen and also the ratification of the charter.

51*Kalender der Neu Braunfelser Zeitung fuer 1918*, 15.

52Seventh Census, Schedule 5: Productions of Industry; Texas State Library. The other industries listed in the census, together with quantity and value of output are: Abel and Andress, saw and grist mill, 10,000 bushels of meal and 100,000 feet of lumber, value $15,000; Hermann Spiess, 100,000 shingles, value $4,000; Frederick Tolle, 150 hides, $800; D. H. Coleman, 1150 saddle trees, value

New immigrants arrived in the winter of 1846 to 1847, some of whom settled in Comaltown, which was laid out by Rafael C. Garza in 1846, across the Comal River, and in Hortontown, on the Horton League across the Guadalupe River along the San Antonio-Nacogdoches road.[53] The state census for 1847 showed that Comal County had 144 voters among its total white population of 533 males and 384 females. There were also 51 slaves.[54]

In 1848 the Western Texas Orphan Asylum was incorporated. L. Bene, H. Spiess, and L. C. Ervendberg were "constituted a body politic and corporate . . . for the purpose of founding, erecting, and maintaining an institution for the protection, support, and education of orphan children." Comal County was named in the act for the site of the asylum. In 1850 a supplementary act allowed the directors to establish an "agricultural school and such other institutions of learning, in any branch of the arts and sciences, as they may deem proper."[55]

On May 1, 1848, an act became effective which was of considerable importance to the immigrants. It authorized the governor to appoint a commissioner to issue certificates for land in the Fisher and Miller grant upon hearing proof that the immigrant was entitled to land. If the grantee did not move on the land within two years from the date of receiving the certificate, the certificate was to lapse. The act was to remain in force for one year only. The commissioner was to have an office both at New Braunfels and Fredericksburg, in order that as many as possible might take advantage of the provisions of the act.[56]

$4,000; E. G. Branch, 200,000 shingles, value $8,000; Henry Kuntz, 50,-000 loaves of bread, value $2,500; August Iwala, blacksmith work, $2,500.

[53]Seele, "Ein Beitrag zur Geschichte von Neu Braunfels," in *Jahrbuch fuer Texas* (*1882*), 41.

[54]*Texas State Gazette*, August 25, 1849, 5, col. 2. For the year 1848 the State census showed that the county had a population of 1465, made up of 796 white males, 614 white females, and 55 slaves. The census figures are quite at variance with the estimate given above, p. 132, which gave 1500. Compared with the census figures for 1848, the figures for 1847 are probably too low.

[55]Gammel, *Laws of Texas*, III, 403-404, 701-702. The census of 1850 showed that this institution had fifty acres of improved and two hundred acres of unimproved land valued together at $5,000, and that four hundred bushels of corn and one hundred pounds of tobacco were raised.

[56]Gammel, *Laws of Texas*, III, 146-149. Seven other acts were passed by the Legislature of Texas bearing on the Fisher and Miller Colony. The first of these was passed on January 21, 1850, and granted 640 and 320 acres of land to heads of families and single men, respectively. The

For the first time since the founding of New Braunfels the settlers had an opportunity in 1848 of expressing their opinions in a
presidential election. The electors for the Democratic nominee,
Cass, received 106 votes, while the Whig electors for Taylor got
only 14.[57]   Thus very early the voters of New Braunfels expressed
a preference for the principles of the Democratic party and, during
the period covered by this study, remained loyal to those principles.

In May, 1849, the cholera broke out in New Braunfels and took
a toll of over forty lives, but precautionary measures were taken at
once. The disease was checked and by the end of June there were
no more deaths from it.[58]

Although the first mass service was held in New Braunfels as
early as March, 1846, by the missionary priest, George Menzel,
under a large oak on the banks of Comal Creek, and other missionary priests served the congregation during the next three years, it
was not until 1850 that the congregation was permanently organized by Bishop Claudius M. Dubuis.   In the same year the Catholics built their first church on a plot of ground which the Society
had set aside for them, the former site of the *Zinkenburg*.[59]

The census of 1850 lists a total population of 1723 for Comal
County, including 927 white males, 735 white females, and 61
slaves. The total foreign population amounted to 1230. There
were 367 families and 367 dwellings.   New Braunfels had a population of 1298 and Hortontown 139, the rest of the people living in
the country. New Braunfels was the fourth largest city in Texas
in 1850, only Galveston, San Antonio, and Houston exceeding her
in population. One hundred and thirty pupils were attending
school and there were only thirteen illiterate persons over the age

act was intended to secure to the German Emigration Company and
their colonists the land to which they were entitled and to adjust the
liabilities of the company. (*Ibid.*, III, 492-497.) For the provisions of
the other laws, see *Ibid.*, III, 1469, 1471, 1479-1480, IV, 1443, V, 478-479,
and VIII, 565-566. Reference is made to the first act in Steinert, W.,
Nordamerika vorzueglich Texas im Jahre 1849, 95.

[57]*Texas State Gazette*, September 1, 1849, 13, col. 1.

[58]Seele, "Ein Beitrag zur Geschichte von Neu Braunfels," in *Jahrbuch
fuer Texas* (*1882*), 42; *Democratic Telegraph and Texas Register*, June
21, 1849, 2, col. 6.

[59]*Neu Braunfelser Zeitung*, July 22, 1926, 9, cols. 4-5. This same
number of the *Neu Braunfelser Zeitung*, 9, cols. 1-2, gives a photographic
reproduction of the first Catholic Church building, which shows also the
palisades of the old "*Zinkenburg*," as well as the large oak tree under
which the first mass was held.

of twenty. There were church accommodations for 900 persons. Fifty-five farms with 1704 acres in cultivation were valued at $81,165, including the improvements and implements. Thirty-seven thousand five hundred seventy-five bushels of corn and ten bales of cotton were produced. Manufactures were valued at $46,800.[60]

The population of New Braunfels and Comal County was increasing steadily. In 1854 J. Eggeling, tax assessor and collector of Comal County, made a report which placed the total population at 2592. There were 565 children under the age of six years, 633 between the ages of six and sixteen years, and the adult population over sixteen years consisted of 1394 persons. The value of all taxable property was $519,586. The 77 negro slaves then in the county were valued at $39,850.[61]

On June 23, 1855, the *Texas State Gazette* printed a word picture of New Braunfels, its inhabitants and its industry, an extract of which follows:

At a short distance from the head of the springs, a portion of the water (of the Comal River) is taken from its natural channel and conveyed to a suitable place to secure a waterfall, sufficient to set in motion a Saw and Grist Mill, Cotton Gin and Sash factory. . . . An enterprising citizen of the place intends soon to build a cotton factory. As this is a good country for growing wool, machinery for its manufacture should be added to the list of improvements.

The town of New Braunfels has a population of thirty-five hundred inhabitants, principally Germans; only eight American families have settled in the place. A company of Germans bought a large body of land, including the site of the town, for the purpose of settling emigrants. Although the first settlers were poor, yet by a few years of persevering industry and rigid economy they have placed themselves in easy and independent circumstances.[62]

[60]DeBow, J. D. B., *Statistical View of the United States. Compendium of the Census*, 309-313, 360, 371; De Bow, *The Seventh Census of the United States*, Table II, p. 504.

[61]*Neu Braunfelser Zeitung*, July 21, 1854, 2, col. 5.

[62]*Texas State Gazette*, June 23, 1855, 339, col. 1. In *Deutsch-Texanische Monatshefte*, XI, 63, the following remarks are made about the large industrial plants of New Braunfels: In the years before and immediately after the war, Merriwether's sawmill, now Landa's flour mills, Koester's mill in Comaltown, and Torrey's mill made use of water power. John Torrey was the most enterprising, for he added a sash and door factory and later a woolen mill, but the elements seemed to have conspired against him. His factory was first destroyed by fire, then by a

During his visit to New Braunfels in 1855, Frederick Law Olmsted gave the following description of the town:

The main street of the town . . . was very wide—three times as wide, in effect, as Broadway in New York. The houses, with which it was thickly lined on each side for a mile, were small, low cottages of no pretensions, yet generally looking neat and comfortable. Many were furnished with verandas and gardens, and the greater part were either stuccoed or painted. There were many workshops of mechanics and small stores, . . . and bareheaded women, and men in caps and short jackets, with pendant pipes, were seen everywhere at work.[63]

Of the people and their occupations, Olmsted wrote:

Half the men now residing in New Braunfels and its vicinity are probably agricultural laborers, or farmers, who themselves follow the plough. The majority of the latter do not, I think, own more than ten acres of land each. Within the town itself, there are of master-mechanics, at least, the following numbers, nearly all of whom employ several workmen: carpenters and builders— 20, wagonmakers— 7, blacksmiths— 8, gun and locksmiths— 2, coppersmiths— 1, tinsmiths— 2, machinists— 1, saddlers— 3, shoemakers— 6, turners— 2, tailors— 5, button and fringe-makers— 1, tanners— 3, butchers— 3, and bakers— 4. There are four grist mills, and a couple of New England men are building a sash and blind factory, and propose erecting a cotton factory. . . . There are ten or twelve stores and small tradesmen's shops, two or three apothecaries, and as many physicians, lawyers, and clergymen.[64]

One other view of New Braunfels is necessary to complete the account of the settlement. In 1860 the census officials found a total population of 3837 white persons and 193 slaves in Comal County. The foreign population of the county amounted to 2186. The entire population of the county was listed under New Braunfels, so that it is impossible to say how many people lived just in New Braunfels alone. Of the 480 farmers listed, all but 23 were Germans. Sixteen thousand five hundred forty-two acres were in

flood, and then by a tornado. "The only disaster that has not overtaken me is an earthquake," he said.

63Olmsted, *Journey Through Texas*, 142-143, quoted in Benjamin, *Germans in Texas*, 76; Olmsted, *Wanderungen durch Texas*, 98.

64Olmsted, *Journey Through Texas*, 177-178; Olmsted, *Wanderungen durch Texas*, 126-127.

cultivation. The farms were valued at $561,527 and the imple-
ments at $41,853. The farmers raised 26,610 bushels of corn, 711
pounds of tobacco, 5005 pounds of wool, 141 bushels of Irish potatoes, and 9059 bushels of sweet potatoes. All of the industrial
establishments, however, were located in New Braunfels itself.
The two brick kilns of Emil vom Stein and Henry Schelper made
160,000 bricks at $1600; the seven flour and grist mills of W. H.
Merriwether, John J. Lacke, John F. Torrey, Friedrich Tolle,
Johann Schickeking, C. A. Porter, and C. W. Thomae produced
29,630 bushels of corn meal at $28,350; the three sawmills of W.
H. Merriwether, John J. Lacke, and John F. Torrey cut 1,100,000
feet of lumber valued at $36,000; John F. Torrey's sash, door, and
blind factory produced 1000 windows at $5,000, 350 doors at $2500,
and 625 window blinds at $2500; the two breweries of Johann
Arnold and H. Guenther & Dambmann made 17,020 gallons of beer
for $6,808; and the soap and candle house of Florenz Kreutz made
550 boxes of soap for $2,337. A total capital of $55,800 was in-
vested in these industries; the raw material consumed was valued
at $64,836; the annual pay roll was $8,484; and the annual output was $103,095.[65]

It has been the object of this chapter to give an account of the
work done by the Society and its agents to get the immigrants into
the interior, to recount the principal incidents connected with the
founding of New Braunfels, and to relate the history of this settlement up to the outbreak of the Civil War. Various descriptions
of New Braunfels were included for the purpose of throwing light
not only on the continued growth of the settlement but also on
the various occupations pursued by the inhabitants of the little
town, which Viktor Bracht, in his generally optimistic turn of
mind, believed would in a very short time become the second or
third largest city in Texas.[66] How much of a prophet Bracht was
has already been noted.

[65]Eighth Census, Schedules 4 and 5, in Texas State Library; Kennedy, Jos. C. G., *Population of the United States in 1860*, 473; Kennedy,
Manufactures of the United States in 1860, 582; Kennedy, *Agriculture
of the United States in 1860*, 140, 141.

[66]Bracht, *Texas im Jahre 1848*, 234. Bracht expressed his belief on
January 11, 1846, less than a year after the settlement was made.

FREDERICKSBURG

From a print in the possession of Mrs. Walter Wuppermann, Austin, Texas. The original was made by Hermann Lungkwitz

CHAPTER VII

FREDERICKSBURG, CASTELL, LEININGEN, SCHOENBURG, AND BETTINA

Mindful of the fact that the Society was planning to send additional emigrants to Texas in the winter of 1845 to 1846, Meusebach left New Braunfels in the latter part of August, 1845, to find a suitable place for establishing another settlement on the way to the Fisher and Miller grant, thus partially carrying out the plan suggested by Prince Solms for establishing various settlements on the way from Carlshafen to the Llano River.[1] Meusebach found a tract of land north of the Pedernales River, about 80 miles from New Braunfels, which he thought most suitable for the next settlement and on his return to New Braunfels about the end of October he immediately bought 10,000 acres of headrights on credit. The land was good, arable land, well watered and with sufficient wood. Meusebach organized a surveying party of 36 men, well equipped with wagons, tools, provisions, and guns, under the command of Lieutenant Bene and the surveyors Groos and Murchison. With instructions to lay out a wagon road from New Braunfels to the new settlement, the expedition left New Braunfels about the middle of December along the route indicated on page 152 of this study.[2]

---

[1]Prince Solms had dropped the plan of making settlements from Carlshafen to New Braunfels, but believed that between New Braunfels and the Fisher and Miller grant several settlements should be made about thirty to forty miles apart, so that each new settlement could depend on the one farther back for protection against Indian attacks and for food supplies.

[2]Meusebach, *Answer to Interrogatories*, 14-15; Roemer, *Texas*, 26-27; Roemer, "Geschichte der deutschen Ansiedlungen in Texas," *Der deutsche Pionier*, VII, 98-99; Penniger, *Fest-Ausgabe*, 48, 59-60; Tiling, *German Element in Texas*, 81, 83-84; Kapp, *Aus und ueber Amerika*, I, 274.

On February 18, 1846, the *Democratic Telegraph and Texas Register*, p. 2, cols. 4-5, reported the expedition as follows: "We learn that Capt. Murchison has lately made an expedition with a party of the German emigrants of New Braunfels to the valley of the Perdinalles with a view to selecting a site for a new settlement. The persons who have visited this valley speak of it in glowing terms and consider it one of the most fertile, healthy, and beautiful sections of the West. This valley in many places is fifteen miles wide, interspersed with woodlands and open grassy fields, at such regular intervals that it seems as if it has at no distant period been the residence of a civilized people. The soil is very fertile and well adapted to the culture of wheat. The water of all the streams is limpid and pure and has few traces of lime that is found in such large quantities in most of the streams of the West. It is believed that the

After the surveying expedition returned to New Braunfels about the middle of February and reported on its work, preparations were made to send the first settlers to the Pedernales. On April 23, 1846, as well as can be ascertained, the first emigrant train of twenty wagons and two-wheeled Mexican carts left New Braunfels for the new settlement of Fredericksburg on the Pedernales.[3] There were about 120 men, women, and children in this train, accompanied by eight men of the Society's military company. On May 8, 1846, after an arduous overland trip lasting sixteen days, the settlers arrived at their destination. One of the delicacies served at the first meal in the settlement was bear meat.[4] Three days later, after all the tents had been pitched and a few huts built for protection against wind and weather, the Society's soldiers, the twenty teamsters, and several young, able-bodied men returned to New Braunfels, leaving the remainder behind in the wilderness.[5]

The complete list of the first settlers of Fredericksburg will probably never be ascertained. In Penniger's *Fest-Ausgabe* a list of twenty-eight survivors of the first settlers is given, but it is not at all certain that even this partial list is accurate, since it was made in 1896, fifty years after the founding of Fredericksburg. The list includes the following names: William Arhelger, August Arhelger, Daniel Arhelger, Lorenz Schmidt, Fritz Lochte, Heinrich Lochte, Mrs. Peter Bonn, *née* Lochte, Heinrich Behrens, John Behrens, Mrs. Carl Schwarz, Sr., *née* Behrens, Heinrich Strackbein, Christian Strackbein, Mrs. John Durst, *née* Strackbein, Mrs. Steubing, *née* Strackbein, Martin Heinemann, Mrs. Anton Novian, *née* Heinemann, Adam Klein, John A. Klein, Mrs. Joseph Leyendecker, *née* Klein, Mrs. Joseph Jung, *née* Klein, Heinrich

apple, pear, and other fruits that are cultivated in northern climates can be cultivated here advantageously. We believe the German emigrants will find this section far more healthy and better adapted to the culture of the articles they have been accustomed to cultivate in Europe than any portion of the country nearer the coast."

[3]Fredericksburg was named after Prince Frederick of Prussia, one of the members of the Society.

[4]John Schmidt, one of the Society's soldiers, had shot a bear that morning on the banks of the Pedernales, when the emigrant train was approaching that stream. It was thought at first that a band of Delaware Indians encamped on the Pedernales had attacked the emigrant train. Fortunately, however, these Indians were friendly disposed. Conrad Merz, another of the Society's soldiers, killed a panther on the Pedernales after the train had crossed the river.

[5]Penniger, *Fest-Ausgabe*, 60-63; Tiling, *German Element in Texas*, 84.

Eckhardt, Jacob Neffendorf, Heinrich Thiele, Mrs. Katharina Schneider, Wilhelm Fritze, Mrs. J. U. Anderegg, *née* Fritze, Theodor Wiedenfeld, Wilhelm Schnautz.[6] A second reason why it is impossible to ascertain the complete list is that in 1850 the store, in which its owner, John Hunter, then county clerk, kept the county records, was completely destroyed by fire, nor is it certain that these records even gave a list.[7] The final reason is the fact that most of the records which the Society kept in Texas have disappeared. It is very likely that the records contained the exact list.

During the summer of 1846 several other large emigrant trains arrived at Fredericksburg. One of these, under Julius Splittgerber, later sheriff of Gillespie County, was in charge of the second group of settlers which left New Braunfels about the middle of June. The population of Fredericksburg was continually increasing. There was much work to be done. The settlers who had arrived in May had gone to work at once to put a small field in cultivation. The later arrivals were at first put in tents in the stockade which had been built for protection and defense near the Society's blockhouse. In the course of time more and more huts were built in order to provide comfortably for all of the settlers. After the town lots were laid out by the surveyor Willke they were distributed to the settlers. Most of them chose lots on Creek Street, because of the black soil there, but others, like Splittgerber, chose lots on the main street of the settlement. The main work was to build the Society's magazines or storehouses, in order to protect the supplies and provisions for the settlers and to take care of the goods which the Society was sending up from New

---

[6] Penniger, *Fest-Ausgabe*, 63-64. This list is in error on at least two names, those of Daniel Arhelger and Lorenz Schmidt. Arhelger had been severely wounded in the right arm by the accidental discharge of a gun when the surveying expedition was returning from the Pedernales and was not allowed to go along with the first emigrant train by Dr. Theodor Koester, the Society's physician. Lorenz Schmidt, also a member of the surveying expedition, remained in New Braunfels to support his mother. (Penniger, *Fest-Ausgabe*, 60.)

[7] In the summer of 1850 John Hunter, who had a store in a log cabin on the main street and adjoining the market place, got into a quarrel with a soldier by the name of Dole and stabbed him to death. The drunken soldier had used insulting words after Hunter had refused to sell him whiskey. The next evening about forty soldiers from Fort Martin Scott set out to wreak vengeance on Hunter. When they were unable to find Hunter, the soldiers set fire to the store, which burned down with all its contents of goods and books, among which were the county records. Hunter was later tried at San Antonio and was acquitted. (Penniger, *Fest-Ausgabe*, 111, 113.)

Braunfels for the trade with the Indians, with whom the settlers
remained on a friendly footing through the judicious distribution
of presents and from whom they bought such articles as they
needed.[8] In spite of their friendly relations with the Indians the
settlers took precautions against an Indian surprise attack. All
of the able-bodied men were organized into one infantry and one
cavalry company. P. Bickel commanded the infantry, and J. L.
Ransleben the cavalry. A cannon shot was to be the signal for
the settlers to assemble fully armed before the Society's buildings.[9]

In the summer and fall of 1846 the terrible epidemic which took
such a heavy toll of lives at Carlshafen and New Braunfels spread
to Fredericksburg, where probably from 100 to 150 persons suc-
cumbed to it.[10] Wm. Hermes, Sr., who some years after his arrival
in Texas in 1846 took up the study of medicine, said that Dr.
Schubert diagnosed the disease incorrectly and prescribed a remedy
that probably increased the number of deaths.[11]

[8]Penniger, *Fest-Ausgabe*, 65-68. (See also Appendix D for a plat of
Fredericksburg.)

On June 3, 1846, the *Democratic Telegraph and Texas Register* reported
upon the Indian situation as follows: "We have heard with pleasure that
the German settlement on the Perdinales is in a remarkable prosperous
condition. The fears that the Comanches would attempt to destroy it are
allayed and the settlers are confident that they will not be molested by
this tribe. They have (received) some injury from a small band of
Wacoes who have killed a few of their cattle; but this has not in the least
discouraged them, and they now have the assurance of the friendly Indians
that if they are again molested, these Indians will combine and extermi-
nate the band of Wacoes that continue hostile. The settlers, we learn,
enjoy excellent health." *(Democratic Telegraph and Texas Register,*
June 3, 1846, 2, col. 5.)

[9]Hermes, "Erlebnisse eines deutschen Pioniers in Texas," *La Grange
Deutsche Zeitung,* August 19, 1915, 11, col. 3.

[10]Meusebach estimated that the total number of deaths did not exceed
850. According to the official list, as he says, 321 died at Carlshafen and
on the way to New Braunfels. Ervendberg, who was probate judge in
New Braunfels, reported a total of 400 deaths at New Braunfels. Thus
the number of deaths at Fredericksburg was between 100 and 150.
(Meusebach, *Answer to Interrogatories,* 21-22; Bracht, *Texas im Jahre
1848,* 244; Penniger, *Fest-Ausgabe,* 50.)

[11]Schubert, so Hermes claims, diagnosed the disease as scurvy of the
mouth and prescribed the wild purslane as a remedy. Hermes claims the
disease was the petechial fever, for which a diet of good, wholesome food,
including fresh meat, should have been prescribed. (Hermes, "Erlebnisse eines deutschen Pioniers in Texas," *La Grange Deutsche Zeitung,*
August 19, 1915, 11, col. 2.)

"Doctor Schubert," whose real name was Friedrich A. Strubberg and
who used the *nom de plume of* Friedrich Armand, was recommended to
Meusebach in Houston in the spring of 1846 by Henry Francis Fisher as
a good doctor. Meusebach appointed him as director of the settlement at

THE VEREINSKIRCHE OR KAFFEEMUEHLE
From a reproduction in Penniger, *Fest-Ausgabe*

In the fall of the year 1846 the Society met its obligation of erecting a building for religious services. All denominations represented among the settlers were allowed to use this church building *(Vereins-Kirche)*. It was built in the shape of a regular octagon according to plans drawn by the colonial director, Doctor Schubert. Each side of the building was eighteen feet long and eighteen feet high. At an elevation of about ten feet above the sides the octagonal roof formed the base of a cupola with eight sides, each ten feet long and ten feet high. Surmounting the cupola was an octagonal roof about seven feet high. Because of its close resemblance to the old-fashioned coffee mill found in many a home up to a quarter of a century ago, this church building was sometimes called the "Coffee Mill," *(Kaffeemuehle)*. The *Vereins-Kirche* stood on the main street of Fredericksburg between the courthouse square and the market square until shortly after 1896.[12] The first Protestant services were conducted in the Vereins-Kirche by Rev. F. Basse, from 1846 to 1849, when Rev. Gottlieb Burchard Dangers succeeded him. The Catholic teacher, Johann Leyendecker, read the Gospel with the explanations and prayed with the Catholics. In 1847 the French priest, C. M. Dubuis, later bishop of Texas, and the Spaniard, Pedro Salazar,

Fredericksburg. Dr. Schubert proved a very unsatisfactory director and was disliked by the majority of the settlers. Late in 1846, without Meusebach's permission, he raised a company of men to go into the grant. He did not dare to cross the Llano River, however, and cowardly returned to Fredericksburg, from where he reported to Meusebach that it was impossible to get into the grant because it was full of hostile Indians. Before Meusebach gave up his position as commissioner general of the Society on July 20, 1847, he fired Doctor Schubert, who thereupon went to Farm Nassau, which he had leased. Hermann Spiess, who succeeded Meusebach as commissioner general, later tried to oust Schubert from Farm Nassau. On this occasion a man by the name of Rohrdorf was killed. Spiess and his men were brought to trial but were acquitted. (Meusebach, *Answer to Interrogatories*, 22-23; Penniger, *Fest-Ausgabe*, 50-53; Tiling, *German Element in Texas*, 111-112; *Democratic Telegraph and Texas Register*, December 2, 1847, 2, col. 3.)

[12]Concerning the destruction of the old church building shortly after the fiftieth anniversary of the founding of Fredericksburg, Rev. H. Gerlach has this to say: "Soon after, the unfortunate idea arose in the heads of a few to tear down this Vereins-Kirche, this reminder of past days, this old venerable witness of so many sorrows and joys, this object of attraction and admiration of all strangers." (Gerlach, H., *Fest-Schrift zum 75-jaehrigen Jubilaeum der St. Marien-Gemeinde zu Friederichsburg, Texas*, 14.)

It should be stated here to the credit of the people of Fredericksburg that in recent years a movement was started to restore the *Vereins-Kirche*.

conducted Catholic services in Fredericksburg during a brief stay of two weeks.[13]

The year 1847 marks the opening of the first privately owned store in Fredericksburg, the Society's store or magazine being the only one up to that time. The owner of the new store was J. L. Ransleben, who kept it only a short while. Chester B. Starks, who opened a store soon afterward, enjoyed a large business from contracts which he made with the United States War Department to furnish the troops in Fort Martin Scott with supplies needed by them. Frank Van der Stucken, who later became one of the most influential men in Fredericksburg, learned the fundamentals of business from Starks. Other storekeepers of Fredericksburg were Louis Martin, John M. Hunter, Wilhelm Wahrmund, Fritz Lochte, and Rev. F. Basse. These men traded not only with the German settlers but also with the Indians and, by a system of barter, exchanged their goods for skins and furs brought to Fredericksburg by the Indians.[14]

Prior to 1847, largely because the Society had not made any agreement with the Indians,[15] the Society did not begin its work of surveying the lands in the Fisher and Miller grant. On June 14, 1847, the *Democratic Telegraph and Texas Register* stated that Mr. Giddings, one of the surveyors of the German colonial grant, reported that the surveyors were making rapid progress, being then engaged in surveying the land between the San Saba and the Concho. Small parties of Comanches belonging to Santa Anna's band, Giddings reported, visited the surveyors frequently and never manifested any uneasiness to see the "land stealers," as

[13]Penniger, *Fest-Ausgabe*, 147-148, 153; Gerlach, *Fest-Schrift zum 75-jaehrigen Jubilaeum der St. Marien-Gemeinde zu Friedrichsburg, Texas*, 14.

Rev. Gerlach's book gives some valuable information about the activities of the Catholics in Fredericksburg from 1846 to 1921. In 1846 the following Catholic families lived in Fredericksburg: Heinemann, Klein, Johann Meurer, Johann Metzger, Johann Friedrich Metzger, the widow Blank, Christian Leyendecker, Jacob Weinheimer, Peter Schmitz, Fuchs, Peter Schandua, Johann Keller, Johann Petsch, Pehl, Besier, Christof Brinkrolf, Johann Fritz, and Vogel. Jacob Metzger, Georg Weber, Johann Roeder, and Peter Burg were the single men of the Catholic faith in Fredericksburg. (Gerlach, *Fest-Schrift*, 10-11.)

[14]Penniger, *Fest-Ausgabe*, 78; Hermes, "Erleibnisse eines deutschen Pioniers in Texas," *La Grange Deutsche Zeitung*, November 19, 1915, 11, col. 2.

[15]For the agreement made with the Indians, see Chapter IX, p. 186, of this study.

the Indians called the compasses, moving into their best hunting grounds.[16]

The settlement at Fredericksburg attracted considerable attention from the forward-looking citizens of Texas. Fifteen stores had been opened by the middle of the year 1847; the population was estimated as exceeding 2000; the settlers were said to have several large fields of corn under cultivation; and the opening of a wagon road from Austin to Fredericksburg was reported.[17] It was even suggested that trade communications might be opened between Houston and Chihuahua by way of Fredericksburg. Concerning this latter point, the *Democratic Telegraph and Texas Register* expressed itself as follows:

It may be of some importance to our citizens to notice, that Fredericksburg is nearly in a direct line from Houston to Chihuahua. The German colonists expect that within a few months, the road will be extended from Fredericksburg to the old San Saba fort, and as the road from that fort to the valley of the Concho, through which the main road to Chihuahua extends, is practicable for wagons, it is by no means improbable that a portion of the valuable trade of Chihuahua will at no distant day be directed by this route to Houston. The distance from Houston to Chihuahua by this route can scarcely exceed 550 miles, and we know of no other point situated on navigable waters which is nearer to Chihuahua than this city, or which can be connected with it by a route so free from obstruction and so convenient for wagoners.[18]

An event of considerable importance to the settlers of New Braunfels and Fredericksburg transpired on July 20, 1847. The Society's second commissioner general, John O. Meusebach, on that day turned over his authority to Hermann Spiess, his successor. Meusebach had served the Society well and had done much for the welfare of the German settlers in West Texas. He had helped the settlements through many trying moments. It is

[16]*Democratic Telegraph and Texas Register*, June 14, 1847, 2, col. 6.
On October 7, 1847, the same paper reported that the Indians had not molested any of the German settlers on the Llano and that several parties of the Comanches had visited Fredericksburg during the two preceding months and "manifested the warmest friendship for the settlers."

[17]*Ibid.*, June 14, 1847, 3, col. 1, and June 28, 1847, 3, col. 4. The estimate on population is too liberal. The state census for 1848 gave Gillespie County credit for a total population of only 966 persons. (*Texas State Gazette*, August 25, 1849, 5, col. 2.)

[18]*Democratic Telegraph and Texas Register*, June 14, 1847, 3, col. 1.

probably not too much to say that his work in straightening out the Society's finances in Texas in 1845 and 1846 actually prevented the abandonment of the settlement of New Braunfels and made possible the founding of Fredericksburg and the continuance of the Society's colonization work. Meusebach's treaty with the Comanches in March, 1847, must ever be regarded as an achievement of incalculable value not alone for the Society but for the state of Texas as well. Many of the settlers regretted that Meusebach was laying down his office. The stockholders of the Society in a general meeting at Biebrich on July 23, 1847, adopted a resolution that their confidence in Meusebach continued unimpaired and that his devotion to the duties of his office was greatly appreciated by them. The resolution was signed by seventeen members of the Society and by Baron Karl von Meusebach, a brother of John O. Meusebach.[19]

Provision was made in 1847 for giving to the people of Fredericksburg and the settlers on the Llano the benefits of organized government by forming the region into a precinct of Bexar County and by letting them elect a justice of the peace. A. Krueger received the office. But the population of the region increased so rapidly and the distance from San Antonio, the county seat of Bexar County, was so great, that in December, 1847, the people drew up a petition and asked the legislature to organize a new county.[20] There were 150 signatures to the petition. As a result

[19]The writer received the manuscript containing the resolution from Mrs. Emmy Marschall, of Cherry Spring, Gillespie County, Texas, one of the daughters of John O. Meusebach. The document recites the fact that the sending of the special commissioner, Cappes, in 1846, was not caused by a lack of confidence in Meusebach, but by the non-arrival of information about the conditions of the Society's affairs in Texas and by the desire to promote its own interests by strengthening its administrative personnel in Texas. The document declares that the report made by Cappes did not result in creating any mistrust in Meusebach and that the Society did not approve the conduct of the special commissioner. Cappes retracted the derogatory statements of his report in an oral statement before a stockholders' meeting on June 15, 1847.

[20]MS. Records Office Secretary of State, Memorial No. 29, File Box No. 28, Letter No. F.

The petition was dated Fredericksburg, December 15, 1847. The list of signers follows: Thomas Thom, F. Tolle, L. Bene, E. Kriewicz, Jacob Wurzbach, Wilhelm Schnautz, Wilhelm Feller, J. W. Jamison, Edward ? Benner, Nikolaus Mosel, Joh. Ludw. Ransleben, Wilh. Becker, Alex. Ferguson, Henry Hesler, James Ferguson, Robert Fraenkel, August Schmidt, St. ? Rudolph, — ? Kolmeier, W. Wahrmund, C. Wissemann, A. Henkel, W. Leilich, Friedrich Kiehne, Friedrich Lochte, Peter Burg, A. Elfeld, L. Poock, L. Schaeper, Andrew Meyer, Louis Martin, G. M.

of the petition the legislature passed an act on February 23, 1848, to create Gillespie County.[21]   The petition recommended the name of Pierdenalis, which was written over Germania, for the new county. Fredericksburg, as the petition had requested, was made the county seat. The chief justice of Comal County was ordered to call an election on the first Monday in June, 1848, to be held at Fredericksburg. Dr. Wm. Keidel was elected chief justice, John M. Hunter county clerk, Louis Martin sheriff, R. W. Cecil assessor and collector, John Leyendecker treasurer, and Friedrich Kiehne, Peter Bickel, John P. Keller, and Peter Schandua county commissioners.[22]

Stebbins, Dr. Mylius, A. Erlmeier, Carl H. Nimitz, Edward Luscher ?, Francis Wurzbach, Ernst Kiesenwetter, Otto Heins, C. Wehmeyer, H. Hitzfeldt, J. M. Caldwell, Ad. Hutzfeld, J. Schmidtzinsky, H. Thiele, C. F. Schulz, J. M. Hunter, G. W. Vandegrift, J. M. Campbell, Richard Baugh, B. L. Posey, John Hamilton, J. Heinrich Goebel, Jacob Jung, Albr. Lincke, George Fritze, Carl Meier, C. Kreissen, Conrad Ahrens, Heinrich Jordan, Peter Keller, Conrad Becker, Jacob Neffendorf, Caspar Danz, Peter Waller, Faehrenhorst ?, Heinrich Mueller, Sr., Heinrich Mueller, Jr., Jacob Weinheimer, Georg Weinheimer, Anton Weinheimer, Franz Gross, Christophal Brinkrolf, Johann Peter Kuhlmann, Mathias Schmidt, Conrad Witterlen ?, Heinrich Witterlen ?, Peter Poetsch, Johannes Poetsch, Gehard Remein ?, P. Schandua, Ph. Fritz, Joh. G. Braun, Johann Georg Weber, Lorenz Schmidt, Ludwig Schmidt, Heinrich Sauer, Wilhelm Keidel, R. W. Cecil, Emil Wahrmund, M. M. Shelley, Jesus Castillo, Rafael Orsina ?, Ysidro Munos, Friedrich Pape, Jacob Luckenbach, N. Mosel, Joh. Masil ?, Frd. Griegmann, Wolfgang Braeutigam, Philip Acker, Fried. Krause, Hein. Jung, Lud. Jung, Karl Kuehn, Andrew Bilo, Cr. Hahn, Herrmann Scheele, Phillip Eschelbach, Heinr. Basse, Jakob Arhelger, Daniel Arhelger, Heinrich Arhelger, Adam Schuessler, Aug. Walch, Nicklaus Jacoby, Georg Karl Stammel, Arnold Fuchs, Friedrich Koetzel, Ch. Gaerdner, Peter Walch, Johann Joseph Walch, Antonio Pena, H. Habenicht, H. Mintzel, J. Leyendecker I, Franz Joseph Leyendecker, Joh. Leyendecker II, J. Heinrich Dietz, J. Georg Dietz, Charles P. Chambers, Daniel Weiershausen, Heinr. Weiershausen, Jul. Wamel, Aug. Spilker, Adolph Schildknecht, August Nette, Th. Specht, R. Schwerin, G. F. Holekamp, Nic. Zink, Adam Bedig, Kaspar Bermann, Johann Bermann, Johann Dietz, Adam Baldus, Adam Belser, Johann Nicholas Schmidt.

[21]Gammel, Laws of Texas, III, 35-36.
    Gillespie County was named after Captain Robert A. Gillespie, who fell in the battle of Monterey, September 20, 1846, during the war between the United States and Mexico.

[22]Penniger, Fest-Ausgabe, 126. The statement in Penniger, Fest-Ausgabe, 126, that the first officers were probably all appointed is based, presumably, on the fact that the election returns had to be sent to the chief justice at New Braunfels who thereupon announced the result. It thus appeared that the officers had been appointed by the chief justice at New Braunfels.
    Penniger, Fest-Ausgabe, 123-139, gives the various lists of county officers from 1848 to 1894. On pages 140-141 appears a tabular list arranged by officers with dates.

In November of 1848 the first United States soldiers appeared at Fredericksburg and established Fort Martin Scott a short distance away.   The building of the fort gave employment to many of the people of Fredericksburg.   The settlers could now sell their surplus agricultural products for cash at the army post.   Some earned money by hauling lumber and hay for the fort.   Members of the nearby settlement of Mormons also found employment in the building of the fort.[23]   The company of mounted infantry at Fort Martin Scott was commanded by Captain Eastman, while Major Merrill commanded several companies of cavalry.[24]

Viktor Bracht, who owned a store in New Braunfels and was conversant with grocery prices there as well as in San Antonio and Fredericksburg, gives the following list of grocery prices for Fredericksburg for 1848.   Meat sold at 4 cents a pound, butter at $37\frac{1}{2}$ cents, ham and bacon at from 15 to 25 cents, eggs at from 25 to $37\frac{1}{2}$ cents per dozen, chickens at from $37\frac{1}{2}$ to 50 cents each, flour at from 15 to 20 dollars a barrel, coffee at 6 to 7 pounds for a dollar, sugar at 5 to 6 pounds for a dollar, rice at 5 pounds for a dollar, beans at 8 to 10 pounds for a dollar, salt at 14 to 15 pounds for a dollar, and corn at $1.25 to $1.75 a bushel.[25]   When the greater purchasing power of money is taken into consideration, it is apparent that the prices of the ordinary necessaries of life were very high.   Fresh meat was the lowest in price, comparatively.

[23]The Mormons established a settlement in 1847 about four miles southeast of Fredericksburg.   There were about 200 persons in their settlement under the leadership of the elder, Lyman Wight.   The Mormons built convenient houses, a large school, and a temple. They built a saw and grist mill on the Pedernales.   They engaged in agriculture, producing corn mostly.   They were on friendly terms with their German neighbors, furnished them with meal and lumber, and instructed them how to cultivate their land advantageously.   Their elder, Lyman Wight, was chief justice of Gillespie County from 1850 to 1851.   In 1853, after their mill on the Pedernales had been destroyed by a flood and there was no more work at Fort Martin Scott for them, the Mormons abandoned their settlement and left.   In 1896 they still possessed one and one-half acres of land on which their cemetery had been located.   (Penniger, *Fest Ausgabe*, 108-109; *Democratic Telegraph and Texas Register*, February 17, 1848, 2, col. 5.) The census of 1850 lists a total of 161 Mormons.   (Photostat Seventh Census, Gillespie County, University of Texas Library.)

[24]Penniger, *Fest-Ausgabe*, 75, 84; Kapp, *Aus und ueber Amerika*, I, 282. The census of 1850 lists 100 officers and soldiers, 4 officers' wives, 1 hospital matron, 9 laundresses, and 7 children.   (Photostat Seventh Census, Gillespie County, University of Texas Library.)

[25]Bracht, *Texas im Jahre 1848*, 216.   The price list for New Braunfels and San Antonio is given in Bracht's book on page 215.   The Mormons sold flour at $20 a barrel and cornmeal at 9 cents a pound in 1850.   (Penniger, *Fest-Augabe*, 83.)

During the year 1849 the cholera broke out in Texas. The German settlements were not spared and, according to the newspaper reports, the cholera was very virulent both in New Braunfels and in Fredericksburg. Many families were reported to have fled from their homes in New Braunfels to the neighboring hills. By the end of June, however, the epidemic had abated in New Braunfels and it disappeared from Fredericksburg about a month later.[26] Splittgerber in an article in Penniger's *Fest-Ausgabe* asserts that the fear of the cholera caused a man by the name of Schumacher, a tailor, to induce Schneider, a Methodist preacher, to come to Fredericksburg to pray every day and every night to prevent the spread of the cholera.[27]

If Fredericksburg had not already attracted attention, it would certainly have become known during 1849, for it was on one of four main roads opened by the United States government to the Rio Grande valley after the treaty of Guadalupe Hidalgo. Fredericksburg lay on the so-called "Emigrant" or "Upper" El Paso road, some miles beyond the junction of the two branch roads from San Antonio and Austin, respectively.[28] Many people were seized with the California gold fever in 1849 and set out for the promised land. Since Fredericksburg was the last town on the "Emigrant" road where supplies could be purchased before reaching El Paso, the storekeepers of the place did a good business.[29]

The statistics of the census of 1850 give a variety of interesting information about Fredericksburg and Gillespie County. The white population consisted of 725 males and 510 females, or a total of 1235 persons, of whom 913 were foreigners. Each of the 274 families had its own home. There were five slaves in Gillespie County that year. The population of Fredericksburg alone was 754.[30] On the 40 farms valued at $26,388 there were 2217 acres

[26]*Democratic Telegraph and Texas Register*, June 14, 1849, 2, col. 4, June 21, 1849, 2, col. 6, and July 26, 1849, 3, col. 1.

[27]Penniger, *Fest-Ausgabe*, 76.

[28]Martin, Mabelle Eppard, "California Emigrant Roads through Texas," *Southwestern Historical Quarterly*, XXVIII, 288. See also Martin, "From Texas to California in 1849:—Diary of C. C. Cox," *Ibid.*, XXIX, 41-42. Cox stated in his diary that Fredericksburg had a population of about 2000, which was 500 more than twice the actual number.

[29]Penniger, *Fest-Ausgabe*, 75-76.

[30]In John R. Bartlett's *Personal Narrative of Explorations and Incidents*, p. 60, appears the statement that the population of Fredericksburg was 500 in 1850. The stores, Bartlett says, were filled with goods for the Indian trade and were enjoying a good business.

in cultivation.   There were 788 meat cattle on the farms.   Fifteen
thousand two hundred forty bushels of Indian corn were produced,
of which the Mormons in their settlement at Zodiac raised 4500
bushels.   The sawmill of Lyman Wight & Company produced lumber valued at $4250 and their grist mill produced corn meal valued
at $600.   Joseph D. Goodale, who operated a turning lathe and
made bedsteads, chairs, and tables, produced $892 worth of finished
products.   Friedrich Winkel, another turner and cabinet-maker,
turned out $1784 worth of finished products.   Friedrich Kiehne, a
blacksmith, had a gross income of $2000, John Schmidtzinsky, a
carpenter, reported an income of $2000, and Nicholas Mosel, a
wheelwright, conducted a business that brought in $1800.[31]

By 1853 the population of Gillespie County had increased to
1600, including 100 Mormons, an increase of 265 over the population of 1850.   The total number of poll taxes paid was 342.   The
taxable property of the county was then valued at $161,328.[32]
Four years later the *Texas Almanac* valued 143,529 acres of land
in Gillespie County at $132,360.   The town lots were valued at
$40,640 and the 63 slaves at $33,800.   The state census of 1858
placed the population of Gillespie County at 2697, including 90
slaves.   There were 450 voters, 718 children under the age of six,
and 644 children between the ages of six and eighteen.   There
were 7227 acres planted in corn but none in cotton.[33]   There was,
then, a steady increase in the population of the county and in the
value of the property as the years went by.

In 1860 the census still reflected the steady increase in the
population.   There were 2703 white persons and 33 slaves.   One
thousand three hundred sixty-three persons were of foreign birth,
but this number does not include the children born in Texas.[34]

[31]Census of 1850, Schedule 4:   Productions of Agriculture, and Schedule
5:   Products of Industry; DeBow, J. D. B., *Statistical View of the United
States.   .   .   .   A Compendium of the Census*, 308-313, 354.

[32]*Neu Braunfelser Zeitung*, September 30, 1853, 2, col. 4.   New Braunfels thought well of the growth of the frontier settlements on the Pedernales and the Llano and wished to see them continue in their growth.
The frontier settlements tended to make the land and products of the
people in and around New Braunfels more valuable and to increase their
trade, since New Braunfels was on the direct road from the Pedernales
to the coast.   The frontier settlements aided also in increasing the political
power of New Braunfels. *(Ibid.*, March 18, 1853, 4, col. 1.)

[33]Records of the Executive Office, 1857-1859, p. 442, Texas State Library.

[34]Schedule I: Free Inhabitants, Census of 1860, distinguished between
children born to German families in Texas and those born in the various

The census of 1860 does not give the population of Fredericks-burg, but it was probably between 1000 and 1200.[35] There were 6645 acres in cultivation valued at $164,695. From this small acreage of cultivated land and the fact that 32,969 cows, oxen, ranch cattle, and sheep were owned in the county, it would seem that the people were engaged in cattle and sheep raising rather than in agriculture. The farmers and ranch owners of the county owned 1002 horses, 55 mules, and 8966 swine. Thirty-eight thou-sand nine hundred sixty-five pounds of butter were made and 5136 pounds of wool were clipped. The farms produced 10,237 bushels of corn, 18,136 bushels of wheat, ten bales of cotton, and 3954 bushels of sweet potatoes. From the schedule for the products of industry it is seen that thirty-eight persons operated ten differ-ent types of industrial establishments and that they employed twenty additional workers. The total amount paid in wages was $25,260, but that sum included wages also for the owners.[36] The capital investment amounted to $26,180; the value of the raw material used was $108,110; and the output was valued at $165,-500. Bernhard Meckel followed the trade of a cooper; Carl Nimitz was a beer brewer; August Kott made soap and candles; Adolf Lungkwitz and Louis Weiss were tinners; Doss, Thomae & Son and Fritz Pape owned sawmills; Franz Staffers and Friedrich Starke made saddles and harness; Doss, Thomae & Son, Fritz Pape, F. Wrede & Company, and Nicolaus Zink owned grist and flour mills; Michael Boos, Henry Dannenberg, Carl Graff, Conrad Meckel, Andreas Moellering, and Henry Wilke were wheelwrights; John Fritz, Valentin Homan, William Isbell, Michael Kaiser, George Leineweber, George Leiter, William Saenger, and Fried-rich Wilke were blacksmiths; and Friedrich Gentemann, John Kunz, William Leilich, John Loeffler, John Petri, Christof

states. The number of persons of German nativity and of German descent, then, was probably as high as 2000. A photostat copy of the schedule is to be found in the University of Texas Library.

[35]The writer bases this estimate on the fact that under the schedule for the productions of agriculture the census lists 317 farmers for Fredericks-burg, Cherry Spring, Grape Creek, and Caldwellshill. If five persons are allowed as the average size of a family, there would remain about 1100 persons for Fredericksburg. The schedule of free inhabitants divided Gillespie County into five precincts, two for Fredericksburg and one each for Cherry Spring, Grape Creek, and Caldwellshill. (Photostat Eighth Census, Gillespie County, University of Texas Library.)

[36]In establishments operated by the owner without additional help wages are always stated in the census. (*Eighth Census*, II, 583-684.)

Schaeper, Jacob Schneider, Christian Staats, Peter Tatsch, and Carl Wendeler were furniture and cabinet-makers.[37]

The German settlements of New Braunfels and Fredericksburg were outside of the limits of the Fisher and Miller grant. The Society, however, founded three settlements on the grant, failed in the attempt to make a fourth settlement, and arranged to let a group of individuals establish a fifth settlement on a communistic plan north of the Llano. These five settlements were Castell, Leiningen, Schoenburg, Meerholz, and Bettina. With the exception of Schoenburg and Bettina these settlements were named after members of the Society, while Bettina was named after the German author, Bettina von Arnim. As far as can be ascertained the work connected with founding these settlements was begun in 1847.

Castell, the only one of these five settlements which exists today as a small town, was laid out before Meusebach retired as commissioner-general.[38] Castell was located on the north bank of the Llano River in what was then Gillespie County. Today it is located in Llano County near the western boundary of the county, but on the south bank of the Llano. Just how many families were placed in the settlement it is not possible to ascertain.[39] The settlers were furnished with wagons, agricultural implements, tents, and provisions and got a good start. The plan of community or group cooking and housekeeping was abandoned by the settlers shortly after they arrived in Castell. In the summer of 1848 the settlers in Castell were notified to appear in Fredericksburg for the purpose of selecting their tracts of land in the grant from a map brought there by Hermann Seele of New Braunfels at the request of the commissioner of the Fisher and Miller colony lands. When the log cabins were completed, an apportionment was made

---

[37]*Eighth Census of the United States*, I, 473, 479, 487; II, 583-584; III, 140-149; Schedule 4: Productions of Agriculture, and Schedule 5: Products of Industry.

[38]Dr. Ferdinand von Herff said that the settlement was founded by Hermann Spiess, the successor of Meusebach. (Herff, *Die geregelte Auswanderung des deutschen Proletariats mit besonderer Beziehung auf Texas*, 62.)

[39]Adolf Paul Weber in his *Deutsche Pioniere*, 31, says that 200 families were settled in Castell and Leiningen together, an estimate which is very likely too high. Wm. Hermes, Sr., who lived in Castell for a few years, says that there were 30 settlers, for each of whom a log cabin was to be built by the Society. (Hermes, "Erlebnisse eines deutschen Pioniers in Texas," *La Grange Deutsche Zeitung*, August 19, 1915, 14, col. 2.)

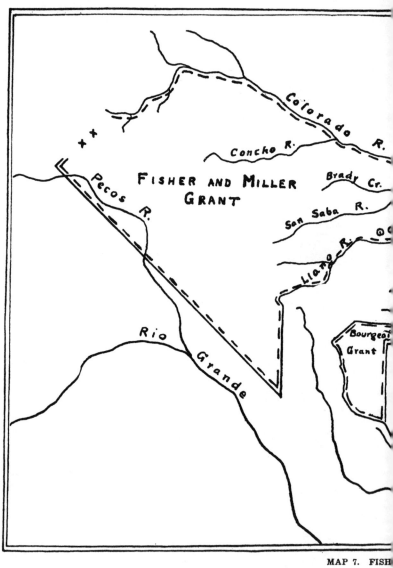

MAP 7.   FISH

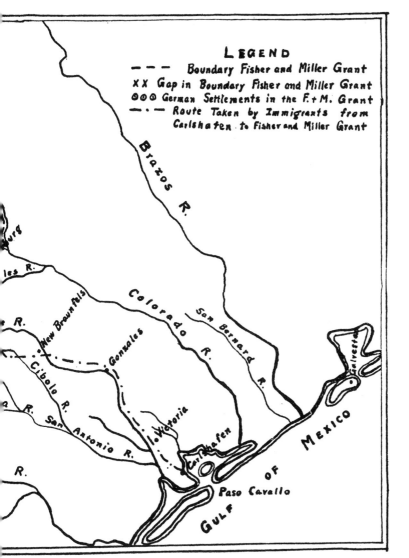

by lot. In addition to his cabin each settler received ten acres of land running back from his cabin. Two and one-half acres of each ten-acre tract were planted in corn.[40] For the protection of Castell and the other settlements north of the Llano a company of rangers under the command of Captain Highsmith was sent to the Llano, but they camped on the south bank of the river, for what reason is not known.[41]

In 1850 the census listed only thirty-two persons living on the Llano River. There were 19 adults and 13 children. One of the seven families had no children. There were five single men. Two of the men were laborers, two were waggoners, one was a carpenter, one was a teacher, one was a blacksmith, one was a farmer, and four were woodchoppers.[42] J. R. Bartlett, who passed some fifteen miles west of the Llano settlements in October, 1850, on his way to New Mexico as a member of the Texas-New Mexico boundary commission, states that there were only nine families in Castell at that time. There were 26 houses, however, a fact which would indicate that the settlement had once been more populous and which is borne out by Bracht, who estimated the population of the Llano settlements in 1848 to be between 230 and 250.[43]

On September 13, 1852, Rev. P. F. Zizelmann, an Evangelical-Lutheran minister who had come on foot from Fredericksburg, conducted religious services and held communion in Castell. He reported that nearly all of the residents were present at the services. The log cabins, which were covered with thatch, were arranged in a single row along the north bank of the Llano. Behind each of them was a small field, in which corn, sweet potatoes, melons, and pumpkins were raised.[44]

[40]Dr. Ferdinand von Herff thought well of the method used by the Society in founding settlements north of the Llano. He pointed out that during the second year more than enough corn and other produce were raised for the needs of the settlers in Castell and Leiningen, while in New Braunfels and Fredericksburg hardly enough food was produced during the second year of their existence. (Herff, *Die geregelte Auswanderung*, 63.)

[41]Penniger, *Fest-Ausgabe*, 52-53, 119; Bracht, *Texas im Jahre 1848*, 135-137; Hermes, "Erlebnisse," *La Grange Deutsche Zeitung*, August 19, 1915, 14, cols. 2-4.

[42]Photostat Seventh Census, Schedule of Free Inhabitants, Gillespie County, University of Texas.

[43]Bartlett, *Personal Narrative of Explorations and Incidents*, 66; Bracht, *Texas im Jahre 1848*, 137.

[44]Mgebroff, *Geschichte der Ersten Deutschen Evangelisch-Lutherischen Synode in Texas*, 142-143.

Not much is known about the settlement Leiningen. It was located on the Llano a few miles below Castell. The first settlers were taken to the place by Emil Kriewicz, who had also conducted the first settlers to Castell. The census of 1850, referred to in connection with Castell, included Leiningen among the Llano settlements. In 1853 a correspondent wrote to the *Neu Braunfelser Zeitung* from Leiningen that corn was then selling at 65 cents a bushel, butter at 25 cents a pound, eggs at 25 cents a dozen, and wool at 50 cents a pound.[45]

Just below Leiningen the little settlement of Schoenburg was made by the Society in 1847, but it did not prosper and soon ceased to exist, the settlers moving away. Only two writers mention the place as a village (Dorf). It is indicated, although without name, on map 5 in Chapter V, page 109.[46]

The Society attempted to found a fourth settlement north of the Llano. This was to be called Meerholz. The place for the settlement was selected by the Society and a number of settlers were taken to the site. After remaining a short while they abandoned the place, because there was not enough timber nearby for the needs of the settlement.[47]

One of the interesting episodes in the history of the Society was the founding of the settlement Bettina[48] through an agreement with a group of forty enthusiastic young men. These men, most of whom were students at the universities of Giessen and Heidelberg and at the industrial school (Gewerbeschule) in Darmstadt, had become interested in Texas through the writings and speeches of Prince Solms and Hermann Spiess, who pictured Texas as the land of opportunity for professional men. Under

[45]Bracht, *Texas im Jahre 1848*, 135; Penniger, *Fest-Ausgabe*, 52, 119; *Neu Braunfelser Zeitung*, September 22, 1853, 2, col. 6; Photostat Seventh Census, Schedule of Free Inhabitants, Gillespie County.

[46]Bracht, *Texas im Jahre 1848*, 135; Hermes, "Erlebnisse," *La Grange Deutsche Zeitung*, August 19, 1915, 14, col. 4.

[47]Bracht, *Texas im Jahre 1848*, 135-136. Bracht says that the settlers, after seeing the scarcity of timber, left the place with the cry: "Mehr Holz! mehr Holz!" (More wood! more wood!") Mehr Holz and Meerholz are pronounced alike in German. Emil Kriewicz says in Penniger, *Fest-Ausgabe*, 119, that the settlement was abandoned because the settlers preferred to live near Fredericksburg, although the Society had been supplying them with provisions for nearly a year.

[48]The settlement was named after the German writer Elizabeth (Bettina) von Arnim.

the leadership of Gustav Schleicher[49] and Dr. Ferdinand von
Herff these young men organized themselves into a society[50] and
on January 11, 1847, "The Forty," *(Die Vierziger)*, as the group
was sometimes called, entered into an agreement with Count Castell to found a settlement on the Fisher and Miller grant. The
contractors were to receive the sum of $12,000 or its equivalent
in live stock, tools, agricultural implements, wagons, and provisions
for one year, in return for which, besides themselves, they were
to settle 200 families on the Fisher and Miller grant.

[49]Gustav Schleicher was born in Darmstadt on November 19, 1823. He
graduated from the gymnasium in Darmstadt and then studied architec-
ture and engineering at the University of Giessen. While still in his
early twenties he found employment with a railroad company which was
then constructing a road from Heidelberg to Frankfurt. Not feeling
satisfied, however, in the cramped conditions of his fatherland he decided
to found a new home in Texas in company with a group of young men
from the educated classes. After the Bettina settlement was abandoned,
Schleicher continued to live in the neighborhood. In 1850, however, he
moved to San Antonio, where in 1853 he was elected a member of the
Texas House of Representatives. From 1859 to 1861 he was a member of
the Texas Senate. He served in the Confederate army and became major
of the "Texas Rangers." After the Civil War he practiced law in San
Antonio. In 1874 he was elected to the House of Representatives in
Washington. As a member of this body he made a noted speech in favor
of hard money, a speech that showed solid academic training, original
thinking, and conscientious research. Responsible newspapers quoted him
as an authority after the speech was printed in the Congressional Record.
He was re-elected in 1876 and 1878. On January 10, 1879, he died in
Washington, D. C. At the memorial services held in the hall of the
House of Representatives on Monday, January 13, 1879, the members of
the House, the members of the Senate, President Hayes and his cabinet,
and the justices of the Supreme Court were all in attendance. Dr. Harrison, chaplain of the House of Representatives, conducted the services and
paid an eloquent tribute to Schleicher. Dr. Harrison said that Schleicher
never stooped to slander his political opponents, that he loved the truth,
that he had a quiet, earnest, and untiring spirit in research, and that he
had an unbending firmness. Schleicher's body was brought by special
train to San Antonio, where on Sunday, January 19, 1879, fifteen thousand
persons attended the services when his body was laid to rest. (Koerner,
Das deutsche Element, 365; Rattermann, H. A., "Gustav Schleicher," *Der
deutsche Pionier*, XI, 84-89, 134-140.)

[50]Seven of the forty members changed their mind and did not go along
to Texas. The remaining thirty-three were: Dr. Ferdinand von Herff,
Leopold Schulz, Gustav Schleicher, Lerch, Philip Zoeller, Wilhelm Zoeller,
Wundt, Fuchs, Theodor Schleuning, Amelung, Christian von Hesse, Julius
Wagner, Herrmann, Friedrich Schenk, Jacob Kuechler, Adam Vogt,
Strauss, Christian Flach, Schunk, Neff, Adam Teichert, Adolf Hahn,
Fritz Louis, Kappelhof, Michel, Ottmer, Peter Bub, Mertins, Backofen,
Lindheimer, Eduard Mueller, and Rock. (Reinhardt, Louis, "The Com-
munistic Colony of Bettina," *Quarterly* Texas State Historical Association,
III, 34-35.)

In his *Deutsche Pioniere in Texas*, 26, Adolf Paul Weber gives the list

Dr. Ferdinand von Herff and Hermann Spiess preceded the others to Texas in order to make the necessary preparations for transporting the others upon their arrival.   In March, 1847, as nearly as can be ascertained, the main group arrived at Galveston.[51] After various delays they reached the Llano in September, 1847. Emil Kriewicz, who knew the country well, since he had lived among the Indians since the making of the Meusebach treaty in March, 1847, was their guide on the way from Fredericksburg to the Llano.

On the north bank of the Llano where Elm Creek flows into it, about a mile below Castell, the settlement was made.   A temporary shed, forty feet long and twenty-two feet wide, covered with reed-grass, was built.   Later an adobe house covered with shingles was built.   About 200 bushels of corn were raised the following year. But late in the summer of 1848 the settlement was abandoned. The communistic experiment had failed.   Some had worked hard, but others had preferred to idle away their time in the shade of live-oak trees, where they dreamed of bygone student days and

of thirty-three members of the society, but he gives seven names which are not on Reinhardt's list.   These are: Hermann Spiess, Kattmann, Kappel, Zentner, Hoerner, Louis Reinhardt, and Obert.   Curiously enough, Reinhardt omits his own name and that of Spiess.   It must be assumed that Reinhardt's list is the more accurate, since he was a member of the group.   For the seven different names which Weber gives, Reinhardt gives those of Ottmer, Mertins, Lindheimer, Fuchs, Herrmann, Schunk, and Rock.   Reinhardt must be mistaken about Lindheimer, however.   Rock, a Canadian, joined the group at Carlshafen, also Vogelsang, but Reinhardt does not mention him.

[51]Reinhardt says July 17, 1847, but he must be mistaken about the date.   He says that they waited several weeks at Galveston in order that the ship, which was to take them to Carlshafen, might be repaired.   They lost some time, however, because the United States government chartered the ship when it was repaired for service in transporting troops to Vera Cruz.   They spent nearly a whole week going from Galveston to Carlshafen after they finally got started.   After a journey of four weeks they reached New Braunfels in August, as Reinhardt says.   In spite of the fact that they were delayed for nearly five weeks at New Braunfels on account of Reinhardt and Schenk getting sick with typhoid, Reinhardt reports that they reached the Llano early in September.   More than likely they reached Galveston in March and New Braunfels in May, for Reinhardt reports that Santa Anna and several other Comanche chiefs arranged a treaty in New Braunfels with Meusebach, von Coll, and Spiess.   (Reinhardt, "The Communistic Colony of Bettina," *Quarterly* Texas State Historical Association, III, 35-37.)   What Reinhardt took for the making of a treaty was simply a visit by the Indians to get their presents which Meusebach had promised to give them in May, if they ratified the treaty which he had made with them in March.   (See Chapter IX, p. 187, of this study.)

lived up to the convenient principle expressed in the words, "Eat and drink, for after death there is no joy" *(Ede, bibe, post mortem nulla voluptas).*[52]

After the settlement was abandoned the members of the group went to the *Darmstaedter Farm,* a few miles from New Braunfels. Dr. Herff went back to Germany and married in Darmstadt. The *Darmstaedter Farm* had been established two and one-half miles from New Braunfels on Comal Creek by three members of the communistic group who had been left there for that purpose. Late in the year 1848 the remnant of "The Forty" were visited at the *Darmstaedter Farm* by six other young men from their native city of Darmstadt. These were Ernst Dosch, Ernst von Lichtenberg, Ludwig von Lichtenberg, von Rotsmann, Hermann Schenck, and a young man by the name of Keller.[53]

The four settlements made by the Society on the Fisher and Miller grant and the communistic settlement founded on the grant with the permission of the Society did not have a very large population in 1850, only 32 persons being listed for the Llano region of Gillespie County in 1850.[54] On February 1, 1856, Llano County was created by an act of the legislature of Texas and took in the region of the German settlements on the Llano.[55] By 1860 the number of persons of German extraction in Llano County was slightly more than three times as large as in 1850. Since the total number of white persons in Llano was 1047, only about one-tenth of the population was of German extraction, which was not a good showing for the colonization work of the Society.[56]

In the period from 1850 to 1860 seven counties, lying either wholly or partly in the Fisher and Miller grant, were organized. These were Llano and San Saba, February 1, 1856, McCulloch, August 27, 1856, Mason, Menard, and Kimble, January 22, 1858, and Concho, February 1, 1858.[57] With the exception of Llano County, the Society founded no settlements in any of these counties

[52]Weber *Deutsche Pioniere in Texas,* 26-31. Penniger, *Fest-Ausgabe,* 52-53, 119; Reinhardt, "The Communistic Colony of Bettina," *Quarterly* Texas State Historical Association, III, 33-40.

[53]Weber, *Deutsche Pioniere in Texas,* 32, 36.

[54]See above, p. 153, in connection with the census of 1850 for Castell.

[55]Gammel, *Laws of Texas,* IV, 224-225.

[56]Kennedy, Joseph C. G., *Population of the United States in 1860,* 475, 488.

[57]Gammel, *Laws of Texas,* IV, 224-226, 487-488, 930-931, 959.

in the Fisher and Miller grant, but it can not be said, therefore, that the Society's activities failed to induce German settlers to go into the other counties of the grant. The number was small, it must be admitted.[58] The census of 1860 does not give any statistics on the German population of McCulloch, Concho, Menard, and Kimble counties. In San Saba County there were only about 20 persons of German extraction out of a total of 824 white persons, a very small proportion. In Mason County, however, there

[58]If the Society had continued to function after 1847 and had been able to stand the financial strain attendant upon a colonization project so far away from Germany, it might have placed more settlers on the grant. The political disturbances in Germany in 1848 and 1849 hindered the Society in its work. An attempt was made to transfer the Society's privileges and— debts— in 1848 to a new colonization company (Deutsche Kolonisationsgesellschaft fuer Texas in Bieberich) organized in that year by Count Castell, Ludwig Martin, an attorney of Freiburg, and Ubaghs, a railroad director, but nothing came of the proposal. In 1850 the Society, through Count Friedrich of Alt-Leiningen, issued a committee report, and Hermann, Count of Neu-Wied, president of the Society, issued a statement in 1851 about the work done by the Society. The Society also published in 1851 a large folder containing instructions for German emigrants to Texas, a large map of the state of Texas, another map showing the surveyed portions of the Fisher and Miller grant, and plans of the towns of New Braunfels, Fredericksburg, and Indianola. This literature all appeared in Wiesbaden. (Rosenberg, Kritik, 22; Parisius, Beitraege zur Geschichte der deutschen Genossenschafts-Bewegung, 46; Benjamin, Germans in Texas, 54.)

While Spiess was commissioner-general, Gustav Dresel was appointed as general business agent, but he failed to bring order into the Society's financial affairs. On October 28, 1847, Spiess, in defending the Society against an attack that had appeared in the Texian Advocate on September 30, 1847, spoke of the Society's financial affairs as follows: Unlike the business of the merchant who expends, but soon again to realize his principal and profits, the company for upwards of three years has been continually disbursing and not a dollar has come into its treasury except from the private fortunes of its members. Owing to causes which could not have been foreseen, the company's expenses have been increased much beyond what could have been anticipated. The political change this country has undergone is inauspicious to emigration from Germany; the Mexican war is also an obstacle and has much increased the expense of subsistence and the cost of transportation from the coast to the interior; the apprehended hostility of the Indians has elicited an admonition from the Executive of the State to the agents of the company advising them not to send emigrants to the upper country and thus hundreds have been detained and subsisted at the expense of the company who might otherwise have been providing for themselves on the colony lands; and ten thousand dollars cash of the company's funds have been spent in presents among the savages of our frontier to conciliate them and keep them from committing open aggressions on the settlements. These and many other causes that might be adduced will show a generous community that it is neither unreasonable nor surprising if there should be a temporary deficit in the treasury of our company. (Democratic Telegraph and Texas Register, October 28, 1847, 3, col. 1-2.) Spiess admitted that the company had

were about 330 persons of German extraction out of a total of 606, or more than one-half.[59]

In summing up the work of the Society, it must be said that it accomplished a great deal. New Braunfels and Fredericksburg, or in a large sense, Comal and Gillespie counties, became the real centers of German life and activity in the western part of the state. They were largely German in population. In 1860 Comal County had a foreign population of 2186 in its total white population of 3837 and Gillespie County 1363 in its total of 2703. The children of German extraction born in Texas, whom the census lists as native-born, numbered about one-half as many as the foreign-born population. Consequently the population of German extraction in Comal County in 1860 was about 3300 and that in Gillespie County about 2000. Approximately 85 per cent of the people of Comal County and 75 per cent of the people of Gillespie County were German.[60]

New Braunfels and Fredericksburg were founded in connection with the work which the Society set out to perform, namely, to direct German emigration toward one place, Texas. The Society did not, by any means, attain the goal which it had in mind, that of directing all German emigrants to Texas. In the very nature of the case, that goal was unattainable. The Society's funds were too limited for such a large undertaking. On the other hand, the Society performed a valuable service to the state by developing a portion of the western part of Texas. Without the effort of the Society to find a home for Germans in Texas, it is safe to say that

drafts outstanding in the amount of about $120,000 but claimed that they would be paid.

Louis Bene succeeded Spiess as commissioner-general in 1848 and authorized Dresel to sell Nassau Farm. Either through carelessness or ignorance Bene neglected to have the Society's premium headrights, which Granville E. Sherwood, the commissioner of the Fisher and Miller colony lands, issued in the name of Henry F. Fisher, annulled by judicial process, thus causing the loss of most of the Society's claims to premium lands. In 1852 Bene went back to Germany and turned his office over to H. Wilke, the Society's surveyor, but Wilke was never empowered by the Society to act as commissioner-general. (Rosenberg, *Kritik*, 22; Penniger, *Fest-Ausgabe*, 53-54; Schuetz, *Texas*, 260; Bracht, *Texas im Jahre 1848*, 271; Herff, *Die geregelte Auswanderung*, 30.)

[59]Kennedy, *Population of the United States in 1860*, 473, 475, 487-488. To the number of foreign-born given in the census the writer has added about half that number for the children born in Texas. Such children are listed as native-born.

[60]Kennedy, *Population of the United States in 1860*, 473, 487-488.

only a very small number of German emigrants would have gone
to Texas and that these few would have gone to the German settlements in the counties of Austin, Colorado, and Fayette. After
the Society had established the settlements of New Braunfels and
Fredericksburg, German emigrants, still following the natural desire to live among relatives, friends, and countrymen, began to go
to these new settlements also. Although after 1847 the Society
was no longer aiding emigrants, the work which it had begun continued unabated. German emigrants continued to go to the western part of Texas and increased the population of New Braunfels
and Fredericksburg. From these two settlements as centers, as
will be shown in the next chapter, other settlements were established, not only in Comal and Gillespie counties, but also in the
counties of Kendall and Guadalupe.

CHAPTER VIII

SISTERDALE, BOERNE, COMFORT, AND OTHER GERMAN SETTLEMENTS IN WEST TEXAS

Although the Society's work to found settlements came to an end in 1847, the influence of the Society did not cease. It was pointed out in the previous chapter that the colonization work of the Society caused many Germans to go into the western part of the State of Texas, where they could be near their relatives, friends, and countrymen. Through the work of the Society and through letters written back home to relatives by emigrants who had gone to Texas under its guidance, Texas became well known in Germany. As a result of the continued emigration of Germans to Texas many other settlements were founded. Two of them, as a matter of fact, came into being before the Society had finished its work, namely, Comaltown and Hortontown.

It was in 1846 that Rafael Garza laid out the settlement of Comaltown across the Comal River from New Braunfels. Some of the Society's immigrants who arrived in New Braunfels in the early spring of 1846 settled in Comaltown and thus helped to found the second German settlement in Comal County.[1] But Comaltown did not long remain a separate settlement, for the legislative act of May 11, 1846,[2] by which New Braunfels was incorporated, made Comaltown a part of New Braunfels. Comaltown had become fairly well settled by 1850. In that year 45 residents of Comaltown petitioned the legislature of Texas for a change in the corporate limits of New Braunfels.[3] Figured at the rate of five persons to a family, Comaltown must have had about 200 persons, more or less, in 1850. The names of the petitioners were: Conrad Holzgraefe, H. R. Crawford, Andrew Spiva, W. G. Ganger, Daniel Murchison, D. H. Coleman, Heinrich Metzing, Friedrich Freitag, Johannes Sebastian, Heinrich Friedrich

---

[1]Seele, "Ein Beitrag zur Geschichte von Neu Braunfels," *Jahrbuch fuer Texas* (1882), 41; Seele, *A Short Sketch of Comal County*, 5.

[2]Gammel, *Laws of Texas*, II, 582-585.

[3]MS. Records Office Secretary of State, Memorial No. 43, File Box No. 14, Letter No. C. The petition dated February 5, 1850, asked that all of that part of New Braunfels lying on the left bank of the Comal River be taken out of the city limits.

Koehler, Heinrich Twiefel, Harm Cordes, Juergen Hinrich Ottens, Heinrich Wesch, David Ely, C. H. Sieber, Ludwig Voigt, Conrad Pape, Andreas Pape, Jacob Rose, G. F. Salziger, J. G. F. Martin Salziger, Daniel Bussmann, H. Krueger, Johann Georg Mueller, J. H. Dedeke, Conrad Engelke, E. Potts, A. Lee, H. Kellermann, David Braunholz, R. A. Robison, Ludwig Kesler, Emile Loep, J. West, Johann Heinrich Petri, Valentin Braunholz, E. Voelcker, W. H. Meriwether, Friedrich Voelkerath, Heinrich Weichold, Johannes Schnautz, Gottlieb Vogt, Heinrich Klingemann, J. H. Holtermann. In 1852 eight of the residents of Comaltown petitioned the legislature for the incorporation of the "Comal Union School." The signers, who, with Julius Harms, were to be created into a body politic, were Daniel Murchison, William Sattler, J. G. Mueller, J. J. Ottens, Conrad Pape, Conrad Engelke, and J. H. Klingemann.[4]

During the summer of 1846, partly because of the dreadful epidemic which had broken out in New Braunfels and partly because of the good land for agricultural purposes available on the high ground east of the Guadalupe River valley directly across from New Braunfels along the San Antonio-Nacogdoches road, some of the Society's immigrants settled on what was known as Horton's League. The new settlement, then in Guadalupe but now in Comal County, was named Hortontown. In the fall and winter of 1846 to 1847 other arrivals at New Braunfels, deciding to engage in farming on Horton's League, settled there.[5] The census of 1850 gave Hortontown credit for one hundred and thirty-nine people.[6] Being strictly an agricultural settlement, Hortontown did not increase rapidly in population. In 1853 the population was about 160. On January 3 of that year 31 settlers of Hortontown and Neighborsville presented a memorial to the legislature asking for a change in the boundaries of Comal and Guadalupe counties so that Hortontown and Neighborsville would be included in Comal County.[7] Neighborsville was an agricultural settlement lying

[4]MS. Records Office Secretary of State, Memorial No. 298, File Box No. 19, Letter No. C. More will be said of the "Comal Union School" in a later chapter.

[5]Seele, A Short Sketch of Comal County, 6; Seele, "Ein Beitrag zur Geschichte von Neu Braunfels," Jahrbuch fuer Texas (1882), 41.

[6]DeBow, J. D. B., Statistical View of the United States. . . . A Compendium of the Seventh Census, 360.

[7]MS. Records Office Secretary of State, Memorial No. 63, File Box No.

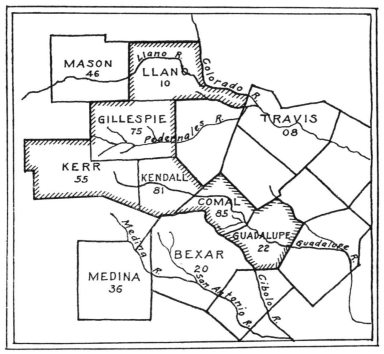

MAP 8

COUNTIES IN WESTERN TEXAS WITH GERMAN SETTLEMENTS AND A
GERMAN ELEMENT BY 1860

The counties which are shaded are those which had definite German settlements by 1860; the others which are named had only a German element.
The figure with each county indicates the approximate percentage ratio
of the German population to the total white population.   See also Table
II on the following page.

Table II.—Percentage Ratio of German Population to Total White Population in Counties of West Texas with German Settlements and a German Element in 1860.

Counties	Native	Foreign	Total*	German†	Percent-age	Corrected Percent-age‡
Comal............	1651	2186	3837	2186	57	85
Gillespie...........	1340	1363	2703	1363	50	75
Guadalupe........	2949	740	3689	570	15	22
Kendall¶.........	250	300	550	300	54	81
Kerr...............	369	216	585	216	37	55
Llano..................	958	89	1047	70	07	10
Bexar..................	7774	5283	10122	1770	13	20
Mason..............	385	221	606	190	31	46
Medina.............	908	824	1732	412	24	36
Travis...............	4371	560	4931	280	05	08

*Figures secured from Kennedy, Joseph C. G., *Population of the United States in 1860*, pp. 487–489.   The figures for the foreign population represent more than only persons of German nativity.

†In Walker, Francis A., *The Statistics of the Population of the United States* (Volume I of the Ninth Census, 1870), pp. 372 and 373, is found a table on Selected Nativities by Counties.   On the basis of figures given in that table the writer estimated the number of Germans in the above Texas counties in 1860, but did not make any changes for Comal and Gillespie counties.

‡For an explanation of this term, see Table I, footnote ‡, on page 62 of this study.

¶The figures for Kendall County are included here, although the county was not organized when the census was taken.   They are based on material available to the writer, which, however, is too involved to explain.   The principal settlements in Kendall County when first organized were Sisterdale and Boerne.   For the material, however, see pages 171 to 173 of this study and Walker, Francis A., *The Statistics of the Population of the United States* (Volume I of the Ninth Census, 1870), pages 322 and 372.

between New Braunfels and Hortontown, as well as to the south of Hortontown, on the left bank of the Guadalupe. In October, 1853, other residents of Hortontown and Neighborsville presented a memorial opposing the change of boundaries,[8] but in August, 1855, when the settlers of Hortontown petitioned the legislature again for a change in the boundaries of Comal and Guadalupe counties, a number of Neighborsville settlers signed the petition.[9] A counter petition signed by 70 settlers from the northern part of Guadalupe County was presented, and, as before, the legislature made no change in the boundaries.

On the counter petition nine German settlers of Yorks Creek, a small German settlement, placed their signatures. These were Leopold Biesele, Friedrich Bading, Franz Eigendorf, Carl Eigendorf, Andreas August Bading, Charles Adolph Bading, Julius Rudolph Bading, August Nolte, and David Braunholz. Four of the Yorks Creek settlers, H. F. Lohrberg, Roman Karolus, H. Blume, and Wm. Flagge, signed the other petition.[10] There seems

33, Letter No. G. The signers of the petition were: Louis Mittendorf, Sr., C. Kramer, L. Mittendorf, Jr., G. A. Mittendorf, E. Mittendorf, H. Mittendorf, H. Loep, Ed. Loep, O. Brinkmann, G. Bodemann, L. Fischer, H. Fischer, H. Richter, C. von Koennecke, Rudolf du Menil, Fr. Voges, W. Voges, H. Allerkamp, Fr. Alves, W. Fehlis, H. Wallhoefer, H. Busch, H. Luersen, Oscar Friedrich, Val. Kirmse, F. Eickenroth, Fr. Eilers, Berthold Ziliax, Hermann Ziliax, Hermann Schenk, Wilhelm Heim. The petition does not distinguish between the residents of Hortontown and Neighborsville, but most of these settlers lived in Hortontown.

[8]MS. Records Office Secretary of State, Memorial No. 63, File Box No. 33, Letter No. G. The names of the following settlers appeared on the petition: Gottlieb Strempel, Fr. Schuenemann, Konrad Schuenemann, Wm. Boerner, Heinrich Specht, Heinrich Winter, Carl Neuse, Friedrich Schulze, Jr., August Albrecht, Friedrich Sorge, August Ebert, Heinrich Wahnschaffe, August Dauer, Christian Dauer, Heinrich Breustedt, Andreas Breustedt, Wilhelm Bock, Ferdinand Willig, Otto Woehler, Friedrich Griche, H. Heinemeier, Ch. Heinemeier, Louis Heinemeier, the widow Neuse, Conrad Brachler, Wm. Fehlis, Charles Krukemeier, H. Boerner, Fr. Timm, Fr. Schulze, August Schulze, Conrad Bormann, Karoline Henze, Conrad Ewald, Johann Ewald, Daniel Thiers, Heinrich Goepf, Heinrich Bruemmer, Martin Engelmann, Leonard Hitzfelder, Leopold Iwonski, Adolph Iwonski, Charles G. Iwonski. Most of these settlers lived in Neighborsville, as far as I have been able to determine.

[9]MS. Records Office Secretary of State, Memorial No. 232, File Box No. 18, Letter No. C.

[10]Ibid.

Leopold Biesele was the writer's paternal grandfather and Charles Adolph Bading his maternal grandfather. At the age of 22 Leopold Biesele took part in the revolution of 1849 in Baden as a lieutenant in the revolutionary forces. After a period of internment he emigrated to Texas in 1851 and settled on the Yorks Creek in the northern part of Guadalupe

to have been no store in the settlement in the early days. Blum
School, founded in 1859, became the gathering place of the settlement. By 1860 there was a total of 37 settlers in the Yorks Creek
settlement.[11]

While these various settlements were forming east of the Guadalupe River two others came into being on its right bank below
New Braunfels. The first of these was Schumannsville, founded
about 1847. The proximity of the settlement to New Braunfels,
the racial and lingual relationship of its settlers and those of
New Braunfels, and the need of crossing the Guadalupe in order
to attend to official business in Seguin, the county seat of Guadalupe County, caused the settlers of Schumannsville on October 29,
1849, to petition the legislature for a change in the boundaries of
Guadalupe and Comal counties so that Schumannsville would be
located in Comal County. The following persons signed the peti-
tion: A. Laechelin, Michael Buchholz, Friedrich Blumberg,
Friedrich Rudeloff, Hermine Schumann, A. W. Schumann, Carl
Koepsel, Johann Leissner, Christoph Maurer, Friedrich Grimm,
Eva Maurer, Eva Zipp, Katherine Ewald, Theodor Buchholz, Carl
Blumberg, Gustav Elley, Jacob Adam, Daniel Koepsel, Friedrich
Koepsel, Johann August Leissner, August Hofmann, Johann Lin-

County. When the Yorks Creek settlement organized a school in 1859
he became one of the first trustees, holding the position for two years.
In 1863 he was elected teacher at a salary of $250.00 per year, part of
which was paid in coin. During the thirteen years of his incumbency
of the position some of his own children and his later sons-in-law and
daughters-in-law were his pupils, as the records of Blum School show.
(Coers, A. C., "Blum School, 1859-1927," *Guadalupe Gazette Bulletin*,
July 28, 1927, 2, col. 4, August 4, 1927, 6, col. 3.) After his retirement
from Blum School he became the teacher of another school located only a
quarter of a mile from his farm. After having served his community for
twenty years he gave up his position in 1883. On June 3, 1905, he died
at the age of over 78 years.

[11]Eighth Census, Schedule 4; Productions of Agriculture; Coers, A. C.,
"Blum School, 1859-1927," *Guadalupe Gazette-Bulletin*, July 28, 1927, 2,
col. 4.

In addition to the settlers already named, these two sources list the
following: Christian Gesche, Dr. Hermann Starcke, F. Freitag, Wm.
Dietert, Andreas Dietert, Gottfried Dietert, Max Starcke, Edward Eber-
hard, Oscar Starcke, Wilhelm Harborth, August Harborth, Heinrich Harborth, Christian Heinemeyer, Conrad Bormann, Heinrich Bauer, ? Rhodius,
the widow Jung, Wilhelm Fehlis, Albert Haseloff, Peter Ernst, ? Wehe,
C. Legrand, C. Lehmann, and D. Peyl. Seven other settlers were Julius
Ploetz, Wilhelm Thormeyer, Louis Stroehmer, Johannes Braunholz,
Johann Karolus, Hannibal Haner, and Jacob Wilhelm.

demann, Johann Zipp, Johann Lindemann, Jr., and Julius Behrendt.[12] The request was not granted.

Lying near Schumannsville to the westward was a small German community that needs mention. It was the agricultural community of Santa Clara on the Santa Clara Creek. By 1860 it had come into definite existence. On January 28, 1860, Johann Nagel, Wilhelm Thiel, Johann Heinrich Schultze, Carl Voges, Ferdinand Weyel, Diedrich Voges, Jacob Orth, Ludwig Kurre, Henry Voelcker, and J. Adams signed a petition to the legislature that Santa Clara and Schumannsville be placed into Comal County.[13] To the list of names so far given must be added the names of John Schnabel, Anton Troeste, Eduard Foerster, and Valentin Klein.

Between 1850 and 1860 a German settlement was formed in the region now occupied by McQueeney and Marion in Guadalupe County. Out of eighty names listed in the census of 1860, fifty-eight are those of German settlers. The census calls the settlement Valley Post Office.[14] This settlement was located in a region where the fertility of the soil was of the first class. Consequently nearly all of the settlers became prosperous.

From New Braunfels there was an expansion of settlement in a westward direction. The principal expansion in an eastward direction resulted in the settlement of Comaltown, Hortontown, and Neighborsville. The westward expansion followed Comal Creek but no definite settlements sprang up. The *Darmstaedter Farm,* located about two and one-half miles west of New Braunfels, failed

[12]MS. Records Office Secretary of State, Memorial No. 32, File Box No. 32, Letter No. G.

[13]MS. Records Office Secretary of State, Memorial No. 63, File Box 33, Letter No. G. Four Schumannsville settlers signed the petition also.

[14]Eighth Census, Schedule 4: Productions of Agriculture; Texas State Library.

The following German names appear on the census of 1860: Robert Hellmann, C. Huthmacher, G. Muehlberg, Agnes Galvin, F. Ehal (Thal?), Jacob Pfeil, Carl Conrad, D. Brotz, A. Schmidt, Jacob Schloder (Schlather?), Geo. Schloder (Schlather?), John Rittemann, M. Amacher, J. G. Bergfeld, A. Pfeil, Wm. Seiler, Christian Schneider, John Rhodius, Christian Baller, Wm. Schloder (Schlather?), A. Rittemann, S. Schraub, L. Stamitz, J. Kneupper, F. Pfannstiel, Henry Acker, F. Reinhardt, George Hild, J. D. Pfannstiel, E. Linne, F. Zuehl, Wm. Zuehl, Charles Saur, Jacob Seiler, V. Klein, F. Weyel, C. Voges, John Orth, D. Voges, Joseph Klein, F. Eberling, B. Schneider, R. Krueger, Adam Becker, J. Hildebrandt, M. Hell, Henry Helmke, J. Schulz, G. Wohlfahrt, H. Stolte, G. Scheffel, A. Markgraf, C. Dittmar, John A. Leissner, F. Koepsel, F. Bocker, Christian Dammann.

to become the center of a settlement. Late in the year 1848 six young men from Darmstadt arrived in New Braunfels and, after having remained at the *"Darmstaedter Farm"* for a few weeks, bought 200 acres of land eight miles west of New Braunfels on Comal Creek. These men were Ernst Dosch, Ernst von Lichtenberg, Ludwig von Lichtenberg, Baron von Rotsmann, Hermann Schenck, and a young man named Keller. This establishment might have become the nucleus of a settlement, but, after farming together for a year, the men abandoned the joint undertaking and sold their farm to S. von Schwartzhoff, a jurist.[15] Other settlers of the locality were L. Grothaus, L. Schuette, C. Riefkohl, H. Bremer, H. Schaefer, Henry Hierholzer, and Conrad Wenzel.

Various other German settlements sprang up in Comal County. Several of them had very few settlers by 1860, but the communities were distinct and definite enough to be called settlements. They show how rapidly all parts of Comal County were being settled by Germans. They were: Comal Creek, Mission Hill, Waco Springs, Buffalo Springs, Cibolo, Smithson's Valley, and Upper Blanco.[16]

The census of 1850 listed the settlers of Gillespie County under the heads of Fredericksburg, Live Oak Settlement, Zodiac Mills, Fort Martin Scott, Pedernales Settlement, and Llano River Settlement. Zodiac Mills was the Mormon settlement, of

---

[15]Weber, *Deutsche Pioniere in Texas*, 36-41. The place is referred to at the present time as Eight Mile Creek *(Acht Meilen Creek)*, but the voting box is called Danville.

[16]The early settlers of these communities were:

Comal Creek: Count Ernst von Coreth, L. Klappenbach, Anton Werner, Charles Fuchs, Anton Schneider, C. Klappenbach, G. Klappenbach, Gustav Hoffmann.

Mission Hill: Hermann Conring, L. Kessler, Adolf Brecher, J. G. Brehmer, H. Dietz, Julius Brehmer, C. Kappmeyer, Johann J. Walzem, J. G. Mueller, G. Starz, Hy. Boehme.

Waco Springs: Hermann Spiess, Wm. Wetzel, Wm. Krueger, J. J. Groos, Fritz Pape, Christian Lohl, Heinrich Meine.

Buffalo Springs: C. Bremer, F. Tausch, John Startz, G. F. Kunz, Johann Alsens, Julius Bose, H. Coers, Gustav Artzt, H. Startz, Friedrich Sattler, Charles Esser, Carl Elmendorf, Gabriel Remmler, Sebastian Schertz, Johann Kleinhaus, Hermann Heffter, Johann Jost Haas.

Cibolo: H. Schulemeyer, J. F. Voges, J. B. Rompel, L. Vogel, C. Wehe, John Kabelmacher, Albert Foerster, Aug. Pieper, Henry Voges, F. Bracht.

Smithson's Valley: Ben Smithson, H. Busch, L. Groenke, Christian Loeffler, Wm. Hillert, C. Ohldrich, Ch. Spangenberg, And. Gass, Bernhard Kuhn, J. Seegers, C. Kuehn.

Upper Blanco: F. Muenzler, Johann Adolf Kneupper, Georg Wuppermann, Meyerhofer, H. Liessmann, Carl Koch, H. Bruemmer, Chr. Lange, August Lange, H. Schmidt, Eduard Schmidt, Gottlieb Elbel, Erdmann Elbel.

which mention was made in the preceding chapter. Attention was also called to the other places, with the exception of the Live Oak and Pedernales settlements. The Live Oak settlement was strictly a German settlement. It was situated to the west of Fredericksburg on Live Oak Creek, a tributary of the Pedernales. In a total population of 126, there were 117 persons of German extraction.[17] In the census of 1860 this region was listed as Fredericksburg, Precinct II.

In the Pedernales settlement there were 44 persons of German descent in 1850. The families living there were those of Adolph Schildknecht, John Klein, Gottfried Herrmann, John Leyendecker, Jr., Dr. William Keidel, William Wahrmund, Auguste Wahrmund, and Charles Feller. The single persons in the settlement were Emilie Wahrmund, William Feller, Susanna Philip, August Kott, and Charles Kraemer.[18]

In 1860 three new German settlements appeared on the census of Gillespie County. These were Grape Creek, northwest of Fredericksburg, on the Grape Creek, Caldwellshill, east of Grape Creek, and Cherry Spring, in the northern part of the county. Out of a total of 308 persons listed for Grape Creek, 281 had names indicating that they were of German descent. William Luckenbach was postmaster for the settlement, and Jacob Brodbeck, E. L. Theuman, and Louis Teschner were listed as school teachers.[19]

---

[17] Photostat Seventh Census, Schedule of Free Inhabitants, Gillespie County, University of Texas.
The following families were listed in the 1850 census: Nicholas Jacoby, Charles H. Nimitz, Henry Miller, William Jenks, Friedrich Pape, Mary Ann Hart, Jacob Roeder, Charles Usener, Peter Bickel, Friedrich Kneese, William Schra, Henry Schrop, William Schrop, Mathias Bonn, Christian Quintell, John Leyendecker, Jacob Luckenbach, Philip Klaerner, Albert Reichenau, Engelhart Weber, Christian Hundhausen, Ferdinand Gellermann, Elizabeth Weber, and Nicholas Schmidt. The single persons listed were: William Mogford, Louisa Keyser, Louisa Mogford, Henry Keyser, Richard Cloudt, Friedrich Wrede, Arthur Cloudt, Minerva Gaertner, Mary Dietz, William Kraemer, Edward Kraemer, Jacob Fiedler, Francis Petermann, and Gottlieb Fischer.
[18] *Ibid.*
[19] Photostat Eighth Census, Schedule of Free Inhabitants, Gillespie County, University of Texas.
The following families were listed: Erasmus Frantzen, John Dechert, Caspar Danz, George Leineweber, Jacob Brodbeck, Gustav Schumann, William Schumann, Daniel Weyershausen, Christian Kusenberger, Henry Beckmann, Philip Beck, Adam Pehl, Peter Pehl, John Blank, Caspar Hopf, August Vater, John Kleck, John Kallenberg, John Rauch, Friedrich Rechenthien, Peter Imhof, John D. Land, Jacob Land, William Mogford, John Schmidtzinsky, Johann Striegler, Jacob Kusenberger, Fried-

In Caldwellshill, which was named after its postmaster, John Caldwell, the number of persons of German descent, including men, women, and children, amounted to 196 out of a total of 335. The majority of the people of the settlement were, therefore, German.[20] The census listed Caldwellshill as the fifth precinct of Gillespie County.

Cherry Spring, which lay almost due north of Fredericksburg on the "Emigrant" Road, was named after Cherry Spring Creek. It was a fairly large settlement by 1860 and had a post office and several stores.[21] Its total population of 202 persons included 130 men, women, and children of German descent.[22] Theodor Huelse-

rich Scharnhorst, Ferdinand Toepperwein, William Luckenbach, August Luckenbach, Jacob Luckenbach, William Diehl, Wolfgang Braeutigam, Valentin Hopf, August Schoenewolf, Henry Minnel, Henry Habenicht, Jost Bohl, Franz Wehmeyer, John Liebeneicher, Johanna Fach, John Poetsch, Peter Poetsch, Louis Doebbler, Albert Molsberger, Christian Ruebsamen, Ferdinand Ruebsamen, Christian Schramm, Christian Baag, Adam Roedig, Christian Gaertner, Henry Taubert, Peter Kuhlmann, Wilhelm Sauer, August Schild, William Feller, Caspar Ressman, Henry Arhelger, Jacob Zanner, Friedrich Kutscher, August Ebers, Ferdinand Doebbler, John Weber, Friedrich Gellermann, Friedrich Meyer. The single persons were: Johanna Hasse, John Immel, William Baetge, Henry Kramm, Emilie Rumpf, Elsie Luckenbach, Mary Braeutigam, Henry Tapperich, E. L. Theuman, Henry Ruetter, Theodor Schild, August Hoffman, and Peter Heep.

[20]Photostat Eighth Census, Schedule of Free Inhabitants, Gillespie County, University of Texas.

The families listed were those of Ernst Schaeper, Henry Grobe, Christian Fahrenhorst, Henry Kamlah, John Ebert, Nicolaus Jacoby, Peter Jacoby, August Decker, Valentin Homan, Henry Kaese, Christian Althaus, Henry Behrens, Jost Stahl, Melchior Bauer, Ludwig Spaeth, Nicolaus Rasche, Friedrich Welgehausen, Gottfried Ottmer, Henry Roeder, Mathias Zenner, Wendelin Mittel, Adam Fries, Friedrich Herbert, Carl Hohenberger, Christian Behrens, William Koennecke, Carl Koennecke, August Koennecke, George Hetzel, Christian Vogel, Henry Weyershausen, Conrad Bock, Fritz Rohde, Michael Vollmer, Ludwig Koenig, Henry Kirchner, Peter Burg, Henry Bruns, and Christian Behrens. The single persons were George Brodbeck, Jacob Welte, Michael Tatsch, John Caldwell, and Hermann Flick.

[21]Cherry Spring lies between Fredericksburg and Mason on the highway which follows, in the main, the old "Emigrant" Road from San Antonio to El Paso. About ten miles beyond it lies Loyal Valley, a little town laid out by John O. Meusebach about the year 1867. A mile beyond Cherry Spring, near the line between Mason and Gillespie counties, Meusebach, who died on May 27, 1897, was buried on a spot selected by himself some time before his death. (Penniger, *Fest-Ausgabe*, 58; *San Antonio Express*, January 10, 1926, 17, cols. 1-2.)

[22]Photostat Eighth Census, Schedule of Free Inhabitants, Gillespie County, University of Texas.

The census listed the following families: Conrad Mund, John Dietz, Carl Kensing, Henry Kensing, Gerhard Rehmann, Henry Bierschwale, Con-

THE OLD NICOLAUS ZINK HOME AT SISTERDALE, TEXAS

From a photograph in the possession of Mr. Alex Brinkmann, Comfort, Texas. The home was built for Nicolaus Zink in 1847 and was sold by him to Edward Degener in 1850

mann and Francis Stein were listed as school teachers in the census
of 1860.

It was the case with nearly every state of the United States in
which German settlements were made in the period from 1830 to
1860 that a so-called "Latin Settlement" came into being.[23] West
Texas was not to be an exception to the rule. Its Latin Settlement was called Sisterdale, situated in what is now Kendall
County. Its history dates back to the year 1847 when Nicolaus
Zink built a log cabin in the beautiful valley of the Sister Creek
near where it flows into the Guadalupe River. Sisterdale derives
its name from its location in the valley of the Sister Creek, formed
by two parallel running brooks, the "Sisters."[24] The next settler
in the valley was Ottomar von Behr.[25] In the years 1848 and 1849
a number of educated Germans settled in this picturesque region.
They were Ernst Kapp, who had been professor in the gymnasium
of Minden, Westphalia, Edward Degener, later a member of Congress from the San Antonio district, Dr. Adolf Douai, who became
editor of the *San Antonio Zeitung* when it was founded in 1853,
Emil Dresel, Julius Dresel, and Rudolph Dresel. In the early

rad Welge, Henry Welge, Christian Evers, Ludwig Evers, Henry Lange,
William Horlen, Henry Marckwardt, Peter Crenwelge, William Marschall,
Mathilde Weiss, William Kothe, Francis Stein, Adam Schuessler, John
Schuessler, Jacob Schuessler, Conrad Schuessler, Gustav Trasch, Dietrich
Rohde, Sophie Dittmar, Henry Ahrens, Henry Bratherich, George Schnei-
der, and Jacob Doering. The single men of the settlement were Henry
Kordzick, Theodor Huelsemann, Christian Pock, Fritz Moos, Michael
Sigmund, and Conrad Behrens.

23Concerning these "Latin Settlements," Bruncken, in his *German Political Refugees*, 18-19, says: These Latin Settlements have played a
part in bringing about a higher standard of civilization in the States
of the Mississippi Valley, which will be appreciated at its true worth
when the history of the cultural development of that section comes to be
written. As farmers, most of the "Latins" were not successes. They
could not be . . . . But during all this time the Latin Settlements
were the centers of light, from which higher ideals of life than were
customary among the ordinary settlers spread among wide portions of
the country. Especially in educational matters, these men set the standard, not only for their German countrymen, but for their American
neighbors.

24Siemering, A., "Die lateinische Ansiedlung in Texas," *Der deutsche
Pionier*, X, 59.

25Ottomar von Behr wrote a book, called *Guter Rath fuer Auswanderer
nach den Vereinigten Staaten von Nordamerika mit besonderer Beruecksichtigung von Texas* (Good Advice for Emigrants to the United States
with Special Reference to Texas), on the title page of which he is
called a practical farmer (*praktischer Landwirth*). The book was written especially for farmers and craftsmen and was based on his own
experience. It was published in Leipzig in 1847.

fifties Dr. W. I. Runge, August Siemering, later a journalist and editor of the *San Antonio Zeitung,* Baron von Westphal, Rudolph Carstanjen, Louis von Donop, Louis von Breitenbauch, Adolph Neubert, Otto Neubert, and Fr. Brunckow settled at Sisterdale.[26]

Of the accomplishments of the settlers of Sisterdale Tiling has the following to say:

The "Latin Settlement" had been born— a library of the ancient and modern classics was to be found in almost every house and the latest products of literature were eagerly read and discussed at the weekly meetings of these gentlemen farmers at the school house. It sometimes occurred at these meetings that Comanches stood listening at the open door, while one of the Latin farmers was lecturing on the socialistic theories of St. Simon or Fourier. Their social life was most refined and reached its climax when Prince Paul of Wuertemberg, brother of the reigning king, arrived at Sisterdale. Prince Paul was a naturalist and botanist of note and during his extensive travels had also come to Texas, where he was highly pleased to find real drawing-room conversation on the borders of civilization.

On October 13, 1850, John R. Bartlett passed through Sisterdale on his way to New Mexico and was agreeably impressed with the intelligence of Prof. Ernst Kapp's wife and daughter and with the comfort and taste of Kapp's house.[27]

In 1849, when Sisterdale was in its infancy and the woods resounded with the "classic" strokes of the Latin scholars, five members of the former Bettina settlement organized another communistic undertaking. They settled about twelve miles from Sisterdale near the present town of Boerne in Kendall County. These men were Philip Zoeller, Adam Vogt, Wilhelm Friedrich, Leopold Schulz, and Christian Flach, joined later by Fritz Kramer, a medical student from Darmstadt. In typical "classical" fashion they named their farm *Tusculum.*[28] After two years, however, they abandoned the experiment and sold their farm to a neighbor for about one-fourth of the purchase price.[29] They had bought two sections of land for another member of "The Forty," Christian von

---

[26]Tiling, *German Element in Texas,* 123; Weber, *Deutsche Pioniere in Texas,* part II, 6; Olmsted, *Wanderungen durch Texas,* 136-141.

[27]Bartlett, *Personal Narrative of Explorations and Incidents,* I, 56.

[28]They borrowed the term from Cicero, who called his country home *Tusculum.*

[29]"Die Lateinische Farm," *Deutsch-Texanische Monatshefte,* II, 239.

Hesse, but when von Hesse's brother did not come to Texas Hesse
sold the tract to Gustav Theissen. On this tract of land on the
Cibolo River, Theissen, who was an admirer of Ludwig Boerne, a
German publicist, laid out the town of Boerne.[30] The surveyor,
John James, assisted Theissen in the work. Adam Vogt, Leopold
Schulz, Wilhelm Friedrich, and Fritz Louis became the first set-
tlers. Later A. Staffel, Julius Fabra, M. Baumann, (Hermann?)
Spitzer, H. Wendler, F. Harz, and C. H. Clauss settled in Boerne.[31]
In December, 1859, the settlers of Boerne, joined by those of Sister-
dale, petitioned the legislature of Texas for the organization of a
new county out of parts of Bexar, Comal, and Blanco counties.[32]
This petition indicates that there were about 400 people in or near
Boerne, since about eighty of the signers lived there. Of the
eighty signers, twenty-eight were American settlers, which indicates that the settlement was remaining German.

The last of the settlements to be discussed in this chapter is
Comfort, which was founded in 1854 by Ernst Altgelt.[33] The

[30]Weber, *Deutsche Pioniere in Texas*, part II, 8.

[31]Clauss, C. Hugo, "Boerne und das Cibolo-Thal in Kendall County,"
Jahrbuch fuer Texas (1882), 29; *Ibid.*, "Aus der Vergangenheit der
Ansiedlung Boerne," *Deutsch-Texanische Monatshefte*, VII, 308.

[32]MS. Records Office Secretary of State, Memorial No. 232, File Box
No. 9, Letter No. B.
The signers of the petition were: George Wilkins Kendall, H. W.
Philipp, F. Wendler, E. Degener, A. Vogt, H. W. Vaughan, Erastus
Reed, August Staffel, S. S. Jamison, F. W. Shaeffer, Seaman Field,
Fisher A. Kibling, Henry Jacobs, H. Meckel, Frederic Meckel, Daniel
Meckel, Karl Wessely, Wm. Wills, Julius Phillips, F. Fabra, W. C. Pren-
tice, Joseph Tait, Gottfried Seewald, W. Kuhfuss, F. Werner, Jacob
Theis, Leopold Schultz, M. Baumann, Gustav Bergemann, Heinrich
Dietert, Fr. Lenz, Joseph Graham, Jacob Sims, A. Pfeiffer, August
Pfeiffer, J. Herff, Carl Adam, Ch. Fritz Louis, H. Dienger, W. Friedrich,
J. D. Johns, E. A. Cooper, Philip Zoeller, Franz Boehm, Augustus Vogt,
E. M. Morehouse, George M. Green, Max Falkenstein, Franz Schwarz,
Mathias Schwarz, George Krause, Carl Seewald, Louis Krause, C. Aman,
Heinrich Vogt, Philip F. Theis, W. Vogt, Joseph Beryman, Wilhelm
Pfeiffer, T. F. Stendeback, Wilhelm Beyer, Fr. Treidmann, John Herman,
John B. Deering, John Yates, Anton Beyer, C. C. Kelley, Franz Riedel,
J. Wenz, J. Scherz, W. G. Kingsbury, Charles M. Palmer, C. (———?),
Karl Heiligromann, Heinrich Heiligmann, Charles Wenzel, W. W. Wil-
liams, Peter Schaefer, F. W. J. Lohmann, Henry Wendler, H. G. Kroebely,
Ignatz Minnich, Conrad Adam, Heinrich Hasenkampe, Gottlieb Stephan,
Julius Dresel, Simon Hernandez, Christoph Rhodius, Hugo Degener,
Hilmar Degener, N. Zink, W. Geissler, G. Bonner, G. Hobart ?, C. Steines,
H. Bitt, Herman Hasenkampe.

[33]Two very readable accounts have been written about the founding
of Comfort. One of these was written by the wife of Ernst Altgelt.
Mrs. Altgelt's account, in manuscript form covering eight pages, is con-

early settlers of the neighborhood were Theodor Wiedenfeld, F. H. Schladoer, Michael Lindner, and C. W. Boerner. The land on which Comfort was laid out was owned by John Vles, president of a New Orleans cotton firm. Ernst Altgelt, who was in the employ of Vles, was sent to Texas by Vles to inspect the land,[34] and if he, Altgelt, found the land suitable for agricultural purposes, he was to have it surveyed and a part set aside for a town. For his services Altgelt was to receive a part of the land and of the proceeds of the sale of land.[35]

Upon his arrival at New Braunfels in 1854 Altgelt organized a surveying party consisting of himself, L. Grothaus, a surveyor, Fritz Goldbeck, Louis von Breitenbauch, Fr. Brunckow, and a few others.[36] Altgelt found the land so desirable that he had it surveyed. He even bought one thousand acres from F. H. Schladoer in order to have a larger tract. He chose a large level tract of land on the left bank of Cypress Creek, just above where it flows into the Guadalupe, for the site of the settlement. Comfort, the name chosen for the new town by Altgelt, expressed the wish of its founder that, after the hardships of founding the settlement had been overcome, the settlers might live there in

tained in a notebook of 147 pages filled with other accounts of incidents in the life of Mrs. Altgelt. The notebook is now in the possession of one of her sons, Mr. Hermann Altgelt of New Braunfels, Texas. Reference to this account will be made as Altgelt, *Comfort*, and the pagination of the notebook will be used. The other account is by Ferdinand H. Lohmann, who was a teacher in Comfort for a number of years and became intimately acquainted with the people and the history of the town. Another, but very brief account, is found in a collection of speeches and writings by Carl Herbst, one of the first settlers of Comfort. The collection is called: Carl Herbst, *Seine Reden und Schriften*. The University of Texas Library has a photostat copy of the collection.

[34]In his *Deutsche Pioniere in Texas*, part II, 10, Weber says that Altgelt had been sent to Texas at an earlier time to inspect the land but that he stopped at San Antonio, since it was too dangerous at that time to go into the region.

In his *Comfort*, Lohmann says that Alexander Rossy of New Braunfels, a relative of Wiedenfeld, found out that Vles was the owner of the land and induced Vles to send Altgelt to Texas to inspect it. The statement is found also in Weber, *Deutsche Pioniere in Texas*, part II, 10.

[35]Altgelt, *Comfort*, 105; Lohmann, *Comfort*, 19. Lohmann gives Altgelt credit for the idea of founding a town, for he says that Altgelt proposed the founding of a town and that Vles gave his consent.

[36]Neither Altgelt nor Lohmann mentions the names of the others, but Weber, in his *Deutsche Pioniere in Texas*, part II, 10, says that Christian Flach, who later married Antonie Kapp, daughter of Ernst Kapp, and Hermann Schimmelpfennig joined Altgelt on the surveying expedition.

ERNST HERMANN ALTGELT
Founder of Comfort
From a photograph in the possession of Mr. Hermann Altgelt,
New Braunfels, Texas

CARL HERBST
Co-editor of *Der Bettelsack*
From a reproduction in Schuetze, *Diamond Jubilee Souvenir Book of Comfort, Texas*

comfort. Besides the members of the surveying party, who remained in Comfort after their work was completed, the early settlers were G. F. Holekamp, Gottfried Schellhase, Carl Herbst, Fritz Sauer, John Hoerner, and Heinrich Wittbold. On August 25, 1854, the *Neu Braunfelser Zeitung* reported that 300 lots had been surveyed, that 30 lots had been sold to actual settlers, and that during the three previous weeks eight houses had been built.[37] In 1855 Christoph Flach and wife, Hermann Wille and wife, G. Vetterlein, and the families of K. Roggenbucke and G. Stieler settled in Comfort. Many other settlers came to Comfort before the Civil War. Some of these were Otto Brinkmann, Adolph Rosenthal, H. Seidensticker, Emil Karger, Carl Heinen, August Faltin, L. Strohacker, Friedrich Perner, Emil Serger, Christian Dietert, Henry Schwethelm, Ernst Schwethelm, Gustav Steves, A. Bohnert, Peter Ingenhuett, and Heinrich Boerner.[38]

Altgelt put up the first store in Comfort and arranged with Vles for building a saw and grist mill. Christian Dietert directed the building of the mill, to which the name "Perseverance Mill" was given. After a few years high water destroyed the dam, whereupon a new dam was built a little farther up. Then a drouth set in, Cypress Creek became almost dry, and the mill had to be abandoned. But during its lifetime Perseverance Mill furnished the lumber for Camp Verde, which was built in 1858 in Kerr County.[39] The principal occupations of the early settlers were shingle making, agriculture, and stock raising. Provisions and other supplies had to be hauled by ox wagons from San Antonio and New Braunfels. In 1856 a rifle club was organized

[37]*Neu Braunfelser Zeitung*, August 25, 1854, 1, col. 5. On November 3, 1854, Altgelt sent the *Zeitung* an article which spoke of the advantages of Comfort, such as good land and the good location. On December 8, 1854, the *Zeitung* commented on Comfort as follows: As we understand, the plan is for Comfort to become a little town. The Germans like to live together in small towns, where, besides the advantages of town life, such as sociableness, the nearness to medical help, and schools, the pleasures and independence of rural life may be enjoyed. . . . May Comfort be for its settlers what its name implies, a comfortable place to live in. As a new addition to the German population of West Texas, we extend to Comfort our best wishes for happiness and prosperity. (*Neu Braunfelser Zeitung*, December 8, 1854, 1, col. 5.)

[38]Altgelt, *Comfort*, 105-107; Lohmann, *Comfort*, 19-20.

[39]One of the interesting sights for the people of Comfort was the camel caravans with which the United States War Department was experimenting in West Texas. (Altgelt, *Comfort*, 110.)

on the farm of Thomas Ingenhuett, and from that year on the club staged a Fourth of July celebration every year. In 1856, also, Herman Schimmelpfennig, who was an excellent musician, organized a quartette in which Ernst Altgelt sang first tenor, Fritz Goldbeck second tenor, C. W. Boerner first bass, and G. F. Holekamp second bass. A written newspaper, known as *Der Bettelsack,* appeared for a while, during which Dr. Otto Mehlis, G. F. Holekamp, Louis von Breitenbauch, Carl Herbst, Fritz Goldbeck, Theodor Goldbeck, and others of the more educated settlers, were regular contributors. The little cabin in which Dr. Otto Mehlis and Carl Herbst corrected and assorted the manuscripts was called the *"Korrektionsbude."* In 1856 an American by the name of Glass organized the first school in Comfort. The younger generation of Comfort took an especial delight to designate some of the houses with droll names, such as "Monkey Cage" *(Affenbude),* "Broken Umbrella" *(Zerbrochener Regenschirm),* "Crystal Palace" *(Krystallpalast),* "Palm Grove" *(Palmenhain),* and "The Dirty Spoon" *(Zum schmierigen Loeffel).* The favorite swimming hole of the settlers was called "Home of the Nymphs" *(Nymphenheim).*[40]

When Kerr County was organized on January 26, 1856,[41] Comfort was put into the new county. In 1860 Comfort became the county seat but it retained this distinction only two years, after which it was placed in Kendall County.[42] While Comfort was the county seat its residents drew up a petition to the legislature protesting against the organization of Kendall County, for which the settlers of Boerne and Sisterdale had petitioned in December, 1859.[43] Out of a total of 89 signatures, 79 were those of German settlers.

[40]Altgelt, *Comfort,* 107-108; Lohmann, *Comfort,* 20-22, 26-27.

[41]Gammel, *Laws of Texas,* IV, 210-211.

[42]Mrs. Altgelt says that it was thought that Comfort would be chosen as the county seat when Kerr County was organized in 1856 but that the American settlers at Brownsborough, a few miles below Comfort, got their non-resident friends and relatives to vote and thus carried the election for Kerrville, the other contestant for the honor. In 1860, after Jonathan Scott, the chief justice had become estranged from the American party, he got the county seat transferred to Comfort. (Altgelt, *Comfort,* 108-109.)

[43]MS. Records Office Secretary of State, Memorial No. 174, File Box No. 8, Letter No. B.

The signers of the petition were: Theodore Wiedenfeld, county clerk, Adolph Rosenthal, county surveyor, Edward Steves, county commissioner, W. Heuermann, county commissioner, Charles Herbst, district clerk, C.

This completes, so far as this study is concerned, the account of the actual founding of settlements. The remaining chapters will deal with the relations between the German settlers and the Indians, with the part played by the German settlers in the politics of Texas, and with the contributions of the German settlers to the economic and cultural life of Texas.

Telgmann, sheriff, Ernst Altgelt, attorney at law, August Faltin, postmaster, Louis Berger, F. Hadenbrock, F. H. Schladoer, Thomas Ingenhuett, L. Strohacker, A. Bohnert, C. Bruckisch, Hubert Ingenhuett, A. Bruns, G. Vetterlein, R. Steves, C. Vetterlein, C. Stieler, G. Steves, Rudolph Voigt, Henry Steves, F. W. Boerner, Ed. Steves, C. W. Boerner, L. Boerner, Heinrich Boerner, Heinrich Wittbold, Ferdinand Schulze, Joseph Grollimund, Gottfried Schellhase, Carl Schmidt, Heinrich Steves, Jr., Henry Schwethelm, Ernst Schwethelm, Carl Heinen, G. Tegener, Peter Ingenhuett, Theodore Bruckisch, M. Ingenhuett, Henry Heinen, M. Weiss, F. Weiss, Ernst Schilling, A. Bebersdorf, G. F. Holekamp, A. Bebersdorf, Jr., C. Bonnet, F. Simon, H. Seidensticker, H. Wille, H. Weber, F. Weber, J. Sieckenius, W. Telgmann, P. H. Oberwetter, Otto Brinkmann, Alexander Brinkmann, Wm. Sieckenius, Chr. Humboldt, C. Schaerter, M. Lindner, L. Wagner, F. Spinacht, L. Kenopky, C. Tegener, Friedrich Perner, Emil Serger, Paul Hanisch, Fritz Delf, R. Pfeifer, H. Klepper, E. Cramer, L. Berner, Gottlieb Bauer, Georg Heinrich Luessmann, John Hoerner, Jonathan Scott, chief justice, E. A. McFadin, Geo. H. Cheney, Charles Pitts, J. Keenan, W. E. Stiles, Christian John, John C. Remick, B. F. Holland, and J. H. Reagan.

CHAPTER IX

THE RELATIONS BETWEEN THE GERMAN SETTLERS
AND THE INDIANS

This chapter will be confined to an account of the relations between the German settlers and the Indians in the counties of Comal, Gillespie, Guadalupe, Kendall, Llano, and Mason. The contact of the Indians with the counties of Austin, Washington, Fayette, Colorado, DeWitt, and Victoria is distinctly a relationship with the Anglo-American settlers. The subject of Indian defense came up for consideration by the provisional government of Texas in 1835 when "a motion was introduced on December 17, to establish a special company of ten men to range on the headwaters of Cummings and Rabb Creeks whenever necessary for the protection of that part of the country. It was referred to the Committee on Military Affairs, which reported on December 18 that 'the corps of rangers already created, is sufficient for the protection of the country, which the said resolution contemplates.' "[1] Such a company would have given protection to the few German settlers on the Mill Creek around Industry, founded by Ernst and Fordtran in 1831, and at Cat Spring, a settlement made by Robert Kleberg in 1834. The Texas government, however, as noted, considered that ample protection for that neighborhood existed. Among the papers in the Texas Archives there are some accounts of the Bureau of Indian Affairs with Mr. F. Dieterich of Washington on the Brazos, but they constitute no relations between the German settlers and the Indians.[2]

The first of the Germans to feel that there would be an Indian problem in connection with the colonization work of the Society was Prince Carl of Solms-Braunfels, its commissioner-general. In

[1]Muckleroy, Anna, "The Indian Policy of the Republic of Texas," in *The Southwestern Historical Quarterly*, XXV, 255-256. Miss Muckleroy cites Gammel, *Laws of Texas*, I, 676, 678-679.

This chapter is, in the main, a reproduction of an article of mine which appeared in the *Southwestern Historical Quarterly* for October, 1927.

[2]Republic of Texas Indian Affairs, 1845-1860; Texas State Library. The six accounts in the list total $260.59 and date from January 24 to June 22, 1845. They deal with articles which Dieterich furnished to the Indian Bureau.

his first report to the Society Prince Solms touched on the subject
with the following words:

Before I close my report, I must urge on the committee to send
me weapons so that I shall be able to make an impression on the
Indians, with whom I hope to get on good terms, and on maraud-
ers and other vagabonds.   I propose, therefore, that those members
of the Society who have in their arsenals many arms no longer
serviceable for Europe may donate them to their emigrating subjects.   Since every man here must be mounted, the most serviceable arms would be a rifle of medium length and a sword.   The
leather accoutrements of the soldier, as well as cartridges, or at
least powder from which to make them, are also necessary.   If in
addition to the two cannon, which I donated to the Society, a small
howitzer were sent along, it would be a very desirable supplement.[3]

It is very significant, as well as prophetic, that Prince Solms used
the words, "with whom I hope to get on good terms," for the relations between the Society and the Indians came to be very cordial.
In his second report Prince Solms pointed out that the proposed
German settlements of from fifty to a hundred families each need
not fear any Indian attacks, but that the fields and herds of the
settlers would not be safe and that the good, unlocated lands situated on the rivers and streams in the mountainous region could be
colonized only after the intervening country had been occupied.[4]
In commenting on the Fisher and Miller grant in his third report,
Prince Solms states that most of the grant comprised the hunting
grounds of the Comanches.   He wrote:

As far as the Indians are concerned, it is particularly the
Comanches, who are numerous and brave, who inhabit the region.
I ask, however, that no offense be taken at these tribes, since I
shall not wait until they look me up in the settlement but shall
call on them first as a matter of politeness.   They will either make
peace and keep it, or I shall try at the very first to administer
such a decisive defeat to them that for a long time, if not forever,
they will be harmless.   Until the winter or spring, when I shall
have enough men, I shall not be able to carry out the plan.   I
shall have to confine myself for the present to patrol the vicinity
with a few mounted men.   This will be necessary in each new
settlement, particularly the nearer it lies to the mountains.

[3]Solms-Braunfels, Carl, Prince of, "Berichte an den Adelsverein," in
Kalender, 18-19.
[4]*Ibid.*, p. 21; Photostat *Original Berichte*, pp. 34-35.

Prince Solms reported that the distance from Carlshafen to the grant was 220 miles and that the Indians would first have to be driven out of the grant.[5] In San Antonio some of Castro's colonists and a few German colonists who had been in Texas since May, 1844, offered their services to Solms for patrol duty against the Indians.[6]

The first three shiploads of approximately 700 colonists of the Society for the Protection of German Immigrants in Texas arrived at Indianola, or Carlshafen, as Solms called it, in November and December, 1844. Early in January, 1845, Prince Solms organized a military company of twenty men. The rest of the men capable of bearing arms, 108 in all, were organized into a reserve company and a militia body. It seems that Prince Solms was a very cautious man in this matter of organizing the available military strength of his first colony. This military force was not to be used for aggression, but was to be used for protection against the Indians.[7] In his *Texas,* Prince Solms says that this company was to be used exclusively for the protection of the settlement and of the settlers on their way thither.[8] Another writer says:

For trying to give the whole settlement a military appearance, he, as an officer, can be pardoned; it is not to be denied that, since the settlement was on the Indian frontier and an invasion of the grant was contemplated, such an organization was appropriate. The whole plan may have been overdone and may have deteriorated through the effect of later influences and conditions; the underlying idea is not to be criticized. Moreover, the newly-arrived immigrants— the prince included— knew nothing at first of the habits of the Indians, and the military demonstrations, together with the daily firing of a cannon at sunset, for the purpose of striking terror into the Indians, were very logical measures of prudence,

---

[5] Solms, "Berichte an den Adelsverein," in *Kalender*, 31-32; Photostat *Original Berichte*, 48-50. The date of this report is August 26, 1844, a little more than two months after the first report was made. The change in attitude toward the Indians may be traced to the influence of Solms's contact with the Texans, who did not have much use for the Indians.

[6] Solms "Berichte an den Adelsverein," in *Kalender*, 33; Photostat *Original Berichte*, 50-51. Castro's colony was at Castroville and his colonists were mainly Alsatians. They spoke German and were willing to join the colony which the Society was to found.

[7] Solms, "Berichte an den Adelsverein," in *Kalender*, 49-50; Photostat *Original Berichte*, 75-76.

[8] Solms, *Texas*, 76.

which, as was soon observed, did not miss their mark, for the Indians remained at a safe distance from the new settlement.[9]

The last mention of the Indians was made by Prince Solms in his tenth report on March 27, 1845, written from his camp on Comal Creek. In describing the tract of land chosen and purchased by him for the site of the first settlement, New Braunfels, the prince wrote:

Everywhere in this whole region there are traces of more or less important Indian camps. The Indians, attracted by the opportunities for hunting and by the excellent water, have put up their tents here. As soon as civilization approaches, they remain away, for the sound of the axe in the forests is calamitous to them. Should some, nevertheless, stray here, I think the clatter of the mills . . . will drive them away. . . .[10]

In addition to the military company, Prince Solms took other precautionary measures for the protection of the New Braunfels settlement. On the site of the present Catholic church a palisade or stockade was built, its north side on the edge of the forty-foot bluff on the south bank of Comal Creek. This stockade was called the *Zinkenburg*,[11] in honor of Nicolaus Zink, the surveyor in the employ of the Society. A quarter of a mile to the south east of the *Zinkenburg*, on a hill rising about thirty feet above the flat on which New Braunfels was built, a large blockhouse, christened the *Sophienburg*, was erected for the protection of the settlement. Plans for building two smaller blockhouses on this same site for use as government buildings and for protection to New Braunfels were not carried out. The cornerstone of the *Sophienburg* was laid on April 28, 1845.[12]

Every evening before nightfall and every morning before daybreak, mounted patrols, generally accompanied by Prince Solms, were sent out. At night sentinels stood guard around the stock-

[9]Penniger, *Fest-Ausgabe*, 40-41.

[10]Solms, "Berichte an den Adelsverein," in *Kalender*, 62; Photostat *Original Berichte*, 92.

[11]Penniger, *Fest-Ausgabe*, 40. In his *Short Sketch of Comal County*, 3, Seele implies that Solms made a treaty with the Lipan Indians before he laid out the city of New Braunfels. Since Solms is silent on this matter the writer believes that no treaty was made.

[12]Kapp, *Aus und ueber Amerika*, 260, gives the date April 22, 1845. The correct date is given by Solms, "Berichte an den Adelsverein," in *Kalender*, 63, also in Penniger, *Fest-Ausgabe*, 44.

ade. During the day long rides for reconnaissance were made to
see if Indians were in the neighborhood. While Prince Solms
was commissioner-general of the Society, not a single person entrusted to his care was killed by the Indians, nor was a single
horse stolen by them.[13]

The German settlers of New Braunfels were not to be long
without a sample of Indian savagery. In October, 1845, two
Germans, Captain Friedrich v. Wrede and Lieutenant Oscar Claren,
were killed and scalped as they were returning to New Braunfels
from Austin. Their companion, Wessel, after killing one of the
Indians, escaped. From Claren the Indians got two scalps, cutting
off also his beard. This sad incident greatly excited the German
settlers. Two days after the scalping Wessel reached Austin and
led a detachment of rangers to Live Oak Spring, the scene of the
scalping. No trace of the Indians could be found, however.[14]
Fredericksburg, which was founded by John O. Meusebach on
May 8, 1846, was some eighty miles above the line of settlements
from Austin to San Antonio and right in the Indian country. Its
location was precarious. The governor of Texas, J. Pinckney
Henderson, heard of the projected movement of settlers to Fredericksburg and took steps to give them protection. On April 13,
1846, Henderson wrote to Major B. L. Beall, U. S. A., stationed
at San Antonio:

Having learned that a number of German emigrants will leave
Braunfels in a few days for the Pierdinales where they intend to
make a settlement and apprehending that they will be exposed to
Indian depredations in that unsettled region I beg leave respectfully to suggest to you the propriety of detaching the company of
rangers now under your command to protect them.

Henderson suggested that, if Col. Harney, commanding at San
Antonio, should send Major Hays on that service, Beall's company
would not be needed.[15] When Beall replied on the 23d that he

---

[13]Solms, *Texas*, 33-34.

[14]Solms, *Texas*, 35; Roemer, *Texas*, 213. See also Bracht, *Texas im
Jahre 1848*, 233. Solms says Live Oak Spring was twenty-five miles from
Austin, but the writer thinks it was not that far. At any rate, Dr. Roemer and companions on horseback, and leading a pack mule, leaving Austin
one morning in June, 1846, reached the place by noon.

[15]Henderson to Beall, Austin, Texas, April 13, 1846; MS. Records Department of State, No. 273, J. P. Henderson and A. C. Horton, 36, Texas
State Library.

would be glad to carry out the governor's orders, Henderson commanded him to order his ranger company to accompany the German settlers on their way to the Pedernales.[16] The settlers in Fredericksburg were in almost constant danger of their lives. "It was indeed a risk, for the Indians made the country unsafe; several times settlers in Fredericksburg, while out in their gardens or near their log houses, were shot at with arrows."[17] This danger ceased, however, when Meusebach made a treaty with the Indians in 1847, of which more presently.

In the autumn of 1846 the governor of Texas advised against the further advance of the German settlers, because a conflict with the Comanches would be unavoidable. According to the terms of the Fisher and Miller grant, the land had to be occupied and surveyed by the fall of the year 1847. For the occupation of the grant, however, the Texas government assured no military assistance to the commissioner-general.[18] Meusebach continued his negotiations with the district surveyor, John James, for the survey of the grant, since he wanted to push the colonization work, but the surveyor declared that his men would not go into the grant until a peace treaty had been made with the Indians.[19] Besides, Dr. Schubert, colonial director of the Society at Fredericksburg, during Meusebach's absence from that place, undertook an expedition to the grant but only reached the border of the Indian country, the Llano River, and then returned. The Indians looked upon this expedition as a hostile invasion; the German settlers, on the other hand, were frightened by Schubert's report that there were from forty to sixty thousand Indians between the Llano and the San Saba. In order to counteract the bad impression which this expedition had created, and mindful of the stipulations of the Fisher and Miller contract, Meusebach decided to go into the Indian country. A mounted company of some twenty men, several volunteers, five Mexicans, and the American surveyors, all well armed, set out from Fredericksburg on January 22, 1847. Meusebach

[16]Henderson to Beall, Austin, Texas, April 24, 1846; MS. Records Department of State, No. 273, J. P. Henderson and A. C. Horton, 36, Texas State Library.

[17]*LaGrange Deutsche Zeitung*, August 19, 1915, 14, col. 1.

[18]Penniger, *Fest-Ausgabe*, 87.

[19]Meusebach, *Answer to Interrogatories*, 23.

joined them in camp two days later.   The expedition crossed the
Llano River at the mouth of Beaver Creek.[20]

Alvin H. Soergel, who was in Fredericksburg when the expedition left, says there were 35 to 40 men in all, with three wagons
and 25 to 30 pack mules, and that Lorenzo de la Rosa, a Mexican
guide, and Young, a Texan guide, accompanied the expedition.
Meusebach planned to go into the Indian country with some twenty
to twenty-five men, leaving the rest of his men and the wagons at
the place which he would choose for the new settlement, Castell.
In New Braunfels Soergel saw Major Neighbors, who was on his
way to Fredericksburg with orders from Governor Henderson to
assist Meusebach.   Neighbors told Soergel that he thought a
separate treaty could be made between the Society and the
Comanches.   At Seguin Soergel saw Major Hays, who also expressed the belief that a separate treaty could be made.[21]

The fullest account of the Meusebach expedition is given by a
member thereof, Dr. Ferdinand Roemer, a geologist and naturalist
of note.   Roemer reports that on February 5, 1847, Major Neighbors, Agent of Indian Affairs, arrived in Fredericksburg from
Austin.   Roemer accompanied Neighbors into the Indian country.
Neighbors had a communication from the governor of Texas in
which Meusebach was advised not to carry out his plan.   The
governor's letter pointed out the dangerous consequences that
might result for the frontier settlements from a possible hostility
of the Comanches, particularly since the war with Mexico was in
progress.   If Meusebach had already left on his expedition, Neighbors had orders to follow and to offer his services to Meusebach,
since Neighbors's personal acquaintance with several of the Indian
chiefs and his intimate knowledge of their customs would make the
negotiation of a treaty easier.[22]

Major Neighbors, who was appointed Special Indian Agent on
March 20, 1847, reported to Col. W. Medill, Commissioner of
Indian Affairs of the United States, on this matter.   He wrote:

For your information, I here state— That Gov. Henderson,
apprehending serious difficulty with the Comanches about the 1st

[20]Meusebach, *Answer to Interrogatories*, 23; Penniger, *Fest-Ausgabe*,
51-52 and 87.

[21]Soergel, Alvin H., *Neueste Nachrichten aus Texas*, 29-31.

[22]Roemer, *Texas*, 283-284.   The account of the expedition covers **pages
283 to 329.**

of Feby last, from the introduction of setlers and the surveying of that section of Country granted to a German Company, by the late Replic (sic) of Texas in 1841-2. Whilst at war with the Comanche Tribe (a part of said Grant being now inhabited by the Comanches) The Said Company was compeled to complete their Surveys by 1st Sept. next or forfeit their claims, they were under the impression that a force would be necessary, and had commenced organizing the German Colonists into companies to force their Surveys— Gov. Henderson solicited my interference. I immediately met the Comanches, and succeeded in forming the preliminaries of a friendly arrangement which is to be carried into effect the 1st of May.[23]

At least two accounts of this expedition disagree with Neighbors that he formed the preliminaries of a friendly arrangement with the Comanches. One of these is by Meusebach, the man in charge of the expedition. These are his words:

When I had been in council for a number of days, with large bands of well-drilled and armed Comanches, and their chiefs, at the San Saba (at the place which is now known as the Camp Colorado crossing), Major Neighbors came on as the bearer of a dispatch from Governor Henderson, dissuading from entering the colony, as the Indians were reported to be on the war path; at the same time recommending the Major as an expert in treating with the Indians— if I would not return. The Major had been Indian agent for the Lipans under the Republic of Texas.[24]

Dr. Roemer, who accompanied Major Neighbors from Fredericksburg, reports that they reached the San Saba on the 10th of February and that a very good understanding existed between Meusebach and the Comanches.[25]

Meusebach completes his rather brief account of his treaty with the Indians with the following words:

I engaged him (Neighbors) for the remainder of the trip, dismissed most of my company with the wagons, keeping only about seven men, agreed with the Indians that at the next full moon the peace council with all the head chiefs of the western bands of Comanches should be held at the lower San Saba, and used the

[23]Neighbors to Medill, Austin, Texas, April 24, 1847; MS. in United States Office of Indian Affairs, Letters 1847-1848. Photostat copies in University of Texas Library.

[24]Meusebach, *Answer to Interrogatories*, 24.

[25]Roemer, *Texas*, 290-291.

time remaining till full moon for an exploration of the lands on
that fabulous San Saba river, Spanish Fort, Brady Creek, and
surrounding places. At full moon we were at the agreed spot on
the lower San Saba, about 25 miles above its mouth into Colorado
river, made a treaty with the head chiefs Buffalo Hump, Santa
Anna, and Mopechucope, and their people, for all the western
bands of Comanches, promised them $3000 worth of presents, for
which consideration they on their part promised and agreed not to
disturb our surveyors in their work, nor to do any harm to our
colonists.[26]

This important council occurred March 1 and 2, 1847. About
twenty chiefs participated. At noon on March 1 the council began. Meusebach opened this momentous meeting with an address,
which the Indian interpreter, Jim Shaw, who was with Major
Neighbors, translated.[27] Meusebach proposed the three following
articles for a treaty:

1.   My countrymen have the permission to go and travel where
they please, and no harm must be done to them, but you must
protect them everywhere. On the other hand, your people can
come to our wigwams and cities without fear and can go wherever
they please and shall be protected.
2.   You the chiefs, and your people will assist us and report to
us, when bad men and redfaces of other tribes steal our horses or
intend other felonies, and we shall do the same, when you are
attacked.
3.   I am going to send men with the thing that steals the land
(compasses), as the red men call it, and will survey the whole
country of the San Saba as far as the Concho and other waters, so
that we may know the boundaries where we can go and till the
soil.   And if you are willing after consultation with your warriors,
to make this treaty, then I will give you and your squaws many
presents, or equal them with the white pieces of metal, that we call
dollars, and give you as many as one thousand and more of them.

[26]Meusebach, *Answer to Interrogatories*, 24.

[27]Tiling, Moritz, *German Element in Texas*, 99-104, gives the translation of the "talks" by Meusebach, Santana, Mopechucope, and Pochana-
quarhip (Buffalo Hump). Penniger, *Fest-Ausgabe*, 101-107, gives these
talks in German from an article which appeared in the *Magazin fuer
die Litteratur des Auslandes*, 1847. The three articles of the treaty
were proposed by Meusebach in his first talk. They are found in Tiling, *German Element in Texas*, 100. A painting of this council, showing Meusebach and the Indian chiefs, was made in 1927 by Mrs. Lucy
Marschall, one of the daughters of John O. Meusebach, and exhibited
in San Antonio and Fredericksburg in the spring of 1928.

Meusebach set the date for the signing of the treaty in the following words: "If we agree on this treaty, I shall go and fetch the presents and will sign the treaty solemnly, at the latest when the disk of the moon has rounded twice." The treaty was ratified at Fredericksburg at the appointed time.

The making of the treaty was a very important accomplishment, both for the German settlers and for the state of Texas. The Fisher and Miller grant at last became valuable for the Society. Without the treaty it would have been dangerous for either the settlers or the surveyors to go into the grant. If the Society could not have had its lands surveyed, the contract would have lapsed. Meusebach was indeed a courageous man and displayed great skill in the making of the treaty with the warlike Comanches, who held him in great respect and called him *El sol colorado,* on account of his great flowing reddish beard.

Did the Indians keep the terms of their treaty with the Germans? The answer is in the affirmative. Viktor Bracht, who was in New Braunfels in 1848, published a letter written at New Braunfels, August 30, 1847, from which the following passage is taken: "Santa Anna, the war chief of the Comanches, was here three days, in order to enjoy himself with his band. . . . He assured us that the friendship for the Germans, whom he respected, would continue to be observed honestly, as had been the case thus far. Mr. Kriewicz of Potsdam has been living for some time with Santa Anna and his tribe,— a remarkable taste, but the affair seems useful."[28] Tiling deals with the matter in the following words:

Through gifts and considerate treatment they succeeded in establishing and maintaining friendly relations with the Indians who were quite numerous, and, like New Braunfels, Fredericksburg suffered very little from Indian depredations. It would have been an easy matter for the Indians of the Llano and San Saba territory to destroy Fredericksburg, as well as the settlements of Betina, Castell and Leiningen, that were established in 1847, but all the Indians had great respect for von Meusebach, whom they called *El Sol Colorado,* from his flowing beard, and the German Indian Agent Emil Krieswitz was very prudent and circumspect in his dealings with the different Indian tribes and secured the friendship of their chiefs for the German pioneers.[29]

[28]Bracht, *Texas im Jahre 1848,* 283-284.
[29]Tiling, *German Element in Texas,* 84-85.

On December 10, 1850, a treaty was made at Spring Creek, near the San Saba River, between John H. Rollins, Special Agent of the United States for the Indians of Texas, and various chiefs, warriors, captains, and councillors of the Indians. The fifteenth article of the treaty is of interest in connection with this chapter, for it read:

It is agreed by the Indians, parties hereto, that they will not go below the present line of Military Posts on the East side of the Colorado River, nor below the Llano River, and a line running West from its headwaters on the West side of said Colorado, without express permission from the Indian Agent or some Officer Commanding a Military Post in Texas, in writing; and that they will give immediate notice to the nearest Military Post should other Indians attempt to do so. The German settlement on the North side of the Llano will be embraced in the Foregoing article, so long as they do not trade with the Indians in any thing except the produce of their farms, nor for any horses or mules which may have been stolen.[30]

This treaty did not in any way set aside the one between the German settlers and the Indians, so far as either side was concerned. It is included in this chapter because of its mention of the German settlements on the Llano.

Some of the German settlers in West Texas were the victims of Indian depredations. The sixteenth article of the treaty just mentioned provided for the delivery by February 5, 1851, to the Officer Commanding at Fort Martin Scott, of the Indians who had murdered a German at Craig's trading house on the Llano. In October, 1851, Emil Wahrmund's horses were stolen from his farm on Bear Creek, near Fredericksburg, by some Lipans who on this occasion also killed an American settler on Goat Creek.[31] Just prior to the organization in November, 1853, of six ranger companies for frontier protection, some horses were stolen from the farms of Dr. Ernst Kapp, Ernst Altgelt, and Julius Dresel at Sisterdale, Kendall County, but then in Bexar County.[32] In 1855 Hermann Runge, the 20-year old son of Dr. W. I. Runge of Sisterdale, was killed and scalped and all of the horses were stolen from

[30]A printed copy of this treaty is found in State Department, Indian Affairs, 1845-1860, Texas State Library.
[31]Penniger, *Fest-Ausgabe*, 188-189.
[32]*Neu Braunfelser Zeitung*, September 22, 1853, 2, col. 3.

the farm.[33] Early in July, 1855, a party of Indians visited the German settlement at Sisterdale and killed some oxen belonging to Julius Dresel. They also stole four mules from Mr. Rhodius.[34] About the same time thirty head of horses were stolen from a Mr. Fischer, a German, living between the Guadalupe and Blanco, about twenty-five miles from New Braunfels.[35] In 1855 the Indians became very active and committed many depredations. On September 13, 1855, a committee of five citizens of New Braunfels sent to Governor Pease a report of a public meeting held at New Braunfels the day before. This meeting adopted measures to co-operate with the citizens of Guadalupe County in raising volunteer assistance to protect the frontier settlements against the marauding incursions of Indians. The committee was instructed to ascertain from Governor Pease to what extent he would furnish such a volunteer company with arms, provisions, and pack mules.[36] In the summer of 1859 Christian and Peter Crenwelge were pursued by Indians near Loyal Valley, now in Mason County. That same night, however, a number of horses were stolen from Fort Mason.[37]

The list of Indian depredations against German settlers is only partial, but even the complete list is small in comparison with that of Indian depredations in the other settled portions of Texas. It is not at all certain that the Comanches, with whom Meusebach had made the treaty, were guilty of all the depredations committed on the Germans. Small bands of Lipans and Wacoes made the country unsafe. In Meusebach's *Answer to Interrogatories* this significant passage is found:

Colonel Jack Hays, the celebrated Indian fighter, when he returned from a trip to El Paso made in the interest of the San Antonio merchants to find the nearest overland road, in 1858 or '59, I believe, stopped at my house at Comanche Springs, and told me that he was astonished that the Indians kept their treaty so

[33]Penniger, *Fest-Ausgabe*, 190.

[34]Jones to Pease, Austin, Texas, July 5, 1855; MS. in State Department, Indian Affairs, 1845-1860, Texas State Library.

[35]Jones to Pease, San Marcos, Texas, July 7, 1855; MS. in *Ibid.*

[36]State Department, Indian Affairs, 1845-1860, Texas State Library. The committee consisted of Robert Bechem, James Ferguson, Ernst Dosch, August Hartmann, and A. Nauendorf.

[37]Penniger, *Fest-Ausgabe*, 191-192. It was supposed that these were Comanches.

well.   That he was never molested nor lost any animals during his travel within the limits of our colony, but as soon as he had passed the line he had losses.[38]

The conclusions of this chapter can be stated briefly.   Separate relations between the German settlers and the Indians in the counties Austin, Fayette, Washington, Colorado, DeWitt, and Victoria did not exist but were especially cordial in the counties Comal, Gillespie, Kendall, Mason, and Llano.   Prince Solms indicated in his first report to the Society that he would try to get on good terms with the Indians.   He took those precautions for dealing with the Indians which prudence dictated.   His prophecy did not come true while he was in Texas.   Meusebach, his successor, made a treaty which placed the Germans and the Indians on a very friendly footing.   Although some of the German settlers in West Texas suffered from Indian depredations, in the main the provisions of the treaty were observed.   A vast territory of over 3,000,000 acres was opened to civilization.   It was the great pioneer work of the German settlers in Texas.

[38]Meusebach, *Answer to Interrogatories*, 25-26.

CHAPTER X

THE GERMAN SETTLERS IN POLITICS

The eighth census of the United States showed that Texas had a total population of 604,215 in 1860. In this number were included 20,553 persons who had been born in various German states. Reduced to a percentage basis, the persons of German nativity constituted 3.40 per cent of the total population of Texas.[1] Although their number was relatively small in comparison with the total population, the German settlers played their part in the political life of Texas. They felt that they had a place in the body politic and assumed the duties and responsibilities of citizenship in their adopted state. When Texas became a member of the Union the German settlers, along with the rest of the population, became interested also in the great political questions of the nation.

In the notes of Judge Robert Kleberg, who came to Texas in 1834, appears the statement that he "wished to live under a republican form of government, with unbounded personal, religious, and political liberty, free from the petty tyrannies and the many disadvantages and evils of the old countries."[2] Kleberg had not long been settled in Texas before he had an opportunity to fight for "unbounded personal, religious, and political liberty." During the Texas Revolution the few German settlers fought for the country of their adoption and helped to win its independence. It was a trying time for them when they had to leave their homes and retreat with Houston's army before the advancing forces of Santa Anna; it was even more trying on the fortitude of some to find their homes in ashes when they returned after the battle of San Jacinto.[3] According to the muster rolls of the participants, about one hundred German settlers were actively engaged in the Texas Revolution.[4] Most of them fought with Houston at the Battle of

[1]Kennedy, *Population of the United States in 1860*, pp. IV and XXIX.

[2]Tiling, *German Element in Texas*, 24.

[3]Kleberg, Rosa, "Some of My Early Experiences in Texas," Texas State Historical Association *Quarterly*, I, 300-302, II, 170.

[4]Tiling, *German Element in Texas*, 34-35. Tiling lists the following German names: Carl Amsler, Louis Amelung, Jacob Albrecht, William Ahlert, Joseph Biegel, Johann Burgiesky, Johann Baumbacher, Thomas

San Jacinto; a few were massacred at Goliad.[5]   The patriotic sentiment of the Germans in the Texas Revolution is perhaps best expressed by the words which Hermann Ehrenberg shouted as he made his escape from the Mexicans at the Goliad massacre: "The Republic of Texas forever!"[6]

While Prince Solms was in Texas late in 1844 making preparations for the reception of the Society's immigrants, he wrote two letters to Anson Jones on the subject of the annexation of Texas to the United States.   In his first letter Prince Solms gave Jones to understand that the Society preferred to see Texas remain out of the Union; in the second he pointed out that advices were reaching him from Europe to the effect that annexation would mean war between Great Britain and the United States.   In order to prove his interest in the welfare of Texas, Prince Solms even offered to go to Mexico to secure Santa Anna's recognition of the independence of Texas.[7]   It is impossible to say whether the So-

Bertram, W. M. Burch, Franz Dietrich, M. Dombriski, George P. Erath, F. G. Elm, Hermann Ehrenberg, Conrad Eigenauer, Bernhard Eilers, Friedrich Ernst, Albert Emanuel, Joseph Ellinger, Carl Fordtran, Carl Felder, Abraham Formann, Peter Fullenweider, Wilhelm Frels, Wilhelm Friedlander, F. W. Grassmeyer, Jacob Geiger, F. Griebenrath, C? Goesecke, J. Herz, Christian Hildebrandt, Moritz Heinrich, G. Herder, Johann Hollien, Johann Heunecke, Edward Harkort, J. A. Heiser, F. Heusemann, H. Halt, C. Hammacher, F. Hellmueller, Conrad Juergens, Thomas Kemp, Louis Kleberg, Robert Kleberg, A. Kinschel, L. Krup, J. Kolmann, Johann Kopf, L. D. Kessler, F. Keller, L. Kranz, A. Lehmkuhl, G. Luckenhoger, C. Luenenburg, William Langenheim, Charles Lantz, G. Luck, F. Lundt, F. Lueders, William Mayer, Peter Mattern, C. Messler, J. Miller, F. Niebling, J. Oberlaender, J. Peske, P. Pieper, W. Preusch, J. Reinhardt, E. Pucholaski, A. C. Redlich, John Reese, G. W. Ricks, Louis von Roeder, Otto von Roeder, Rudolph von Roeder, Joachim von Roeder, William von Roeder, L. Schulz, H. Schultz, J. Schur, A. Stern, A. Stolke, F. Schrack, C. Schultz, F. Schroeder, B. Strunck, G. Sullsbach, H. Thuerwaechter, C. Tapps, J. Volkmar, Sam Wolfenberger, William Wanger, Henry Wilke, Philip Weppler, J. Wilhelm, R. Wilhelm, A. Winter, L. von Zacharias, J. Zekainski, William Zuber.

[5]*Telegraph and Texas Register*, November 9, 1836, 1, cols. 1-2.
Sixteen Germans are listed by the *Register* as being in Fannin's corps. Of these, Franz Dietrich, George Voss, and Wm. Rosenberg were detained by the Mexicans as surgeons and laborers; Wm. Preusch. Hermann Ehrenberg, and Joseph H. Spohn escaped; and Wm. Mayer, J. Q. Volkmar, H. Schultz, Charles Lantz, N. Dombrinski, F. Griebenrath, F. Peterswich, Peter Mattern, Conrad Eigenauer, and B. Strunck were killed.

[6]Ehrenberg, H., *Der Freiheitskampf in Texas im Jahre 1836*, 168.

[7]Jones, *Memoranda and Official Correspondence*, 392, 407. The letters were written from Houston, November 2, and from Galveston, December 3, 1844.

ciety changed its views on annexation or not, since, so far as is known, no election was held in New Braunfels on October 13, 1845, when the people of Texas were called on to determine whether the terms of annexation offered by the Congress of the United States were to be accepted or rejected. At Industry seventeen German settlers voted in favor of annexation, as the election report signed by Friedrich Ernst shows. Carl Amsler's house was used for the voting place in Cat Spring.[8]

When war was declared on Mexico by the United States in May, 1846, the Society had a considerable number of immigrants at Carlshafen (Indianola) whom it had been unable to transport into the interior on account of almost impassable roads. Eighty-eight of the immigrants enlisted in a company which Augustus Buchel, one of their number, organized.[9] This company was ordered into

[8]Trenckmann, *Austin County*, 17-18. The seventeen German voters at Industry were: Friedrich Ernst, John Koehler, Jacob Wolters, Heinrich Stuessy, J. G. Sieper, H. Schmidt, C. Fordtran, C. Giesecke, E. Franke, Jacob Rehm ?, J. Vanderwerth, Conrad Stoehr, J. Grunder, A. Rothermel, A. von Roeder, Otto Henkhaus, and J. G. Schwarting. The eight German voters at Cat Spring were C. Amsler, M. Amsler, J. Hollien, Levermann, Weltt ?, C. A. Mattern, Louis Kleberg, and Robert Kleberg.

[9]Augustus Buchel was born at Mainz on the Rhine in 1811. He was educated at the military academy of his native city and at the "Ecole Militaire" of Paris. For a while he was military instructor of the Turkish army, but his attachment to the Christian religion prevented his advancement above the rank of colonel. He fought in the Carlist war in Spain and was rewarded for meritorious service with the Knight Cross of the Order of the Golden Crosses. In 1845 he emigrated to Texas, his immigration agreement with the Society for the Protection of German Immigrants in Texas being issued on October 1, 1845, at Antwerp by Gustav Merz, the Society's agent at that port. He fought with distinction in the Mexican war, was transferred to General Taylor's staff, was promoted to major, and was cited for meritorious service at the Battle of Buena Vista by General Taylor. He was slated for appointment as minister to Brazil, but President Taylor's death prevented it. President Pierce appointed him collector for the port of Lavaca. In the late fifties he took a leading part in the suppression of the banditry carried on by Neptuna Cortina along the Rio Grande. In the Civil War he distinguished himself for the Confederacy, became lieutenant-colonel in Col. Philip N. Luckett's Third Texas Infantry Regiment, and was later made colonel of the First Texas Cavalry Regiment, in command of which he was fatally wounded on April 9, 1864, at Pleasant Hill, Louisiana. He died from his wound a few days later at Mansfield. The Legislature of Texas voted an appropriation to have his remains removed to the State Cemetery at Austin and to have a monument erected over his last resting place. (Johnson, Sid S., *Men Who Wore the Grey*, 1, 62-63; Talbot, Harriet, "General Augustus Buchel," *Houston Post*, December 27, 1903, p. 2, cols. 1-2; Flood, Corinne

the service of the United States by Governor J. Pinckney Henderson on May 22, 1846, for a period of six months.   It formed a part
of the first brigade of Colonel A. S. Johnston's regiment of *Texas
Foot Volunteer Riflemen.*   The commissioned officers of the company were Augustus Buchel, captain, Rudolph Binderwald, first
lieutenant, and Charles Kind, second lieutenant.   There were four
sergeants, four corporals, and seventy-seven privates in the company.   The muster roll of the company shows that they enlisted
on May 1, 1846.[10]

On May 20, 1846, the *Democratic Telegraph and Texas Register*
announced that General Taylor had asked Governor Henderson,
through Colonel Harney, that seven companies be organized and
stationed at San Antonio, New Braunfels, and Austin.   The editor
expressed the belief that the German and French immigrants of
West Texas would "probably fill the rolls of the companies as soon
as the Governor's order" was issued.[11]

On October 21, 1846, the Germans of Galveston held a mass
meeting at the Wilhelm Tell Inn.   A committee consisting of A.

L., "General Buchel Unknown to History," *Galveston Daily News*, May
29, 1921, p. 33, cols. 1-5.)

Reference is also made to Augustus Buchel in *Texas Vorwaerts*, January
18, 1884, p. 2, col. 6.

[10]The writer secured his information on Captain Buchel's Company
from a photostatic copy of the muster roll furnished by the Secretary
of War. Besides the commissioned officers already mentioned, the fol-
lowing men belonged to it: Sergeants—Emil Kriewicz, Charles Valen-
tine, W. B. Graefenhaim, Adolph Herrman; Corporals—George Dalwick,
Adolph Hoepfner, Charles Weirich, William Leilich; Privates—George
Amschutz, Alexander Ainsperger, Conrad Bloenecke, Louis Boedecker,
August Boettcher, Theodore Brandes, George Bohl, John G. Benner, Henry
Martin Bruch, Albert Braess, Christian Corin, John H. Doedeke, Philip
J. Dietz, David Elze, Conrad Engelke, Louis Elbert, Philip Eschelbach,
Philip Fritz, Frederick Freitag, Henry Finkenstein, Jacob Fiedler,
Francis Fink, Jacob Gebhardt, Gustav Gotthardt, Friedrich Gempel,
Henry Goericke, George Heberer, Clemens Hartmann, Jacob Hutschmann,
Christian Heuer, Francis Hoppe, John Jost Hof, Henry Habenicht, Henry
Jellermann, Edward Kahler, William Keidel, Friedrich Koch, Louis
Kuhn, John Kohler, Charles Kuhn, Charles Krause, Henry Laesecke,
Henry Leifeste, David Meyer, Ludolph Meyer, Ernst Mittelegge, Augustus
Meinert, Friedrich Merkel, Friedrich Muench, Charles Miller, William
Palm, Christian Peters, Lorenz Rehner, Friedrich Roode, Edward Ruckes,
Henry Salge, John H. Schneider, Nicolas Sittig, Friedrich Stelter, John
George Storch, Friedrich Schulz, Henry Schroeder, Henry Schogke
(Schocke), Friedrich Schrader, August Smith (Schmidt), John Schmidt,
John Henry Taps, Ferdinand Traub, Wolfgang Taubert, Henry Theiss,
Michel Ulrich, Henry Vogt, Gottfried Vollmar, Guenther Weiss, Ernst
Wittenbert, Jost Henry Zollner, Jacob Schneider.

[11]*Democratic Telegraph and Texas Register*, May 20, 1846, 2, col. 4.

Rossy, M. Seligson, John Kaller, G. Brock, and J. E. Rump drew up and the meeting adopted resolutions to support Timothy Pillsbury for the United States Congress from the second congressional district, to oppose all candidates who favored privilege and monopolistic control, and to send a copy of the resolutions to all of their German fellow-citizens.[12] Pillsbury had voted against the Wilmot Proviso.[13]

When the election was held in Texas on the approval of that provision of the Compromise of 1850 by which Texas was to receive $10,000,000 for the surrender of her claims to territory in New Mexico, the people of Gillespie County cast fifty-four votes in favor of and forty-four votes against the proposal, while the vote stood thirty-six for and thirty-two against in Comal County.[14] These votes were fairly light in proportion to the whole number of eligible voters. They indicate that the German settlers of West Texas had not yet begun to be interested in national political affairs to any extent. Olmsted comments that in social and political affairs the German settlers did not occupy the position to which their numbers and their character entitled them.[15]

The German settlers in Texas generally affiliated themselves with the Democratic party, because the principles and tendencies of that party appealed to them. They believed with the Democratic party in the equality of men. When the German settlers in Texas had their first opportunity to take a stand in national politics they voted the Democratic ticket. In Comal County the Democratic electors received 106 of the 120 votes cast in the election of 1848.[16] It was not until the middle of the fifties that some of the Germans broke away from the Democratic party. They did not take this step, however, because they no longer agreed with the basic principles of the Democratic party. They were just as true Democrats as before, but they feared the disruption of the Union and took their stand for the preservation of the Union. Their vote against secession did not mean that they were in favor of abolition but they wanted to preserve the Union, as will be shown later.

[12]*Ibid.*, October 21, 1846, 3, col. 2.

[13]*Ibid.*, 3, col. 1.

[14]*Democratic Telegraph and Texas Register*, November 16, 1850, p. 99, col. 2, and December 14, 1850, p. 131, col. 1.

[15]Olmsted, *Wanderungen durch Texas*, 261.

[16]*Texas State Gazette*, September 1, 1849, p. 13, col. 1.

The fact that the Democratic party in Texas supported slavery did not especially disturb the German settlers. They regarded slavery as an institution with which the federal government had nothing to do. Generally speaking, the German settlers had no slaves, for the idea of human bondage was repugnant to them. In speaking of the Germans of San Antonio and New Braunfels, Bruncken says that "among them slavery was practically unknown."[17] The largest slaveowner among the Germans in Texas was the Society for the Protection of German Immigrants in Texas, which had twenty-five slaves on Nassau Farm in 1848 when Otto von Roeder bought this plantation.[18]

The first political organizations among the German settlers of Texas were formed in 1853. In the *Neu Braunfelser Zeitung* of August 12, 1853, Rev. L. C. Ervendberg advocated the organization of a political club *(Demokratischer Verein)* and called a meeting for the following Sunday afternoon at Neu Wied, near New Braunfels on the Guadalupe. At the meeting on August 14, L. C. Ervendberg was elected president and G. F. Holekamp secretary. It was decided to have a social club *(Geselliger Verein)*, but to have political discussions at each regular monthly meeting, thus attaining the desired object. Ervendberg hoped that the club would enable the Germans to act in unison in political affairs.[19] In the same year also another political society, *Der freie Verein,* was organized at Sisterdale. Ernst Kapp was elected president and A. Siemering secretary.[20] The writer surmises that *Der freie Verein* became a branch of the *Bund Freier Maenner,* a national organization which was founded at Louisville, Kentucky, in

---

[17]Bruncken, *German Political Refugees,* 58. Bruncken's view is borne out by Anna Irene Sandbo in her article, "The First Session of the Secession Convention in Texas," *Southwestern Historical Quarterly,* XVIII, 175.

Olmsted says that on his journey through Texas in 1855 he made inquiries about slave-owning among the German settlers and was told that as soon as they became financially able they bought slaves. (Olmsted, *Wanderungen durch Texas,* 91.) At another point, however, Olmsted says that a German butcher, whom he met on the road near New Braunfels, told him that he, the butcher, knew of only one German who had bought a slave. (*Ibid.,* 97.)

[18]See above, Chapter IV, p. 68, footnote 5.

[19]*Neu Braunfelser Zeitung,* August 12, 1853, 2, cols. 3-4, and August 19, 1853, 2, col. 5.

[20]Siemering, A., "Die lateinische Ansiedlung in Texas," *Der deutsche Pionier,* X, 60.

1854.[21] *Der freie Verein,* like the national organization to which it belonged, took a stand against slavery. Early in the following year two societies were organized in Gillespie County. One of these, the Society for Good Fellowship and the Promotion of General Information *(Verein fuer Geselligkeit und zur Befoerderung gemeinnuetziger Kenntnisse),* was organized by the settlers on the Pedernales and Live Oak Creek, the other, the Reform Club *(Reform Verein),* was organized in Fredericksburg. Both of these societies strove to interest their members in political questions through public discussions, debates, and the reading of newspapers, magazines, and books.[22]

Under date of March 15, 1854, *Der freie Verein* called a meeting of all Germans in Texas for May 14 and 15 on the occasion of the approaching second *Staats-Saengerfest.*[23] The *Politischer Verein* of New Braunfels called a special meeting for April 9 to deliberate on the instructions for the delegation to the San Antonio meeting.[24] On April 21 the *Neu Braunfelser Zeitung* published an article by A. Siemering in which the object of the San Antonio meeting was discussed. Siemering declared that the object was to secure for the Germans the position in political affairs to which their intelligence and power entitled them.[25] A week later the Louisville platform, which the *Bund Freier Maenner* had adopted at its meeting in 1854, was discussed in the *Neu Braunfelser Zeitung.* The contributor of the article said that the American population, misinterpreting the demand for the abolition of slavery, believed that the Germans were abolitionists. The contributor asserted that the sudden abolition of slavery was considered to be neither possible nor advisable and that the platform asked only for the adop-

[21]Bruncken, *German Political Refugees,* 44. Bruncken says that the *Bund Freier Maenner* held state conventions in Kentucky, Wisconsin, Ohio, Indiana, Illinois, and Texas in the summer of 1853. At these conventions resolutions were adopted favoring the direct election of the President and the United States Senators and the abolition of slavery. Bruncken must be mistaken about the date of the convention in Texas, for such a convention was not held until 1854.

[22]*Neu Braunfelser Zeitung,* January 20, 1854, 4, col. 2, and January 27, 1854, 3, col. 3.

[23]*Ibid.,* March 24, 1854, 2, cols. 3-4.

[24]*Neu Braunfelser Zeitung,* April 7, 1854, 3, col. 6. The *Politischer Verein* announced also that its reading room was open daily from nine o'clock in the morning until six o'clock in the afternoon and evenings also on Sunday, Wednesday, and Saturday.

[25]*Neu Braunfelser Zeitung,* April 21, 1854, 2, col. 4.

tion of measures which would prepare for and make possible the abolition of slavery at a future time. The object of the organization, he said, seemed to be misunderstood also by the Germans of West Texas. The real object, he said, was to unite the Germans so that they would concentrate their votes on those aspirants for office who held the same political views as they did. He regarded this action not only as a right, which all citizens except the Germans exercised, but also as a civic duty under the oath which every citizen takes to do all in his power to promote the welfare of the state.[26] Julius Schlickum of Fredericksburg was of the opinion that the Germans should be careful in going from the one extreme of very little participation to the other extreme of a full participation in the political affairs of their adopted state.[27]

The mass meeting was held at San Antonio at the appointed time. Various German clubs and organizations sent delegates. The following officers were elected: H. Guenther of New Braunfels, president; Wm. Keidel of Fredericksburg and H. Fr. Osswald of San Antonio, vice-presidents; Dr. Hertzberg of San Antonio, A. Siemering of Sisterdale, Julius Schlickum of Fredericksburg, and Louis Schuetze of Coletoville, secretaries. These officers also constituted the committee on resolutions. A considerable amount of discussion took place on the adoption of the platform, as the resolutions came to be called. The platform dealt with three large subjects: political reforms, social reforms, and religious reforms. Preceding the main part of the platform the statement was made that it was not the intention to create a German party and that the main reason for this organization of Germans was a linguistic one. Under the head of political reforms the platform advocated the popular election of the President, United States senators, judges, and postal, revenue, and administrative officers, exclusive of cabinet members and ministers to foreign countries, the upholding of the Monroe Doctrine, a graduated income tax, and a graduated inheritance tax. Under the head of social reforms, to which the most space was given, the platform declared: "Slavery is an evil, the removal of which is absolutely necessary according to the principles of democracy. Since slavery concerns only the states, we demand that the federal government refrain from all interference

[26]*Neu Braunfelser Zeitung*, April 28, 1854, 1, col. 4.
[27]*Ibid.*, May 12, 1854, 2, col. 1.

in matters pertaining to slavery. However, if a state determines on the removal of this evil, it may call on the federal government for aid in the execution of its decision."[28] Some of the more conservative delegates in attendance at the convention tried to temper the radical nature of the plank on slavery but failed in two efforts to get a substitute passed.[29]

The remaining work of the convention was of a routine nature. A motion was adopted to work for a convention of all German-Americans to be held at St. Louis early in November, 1854. Edward Degener of Sisterdale was chosen delegate with C. N. Riotte, a lawyer, of San Antonio, and Dr. Nohl of New Braunfels as first and second alternates. Der freie Verein of Sisterdale subscribed one hundred dollars of the four hundred dollars required for defraying the expenses of the delegate to the St. Louis convention. H. Guenther, Dr. Nohl, and L. C. Ervendberg, all of New Braunfels, were appointed a central committee to formulate plans to get the convention called.[30]

When the San Antonio platform was given to the public, a veritable storm broke loose. In many respects the resolutions appeared to be ultra-radical. The storm of protest centered about the slavery plank. The time for issuing such a platform was highly inopportune, because the Know-Nothing movement was just getting a good start. The platform placed the entire German population of Texas in a bad light. The more conservative Germans wished to set themselves right with their American neighbors,

[28]Neu Braunfelser Zeitung, May 19, 1854, 2, cols. 2-3; San Antonio Zeitung, May 20, 1854, p. 2, cols. 2-5. A translation of the platform is found in The Western Texan in its issue of June 1, 1854. This paper was published in San Antonio, Texas. The Texas State Library has the only copy of which the writer knows.

For an extended discussion of the San Antonio meeting and of the platform, read my article, entitled "The Texas State Convention of Germans in 1854," in The Southwestern Historical Quarterly for April, 1930.

[29]Olmsted, Wanderungen durch Texas, 264-265. One of the substitute proposals read: "According to our opinion, slavery is a social evil which may get into conflict with white labor. However, this question affects the Germans too little and is interwoven too much with the interests of our fellow-citizens for us to take the initiative in this matter or to let it determine our political stand." The other read: "Negro slavery is an evil which threatens the continued existence of the Union. Its abolition must be left to the several states in which it exists. We German-speaking Texans are not in a position to suggest a solution but feel that the federal government should not interfere in this question."

[30]Neu Braunfelser Zeitung, May 26, 1854, 2, col. 2.

with whose affairs it was not their intention to meddle. The first protest came from these conservative German settlers. On May 26, 1854, the *New Braunfelser Zeitung* printed a long protest from a correspondent who signed himself R., presumably Alexander Rossy, of New Braunfels. In the first place Rossy, if it was he, protested that New Braunfels had no regularly chosen delegates at the convention; in the second place he spoke very strongly against various planks in the platform, as for instance that suggesting the abolition of the grand jury system. His main attack was against the slavery plank, which he regarded as useless and impolitic, since it was impossible to abolish slavery at any time in the near future. He regretted that the Germans allowed themselves to be led by abolitionists of the North and that they did not understand that, as he declared, most of the abolitionists were nativists besides. Rossy thought that abolition would endanger the free institutions of the United States and bring ruin to the richest section of the country. He said that the Germans of the South had an identity of interests with the slaveowners.[31] In the same number a protest signed by 135 residents of New Braunfels said that the German communities were not represented by delegates duly elected, that they did not wish to have the San Antonio platform regarded as the political opinion of the Germans in Texas, and that the other German communities should join in the protest. Lindheimer, the editor of the *Neu Braunfelser Zeitung,* also expressed himself against the action of the convention.[32] These charges were all answered by Hermann Spiess in an article in which he said that the *Politischer Verein* had elected a delegate, that residents of Sisterdale had gone to New Braunfels to discuss the approaching San Antonio convention, and that the non-citizens referred to by Rossy had all refused to accept the positions entrusted to them but had finally been persuaded to accept them.[33]

---

[31]*Neu Braunfelser Zeitung*, May 26, 1854, p. 2, cols. 2-4. Rossy charged that only one of the seven officers of the convention was a citizen, that only one of the central committee appointed to arrange for the St. Louis convention was a citizen, and that neither Degener, the delegate to the convention, nor either of his two alternates, was a citizen.

For several weeks the San Antonio platform was the subject of articles contributed to the *Neu Braunfelser Zeitung* and the *San Antonio Zeitung*. At times some of the statements were quite personal and very caustic.

[32]*Neu Braunfelser Zeitung*, May 26, 1854, p. 2, cols. 5-6. German citizens of Houston and sixteen residents of Comaltown also sent in protests. (*Ibid.*, June 30, 1854, p. 2, col. 5, and July 7, 1854, p. 2, col. 2.)

[33]*Ibid.*, June 2, 1854, p. 1, col. 5 to p. 2, col. 2.

FERDINAND JACOB LINDHEIMER
First Editor of the *Neu Braunfelser Zeitung*
From a photograph in the possession of Miss Lillie E. Simon,
New Braunfels, Texas

KARL DANIEL ADOLF DOUAI
First Editor of the *San Antonio Zeitung*
From a reproduction in *Transactions* of the Illinois State
Historical Society for 1928

Writing from Mill Creek on May 26, 1854, Friedrich Ernst also spoke for the opposition. He said that it was very unwise for the Germans to take such a defiant stand against slavery and feared that the slaveowners and nativists might deny the German immigrant all political rights in order to protect themselves. Ernst believed that political clubs were good for those who interested themselves little in politics.[34]

The San Antonio *Western Texan* and the *Texas State Gazette* represented the opposition of the American settlers. In its issue of June 8, 1854, the *Western Texan* said that for several years the Germans had been organizing singing societies in Texas, that there had always been ultra-radicals among them who, not satisfied with the views of their fellow-countrymen on the prevailing conditions, passed resolutions of a radical character and then sent them out as the views of all of the Germans. The great mass of the Germans in Texas, said the *Western Texan,* were enterprising and useful citizens, who knew the laws and recognized the value of the existing institutions. While this paper spoke against the ultra-radicals among the Germans, it also spoke a good word for the great mass of the German settlers.[35] The *Texas State Gazette,* after averring that it had always defended the German population against the charge of abolitionism, said that if it were true, as an article in the *Victoria Advocate* stated, that the Germans were organizing singing societies for the purpose of spreading political propaganda, then it was high time for the people of Texas to know about it. A crusade against slavery, the laws, and religion in Texas would create a storm of opposition among the American settlers, the *Texas State Gazette* said.[36]

Lindheimer, the editor of the *Neu Braunfelser Zeitung,* accused the *Texas State Gazette* of acting in an unrepublican, inquisition-like, and illogical manner in casting suspicion on the German settlers. The reply of the "Political Society" *(Politischer Verein)* of New Braunfels to the article in the *Texas State Gazette* is very interesting in this connection. The reply stated that the object of the society was to instruct the members by public debates and

[34]*Ibid.,* June 9, 1854, p. 2, col. 2.

[35]*Neu Braunfelser Zeitung,* June 16, 1854, 2, cols. 2-3. The *Zeitung* printed a translation of the article in the *Western Texan.*

[36]*Neu Braunfelser Zeitung,* June 23, 1854, 3, cols. 2-3. The *Zeitung* published a translation of the article in the *Texas State Gazette.*

explanation of political and social questions. The society desired the American citizens of New Braunfels to join in the proceedings and to contribute to the good project, thus proving that it was not working secretly. The reply, signed by H. Guenther, Dr. Wm. Remer, Dr. Nohl, and Hermann Spiess, said that the suspicion of the *Texas State Gazette* was absolutely without foundation.[37]

The protests of the Germans were directed against the platform primarily because they felt that it was impolitic to antagonize the American settlers and to meddle in their affairs. They claimed also that the convention was not representative of all of the Germans.[38] The American protests stressed the political propaganda of the Germans in favor of abolitionism and told the Germans to beware of the slaveholders, lawyers, and preachers. The protests against the political propaganda would have been unnecessary if any pains had been taken to find out what the abolition plank of the San Antonio convention meant. Lindheimer, after inquiring about the real meaning of the plank, learned that by "federal aid" the convention meant the compensation of the slaveowners for the liberation of their slaves.[39] The *Texas State Gazette*, however, again referred to the "recent injudicious and anti-American demonstration," although it expressed satisfaction over the "firm repudiation by the masses of the German people." It warned against drawing a distinction between *Germans* and *American citizens,* and against the "object of overturning our social and domestic institutions."[40]

The protests against the San Antonio platform might have ended at this point if Dr. Adolf Douai, the editor of the *San Antonio Zeitung,* had not kept on agitating for abolition. Douai discussed all questions of public interest in the light of social progress and came out strongly in favor of abolition. The effect of his abolition agitation was to make the American press, generally speaking, believe that all Germans were abolitionists.[41] The

[37]*Neu Braunfelser Zeitung,* June 23, 1854, 3, cols. 2-3.

[38]Interesting in this connection, and corroborative as well, is the statement that only New Braunfels, San Antonio, Seguin, LaGrange, Austin, Victoria, Indianola, Fredericksburg, and Sisterdale had sent delegates. (*Neu Braunfelser Zeitung,* June 16, 1854, 2, col. 1.)

[39]*Neu Braunfelser Zeitung,* July 7, 1854, 2, col. 5.

[40]*Texas State Gazette,* September 9, 1854, 20, cols. 1-2.

[41]The principal newspapers attacking the *San Antonio Zeitung* and its

Germans of New Braunfels met in a mass meeting on June 25, 1855, and "passed resolutions, the purport of which was that, as they had been attacked by the newspapers of the state, they wished to say that they acknowledged their allegiance to the Constitution and laws of the state, that they were not responsible for the sentiments expressed in the *San Antonio Zeitung,* and that it was both unjust and untrue that they had feelings inimical to Americans."[42] At a mass meeting of Germans in Lockhart it was resolved, among other things, to recommend to their German countrymen to discountenance and suppress all attempts to disturb the institution of slavery.[43]

In the great crusade which Knownothingism waged against the foreign element in the United States the Germans of Texas accepted the gage of battle and defended themselves nobly. In La Grange, not a German settlement, but a town with a strong German element, the first steps to form a political club were taken on June 9, 1855. At a meeting held on that day the following resolution was passed: "*Resolved,* that a committee be appointed to draw preliminary articles of a constitution for a Society, to be called 'Social Democratic Society,' which has in view to unite the German population as a body, encourage and assist the more ignorant and indifferent of their countrymen to become citizens of the United States, and use all means, as a political body, to defend and uphold Democratic principles."[44]

On the occasion of a great celebration in New Braunfels in honor of the fiftieth anniversary of its founding, Hermann Seele made one of the principal addresses and said: "True to the character of the German people, with whom love of truth and right is second nature, New Braunfels stood together with the German population of the state and with other citizens of the same convictions in the great struggle against the approaching avalanche of

abolitionist editor were the *Galveston News, Goliad True American, La Grange Paper, Gonzales Enquirer,* and *Texas State Gazette.*
An interesting characterization of Dr. Adolf Douai by Julius Schuetze appeared in *Texas Vorwaerts,* February 15, 1884, p. 3, col. 1.

[42]Sandbo, Anna Irene, "The First Session of the Secession Convention of Texas," *The Southwestern Historical Quarterly,* XVIII, 175. The article refers to the *Galveston News,* July 17, 1855. The resolutions of the New Braunfels meeting appeared in the *La Grange Paper,* July 7, 1855, 2, cols. 5-6, and in the *Texas State Gazette,* July 11, 1855, 1, col. 4.

[43]*Texas State Gazette,* July 25, 1855, 4, col. 2.

[44]*La Grange Paper,* June 16, 1855, 2, col. 4.

Knownothingism. In recognition of its work and as a sign of victory, Comal County received a large banner which the ladies of Austin had embroidered. On the banner appeared in large gold letters the motto of the German Democrats: 'Democrats worship no man; they pay their homage to God and principles.' "[45]

On the question of slavery in the territories the German settlers of Texas, generally speaking, favored the view held by John C. Calhoun and Jefferson Davis, namely, that the territories were open to the slaveowners and that Congress had no right to exclude slave property from the territories. Lindheimer, who may be called the political barometer of the Germans in Texas, voiced his opposition to the Kansas-Nebraska Bill in no uncertain terms, since he thought that sovereignty was acquired only when a territory was admitted as a state. Hence he claimed that popular sovereignty was an absurdity.[46] Lindheimer was quite satisfied with the decision of the Supreme Court in the Dred Scott case. To his brief mention of the decision Lindheimer added his private opinion that the single purpose of the Dred Scott case was to provoke the South.[47]

When the presidential campaign of 1860 was in progress Lindheimer, who was supporting Breckinridge, again defended the right of the citizen to have slave property in the territories.[48] On the evening of October 4 Dr. Felix Bracht made a strong Breckinridge speech at New Braunfels and answered the arguments presented by Houston earlier in the day in behalf of Bell's candidacy.[49] On October 29 Jacob Waelder, member of the legislature from San Antonio, made a speech for Breckinridge at New Braunfels. The election produced only a light vote at New Braunfels, Breckinridge getting 137 votes against 15 for Bell. In Comaltown Breckinridge got sixty-four votes and Bell seven.[50] It is to be noticed that neither Lincoln nor Douglas got a single vote in New Braunfels and Comaltown. At Schumannsville Breckinridge got every one

[45]*Neu Braunfelser Zeitung*, May 22, 1895, 1, col. 4.

[46]*Neu Braunfelser Zeitung*, May 5, 1854, 2, col. 3, and September 12, 1856, 2, col. 1.

[47]*Ibid.*, April 3, 1857, 2, col. 1.

[48]*Ibid.*, September 28, 1860, 2, col. 1.

[49]*Neu Braunfelser Zeitung*, October 12, 1860, 3, col. 1.

[50]*Ibid.*, November 9, 1860, 3, col. 1, and November 16, 2, col. 6. Lindheimer was not pleased with the "light vote on such an important election."

of the thirteen votes cast, but at Fredericksburg Bell got a majority of nine votes.[51]

When the election was over and secession became the topic of the day, Lindheimer and some of his fellow-citizens called a mass meeting for December 9, 1860, to determine the stand of Comal County on calling a convention.[52] Dr. Felix Bracht was made president of the meeting, Wm. Ludewig, J. Landa, Dr. Wm. Remer, and Wm. Clemens were chosen vice presidents, and H. Seele was made secretary. A committee of eleven drew up the following resolutions:

Whereas, The election of Abraham Lincoln endangers the institutions of the South, and whereas, the people are entitled to defend their rights; be it resolved that the governor of Texas call the legislature of Texas in special session to consider calling a convention and that, if the rights and institutions are not sufficently guaranteed by the North, to claim for Texas the right peacefully or by force to demand a return of all of the powers and rights delegated to the United States and to recommend the organization of the whole population in defense of those rights.

Dr. F. Bracht said that the people were not to be deceived by the talk of union, that Comal County, indeed, wanted to see the Union preserved but with the full rights of the people respected.[53]

On January 1, 1861, the citizens of Gillespie County assembled in mass meeting. Fr. van der Stucken was made chairman and H. Ochs and R. J. Radeleff secretaries. The meeting was addressed by N. M. Dennis, Fr. Wrede translating the speech for the benefit of those who could not understand English. It was resolved, among other things, first, to approve Houston's action in calling a special session of the legislature, second, to join in a call for a

[51]*Ibid.*, November 16, 1860, 2, col. 4, and November 30, 2, col. 5.

[52]*Neu Braunfelser Zeitung*, December 7, 1860, p. 3, col. 3. The call was signed by the following: F. Lindheimer, J. Schuhmacher, Bernhard Holtz, Edward Kirchmann, Michael McCarty, W. Forest Holly, Mathew Taylor, Sam S. Frank, J. Schmitz, F. Simon, W. Ludewig, J. Eggeling, C. Kramer, J. A. Staehely, H. J. Offer, C. Prinz, Georg Pfeuffer, J. J. Meyer, D. Elze, C. Bardenwerper, J. J. Thomas, A. Schlameus, Gustav Conrads, Johann Arnold, F. Kreuz, H. Guenther, J. J. Barbee, P. Linnartz, J. Mattfeld, F. Bartels, H. Lux, Johann Kneuper, Val. Klein, Karl Stahl, Johann P. Nuhn, W. H. Henk, Christian Pape, Conrad Pape, L. Pape, Chr. Jentsch, J. J. Walzem, Jacob Heidrich, Gottlieb Arnold, H. Adams, Victor Boehme, Friedrich Michel.

[53]*Neu Braunfelser Zeitung*, December 14, 1860, p. 2, col. 3, and p. 2, col. 6 to p. 3, col. 1.

convention of slave states to consider what steps to take, and third, to support secession as a last means and to favor settlement of the issues by remaining in the Union, if it could be done with safety and honor.[54]

Dr. Theodore Koester and W. F. Preston, representing the more conservative group among the citizens of Comal County, were elected delegates to the convention over Dr. F. Bracht and Gustav Dreiss.[55] Koester and Preston favored using every honorable means to secure promises from the North to respect the rights and institutions of the South. In the convention they voted for secession.[56]

In the election of February 23, 1861, on the adoption of the ordinance of secession, the Germans sided with the anti-secessionists. Comal County, where 239 votes were cast for and only 89 against secession, formed an exception. In Gillespie County 17 were for and 400 against secession; in Boerne only 6 were in favor while 85 were opposed; and in Comfort the vote stood 15 for and 42 against withdrawal from the Union. At New Ulm in Austin County, where there was a strong Union feeling early in 1861, the sentiment changed when the people felt that Texas could not honorably remain in the Union. A majority of six voted for secession.[57] At the Cat Spring-Millheim box, on the other hand, 99 votes were cast against and only 8 for withdrawing from the Union.[58] The vote against secession does not indicate opposition to slavery but a desire to preserve the Union. The people of Comal County demanded that the "rights and institutions" of the South be guaranteed by the North, and the people of Gillespie County favored a convention of slave states. Certainly nothing would have been done against slavery by such a convention.

The Germans, then, assumed the duties and responsibilities of citizenship. They took part in the Texas Revolution and fought for the United States in the war against Mexico. In state and national politics they upheld the principles of the Democratic party and regarded Knownothingism as an attack upon their rights.

[54]*Ibid.*, January 18, 1861, 2, col. 3.

[55]*Ibid.*, January 25, 1861, 3, col. 2.

[56]*Neu Braunfelser Zeitung*, February 1, 1861, 2, col. 5.

[57]*Ibid.*, March 8, 1861, 2, cols. 4-5.

[58]Regenbrecht, "The German settlers of Millheim before the Civil War," *Southwestern Historical Quarterly*, XX, 30.

They were opposed to slavery as a matter of principle and would gladly have seen the institution disappear, but they believed that the states should be allowed to solve the problem without federal interference. Most of them regarded the slavery plank of the San Antonio platform as unwise and impolitic. The majority voted against secession because they wanted to preserve the Union.

CHAPTER XI

ECONOMIC AND SOCIAL LIFE AMONG THE GERMAN SETTLE-
MENTS

The German settlers were hard workers and their perseverance helped them to overcome the discomforts and hardships of frontier life. Most of them engaged in agriculture and stock raising and organized agricultural societies for the discussion of topics related to their major occupation. A few of them engaged in manufacture and trade and thus helped in the industrial development of the state. They exhibited an especial interest in education and religion. They enjoyed music and dramatic art and had their dramatic, literary, and singing societies. They founded several newspapers for the discussion of local matters and for arousing an interest in the public affairs of the state and nation. It is the object of this final chapter to present the activity and interest of the German settlers in these matters.

In order to improve their methods of farming and to be better informed on this occupation and on stock raising, agricultural societies were organized in several of the German settlements. The first society of this nature was the Agricultural and Horticultural Society of Comal County *(Land- und Gartenbau Verein von Comal County),* organized on May 1, 1852.[1] Olmsted reports that this society spent $1200 in one year on trees and shrubs which it had shipped into New Braunfels.[2] The following March the Shepherds Society *(Hirtengesellschaft)* of New Braunfels was organized mainly for coöperation on the question of grazing the cattle and herding them. It was agreed that shepherds employed by the society should receive ten cents per head per month.[3] In April, 1853, the farmers around New Braunfels suggested the holding of a weekly market day so that the producer and consumer could get together and cut out the middleman, or merchant, to a large extent.[4] On January 4, 1854, the Reform Club *(Reform*

---

[1] *Neu Braunfelser Zeitung,* November 19, 1852, 2, col. 4.
[2] Olmsted, *Wanderungen durch Texas,* 127.
[3] *Neu Braunfelser Zeitung,* March 11, 1853, 3, cols. 5-6.
[4] *Neu Braunfelser Zeitung,* April 8, 1853, 3, cols. 2-3.

Verein) was organized at Fredericksburg. Among its objects are found the discussion of agricultural problems and the procuring of newspapers, magazines, and books devoted to agriculture.[5] About the same time the Society of Good Fellowship and the Promotion of General Information *(Verein fuer Geselligkeit und zur Befoerderung gemeinnuetziger Kenntnisse)* was organized in the settlements on the Pedernales and Live Oak Creek. Its purposes were in the main similar to those of the Reform Club of Fredericksburg. Wm. Wahrmund, the secretary, in reporting on its organization said that it had about fifty members.[6] The outstanding example of these societies, however, was the Agricultural Society of Austin County *(Landwirthschaftlicher Verein fuer Austin County),* which was organized on June 7, 1856, at Cat Spring at the suggestion of Andreas Friedrich Trenckmann of Millheim. The object of the society was to promote agriculture in its broadest sense through instructive and entertaining addresses and discussions on subjects related to agriculture. The Society subscribed to various agricultural papers and magazines, among which was the *Southern Cultivator.* Regenbrecht says that in this society the book farmers of Millheim exchanged ideas with the practical farmers of Cat Spring.[7]

In the sixth and seventh chapters of this study attention was called to the reports of the census on the products of industry in Comal and Gillespie counties for 1850 and 1860. Exclusive of the manufacturing establishments and small shops of the American settlers, there were two millers, two shingle makers, one tanner, one saddletree maker, one blacksmith, and one baker among the Germans in Comal County in 1850; and two brick makers, two brewers, four millers, one soap boiler, and one sawmill owner in 1860. In Gillespie County there was one blacksmith, one wheelwright, one carpenter, and one turner listed in 1850; and one soapboiler, one cooper, one brewer, one sawmill owner, two turners, two tinners, three saddlers, four millers, six blacksmiths, eight wheelwrights, and eight cabinet-makers in 1860. Charles Kesler was listed as a sawmill owner in Colorado County in 1850 and

---

[5] *Ibid.,* January 27, 1854, 3, col. 3.

[6] *Ibid.,* January 20, 1854, 4, col. 2.

[7] Photostat Minutes Agricultural Society of Austin County, University of Texas; Regenbrecht, "The German Settlers of Millheim before the Civil War," *Southwestern Historical Quarterly,* XX, 30.

1860 and Charles Ehlinger as a sawmill owner and ginner in 1860. In Fayette County August Beyer owned a blacksmith shop, Henry Frosch, Sr., a sawmill, and Andrew Frenzel a grist mill in 1860.[8] The census records make no mention of the first gin that was built by F. B. Hoffmann and Theodore Diesselhorst in Comal County in 1855 four miles west of New Braunfels at a place now called Solms.[9] An effort was made early in 1854 to secure a charter for the Comal Cotton and Woolen Mills, but lack of time killed the proposition in the legislature. It was not until the Civil War that the cotton mill was built.[10]

In connection with trade and manufacture must be mentioned two societies of workingmen formed at New Braunfels early in 1854. The Tradesmen's Club *(Gewerbe-Verein)* was organized on January 11 for the purpose of encouraging the various trades and provision was made for subscribing to technological and agricultural journals. The Workingmen's Club *(Handwerker-Bund)* was founded on February 5 to provide for a workmen's sick-fund, for social entertainments and instruction in the English language, essay-writing, arithmetic, and drawing, and for the continuation of technical education through the reading of workingmen's journals.[11]

Railroad building proved to be a topic of interest to the Germans in Texas. Late in 1844 Prince Solms suggested that the Society should build a railroad from Carlshafen to New Braunfels in order to save time, labor, and expense. He recommended live-oak rails and thought that horses should be used to draw the cars until the Society could secure locomotives.[12] D. H. Klaener, the Society's agent in Galveston, said in a letter to Mayor Schmidt of Bremen that he was working on the project of a railroad from Carlshafen to the settlements so that the Society could move its settlers more rapidly.[13] This idea persisted for some time. In fact, the Society was known in Texas as the Lavaca, Guadalupe,

[8]Seventh and Eighth Census, Texas State Library.

[9]*Neu Braunfelser Zeitung*, July 22, 1926, 5, col. 1.

[10]*Neu Braunfelser Zeitung*, February 17, 1854, 2, col. 2, and July 22, 1926, 5, col. 1.

[11]*Neu Braunfelser Zeitung*, January 20, 1854, 2, cols. 4-5, and February 10, 1854, 3, col. 3.

[12]Solms, "Berichte an den Adelsverein," in *Kalender*, 45.

[13]Klaener to Schmidt, Galveston, September 5, 1846. The letter was published in the *Weser Zeitung*, November 8, 1846.

and San Saba Railroad, under which name it sold Nassau Farm in 1848.[14]

On November 16 and 29, 1852, the people of New Braunfels held mass meetings in the interest of getting the Houston and San Antonio Railroad to build its line through New Braunfels. Dr. Wm. Remer, John F. Torrey, and Hermann Seele were appointed a committee of correspondence. Nothing, however, was done and New Braunfels did not get a railroad at that time.[15]

It is very difficult to estimate the importance and the extent of the influence of the Germans on the social life of Texas. It is fairly easy, however, to state what they did for themselves in this respect. One of their own number said that their interest in schools and in the organization of societies allowed their cultural development to keep pace with their material advancement.[16]

A good number of the German settlements provided themselves with elementary schools. The first of these were founded by Rev. L. C. Ervendberg and Dr. Johann Anton Fischer at Industry, Cat Spring, Biegel, La Grange, and Columbus in the period from 1840 to 1844 in connection with Protestant congregations which Ervendberg organized at these places.[17]

The next school of which the writer found any record was that which was opened on August 11, 1845, under the large oaks and elms at the foot of the Vereinsberg in New Braunfels. The Society for the Protection of German Immigrants in Texas, which, it will be recalled, promised to provide for schools in its settlements, employed Hermann Seele as the first teacher of this school.[18] When winter came it was necessary to discontinue this school since no building had been erected which could serve as a schoolhouse. From March 22, 1846, on, however, the newly completed church which the Society erected was used as a schoolhouse. L. C. Ervendberg took over the school as part of his work as Protestant pastor. In 1851 Gustav W. Eisenlohr succeeded Ervendberg as pastor and

[14]See above, Chapter IV, p. 68, footnote 5.

[15]*Neu Braunfelser Zeitung*, December 10, 1852, 1, cols. 3-4.

[16]Editorial by Lindheimer, *Neu Braunfelser Zeitung*, January 20, 1854, 2, col. 6.

[17]Mgebroff, *Evangelisch-Lutherische Synode in Texas*, 8.

[18]Seele, "Ein Beitrag zur Geschichte von Neu Braunfels," **Jahrbuch fuer Texas** (1882), 39.

teacher, but in 1853 the church school, which never was denominational, was discontinued.[19]

A school was organized in connection with the Western Texas Orphan Asylum at Neu Wied a few miles from New Braunfels on the Guadalupe. In 1850 an amendment to the charter of the asylum authorized the directors to establish an agricultural school and such other institutions of learning, in any of the arts and sciences, as they deemed proper.[20]

Two private schools were organized in New Braunfels in 1852 and 1853, one by Dr. Adolf Douai, the other by Adolf Schlameus. Douai's school was opened in December, 1852, but was discontinued the following year when Douai moved to San Antonio. Schlameus opened his school about May 16, 1853, but discontinued it the same year when he was elected as one of the first two teachers of the City School (*Stadtschule*).[21]

Late in 1851 the residents of Comaltown petitioned the legislature for the incorporation of "Comal Union School."[22] The legislature granted the request and incorporated the school on February 13, 1852.[23] This school was kept up as a separate school for about thirty years, after which it became a ward school.

The first steps to organize a city school in New Braunfels were taken on February 17, 1853, when the city council appointed a committee consisting of Conrad Seabaugh, Julius Eggeling, and James W. Ferguson to submit proposals for such a school. L. C. Ervendberg, a member of the school board, drew up the regulations and these the city council adopted unanimously on May 9, 1853. The first teachers of the City School were Heinrich Guenther and

[19]Roemer, *Texas*, 120. Dabney, E. R., *The Settlement of New Braunfels and the History of Its Earlier Schools*, 40-43. Dabney's account is a thesis accepted by the Graduate School of the University of Texas in August, 1927.

[20]Gammel, *Laws of Texas*, III, 701. The original charter was granted on March 16, 1848. (*Ibid.*, III, 403-404.) See also Dabney, *The Settlement of New Braunfels and the History of Its Earlier Schools*, 45-46.

[21]*Neu Braunfelser Zeitung*, December 17, 1852, 4, col. 4, and April 29, 1853, 2, col. 5; Dabney, *The Settlement of New Braunfels and the History of Its Earlier Schools*, 55.

[22]MS. Records Office Secretary of State, Memorial No. 298, File Box No. 19, Letter No. C. The memorial contains a copy of the constitution which the petitioners desired.

[23]Gammel, *Laws of Texas*, III, 1175-1176. The act names Daniel Murchison, David H. Coleman, William Sattler, J. G. Mueller, J. J. Ottens, Conrad Pape, C. Engelke, J. H. Klingemann, and Julius Harms as incorporators.

Adolf Schlameus.[24]   This school was in operation until 1858 when
it was replaced by the New Braunfels Academy, which was incorporated on February 5, 1858.[25]   The first teachers of the academy
were Adolf Schlameus, S. H. Franks, and C. H. Holtz.   When
Olmsted was in Texas in 1855 he was impressed with the interest
which was taken in schools in and around New Braunfels.   At
that time there were five public schools in the neighborhood, a
Catholic school and the City School in New Braunfels, and a
private school for the study of Greek and Latin.[26]

The first school in Fredericksburg was organized in 1846 by the
Society for the Protection of German Immigrants in Texas.
Johann Leyendecker held school in the *Kaffeemuehle,* the Society's
church building.   In 1847 he was succeeded by Jacob Brodbeck.
The first city school was organized in 1856 and August Siemering
was chosen as teacher.[27]   Schools were organized also in the settlements around Fredericksburg and in 1860 there were ten schools
in the county with ten teachers and an enrollment of 290 pupils.
The teachers listed for Cherry Spring were Theodor Huelsemann
and Francis Stein and for Grape Creek the census named Jacob
Brodbeck, E. L. Theuman, and Louis Teschner.[28]

On October 29, 1849, Adolphus Fuchs petitioned the legislature
in the name of thirty German families of Cat Spring and neighborhood for aid in maintaining a school.   Fuchs, who was the
teacher at Cat Spring, stated that English schools were "unde-
niably the best way to Americanize the German population of
Texas and to make good citizens of them."[29]   In another settlement of Austin County, Shelby *(Roedersmuehle),* a school was
built in 1854.   A few years before the Civil War began one of the

[24]*Neu Braunfelser Zeitung,* September 16, 1853, 3, col. 4, and June 1,
1905, 7, col. 1.   For a copy of the regulations (also called constitution)
and the history of the school, see Dabney, *The Settlement of New Braunfels and a History of its Earlier Schools,* 53-66.

[25]Gammel, *Laws of Texas,* IV, 1273-1274.

[26]Olmsted, *Wanderungen durch Texas,* 128.

[27]Penniger, *Fest-Ausgabe,* 143-145; Gerlach, *Fest-Schrift zum 75-
jaehrigen Jubilaeum der St. Marien-Gemeinde zu Friedrichsburg, Texas,*
48-49.

[28]Eighth Census, Schedule 6:   Social Statistics for Gillespie County;
Photostat Eighth Census, Schedule of Free Inhabitants for Gillespie
County.

[29]MS. Records Office Secretary of State, Memorial No. 31, File Box
No. 1, Letter No. A.

best elementary schools of Texas was opened at Millheim by E. G.
Maetze. Many of his pupils became prominent, among them
Charles Nagel, Secretary of Commerce and Labor under President
Taft, and W. A. Trenckmann, at present editor of the *Austin
Wochenblatt.*[30]

Two schools were organized in the fifties by ministers of the
Evangelical-Lutheran Church. Rev. P. F. Zizelmann conducted a
school at La Grange for a few months early in 1852 and Rev.
Johann Georg Ebinger was in charge of a school at Berlin, near
Brenham, during his pastorate from 1855 to 1856.[31]

In Comfort the first school was organized in 1856 by a Mr. Glass,
an American. The schoolhouse was a small log cabin with only one
window and a door and no floor. It had neither crayon nor a
blackboard and the seats on the benches had no backs.[32] In 1859
the settlers of the Yorks Creek community organized a school and
chose Robert Bodemann of Hortontown as the first teacher at a
salary of $200 for nine months.[33] On the first Monday in April,
1860, a school was opened in Boerne. H. W. Toepperwein of
Grape Creek, Gillespie County, taught the school for one year at a
salary of $25.00 per month and all the school money furnished by
the state. The tuition was one dollar per month. McGuffey's
Speller and *Reader* and a series of German books published in
Cincinnati were used in this school.[34]

In other communities where the German element was well repre-
sented schools were organized for the education of their children.
In 1846 a German school was dedicated with great ceremony at
Galveston.[35] In 1858 the German Free School Association of
Austin was incorporated by the legislature. Wm. von Rosenberg,
Charles Pressler, Joseph Martin, H. Steussy, Dr. J. A. Brown,
Wm. Sattler, and Christian Wilhelm were named as incorporators.
The charter said that the object of the association was the "educa-

---

[30]Regenbrecht, "The German Settlers of Millheim before the Civil
War," *Southwestern Historical Quarterly*, XX, 30.

[31]Mgebroff, *Evangelisch-Lutherische Synode in Texas*, 41, 72; *Brenham
Banner-Press*, January 27, 1916, 24, col. 3.

[32]Lohmann, *Comfort*, 27.

[33]Coers, "Blum School, 1859-1927," *Guadalupe Gazette-Bulletin*, July
28, 1927, 2, col. 4.

[34]Lohmann, "Die erste Schule in Boerne," *Deutsch-Texanische Monatshefte*, VII, 210-214.

[35]Koerner, *Das deutsche Element*, 365.

tion of the youth, the promotion of useful knowledge, and the advancement of the sciences" and that the school was to be "accessible to all alike without regard to religious opinions."[36] On February 2, 1860, the German-English School of San Antonio received a charter for twenty years. C. N. Riotte, Dr. A. Nette, W. Friedrich, Gustav Theissen, J. H. Kampmann, G. Freiesleben, and Julius Berends were constituted a body corporate and politic for the purpose of organizing the school.[37] Julius Berends was the first teacher of this school. The "La Grange Casino," which was incorporated on February 11, 1860, was authorized by its charter to "establish, manage, and carry on . . . a free school."[38]

The Germans exhibited an interest also in the matter of higher education. In September, 1842, 38 residents of Austin County petitioned the Congress of Texas for the incorporation of Hermann's University. The memorial read as follows:

The undersigned, citizens of the Republic of Texas, would respectfully represent to Your Honorable Bodies—

That, with hardly one exception, they are natives of Germany who have emigrated to Texas with the motives and for the purposes that usually induce emigration from other countries;

That while they have endeavoured to secure the political, religious, and social privileges presented them by a free and tolerant Government, they have not been able, nor have they desired, to forget the many and perhaps unequally *(sic)* advantages for the education of Youth afforded by the schools and higher seminaries and universities of their native country;

That unable as they are at present to educate their children in a manner agreeable to their wishes, and desiring to remove this inability as also to extend a further and not unimportant inducement for their countrymen to come and settle among them, and for other and weighty reasons, obvious without further allusion;

Therefore, they respectfully ask of the Honorable Congress for an Act incorporating an Institution of Learning, to be known by the name of "Hermann's University" and of which the main peculiarities and objects are more fully set forth in the Bill herewith respectfully proposed, hoping by the passage of that or of a similar bill, that they and others in like condition may be able to educate

---

[36]Gammel, *Laws of Texas*, IV, 1223.

[37]Gammel, *Laws of Texas*, V, 125-126. A long account of the history of this school appeared in the *San Antonio Express* in its issue of March 4, 1928.

[38]*Ibid.*, V, 263.

their youth in a manner alike worthy of the country whence they have their origin and of that to which they have voluntarily transferred their allegiance and their fortunes.[39]

On January 27, 1844, Hermann's University was incorporated and a league of land was donated to it by the Congress of Texas. The university was to be located somewhere between Mill and Cummins Creeks. The management was to be in the hands of a president and twelve trustees, and this body was given authority to levy an excise on spirituous liquors within a radius of fifty miles from the university. The professors in each of the faculties of philosophy, medicine, theology, and jurisprudence had to be able to understand both English and German, but the trustees were allowed to waive this qualification by a unanimous vote.[40] The charter was amended on April 11, 1846. The theological faculty was no longer to be known as Protestant Faculty and the president and trustees were no longer restricted in locating the university near Mill or Cummins Creek.[41] A two-story stone building was erected at Frelsburg, but no classes were ever conducted in it by Hermann's University. Later on this building was used for a public school.[42] Another charter was secured on February 11, 1860, but the Civil War spelled failure for the undertaking and Hermann's University remained a beautiful dream.[43]

On January 19, 1850, the charter of the Western Texas Orphan Asylum was amended to the effect that the directors were authorized to establish an agricultural school and such other institutions of learning as they might deem proper. The directors were to

---

[39]MS. Records Office Secretary of State, Memorial No. 61, File Box No. 39, Letter No. H.
The memorial was signed by the following: L. C. Ervendberg, Friedrich Ernst, H. Schmidt, F. W. Huesman, Henry Amthor, Adam Kuhn, W. Wadhain, D. J. F. Jordt, H. Krey, H. Droop, John Koller, J. G. Sieper, Frd. Ed. Miller, Geo. Dannker, F. Frede, U. Algauer, A. Franke, C. Stoehr, S. Gruebler, Jacob Wolters, C. P. Allbright, George Bondeis, Fr. Zimmerscheit, Charles F. J. Jordt, Philip Biegel, ———? Beumer, W. Brodbeck, George Wrede, H. Buhl, A. Rohde, O. Henkhus, W. Ruhmann, Paul Mallich, H. H. Honnen, Anton Pieper, J. Hellmiller, R. Stoeltge, C. H. Weyer (Meyer ?).

[40]Gammel, *Laws of Texas*, II, 948-950. The league of land was located in Gillespie County, as an old map of the county on file in the General Land Office at Austin shows.

[41]*Ibid.*, II, 1384.

[42]*Deutsch-Texanische Monatshefte*, XIII, 88.

[43]*Deutsch-Texanische Monatshefte*, XII, 88; Gammel, *Laws of Texas*, V, 256-258.

appoint the president, all other officers, and professors, to regulate and prescribe their duties, and to grant degrees in conjunction with the faculty. No religious qualification or test, whatsoever, was to be required either of the professors or of the students.[44] In pursuance of the amended charter the directors organized the West Texas University at Neu Wied and appointed L. C. Ervendberg president. A preparatory school, divided into elementary, grammar, and high school grades, was conducted in connection with the university. As late as 1855 Ervendberg was still the only professor in the institution.[45]

On the occasion of the first German-Texas Saengerfest (*deutsch-texanisches Saengerfest*) at New Braunfels a meeting was held on October 17, 1853, and a number of resolutions were adopted. One of these called for the appointment of a committee to secure a charter for founding a higher middle-class, German-English school in West Texas. Ottomar von Behr, Dr. Adolf Douai, C. N. Riotte, Gustav Theissen, C. G. Guenther, and H. F. Osswald were appointed for this committee.[46]

The earliest record of religious services among the Germans in Texas is found in the *Morning Star* of December 24, 1839, which stated that two days earlier a German minister had preached to a congregation of immigrants in Houston. The same paper two weeks later announced regular services of the German Protestant congregation every Sunday morning at the home of Mr. Thiel.[47] Although the name of the minister is not given, the writer believes that it was L. C. Ervendberg, who came to Houston from Illinois in 1839.[48]

In the period from 1840 to 1844 L. C. Ervendberg and Dr. Johann Anton Fischer organized Protestant congregations in Industry, Cat Spring, Biegel, La Grange, and Columbus. During the same period there were Free Protestant congregations at Galveston and Frelsburg. Fiebiger was pastor at Frelsburg but

[44]Gammel, *Laws of Texas*, III, 701-702.

[45]*Neu Braunfelser Zeitung*, November 12, 1852, 4, col. 1; Olmsted, *Wanderungen durch Texas*, 119.

[46]*Jahrbuch fuer Texas* (1882), 45; *Deutsch-Texanische Monatshefte*, IX, 25-26.

[47]*Morning Star*, December 24, 1839, 2, col. 1, and January 11, 1840, 3, col. 2.

[48]Mgebroff, *Evangelisch-Lutherische Synode in Texas*, 8.

died soon after organizing the congregation.[49]   At a synodal meeting of German ministers at Industry on November 1, 1841, a constitution for the regulation of the different churches was drawn
up.   It was signed by Dr. Johann Anton Fischer as president and
by L. C. Ervendberg as secretary of the synod.[50]

In December, 1844, Prince Solms secured L. C. Ervendberg to
look after the religious needs of the settlers brought to Texas by
the Society for the Protection of German Immigrants in Texas.
Ervendberg preached the first sermon to his new flock on December 23 at Port Lavaca.   He conducted services for the Society's
settlers in New Braunfels under the great oaks and elms at the
foot of the *Vereinsberg* and dedicated the *Vereinskirche* on March
22, 1846.   When the Society discontinued its work early in 1848
Ervendberg became the pastor of the Protestant congregation,
which really was affiliated with the Evangelical Church.   On March
30, 1851, Gustav W. Eisenlohr succeeded him.[51]   When the Society
founded the settlement at Fredericksburg it engaged Rev. F.
Basse, one of its immigrants, to carry on the religious work.
Basse conducted services in the old *Kaffeemuehle* until 1849, when
Rev. B. Dangers succeeded him.[52]

Besides the Protestants the Catholics also had churches in New
Braunfels and Fredericksburg.   The first mass was celebrated in
New Braunfels early in 1846 by the missionary priest, George
Menzel, but the first church was not built until 1850.[53]   In Fred-
ericksburg the Catholics built a church in 1848 under Father
George Menzel, who, in the same year, erected a cross as a sign of
salvation and civilization on the *Kreuzberg,* a hill to the northwest
of Fredericksburg.[54]

---

[49]*Ibid.*, 8, 11.

[50]Wrede, *Lebensbilder*, 253-254.   The constitution which consisted of
seven articles, was called "Konstitution der vereinigten christlichen
Kirche der Deutschen in Texas und den Vereinigten Staaten."

[51]Seele, "Beitrag zur Geschichte von Neu Braunfels," *Jahrbuch fuer
Texas* (1882), 43; *Neu Braunfelser Zeitung*, September 18, 1895, 4, col.
4; Solms, "Berichte an den Adelsverein," *Kalender*, 45.   The Protestant
congregation received a charter on November 6, 1845.   This charter is
recorded in Bexar County Deed Records, Book C, No. 2, 184-185.

[52]Penniger, *Fest-Ausgabe*, 147, 153.

[53]*Neu Braunfelser Zeitung*, July 22, 1926, 9, col. 5.

[54]Penniger, *Fest-Ausgabe*, 153-154.   The fullest treatment of the activities of the Catholics in Fredericksburg is found in Gerlach, *Fest-
Schrift zum 75-jaehrigen Jubilaeum der St. Marien-Gemeinde zu Friedrichsburg, Texas.*

The first German Methodist congregation in Texas, as far as the writer was able to ascertain, was founded in La Grange in 1847 and Rev. G. Rottenstein set to work immediately to secure funds for building a church.[55] In Fredericksburg a Methodist congregation was founded by Rev. Eduard Schneider in 1849. Services were held in the Society's *Kaffeemuehle* until 1855, after which the congregation held its services in a new church built of rock.[56]

The most active of the Protestant churches was the Evangelical-Lutheran. In the winter of 1849 one of the Society's immigrants wrote a letter to his relatives in Switzerland and described the religious needs of the people. C. F. Spitteler of Basel, to whom the letter was given and who was the benefactor of a missionary school in Crishona, Switzerland, sent Theobald Kleis of Baden and Christoph Adam Sager of Wuertemberg to Texas in response to the appeal. Sager began his work in Victoria, where there was a considerable German element and also served Meyersville, Yorktown, and Goliad. Kleis went to New Braunfels, founded a small congregation, built a church, and made occasional missionary trips to Seguin, San Antonio, Castroville, and Quihi. Besides these two men, Rev. G. F. Huebner served in Galveston, Rev. Caspar Braun in Houston, and H. Braschler in Spring Creek near Houston. In the following year, 1851, Johann Conrad Roehm, Johann Georg Ebinger, Philip Friedrich Zizelmann, Wilhelm T. Strobel, Christian Oefinger, and Heinrich Wendt were sent to Texas from Germany. On November 10-12, 1851, the first German Evangelical-Lutheran Synod of Texas was organized at Houston by Roehm, Zizelmann, Strobel, Ebinger, Oefinger, Braun, and Braschler. The Evangelical-Lutherans built a number of churches in Texas in the period from 1850 to 1860 and organized many small congregations which were served occasionally either by ministers on circuit or by ministers definitely stationed at a nearby settlement. In all there were thirty-three ministers of this denomination actively at work in Texas in the period mentioned and congregations were organized at thirty-seven places.[57]

[55]*The Far West*, April 10, 1847, 2, col. 2. This newspaper was published at La Grange, Texas.

[56]Penniger, *Fest-Ausgabe*, 157.

[57]Mgebroff, *Evangelisch-Lutherische Synode in Texas*, 12-36, 346-348; *Brenham Banner-Press*, January 27, 1916, 24, cols. 1-4. The early history

One of the distinguishing characteristics of the German settlers was the attention which they gave to the founding of clubs (*Vereine*). Some of these, the social clubs, were formed for the purpose of promoting the spirit of good fellowship (*das gesellige Leben*). The meeting of a *Verein* for *einen geselligen und gemuethlichen Abend* was always an occasion to which the members looked forward with genuine pleasure. Others, as the literary, dramatic, and singing societies, were formed to promote the cultural development of their members. Even the agricultural, workingmen's, and political clubs, aside from their main purpose, aimed to further the cause of cultural progress.

The first society which was organized to promote good fellowship was the German Union for Texas, an association formed at Houston in 1840 with George Fisher as president and Henry Francis Fisher as secretary. On January 21, 1841, the association received the charter for which it had petitioned the Congress of Texas on December 8 of the previous year. The main purpose of the German Union seems to have been to assist immigrants and to minister to the sick and needy.[58]

On the evening of Whitsuntide, 1841, the Germans of Industry and Cat Spring under the leadership of Friedrich Ernst organized the Teutonic Order (*Teutonia Orden*). Within a month the order had fifty-three members. Aside from bringing the Germans together, the order wished to further immigration, facilitate correspondence between Texas and Germany, practice philanthropy, and preserve the German traits of character. The order was made up of many degrees. Talent, ability, and education were requisites for admission to the second and third classes in the order. Intellectual entertainment to compensate for the lost joys of the Fatherland was provided for.[59] The order existed only a few years. On Palm Sunday, 1842, it had a great celebration on Mill Creek.[60]

---

of Trinity Church of this denomination at Victoria, Texas, is given in an account by C. A. Leuschner. (See Victor Rose Papers, University of Texas.)

[58]MS. Records Office Secretary of State, Memorial No. 12, File Box No. 32, Letter No. G; Gammel, *Laws of Texas*, II, 553-554; Tiling, *German Element in Texas*, 48-51.

[59]Benjamin, *Germans in Texas*, 8 (quotes from *Deutsch-Amerikanische Geschichtsblaetter*, January, 1906, 21-22); Koerner, *Das deutsche Element*, 359.

[60]Entry in Diary of Adolphus Sterne, April 22, 1842.

On March 2, 1843, the members gave proof of their patriotism by celebrating the anniversary of the Texas Declaration of Independence.[61]

The Social Club *(Geselliger Verein)* and the Workingmen's Club *(Handwerker-Bund)* of New Braunfels, the Society of Good Fellowship and the Promotion of General Information *(Verein fuer Geselligkeit und zur Befoerderung gemeinnuetziger Kenntnisse)* of the Pedernales and Live Oak Creek settlements, and the Reform Club *(Reform-Verein)* of Fredericksburg, which were organized in 1853 and 1854, made it a point to foster social life in addition to other work which each promoted.[62]   The Casino Association of San Antonio, incorporated December 7, 1857, the Galveston Casino, incorporated February 3, 1860, and the La Grange Casino, incorporated February 11, 1860, were formed for promoting social entertainments.[63]

During the fifties, in what year is not certain, Johannes C. N. Romberg organized a literary society among the settlers on Black Jack Creek in Fayette County.   This Society had the very appropriate name of Prairie Flower *(Prairieblume)*.   On the occasion of the first meeting Romberg read the following poem:

> "Bluemelein,
> Zart und klein,
> Wuensch' dir gutes Wetter,
> Moegst gedeihn
> Auf texanischer Prairie.
> Prosa deuten deine Blaetter,
> Deine Blueten Poesie."

Romberg, as the poem indicates, wished the society to study both prose and poetry.[64]   It is not stated in the introduction to the *Gedichte* that the society was to present plays, but the writer surmises that it did.   On October 21, 1854, H. Schulz, H. Remer, and H. Seele organized the New Braunfels Dramatic Society *(Neu Braunfelser Theater-Gesellschaft)*.   The proceeds from the first six performances of this society were donated to the school board for the building fund of the first public school in New

---

[61]*Telegraph and Texas Register*, March 29, 1843, 2, col. 4.

[62]*Neu Braunfelser Zeitung*, August 19, 1853, 2, col. 5, January 20, 1854, 4, col. 2, January 27, 1854, 3, col. 3, and February 10, 1854, 3, col. 3.

[63]Gammel, *Laws of Texas*, IV, 1185-1186, V, 136-137, 263.

[64]Romberg, *Gedichte*, p. IX.

Braunfels.[65]   The Casino clubs of San Antonio, Galveston, and La Grange, of which mention was made on the preceding page, also had the object of promoting literary pursuits, by which expression was understood the presentation of plays.

The love for music is one of the distinguishing characteristics of the German people. This inherent musical sentiment followed them to Texas. "It may be of some interest to note," says Moritz Tiling, "that the first piano on Texas soil was brought here by Robert Kleberg, Sr., . . . in 1834."[66] Other German families had pianos. On the piano in the home of Adolphus Fuchs at Cypress Mill lay such musical compositions as Mozart's *Don Juan* and *The Magic Flute (Die Zauberfloete)* and Haydn's *Creation.* Fuchs was an excellent singer and on the occasion of a visit to the Amthor's at Cat Spring in 1859 he sang arias from Haydn's *Creation* and Beethoven's *Adelaide,* while Mrs. Amthor accompanied him on her piano.[67]

Singing societies were formed in nearly every German settlement. One writer says: "The German immigrants who came to Texas in great numbers from 1845 to 1850 brought along an invisible passenger, the German song *(das deutsche Lied).* It accompanied them westward on their dreary march across the broad prairies . . . and established itself with the sturdy pioneers on the beautiful banks of the Comal and Pedernales, to cheer them in their daily toil and brighten their evenings at the fireside."[68] The first singing society in Texas, the *Germania,* was organized at New Braunfels on March 2, 1850. Some of its early directors were Petmecky, C. F. Blum, Dr. Adolf Douai, and H. Guenther. On July 1, 1853, the *Germania* announced a celebration for July 4 at Seele's Place on the right bank of the Guadalupe just north of where the Missouri Pacific now crosses the river. Speeches and the reading of the Declaration of Independence were to be included in the program.[69] Besides the *Germania* two other singing

---

[65]*Jahrbuch fuer Texas* (1882), 46; *Neu Braunfelser Zeitung*, December 22, 1854, 2, cols. 2-3.

[66]Tiling, *German Element in Texas*, 136. See also Kleberg, Rosa, "Some of My Early Experiences in Texas," Texas State Historical Association *Quarterly*, I, 298.

[67]Goeth, *Was Grossmutter erzaehlt*, 43-47.

[68]Tiling, *German Element in Texas*, 136.

[69]*Neu Braunfelser Zeitung*, July 1, 1853, col. 3, and July 22, 1926, 4, col. 3; Tiling, *German Element in Texas*, 136-137; *Jahrbuch fuer Texas*

Ed. Rische   F. Moureau H. Conring C. H. Holtz Jul. Bremer H. Seele E. vom Stein G. Eisenlohr   J. Rennert   A. Hartmann
           A. Baier   Aug. Bechstedt   A. Schlameus   H. Schimmelpfennig

GERMANIA GESANGVEREIN OF NEW BRAUNFELS

GRUENDER DES TEXANISCHEN SAENGERBUNDES

From a print in the possession of Miss Georgine Holtz, San Antonio, Texas. The original was made
by Carl G. Iwonski in 1857

clubs were organized in New Braunfels before 1861, the *Lieder-tafel* and a chorus of men and women, the *Concordia*. A quartette existed at Sisterdale from 1852 to 1857, while at Comfort, under the direction of Herman Schimmelpfennig, there was a quartette from 1855 to 1858 with Ernst Altgelt, Fritz Goldbeck, C. W. Boerner, and Fritz Holekamp as members. Before the Civil War there were singing societies at San Antonio (1852), Austin (1852), Shelby (1852), La Grange (1853), Indianola (1854), Columbus (1854), Coleto (1854), Welcome (1856), Fredericksburg (1858), Pedernales (1858), Grape Creek (1858), and Comfort (1858).[70]

In August, 1853, plans were made in New Braunfels for holding a state song festival *(Staats-Saengerfest)* to which all the singing societies of the state were to be invited. The committee on arrangements consisted of Rev. G. Eisenlohr, F. Moureau, H. Seele, J. Eggeling, and F. Mueller. Participating in this first *Saengerfest,* which was held in New Braunfels on October 16, 1853, were the *Germania,* the Sisterdale quartette, and the singing clubs of San Antonio and Austin. A very excellent program was rendered, everybody was enthusiastic, and a genuine German *Volksfest* followed the concert. The second *Saengerfest* was held at San Antonio, May 14-16, 1854, and steps were taken to form the German State Singers' League *(Deutsch-Texanischer Staats-Saengerbund).* When the third *Saengerfest* was held at New Braunfels in May, 1855, Hermann Seele's *Saengerhalle,* a brick building 30 feet by 80 feet which had been built that spring, was used for the meeting place.[71] Four other meetings were held before 1861, namely at New Braunfels, 1856, 1858, and 1860, and at Fredericksburg, 1859.[72]

The German newspaper is another evidence of culture among the early settlers. According to Ferdinand Lindheimer, the *Galveston Zeitung,* the first of these, was published as early as 1846. C. W. Buechner was editor in 1853.[73] The *Democratic Telegraph and*

(1882), 44. On the same day with the Fourth-of-July celebration of the *Germania* a political rally was announced for Neu Wied in connection with a *Volksfest.*

[70]Tiling, *German Element in Texas,* 137-142; Lohmann, *Comfort,* 27; Trenckmann, *Austin County,* 25 and 28.

[71]*Neu Braunfelser Zeitung,* March 9, 1855, 2, col. 4, and May 25, 1855, 2, col. 2.

[72]Tiling, *German Element in Texas,* 137-142.

[73]*Neu Braunfelser Zeitung,* February 11, 1853, 3, col. 3.

Texas Register hoped the new journal would "solace the German immigrants in the distant wilds" and "come to them like the sunbeams to gladden their hearts with sweet thoughts of Faderland."[74] W. Steinert, who made a trip through Texas in 1849, characterized the paper as rather dry *(ziemlich trocken),* but an article which it published on Texas in 1848 is anything but dry.[75] As far as the writer knows, no files of the *Galveston Zeitung* have been preserved.

Although the project of founding a newspaper in New Braunfels was mentioned as early as 1851, it was not until April 3 of the next year that a mass meeting was held and steps were taken to establish the *Neu Braunfelser Zeitung.* Dr. Ferdinand Jacob Lindheimer[76] was chosen editor and a committee was appointed to secure donations for the purchase of a press and other equipment. On November 12, 1852, the *Neu Braunfelser Zeitung* made its initial appearance and has remained in continuous publication up to the present time. The *Zeitung* was to be the official organ of the Germans in West Texas, as its sub-title indicated. The main objects in founding the paper were: *first,* to stimulate the Germans to think about and to participate in public affairs; and *second,* to have a paper for the discussion of local interests. It was not the intention of the founders that the paper should be the organ of any political party, as its initial issue stated.[77] However, as was noticed in the preceding chapter, the *Neu Braunfelser Zeitung,* in its editorial columns, championed the cause of the Democratic

[74]*Democratic Telegraph and Texas Register,* August 9, 1847, 3, col. 2.

[75]Steinert, *Nordamerika, vorzueglisch Texas, im Jahre 1849,* 60. The article on Texas, which is reproduced in Bracht, *Texas im Jahre 1848,* 299-303, appeared on June 7, 1848, over the signature of thirty-three German settlers.

[76]Dr. Ferdinand Jacob Lindheimer was born at Frankfort on the Main in 1801. He studied law in Jena. He was a Liberal in politics and took part in the *Frankfurter Putsch* of 1833. He fled to the United States and remained in New Orleans until early in 1836, when he went to Texas to take part in the revolution. After Texan independence was won he went to Mexico with his friend, Otto Friedrich. Soon, however, the two returned. Lindheimer studied the flora of Texas and organized it into a system. Many of the plants discovered by him carry the name of *Lindheimeriana* along with their regular botanical names. Prince Solms and John O. Meusebach cultivated his friendship and made good use of his advice. He edited the *Neu Braunfelser Zeitung* continuously until August 30, 1872, when he was succeeded as editor by A. Eiband. *(Der deutsche Pionier,* XI, 380-382; *Neu Braunfelser Zeitung,* September 6, 1872.)

[77]*Neu Braunfelser Zeitung,* November 12, 1852, 1, col. 5, and November 24, 1854, 1, cols. 1-3; *Jahrbuch fuer Texas* (1882), 42-43.

party and upheld the views of John C. Calhoun and Jefferson Davis on the question of slavery in the territories.

Dr. Adolf Douai began publication of the *San Antonio Zeitung* about the first of July, 1853. Olmsted, who read a copy of the paper at Bastrop, Texas, early in 1854 said that it contained more new, important, and interesting information than all the Texan newspapers which he had seen up to that time. Douai was an ardent opponent of slavery and advocated abolition in the columns of his paper. In New Braunfels the Germans met in mass meeting on June 25, 1855, and declared that they were not responsible for the "opinions and sentiments promulgated in the *San Antonio Zeitung.*" In Lockhart the Germans demanded that Douai be removed from the editorship and even said that they would heartily join with their American fellow-citizens to put him down. Douai finally aroused so much opposition that he was forced to sell his paper and leave Texas.[78]

At the annual meeting of the Evangelical-Lutheran Synod in 1854 it was decided to issue a monthly paper for the purpose of working up an interest in a theological and classical seminary. This paper was called *Der Pilger im Sueden der Union* and more than likely was published at Galveston, since Rev. Heinrich Wendt of that place was made editor, with Revs. Wilhelm Strobel and Heinrich Bohnenberger as assistants. The paper was published for one year, but, it is said, not a single copy is to be found.[79]

Unique among the newspapers of Texas, however, was *Der Bettelsack*, issued at Comfort. This paper was not printed but simply written and circulated in that fashion. Its principal contributors were Dr. Otto Mehlis, Fritz Holekamp, Louis von Breiten-

[78]*Neu Braunfelser Zeitung*, July 8, 1853, 2, col. 2; Olmsted, *Wanderungen durch Texas*, 90-91; Tiling, *German Element in Texas*, 122; Benjamin, *Germans in Texas*, 100-101; *Texas State Gazette*, July 11, 1855, 1, col. 4, and July 25, 1855, 4, col. 2; *La Grange Paper*, July 7, 1855, 2, cols. 5-6. In its issue of June 30, 1855, the *La Grange Paper* quoted from the *Gonzales Inquirer* as follows: "A report reached here a day or two since that the printing office of the *San Antonio Zeitung*, a German abolition concern, had been destroyed by the citizens of that town. Generally speaking, we are opposed to mobs, but if the report be true, this is one case where the nature of the circumstances will, we think, justify their course. The *Zeitung* has for some time past advocated doctrines entirely contrary to the spirit of our institutions, and if the office is not destroyed it should be. It would teach the editor a wholesome lesson and prove a worthy example to all similar evil-doers." (*La Grange Paper*, June 30, 1855, 3, cols. 1-2.)

[79]Mgebroff, *Evangelisch-Lutherische Synode in Texas*, 136-140.

bauch, Fritz Goldbeck, Theodor Goldbeck, and Carl Herbst.   The
log cabin inhabited by Herbst and Mehlis was the editorial room
and was nicknamed the *Korrektionsbude*.[80]

Culture manifested itself among the German settlers also through
the art of painting.   In Hortontown, northeast of New Braunfels,
lived Carl G. Iwonski, a painter, who engaged mostly in portrait
painting.   As far as I have been able to determine his first painting
was done in 1855.   It was a water color portrait of a sixteen-year-
old girl.   In April, 1857, he made a pencil portrait of the Germania Gesangverein of New Braunfels.   The faces on this portrait
are said to be true likenesses.   About this same time, too, he made
a pencil sketch of New Braunfels.[81]   In 1864 he made a pencil
portrait of Mrs. Heinrich Schuetze, her son, Julius, and her daughter, Emilie.   Another of his pencil sketches was called *Texanische
Wolken*.   Iwonski returned to Germany after the Civil War and
is said to have become a well-known artist.

Another portrait painter of considerable talent was Richard
Petri, who had studied art in Germany before going to America.
In 1849 he moved from Wheeling, then in Virginia, to Fredericksburg, Texas.   He made separate portraits of himself, of his sister,
Marie, who became Mrs. Jacob Kuechler, and of his sister, Elise,
who married Hermann Lungkwitz.   His favorite subject seems to
have been the Biblical scene, with the Indian as his second choice.
His best Biblical picture is one showing Simon, the sorcerer, before
the Apostles Peter and John offering them money to grant to him
the gift of God.   Petri painted a very good portrait of an Indian
living on the Pedernales.   Another painting shows the head of
Shylock.   Petri left unfinished a painting of a scene near Fredericksburg showing soldiers, settlers, and Indians.

In landscape painting Hermann Lungkwitz[82] did excellent work.
He was born at Halle-an-der-Saale, Germany.   He came to America
in company with his sister, Therese, Richard Petri, and Elise Petri.
After having lived for a while at Wheeling, then in the state of
Virginia, he moved to Fredericksburg in 1849 and married Elise
Petri.   While studying art in Germany he had become acquainted

[80]Altgelt, *Comfort*, 106-107; Lohmann, *Comfort*, 21.

[81]For copies of these two paintings, see pages 111 and 222.

[82]For the information about Richard Petri and Hermann Lungkwitz I
am indebted to Mrs. Walter Wuppermann of Austin, a granddaughter of
Hermann Lungkwitz.   A copy of the pencil sketch of Fredericksburg is to
be found on page 139.

with Richard Petri. Some of his paintings represent scenes in Germany, the best of which is probably that of the city Freiburg. Others of his paintings represent scenes in Texas, among them being Bear Mountain near Fredericksburg, the Pedernales River, West Cave on the Pedernales River, Marble Falls on the Colorado River, and Waller Creek at Austin. A pencil sketch shows Fredericksburg about the year 1850. A good part of his work was done in Austin, where Lungkwitz lived in the later years of his life. It is not generally known that two of his great landscape paintings are on public exhibit in Austin. In the south entrance to the Capitol are to be seen two large paintings. The one is that of David Crockett, the other shows the surrender of Santa Anna to General Sam Houston. The portraits of these paintings were done by the artist Huddle, but the landscapes are the work of Hermann Lungkwitz.

Generally speaking, the German settlers bore the burdens and discomforts of founding a new home on the frontier of Texas with the true spirit of the American pioneer. Their schools, churches, societies, and newspapers added a touch to frontier life which made them feel at home in Texas. They came to have a high regard for their adopted state, a feeling to which Viktor Bracht gave expression in the last sentence of his book, *Texas im Jahre 1848*, with the words:

"All for Texas and Texas forever!"

BIBLIOGRAPHY

I. BOOKS AND PAMPHLETS

Contemporary

Bartlett, John Russell, *Personal Narrative of Explorations and Incidents in Texas, New Mexico, California, Sonora, and Chihuahua*, Connected with the United States and Mexican Boundary Commission During the Years 1850, '51, '52 and '53. In two volumes. New York, 1854.

Behr, Ottomar von, *Guter Rath fuer Auswanderer nach den Vereinigten Staaten von Nordamerika mit besonderer Beruecksichtigung von Texas. Vorgueglich fuer Landleute und Handwerker nach eigener Erfahrung geschrieben.* Leipzig, 1847.

Beyer, Moritz, *Das Auswanderungsbuch oder Fuehrer und Rathgeber bei der Auswanderung nach Nordamerika und Texas.* Leipzig, 1846. Baumgartner's Buchhandlung.

Bracht, Viktor, *Texas im Jahre 1848.* Elberfeld u. Iserlohn, 1849.

Bromme, Traugott, *Hand- und Reisebuch fuer Auswanderer nach den Vereinigten Staaten von Nord-Amerika.* Bayreuth, 1849.

Bromwell, William J., *History of Immigration to the United States.* New York, 1856.

Buettner, Prof. Dr. J. G., *Briefe aus und ueber Nordamerika.* Dresden und Leipzig, 1845.

Chickering, Jesse, *Immigration into the United States.* Boston, 1848.

Comite-Bericht des Vereins zum Schutze deutscher Einwanderer in Texas. Wiesbaden, 1850.

Constant, L., *Texas. Das Verderben deutscher Auswanderer in Texas unter dem Schutze des Mainzer Vereins.* Berlin, 1847.

DeBow, J. D. B., *Statistical View of the United States . . . A Compendium of the Seventh Census.* Washington, 1854.

De Bow, J. D. B., *The Seventh Census of the United States.* Washington, 1853.

Duden, Gottfried, *Bericht ueber eine Reise nach den westlichen Staaten Nordamerika's und einen mehrjaehrigen Aufenthalt am Missouri* (in den Jahren 1824, 1825, 1826, 1827). · · · · Bonn, 1834.

Dunt, Detlef, *Reise nach Texas.* Bremen, 1834.

Ehrenberg, H., *Der Freiheitskampf in Texas im Jahre 1836.* Leipzig, 1844.

Ehrenberg, H., *Fahrten und Schicksale eines Deutschen in Texas.* Leipzig, 1845.

Ehrenberg, H., *Texas und seine Revolution*. Leipzig, 1845.
Fleischmann, C. L., *Wegweiser und Rathgeber nach und in den Vereinigten Staaten von Nord-Amerika*. Stuttgart, 1852.
Franz, Georg, *Die Auswanderung der Deutschen nach Texas, Nordamerika und Ungarn*. Eine Mahnung an die Nation. Muenchen, 1844.
Gesammelte Aktenstuecke des Vereins zum Schutze deutscher Einwanderer in Texas. Nebst einer Karte. Mainz, 1845.
Hecke, J. Val., *Reise durch die Vereinigten Staaten von Nord-Amerika in den Jahren 1818 und 1819*. Berlin, 1820.
Herff, Dr. Ferdinand von, *Die geregelte Auswanderung des deutschen Proletariats mit besonderer Beziehung auf Texas*. Frankfurt am Main, 1850.
Jones, Anson, *Memoranda and Official Correspondence Relating to the Republic of Texas, Its History, and Annexation*. Including a brief autobiography of the author. New York, 1859.
Kapp, Ernst, *Der Constituirte Despotismus und die Constitutionelle Freiheit*. Hamburg, 1849.
Keene, Don Ricardo Reynal, A. M., *Memoria Presentada a S. M. C. El Senor Don Fernando VII, Sobre el Asunto de Fomentar la Poblacion y Cultivo en los Terrenos Baldios en las Provincias Internas del Reyno de Mexico*. Madrid, 1 de Enero de 1815.
Kennedy, Jos. C. G., *Agriculture of the United States in 1860*. Washington, 1864.
Kennedy, Jos. C. G., *Population of the United States in 1860*. Washington, 1864.
Kennedy, Jos. C. G., *Manufactures of the United States in 1860*. Washington, 1864.
Kennedy, Jos. C. G., *Preliminary Report on the Eighth Census, 1860*. Washington, 1862.
Kennedy, Wm., *Geographie, Naturgeschichte, und Topographie von Texas*. Aus dem Englischen von O. von Czarnowsky. Frankfurt am Main, 1846.
Kennedy, Wm., *Texas: the Rise, Progress, and Prospects of the Republic of Texas*. London, 1841.
Loeher, Franz, *Geschichte und Zustaende der Deutschen in Amerika*. Cincinnati, 1847, and Leipzig, 1847.
Ludecus, Eduard, *Reise durch die mexikanischen Provinzen Tumalipas, Cohahuila und Texas im Jahre 1834*. Leipzig, 1837.
Olmsted, Frederick Law, *A Journey Through Texas; or A Saddle-Trip on the Southwestern Frontier;* with a statistical appendix. . . . New York, 1857.
Olmsted, Frederick Law, *Wanderungen durch Texas und im mexikanischen Grenzlande*. Leipzig, 1857.

Roemer, Dr. Ferdinand, *Texas*. Bonn, 1849.

Ross, George M. von, *Der Nordamerikanische Freistaat Texas*. Rudolstadt, 1851.

Scherpf, G. A., *Entstehungsgeschichte und gegenwaertiger Zustand des neuen, unabhaengigen, amerikanischen Staates Texas*. Augsburg, 1841.

Schmoelder, B., *Neuer praktischer Wegweiser fuer Auswanderer nach Nord-Amerika*. Mainz, 1849.

Schuetz, Kuno Damian Freiherrn von, *Texas. Rathgeber fuer Auswanderer nach diesem Lande*. Wiesbaden, 1847.

Schultz, Joh. Heinr. Siegfried, *Die deutsche Ansiedlung in Texas*. Bonn, 1845.

Soergel, Alwin, *Fuer Auswanderungslustige!* Briefe eines unter dem Schutze des Mainzer Vereins nach Texas Ausgewanderten. Erste Lieferung. Leipzig, 1847.

Soergel, A. H., *Neueste Nachrichten aus Texas*. Eisleben, 1847.

Solms-Braunfels, Carl, Prinzen zu, *Texas*. Geschildert in Beziehung auf seine geographischen, socialen und uebrigen Verhaeltnisse mit besonderer Ruecksicht auf die deutsche Colonisation. Ein Handbuch fuer Auswanderer nach Texas. Frankfurt am Main, 1846.

Steinert, W., *Nordamerika vorzueglich Texas im Jahre 1849*. Berlin, 1850.

Texas. Ein Handbuch fuer deutsche Auswanderer. Bremen, 1846.

Thrau, Jacob, *Meine Auswanderung nach Texas unter dem Schutze des Mainzer Vereins*. Berlin, 1848.

Treu, Georg, *Das Buch der Auswanderung*. Bamberg, 1843.

Walther, F. E., *Texas in sein wahres Licht gestellt*. Dresden und Leipzig, 1848.

Wrede, Fr. W. v., *Lebensbilder aus den Vereinigten Staaten von Nordamerika und Texas*. Cassel, 1844.

Later

Adams, Ephraim Douglass, *British Diplomatic Correspondence Concerning the Republic of Texas, 1838-1846*. (Edited by Ephraim Douglass Adams. Reprinted from *The Quarterly* of the Texas State Historical Association, XV, Nos. 3 and 4, and from *The Southwestern Historical Quarterly*, XVI, No. 1-XXI, No. 2. January, 1912-October, 1917. The Texas State Historical Association, Austin, Texas.

Barker, E. C., *The Life of Stephen F. Austin*. Founder of Texas, 1793-1836. A Chapter in the Westward Movement of the Anglo-American People. Nashville and Dallas, 1925.

Benjamin, G. G., *The Germans in Texas. A Study in Immigration*. Philadelphia. (Reprinted from *German American Annals,* Vol. VII), 1909.

Biedermann, K., *Deutsche Volks- und Kulturgeschichte fuer Schule und Haus*. Zweite, verbesserte und vermehrte Auflage. Wiesbaden, 1891.

Binkley, William Campbell, *The Expansionist Movement in Texas, 1836-1850*. Berkeley, Cal., University of California Press, 1925.

Bosse, Georg von, *Das deutsche Element in den Vereinigten Staaten*. New York and Stuttgart, 1908.

Brown, John Henry, *Indian Wars and Pioneers of Texas*. Austin, Texas.

Bruncken, Ernest, *German Political Refugees in the United States during the Period from 1815-1860*. (Special Print from *"Deutsch-Amerikanische Geschichtsblaetter."*) Milwaukee?, 1904.

Cronau, Rudolf, *Drei Jahrhunderte deutschen Lebens in Amerika: Eine Geschichte der Deutschen in den Vereinigten Staaten*. Berlin, 1909.

Cronau, Rudolf, *German Achievements in America*. New York, 1916.

Dabney, Edgar Robert, *The Settlement of New Braunfels and the History of its Earlier Schools*. Austin, Texas, 1927. Master of Arts Thesis in the University of Texas.

Davis, Philip, *Immigration and Americanization*. Selected Readings. Compiled and Edited by ————, Boston and New York, 1920.

Eickhoff, Anton, *In der neuen Heimath*. New York, 1884.

Fairchild, Henry Pratt, *Immigrant Backgrounds*. New York, 1927.

Faust, A. B., *Charles Sealsfield (Carl Postl), der Dichter beider Hemisphaeren. Sein Leben und seine Werke*. Weimar, 1897.

Faust, A. B., *Das Deutschthum in den Vereinigten Staaten in seiner geschichtlichen Entwickelung*. Leipzig, 1912.

Faust, A. B., *Das Deutschthum in den Vereinigten Staaten in seiner Bedeutung fuer die amerikanische Kultur*. Leipzig, 1912.

Faust, A. B., *The German Element in the United States with special reference to its political, moral, social, and educational influence*. Boston and New York, 1909.

Gerlach, Rev. H., *Festschrift zum 75-jaehrigen Jubilaeum der St. Marien-Gemeinde zu Friedrichsburg, Texas*. Fredericksburg, 1921.

Goeth, Ottilie, *Was Grossmutter erzaehlt*. San Antonio, 1915.

Gammel, H. P. N., *The Laws of Texas, 1822-1897* . . . compiled and arranged by H. P. N. Gammel. . . . With an introduction by C. W. Raines. Austin, 1898.

Goldbeck, Fritz, *Seit fuenfzig Jahren.* San Antonio, Texas, 1895.

Hatcher, Mattie Austin, *The Opening of Texas to Foreign Settlement, 1801-1821.* University of Texas Bulletin No. 2714. Austin, Texas, 1927.

Henderson, Ernest Flagg, *A Short History of Germany.* New York, 1906.

Herbst, Carl, *Seine Reden und Schriften.* Comfort, Texas. This is an unpublished compilation of Herbst's speeches and writings. Date unknown.

Johnson, Sid S., *Texans Who Wore the Gray,* Vol. I. (Tyler?), Texas, 1907.

Kapp, Friedrich, *Aus und ueber Amerika. Thatsachen und Erlebnisse.* Berlin, 1876.

Kaufmann, Georg, *Politische Geschichte Deutschlands im Neunzehnten Jahrhundert.* Berlin, 1900.

Kenney, Martin M., *An Historical and Descriptive Sketch of Austin County, Texas.* Centennial Address delivered at the celebration near Bellville, July 4, 1876.

Koerner, Gustav, *Das Deutsche Element in den Vereinigten Staaten von Nordamerika, 1818-1848.* Cincinnati, 1880.

Koerner, Gustav, *Memoirs of Gustav Koerner,* 1809-1896, I. (Edited by Thomas J. McCormack.) Cedar Rapids, Iowa, 1909.

Lohmann, F. H., *Comfort. Festschrift zur fuenfzigjaehrigen Jubelfeier der Ansiedelung.* Comfort, Texas, 1904.

Lohmann, F. H., *Texas-Blueten.* Utica, N. Y., 1906.

Lotto, F., *Fayette County, Her History and Her People.* Schulenburg, Texas, 1902.

Maris, M., *Souvenirs D'Amerique. Relations D'Un Voyage au Texas et en Haiti.* Bruxelles, 1863.

Meister, Aloys, *Gebhardts Handbuch der deutschen Geschichte.* (Sechste Auflage. Dritter Band.) Stuttgart, Berlin, Leipzig, 1923.

Meusebach, John O., *Answer to Interrogatories.* Austin, Texas, 1894.

Mgebroff, J., *Geschichte der Ersten Deutschen Evangelisch-Lutherischen Synode in Texas.* Chicago, 1902.

Penniger, Robert, *Fest-Ausgabe zum 50-jaehrigen Jubilaeum der Gruendung der Stadt Friedrichsburg.* Fredericksburg, 1896.

Pennington, Mrs. R. E., *The History of Brenham and Washington County.* Houston, Texas, 1915.

Rives, R. L., *The United States and Mexico, 1821-1848.* New York, 1913.

Romberg, Johannes, *Gedichte.* Dresden und Leipzig, 1900. Alfred Wagner of Black Jack Springs, Fayette County, appears to have edited the *Gedichte,* since he wrote both a "Vorwort" and a "Biographische Skizze."

Rosenberg, W. von, *Kritik. Geschichte des Vereins zum Schutze der Deutschen Auswanderer nach Texas.* Austin, Texas, 1894.

Sandbo, Anna Irene, *The Beginnings of the Secession Movement in Texas, and the first Session of the Secession Convention.* Austin, Texas, 1913. Master of Arts Thesis in the University of Texas.

Sealsfield, Charles, *The Cabin Book; or National Characteristics.* New York, 1871.

Seele, H., *A Short Sketch of Comal County, Texas.* New Braunfels, 1885.

Seidensticker, Oswald, *Geschichte der Deutschen Gesellschaft von Pennsylvanien.* Philadelphia, 1876.

Steinhausen, Georg, Prof. Dr., *Geschichte der deutschen Kultur,* II. Leipzig und Wien, 1913.

Tiling, Moritz, *History of the German Element in Texas from 1820-1850 and Historical Sketches of the German Texas Singers' League and Houston Turnverein from 1853-1913.* First Edition. Houston, Texas, 1913.

Treitschke, Heinrich von, *Deutsche Geschichte im Neunzehnten Jahrhundert.* Leipzig, 1889.

The Papers of Mirabeau Buonaparte Lamar, Edited from the original papers in the Texas State Library by Charles Adams Gulick, Jr., and Katherine Elliott, Archivist, Texas State Library. Austin, Texas (1923).

Trenckmann, W. A., *Austin County.* Beilage zum *Bellville Wochenblatt,* den alten Texanern gewidmet und den jungen Texanern zu Nutz' und Frommen. Bellville, Texas, 1899.

Urbantke, Rev. C., *Aus meinen Lebensfuehrungen.* Cincinnati, 1902.

Weber, Adolf Paul, *Deutsche Pioniere. Zur Geschichte des Deutschthums in Texas.* San Antonio, Texas, 1894.

Wiggin, Edith E., *Anstandslehre fuer Schule und Haus.* Uebersetzt von Wilhelm Eilers. Nebst einem Anhang, enthaltend Geschichte und Biographien prominenter Deutsch-Texaner, gesammelt und bearbeitet durch W. Eilers. Austin, Texas, 1905.

Wislizenus, Dr. F. A., *A Journey to the Rocky Mountains in the Year 1839.* St. Louis, 1912.

Ziegler, Theobald, *Die geistigen und sozialen Stroemungen des Neunzehnten Jahrhunderts.* Berlin, 1910.

II. MAGAZINE ARTICLES

Baker, T. S., "America as the Political Utopia of Young Germany," *Americana Germanica,* I.

Biesele, R. L., "The German Settlers and the Indians in Texas, 1844-1860," *Southwestern Historical Quarterly,* XXXI.

Biesele, R. L., "The San Saba Colonization Company, *Southwestern Historical Quarterly,* XXXIII.

Biesele, R. L., "The Texas State Convention of Germans in 1854," *Southwestern Historical Quarterly,* XXXIII.

Kleberg, Rosa, "Some of My Early Experiences in Texas," *Quarterly* of the Texas State Historical Association, I-II.

Koch, Clara Lena, "The Federal Indian Policy in Texas, 1845-1860," *Southwestern Historical Quarterly,* XXVIII-XXIX.

Martin, Mabelle Eppard, "California Emigrant Roads through Texas," *Southwestern Historical Quarterly,* XXIX.

Muckleroy, Anna, "The Indian Policy of the Republic of Texas," *Southwestern Historical Quarterly,* XXV.

Regenbrecht, Adalbert, "The German Settlers of Millheim before the Civil War," *Southwestern Historical Quarterly,* XX.

Reinhardt, Louis, "The Communistic Colony of Bettina," *Quarterly* of the Texas State Historical Association, III.

III. NEWSPAPERS

Contemporary (Published in Germany)

Augsburger Allgemeine Zeitung, 1844.
Frankfurter Journal, January 21, 1844-July 17, 1844.
Karlsruher Zeitung, July 23, 1844.
Mainzer Zeitung, June 16, 1844.
Weser Zeitung, July 15, 1846-November 8, 1846.

Contemporary (Published in Texas)

Democratic Telegraph and Texas Register, 1846-1861.
La Grange Intelligencer, January 24, 1846.
La Grange Paper, 1855.
Morning Star, 1839-1843.
Neu Braunfelser Zeitung, November 12, 1852-March 18, 1861.
San Antonio Zeitung, July 5, 1853-March 29, 1856.
Telegraph and Texas Register, 1836-1845.
Texas National Register, December 7, 1844.
Texas State Gazette, 1849-1860.
The Western Texan, June 1, 1854.

Later

Frontier Times, February, 1927.
Galveston Daily News, May 29, 1921, July 31, 1921.
Guadalupe Gazette-Bulletin, July 28, 1927-August 11, 1927.
Houston Post, December 27, 1923.
Neu Braunfelser Zeitung, May 27, 1870, August 30, 1872, September 7, 1872, May 8, 1895, July 22, 1926.
San Antonio Express, January 10, 1926, March 4, 1928.
Texas Vorwaerts, October 26, 1883-September 4, 1914.
Wochenblatt der Union, September 12, 1869.

IV. PERIODICALS

Americana Germanica, I.
Der deutsche Pionier, Vols. I-XVIII.
Deutsch-Texanische Monatshefte, Vols. I-XIII. Library of Mr. S. V. Pfeuffer, New Braunfels, Texas.
Jahrbuch fuer Texas und Emigrantenfuehrer fuer 1882. (Albert Schuetze, editor.)
Jahrbuch fuer Texas und Emigrantenfuehrer fuer 1883. (Albert Schuetze, editor.)
Jahrbuch fuer Texas und Emigrantenfuehrer fuer 1884. (Albert Schuetze, editor.)
Kalender der Neu Braunfelser Zeitung fuer 1914.
Kalender der Neu Braunfelser Zeitung fuer 1916.
Kalender der Neu Braunfelser Zeitung fuer 1918.
Niles's Weekly Register, Vol. XLVIII.
Quarterly Texas State Historical Association, Vols. I, II, III.
Southwestern Historical Quarterly, Vols. XVIII, XX, XXV, XXVIII, XXIX, XXXI, XXXIII.
Texas Almanac for 1857.
The Annual Register for 1832.

V. ORIGINAL DOCUMENTS AND MANUSCRIPTS

Altgelt, Mrs. Ernst, *Comfort.* A collection of prose and poetry. Possession of Hermann Altgelt, New Braunfels, Texas.
Austin Papers. University of Texas.
Austin, Stephen F., *List of Titles.* University of Texas.
Barry, James Buckner, *Reminiscences.* Typewritten copy in University of Texas Library. Date not known, but after the Civil War.
Colonization Papers, Republic of Texas. Texas State Library.
Comal County Deed Records, Book L, Book N, Vol. E. New Braunfels, Texas.
Comal County District Court Minutes, Book E. New Braunfels, Texas.

Correspondence Secretary of State of Texas, Consular Letters, Vol. 57. Office Secretary of State, Austin, Texas.

Correspondence Secretary of State of Texas, Foreign Letters, Vol. 44. Texas State Library.

Diary of Adolphus Sterne. Texas State Library.

Domestic Correspondence, Republic of Texas. Texas State Library.

Dunn Transcripts, 1821. *Archivo General de Indias, Sevilla: Audiencia de Guadalajara.* University of Texas.

Fayette County Deed Records, Books C, E, G, I. La Grange, Texas.

Henry Francis Fisher Papers. University of Texas.

Indians Affairs, 1845-1860, Department of State. Texas State Library.

Maverick, Sam, *Reminiscences.* Typewritten copy in University of Texas Library.

Memorials to the Congress and to the Legislature of Texas. Office Secretary of State, Austin, Texas.

Nacogdoches Archives. Texas State Library.

Original Berichte des Prinzen Karl zu Solms-Braunfels an den Mainzer Adelsverein. Office City Secretary, New Braunfels, Texas.

Records of the Executive Department, Vol. 40. Texas State Library.

Records of the Executive Office, 1857-1859. Texas State Library.

Records of the Executive Office, Vol. 273. Texas State Library.

Records of the German Emigration Company. General Land Office, Austin, Texas.

Translations of Empresario Contracts. General Land Office, Austin, Texas.

United States Census for 1850; Schedule 4: Productions of Agriculture, and Schedule 5: Products of Industry. Texas State Library.

United States Census for 1860; Schedule 4: Productions of Agriculture, and Schedule 5: Products of Industry. Texas State Library.

Victor Rose Papers. University of Texas.

West Transcripts, 1822-1835, 1833-1834, Department of *Fomento* on Colonization. University of Texas.

VI. PHOTOSTATS

Augustus Buchel's Company of Col. Albert Sidney Johnston's Texas Foot Volunteer Riflemen. University of Texas.

Minutes of the Agricultural Society of Austin County. University of Texas.

Original-Berichte des Prinzen Karl zu Solms-Braunfels an den
Mainzer Adelsverein. University of Texas.

Records United States Office of Indian Affairs, Letters, 1847-1848.
University of Texas.

United States Census for 1850. Schedule 1: Free Inhabitants
of Gillespie County, Texas. University of Texas.

United States Census for 1860. Schedule 1: Free Inhabitants
of Gillespie County, Texas. University of Texas.

APPENDIX A

The three maps on pages 72, 80, and 109 of this study show what the Society believed were the location and extent of both the Bourgeois-Ducos and the Fisher and Miller grants. The mistakes which occur on the maps are due to the fact that very little was known of the topography of western Texas at the time when the maps were made. A comparison with the map on page 152 will show the mistakes.[1]

The second map is nearly correct about the location and general shape of the Bourgeois-Ducos grant; maps 3 and 5 do not even show this grant.

The first Fisher and Miller grant, dated June 7, 1842, stated that the grant should be bounded by a line beginning at the mouth of the Llano River, thence running to the source of the northern branch of the Llano, thence due south fifty miles, thence due west to the Colorado, and with the meanders of this river to the place of beginning. Maps 2 and 5 use the boundary set forth in the first grant. The renewal grant with Fisher and Miller, dated September 1, 1843, specified that the boundary should be a line beginning at the mouth of the Llano, thence running to the source of the southern branch of the Llano, thence due south fifty miles, thence due northwest (North 45° West) to the Colorado, and with the meanders of this river to the place of beginning. Map 3 uses the revised boundary.

All three of the maps faithfully show the lower boundary striking the Colorado. According to the topography of western Texas, however, the lower boundary as specified in either the first or the second Fisher and Miller contract could not have touched the Colorado. The map on page 152 shows the boundary line running off into space and leaving a gap between it and the Colorado River.

APPENDIX B

VEREIN ZUM SCHUTZE DEUTSCHER EINWANDERER IN TEXAS

Im Fruehling des Jahres 1844 brachten die oeffentlichen Blaetter nachfolgende Bekanntmachung:

Ein Verein hat sich gebildet, dessen Zweck es ist, die deutsche Auswanderung so viel als moeglich nach einem einzigen, guenstig gelegenen Punkte hinzuleiten, die Auswanderer auf der weiten Reise und in der neuen Heimath zu unterstuetzen und nach

---

[1]Maps 2 and 3 are taken from Solms, *Texas*, published in 1846; Map 5 is contained in a folder of instructions issued by the Society in 1851.

Kraeften dahin zu wirken, dass ihnen jenseits des Meeres eine neue
Heimath gesichert werde.

Der Verein erlaesst diese Bekanntmachung nicht in der Absicht,
Geldkraefte fuer sein Unternehmen zu gewinnen; das Geschaefts-
Kapital ist bereits vollstaendig gezeichnet. Allein im Bewusstsein
des guten Zweckes, ist er es dem Publikum und sich selbst
schuldig, die Gruende, welche den Verein in's Leben gerufen, die
Art und Weise, wie er seine Aufgabe zu loesen hofft, und die
Grundsaetze, die ihn dabei leiten, offen darzulegen.

Der Verein will den Trieb zur Auswanderung weder anregen,
noch entschuldigen. Genug, das Beduerfniss besteht einmal, and
laesst sich leider eben so wenig weglaeugnen, als es moeglich ist,
jenem immer lebendigeren Triebe Einhalt zu thun. Vielfaeltige
Ursachen wirken dabei zusammen; die Verdraengung der Hand-
arbeit durch das Maschinenwesen, die grossen, fast periodischen
Unfaelle, die den Handel heimsuchen, die zunehmende Verarmung,
eine Folge der Uebervoelkerung und des Mangels an Arbeit; end-
lich wohl auch der geruehmte Reichthum des Bodens im neuen
Lande und die manchmal belohnte, oft getaeuschte Hoffnung auf
ein besseres Seyn und Wirken jenseits der Meere.

Unter solchen Verhaeltnissen muessten die Auswanderer in der
That einem besseren Loose entgegen gehen, wenn sie, in wohl-
geordneter Masse zusammenhaltend, eine richtige Leitung und
einen wirksamen Schutz in der Fremde faenden. Und somit ist
die Nothwendigkeit, wie der Zweck des Vereins von selbst gegeben;
er will es versuchen, die Auswanderung zu regeln, und zu leiten,
damit die Moeglichkeit gegeben werde, dass die Deutschen in
Amerika eine deutsche Heimath wiederfinden, und aus dem ununi-
terbrochenen Zusammenhange unter sich und mit dem alten Vater-
lande ein gewerblicher und Handelsverkehr entstehe, der beiden
zum materiellen und geistigen Gewinn gereichen muss. Auf diese
Weise wuenscht der Verein das Seinige zu thun zu Deutschlands
Ehre und Wohl beizutragen, um vielleicht den deutschen Armen
eine belohnende Thaetigkeit, dem deutschen Gewerbfleiss neue
Maerkte, dem deutschen Seehandel eine weitere Ausdehnung
dereinst zu eroeffnen.

Nach langer, sorgfaeltiger Pruefung hat sich der Verein dafuer
entschieden, dass Texas dasjenige Land ist, welches dem deutschen
Auswanderer am besten zusagen moechte. Das gesunde Clima,
die Fruchtbarkeit des Bodens, der Reichthum seiner Erzeugnisse
und die Leichtigkeit der Verbindungen mit Europa haben schon
seit laengerer Zeit eine grosse Zahl von auswanderungslustigen
Deutschen dahin gezogen, die jedoch, ohne Schutz und Schirm,
sich vereinzelten, und leider oft ganz zu Grunde gingen. Um so
mehr musste sich die Aufmerksamkeit des Vereins nach diesen
Gegenden wenden. Durch erfahrene und des Landes kundige

Maenner hat er das texanische Gebiet bereisen lassen, und so vollstaendige Aufschluesse erhalten, dass er mit gutem Gewissen und voller Ueberzeugung seine Wahl treffen konnte.

Der Verein hat im Westen, im gesundesten Theile, ein zusammenhaengendes noch unbebautes Gebiet von betraechtlichem Umfang erworben, wird dort die Ansiedlung derjenigen Deutschen die das alte Vaterland verlassen, nach Kraeften befoerdern, und hierzu die von den Verhaeltnissen gebotenen, zweckdienstlichsten Mittel anwenden.

Vor dem Abgange wird jedem Auswanderer eine Strecke gütes Land schriftlich zugesichert, welches er bei seiner Ankunft als Geschenk, ohne alle jetzige oder kuenftige Verguetung, vom Vereine erhaelt. Dieser Boden, dessen groesserer oder geringerer Flaechenraum sich nach der Groesse der Familie richtet, wird freies Eigenthum des Auswanderers, sobald er drei Jahre lang auf seinem Gute gewohnt. Aber auch vor Ablauf dieser drei Jahre gehoeren ihm die Erzeugnisse seines Bodens, und der Verein macht weder auf jene, noch auf diesen den geringsten Anspruch.

Der Verein ist ferner dafuer bemueht, gute und geraeumige Schiffe fuer die Ueberfahrt auszuwaehlen; er sorgt dafuer, dass es an gesunder, wohlfeiler Nahrung nicht fehle, und die Reisekosten so gering als moeglich ausfallen. An den Landungsplaetzen sind besondere Agenten damit beauftragt, den Auswanderern mit Rath und That an die Hand zu gehen; die Letzteren finden hier Wagen bereit, die sie mit ihrer Habe unentgeltlich an den Ort ihrer Ansiedlung fuehren. Auch fuer ihre Beduerfnisse unterwegs wird Vorsorge getroffen. So wie sie an Ort und Stelle anlangen, wird jeder Familie ein eigenes Haus eingeraeumt, versteht sich, nur nach dortiger Art aus aufeinander gelegten Balken gezimmert; Vorrathshaeuser mit Lebensmitteln, Werkzeugen fuer Garten und Ackerbau, Samen und Pflanzen aller Art wohl versehen, sichern ihnen Alles, was sie zur Arbeit und zum Leben beduerfen; ebenso finden sie die noethigen Hausthiere, als Pflugochsen, Pferde, Kuehe, Schweine, Schafe, schon an Ort und Stelle. Alles dies wird ihnen zu einem viel geringeren Preise verkauft, als die naemlichen Gegenstaende auf den naechstgelegenen Maerkten zu haben sind. Solche Auswanderer, deren Betragen und Thaetigkeit sich besonders bewaehrt, erhalten von Seiten der Verwaltung Vorschuesse, die von der ersten Ernte zurueckzuzahlen sind.

Den Auswanderern steht es frei, die Erzeugnisse ihres Ackerbaues und ihrer Gewerbsthaetigkeit an die Magazine des Vereins zu veraeussern.

Fuer sittliche und religioese Erziehung der Kinder zu sorgen, betrachtet der Verein als eine heilige Pflicht; er wird daher, je nach den Beduerfnissen der Bevoelkerung, Kirchen und Schulen in der Kolonie errichten lassen. Er wird nicht minder fuer die Anstellung von Aerzten und Apothekern, so wie fuer Gruendung eines Krankenhauses Sorge tragen.

Eine Gemeindeverfassung und eine Gerichtsordnung, beide nach dem Vorbilde der in Texas anerkannten englischen, werden, sobald es nur thunlich, durch die Verwaltung der Ansiedlungen hergestellt.

Sollten sich unter den Auswanderern einzelne zur Rueckkehr nach Europa bewogen finden, so wird ihnen die Heimfahrt zu den naemlichen Preisen, wie die Hinfahrt, auf den Schiffen des Vereins zugesichert.

Der erste Zug von Auswanderern geht im September dieses Jahres 1844 ab; allein schon im Mai werden zwei Mitglieder des Vereins nach Texas reisen, um dort Vorbereitungen zur Aufnahme der Auswanderer zu treffen und die Verwaltung der Ansiedelungen vorlaeufig einzurichten.

Der Verein wird drei Prozent seiner Einnahme dazu verwenden, um duerftigen Auswanderern die Ueberfahrt und Ansiedelung zu erleichtern. Vorlaeufig jedoch und bis er diese Absicht zu wirklichen im Stande ist, kann die Niederlassung in der Kolonie nur Denjenigen zugestanden werden, welche die unumgaenglich erforderlichen Geldmittel besitzen.

Der unverheirathete Einwanderer bedarf wenigstens ein Capital von 300 Gulden.

Das Haupt einer nicht zahlreichen Familie ein Capital von 600 Gulden.

Um aber auch einer wenn gleich nur kleinen Anzahl von aermeren Familien sogleich die Ansiedelung moeglich zu machen, wird der Verein— indem er glaubt, den edlen Gesinnungen, die man ihm bereits zu erkennen gegeben, dadurch am besten entgegen zu kommen— eine Liste zu freiwilliger Unterzeichnung eroeffnen, deren Ertrag ausschliesslich zu diesem Zwecke destimmt ist. Jaehrlich sollen sodann die Beitraege und deren Verwendung, so wie die Namen der Wohlthaeter in den gelesensten Blaettern Deutschlands bekannt gemacht werden.

Wenn der Verein auf diese Weise, so viel in seinen Kraeften steht, dem Unternehmen einen gluecklichen Erfolg zu sichern bemueht ist, so beruht doch das Gelingen am meisten auf der ernsten unverdrossenen Thaetigkeit der Auswanderer selbst. Das neue Vaterland jenseits des Oceans wird nur dann gedeihlich emporbluehen, wenn die Deutschen auch dort sich bewaehren, wie sie stets in der Heimath waren: arbeitsam, beharrlich, treu der guten Sitte und dem Gesetze. Darf der Verein auch hieran nicht zweifeln, so wird er doch, um nicht das Wohl und Wehe deutscher Landsleute den Zufaelligkeiten eines Versuches preiszugeben, im Laufe diese Jahres fuer's erste nur ein Hundert und fuenfzig

Familien zur Uebersiedelung zulassen, und erst dann, wenn diese
eine wohlgesicherte Niederlassung gegruendet haben, einer
weiteren Auswanderung mit Rath und That an Handen gehen.

Genauere Aufschluesse und Auskunft jeder Art werden auf
frankirte briefliche Anfragen ertheilt:

Zu Mainz bei der Verwaltung des Vereins zum Schutze deutscher
Einwanderer in Texas.

Zu Frankfort a. M. bei Hrn. L. H. Flersheim, Banquier des
Vereins.

Gefertigt durch den leitenden Ausschuss des Vereins.

Mainz, den 9. April 1844.

(gez.) Fuerst zu Leiningen.

In Verhinderung des Grafen Carl zu Castell:

Graf zu Isenburg-Meerholz.

APPENDIX C

FORM OF IMMIGRATION AGREEMENT USED IN 1846

Verein zum Schutze Deutscher Einwanderer in Texas
Einwanderer-Vertrag

Zwischen dem unterzeichneten Agent, als Bevollmaechtigten des
Vereins, einerseits, und dem.............. ...., anderer-
seits, ist nachstehender Vertrag abgeschlossen:

Par. 1.

Der Verein schenkt dem................hierdurch........
(no. of acres) von seinen in der County Travis in Texas, belegenen,
durch Congress-Beschluss d. d. Washington den 1. September 1843
bewilligten Laendereien, als unbeschraenktes Eigenthum, und
erfolgt die Anweisung dieser Grundflaeche, sobald deren Ver-
messung durch die texanische Regierung vorgenommen und die
dem .... pro rata zur Last fallenden des-
fallsigen Kosten berichtiget sein werden. Der betreffende Rechts-
titel wird ihm jedoch gleich bei seiner Ankunft in Texas durch die
Colonial-Direction des Vereins uebergeben, und dieser, nach Ablauf
von drei Jahren, gegen eine wirkliche Erwerbsurkunde des texanischen Gouvernements ausgetauscht.

Par. 2.

Ausserdem erhaelt der .... gleich bei
seiner Ankunft in der neu zu gruendenden Niederlassung 10 Acres
Landes (17 Morgen) als unbeschraenktes Eigenthum zur sofortigen
Benutzung in dem Falle, dass ihm nicht sogleich die statuten-
maessig zugesicherte Quote Landes ueberwiesen werden koennte;

ohne dass diese Donation seine Ansprueche an die Par. 1. gemachte
Schenkung in irgend einer Weise schmaelern soll; vielmehr erhaelt
er diese als Geschenk, um sofort eine Ernte machen zu koennen.

Par. 3.

Der . . . . nimmt diese Schenkungen fuer
sich, seine Familie, Erben und Rechtsinhaber in bester Form
Rechtens an, und benutzt die ihm zu ueberweisenden Grundstuecke
ungefaehrdet aller im Eigenthum liegenden Rechte, darf dieselben
aber vor Ablauf von drei Jahren nach der Besitzergreifung nicht
verkaufen, ist vielmehr verpflichtet, in diesem Zeitraume darauf
ein Haus zu erbauen, 15 Acres im Ganzen zu kultivieren und nach
landesueblicher Sitte einzufriedigen, wonach derselbe den in Par. 1.
erwaehnten direkten Besitzstitel von der texanischen Regierung
erhaelt. Sollte derselbe aber dennoch vor Ablauf dieser Frist die
ihm ueberwiesenen Grundstuecke verlassen, so fallen dieselben,
nebst den darauf befindlichen Gebaeuden, dem Verein anheim, ohne
dass der fruehere Besitzer wegen etwaiger Meliorationen einen
Anspruch auf Entschaedigungen zu machen berechtigt ist.

Par. 4.

Sollte der . . . . vor Ablauf dieser drei
Jahren sterben, so gehen dessen Rechte und Verpflichtungen auf
seine Familie oder naechsten Erben in Texas, nach Ablauf dieser
Frist aber, und nachdem er die uebernommenen Verbindlichkeiten
erfuellt, auch auf dessen Erben in Europa ueber, insofern keine
Erbnehmer in Texas vorhanden sein sollten.

Par. 5.

Die betreffenden Landesvermessungskosten fallen, wie Par. 1.
besagt, dem . . . . zur Last und haften
fuer diese sowohl, als fuer etwa von dem Vereine erhaltenen
Vorschuesse die dem Contrahenten geschenkten Laendereien und
dessen Gebaeude als Pfand, bis zur gaenzlichen Tilgung.

Par. 6.

Der Verein uebernimmt den Transport und den Unterhalt vom
Tage der Einschiffung bis nach Neu-Braunfels gegen acht und
neunzig Gulden und ein Dollar Hospitalgeld per Kopf. Es wird
dieses Hospitalgeld jedoch im Abrechnungsbuechelchen des Contrahenten besonders bemerkt und nur mit dem Vorbehalte quittirt,
dass, falls die mit Vereinsschiffen in Galveston ankommenden Einwanderer von dieser Abgabe befreit bleiben sollten, dassselbe ihm

bei seiner Ankunft in der Colonie wieder zu gute gerechnet werden
solle.

Par. 7.

Nachdem die Ankunft in der Niederlassung erfolgt und dem
Contrahenten 10 Acres Landes ueberwiesen worden, hat derselbe
durchaus keine Ansprueche auf Unterhaltung Seitens des Vereins,
sondern es koennen ihm die Provisionen und andere Gegenstaende
aus den Magazinen der Colonie nur gegen Zahlung verabfolgt
werden.— Sollte derselbe aber alsdann die erforderlichen Mittel
nicht mehr besitzen, so wird die Colonial-Direction so viele Arbeit
ihm anweisen, dass er durch deren Ertrag in den Stand gesetzt
wird, sich die noethigen Existenzmittel zu verschaffen.

Par. 8.

Der Verein uebernimmt den Contrahenten . . . .
. . . . vom siebenten Tage an, nach seiner Ankunft am
Einschiffungsorte, d. h. von dem in seinem Aufnahmeschein
enthaltenen Datum gerechnet, auf seinen Kosten unterhalten zu
lassen, dagegen ist das Pfandgeld verfallen und kann nicht
reclamirt werden, wenn derselbe nicht an dem bestimmten Termine
zur Einschiffung eintreffen sollte.

Par. 9.

Sobald das Schiff den Hafen verlassen, hat der Verein fuer die
Dauer der Seereise keine Verantwortlichkeit; es koennen auch
keinerlei Ansprueche wegen erlittener Unfaelle oder deren Folgen
an ihn gestellt, und ueberhaupt nur die in diesem Vertrag ange-
fuehrten gegenseitigen Ansprueche und Verpflichtungen geltend
gemacht werden.

Par. 10.

Diesen in duplo auf guten Glauben ausgefertigten und von
beiden Theilen unterschriebenen Vertrag versprechen die Contrahenten puenktlich zu erfuellen, gleichzeitig aber auch nur die in
demselben enthaltenen wechselseitigen Verpflichtungen in Anspruch zu nehmen, und verzichten deshalf auf alle Einreden, sie
moegen Namen haben, wie sie wollen.

. . . . den. . . . . 1846.

Der bevollmaechtigte Agent
Hill

. . . .

Der Auswanderer

. . . .

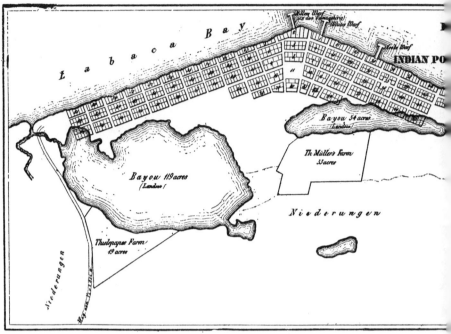

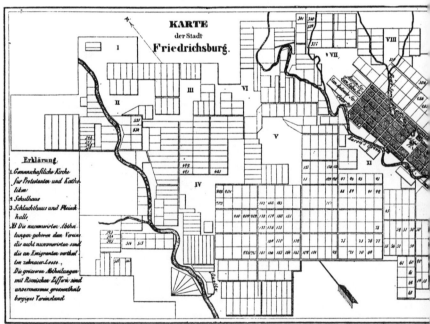

MAP 9.   PLATS OF NEW BRAUNFEL
From a folder of instructic

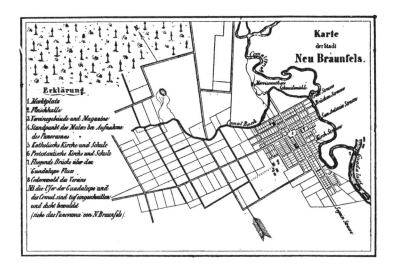

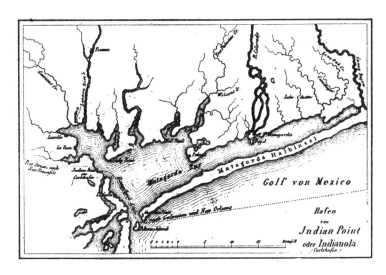

Wie ersichtlich sind diese Pläne nach verschiedenen Maasstaabe aufgenommen.

APPENDIX E

The following lists of names are taken from four issues of the *Neu Braunfelser Zeitung*, namely, May 27, 1870, May 8 and 15, 1895, and July 22, 1926. They contain the names of the early settlers of New Braunfels. They are given for the sake of making my account more nearly complete and for the purpose of preserving these names in book form. I do not contend that the persons whose names are listed were all present when New Braunfels was founded on March 21, 1845.

B. Albrecht, J. Arnold, P. Arnold, H. von Assel.

G. Baldus, Carl Bellmer, G. Benfer, A. Benner, H. Bevenroth, F. Bodmer, — Brasche, G. Brecher, G. A. Breilipper, C. H. Bremer, C. Brockheim, G. Brune, F. Burg, H. Burkhard.

Oscar von Claren, Richard von Cloudt, Jean J. von Coll.

Andreas Eikel, C. Elmendorf, Chr. Engel, E. Ernst, L. C. Ervendberg.

Valentin Fey, C. Feyck, F. Fischer, Ch. Fortemps.

Theodor Goldbeck.

F. Haemmerle, Chr. Hans, Fr. Hartung, H. Hartung, J. Chr. Hartung, Ludwig Hartwig, E. von Hartz, Johann Hassler, F. Heidemeyer, H. Heitkamp, M. Hellmuth, A. Henkel (von Donnersmark), H. Herbst, J. Heym, Chr. Hof, Gustav Hoffmann, G. F. Holekamp, J. Holzapfel, Peter Horne, George Humar.

J. Jahn.

Jacob Kaderli, Chr. Kaiser, G. Kirchner, Jos. Klein, N. Klein, St. Klein, W. Koch, Dr. Theodor Koester, W. Kracke, H. Kraft, C. Kreitz, J. M. Kreitz, J. Kuehne.

F. Lindheimer, Chr. Loeffler, C. Luck, Th. Luck, Chr. Luentzel, J. H. Lux.

F. Marheinicke, L. Martin, Andreas Mattern, A. Meixner, E. Mergele, J. Mergele, P. Mergele, J. Mertz, J. C. Moeschen, F. E. Mueller, J. Mueller, Wm. Mueller. Fr. Muenzler.

L. Negedank, P. Neis, Dr. A. Nette.

A. Pelzer, G. Peter, L. Pook.

J. Rahn, A. Ram, G. Reeh, — Reinhard, H. Reininger, J. W. Reinartz, Dr. Wm. Remer, G. Remmler, J. Rennert, W. Reuter, J. Rieck, A. Riedel, N. Riedel, H. Roege, H. Roeser.

F. Saalmueller, G. Sacherer, M. Sanders, A. Sauerborn, C. Schaefer, H. Schaefer, Ph. Schaefer, Jean Scherz, J. Scherz, Jos. Scherz, Seb. Scherz, F. Schlicking, L. Schmidt, Leonhard Schmidt, E. Schmitz, J. Schmitz, Johann Schneider, J. V. Schulmeier, J. H. Schutze, Th. Schwab, H. Seele, C. H. Seibert, E. Siehn, N. Siering, Sylvester Simon, H. Startz, C. Stock, P. Stock.

F. Tausch, Chr. Thiel, G. Thielepape, C. W. Thomae.

G. Ulrich.

J. Voelcker, L. Vogel, A. Vogt.

A. Wedemeyer, Ph. Weil, Th. Weil, J. Wengeroth, G. Wenzel,. Ignaz Wenzel, G. Wersdoerfer, W. Wetzel, A. J. Weyel, H. Willke,. L. Willke, J. Winkler, F. W. von Wrede, J. A. Wuest.

Nicolaus Zink, N. Zucher, N. Zuercher, H. Zuschlag.

In addition to the above names the *Neu Braunfelser Zeitung,* in its issues of May 8 and May 15, 1895, gave the following:

Johann Baldus, Alexis von Bauer, J. G. Beckel and wife, Julius von Bose, H. Bothmer, Viktor Bracht, Johann J. Brecher, J. K. Breilipper, C. Brockhuisen, Peter Burg, Daniel Bussmann and wife.

Mrs. Andreas Eikel.

Gottlieb Fischer, George Fritze and wife, Ludwig Fr. Fritze.

Peter Gerlach, Maurice Germain, Mrs. M. Guenther.

John Hartung, Mrs. F. Heidemeyer, Otto Heins, C. H. Heitkamp, Caspar Herber and wife, Justus Herber and wife, Peter Hermani, Elizabeth Hobarth, Joseph Hoffmann, Wilhelm Holzmann and wife.

Heinrich Imhof, Peter Imhof.

Anna Jokel, Joseph Jung.

Johann Kaderli, Jacob Klein, Valentin Klein, J. Andreas Koch,. Mrs. Sophie Koester, Conrad Kraushaar, Marianne Kuhn.

Catharine Langguth, Daniel Letsch, E. von Lochhausen, Chr. Luck, Louis Luck, Ph. Luck.

Conrad Mertz and wife, John Merz, John O. Meusebach, Dr. Emil Meyer.

H. L. Nix.

Joseph Peters, Johann Petri.

John Rahn, F. W. Reese, H. Fr. Th. Reiche, Alois Russer.

J. G. Salziger and wife, Mrs. M. Sanders, Alexander Sartor and wife, Johann Sauerborn, Philip H. Schaaf and wife, Chr. Schellentraeger, Heinrich Schelper and wife, Napoleon Schippach, Fr. Schlichting, Carl Schloesser, Ed. Schmidt, H. Schoene,. H. Sowersby, Chr. Spangenberg and wife.

August Tolle, Chr. Tolle, Georg Fr. Tolle and wife, Mrs. Anton Troeste.

Fr. Utermoehlen and wife.

Gustav von Vechten, Ludwig Voigt and wife.

August Weinert, Reinhard Weinert and wife, Joseph Wersdoerfer, Wessels, Wilhelm Weyel, Theodor Wiedenfeld, Wm. Wiedenfeld and wife.

Conrad Zuschlag.

In a list of early settlers published by the *Neu Braunfelser Zeitung* on July 22, 1926, the following names, not given in the two lists above, appear:

Mrs. Fr. Marheinicke, Carl C. Mertz and wife, P. H. Metz and wife, Johann Ruck, Mrs. F. Saalmueller, Carl Schertz, Johann J. Weyel.

INDEX

AFTERWORD

Rudolph Biesele's study of German settlements in Texas has been the starting point for all those who have subsequently tried to learn and write about the topic. In its general outlines it has not been surpassed, and there is little likelihood it will ever be supplanted. Later writers on the early history of the Germans in Texas have added many interesting details and some new perspectives, but they have not unearthed any sources that would have forced Biesele to reconsider his information in any fundamental manner. For that reason all of us who are interested in German Texan history welcome this reprint. The biographical sketch by Biesele's son enhances its value, especially since the author's love for his family's heritage clearly played an important role in its in - ception.

The list of writings on the history of German settlements in Texas Biesele consulted was remarkable, but it did not exhaust all possible sources; some were simply not available to him. For example, he was not able to consult several older publications, such as:

Heffter, Hugo Oswald. *Mein Lebenslauf bis zum Goldenen Hoch - zeitsmorgen 1837-1916.* [Leipzig, 1916.]

Sommer, G. v. *Bericht über meine Reise nach Texas im Jahre 1846.* Bremen, 1847.

Struve, Heinrich von. *Ein Lebensbild.* Leipzig, 1896.

Morever, an almost endless number of subsequent studies, generally more limited in focus but for that very reason frequently more detailed, have taken up where Biesele left off. Some of the first such studies were, of course, articles by Biesele himself. In addition, there have been translations of many of the sources he used, and in several instances these translations contain additional material. (Some, to be sure, such as the adaptation and translation of Ehrenberg's memoirs, are distortions of their originals and scarcely better for historians than no translation at all.) Those who wish to take up where Biesele left off will find an excellent general survey in

Lich, Glen E. *The German Texans.* San Antonio: Institute of Texan Cultures, 1981.

An exhaustive bibliography, which does not restrict itself to the period of Biesele's study, can be found in

> Lich, Glen E. and Dona B. Reeves. *German Culture in Texas. A Free Earth; Essays from the 1978 Southwest Symposium.* Boston: Twayne, 1980.

Excellent sources for further information are

> *The Handbook of Texas.* Volumes 1 and 2 edited by Walter Prescott Webb and H. Bailey Carroll; volume 3, by Eldon Stephen Branda. Austin: Texas State Historical Association, 1952, 1976.
>
> *Yearbook of the Society for German-American Studies.* (Annual bibliography.)
>
> *Southwestern Historical Quarterly.* (The indices include announcements of related studies elsewhere.)
>
> *German-Texan Heritage Society Newsletter.* (Primary strength in genealogy; some historical articles and translations of diaries and memoirs; reviews of recent publications.)

Numerous books have appeared since the bibliography in Lich/Reeves. Three that not only relate to the period of Biesele's study but also contain valuable references to other works and sources are

> McGuire, James Patrick. *Hermann Lungkwitz: Romantic Landscapist on the Texas Frontier.* Austin: Institute of Texan Cultures, 1983.
>
> Buenger, Walter L. *Secession and the Union in Texas.* Austin: University of Texas Press, 1984.
>
> Gish, Theodore and Richard Spuler, eds. *Eagle in the New World: German Immigration to Texas and America.* College Station: Texas A&M University Press, 1986.

Hubert P. Heinen

July 7, 1987

MAPS

ILLUSTRATIONS